The Austrian Enlightenment and its Aftermath

Edited by Ritchie Robertson and Edward Timms
AUSTRIAN STUDIES 2

The Austrian Enlightenment and its Aftermath

Edited by Ritchie Robertson and Edward Timms

AUSTRIAN STUDIES 2

EDINBURGH UNIVERSITY PRESS

© Edinburgh University Press, 1991
22 George Square, Edinburgh

Set in Linotron Ehrhardt by
Koinonia, Bury, and
printed in Great Britain by
The University Press, Cambridge

British Library Cataloguing
  in Publication Data
The Austrian Enlightenment and its
  Aftermath – (Austrian studies).
I. Robertson, Ritchie II. Timms,
  Edward III. Series
  943.6

ISBN 0 7486 0231 3 (cased)

Contents

List of illustrations — viii
Notes on contributors — ix
Preface — xiii

PART ONE

Derek Beales — 1
Was Joseph II an Enlightened Despot?

Ritchie Robertson — 22
Joseph Rohrer and the Bureaucratic Enlightenment

Peter Horwath — 43
The Altar of the Fatherland: Wilhelm Friedrich von Meyern's Utopian Novel *Dya-Na-Sore*

Joseph P. Strelka — 59
Gottlieb von Leon and his *Rabbinische Legenden*

Ewan West — 71
Masonic Song and the Development of the *Kunstlied* in Enlightenment Vienna

Roger Paulin — 88
The Biedermeier Anomaly: Cultural Conservatism and Technological Progress

Eve Mason — 102
Stifter and the Enlightenment

Eda Sagarra — 117
Marie von Ebner-Eschenbach and the Tradition of the Catholic Enlightenment

Hartmut Steinecke (translated by Ritchie Robertson) — 132
Charles Sealsfield and the Novel as a Means of Enlightenment

R. J. W. Evans — 145
Josephinism, 'Austrianness', and the Revolution of 1848

Austrian Writers of the Enlightenment and Biedermeier: 161
A Biographical Directory

PART TWO: REVIEW ARTICLES

Leslie Bodi 171
The Austrian Enlightenment: An Essay on Publications,
1975–1990

Peter Branscombe 188
The Mozart Bicentenary

Sander L. Gilman 194
Histories of the Viennese Jews

PART THREE: REVIEWS

Ewan West 201
H. C. Robbins Landon and David Wyn Jones, *Haydn: His Life and Music*

W. E. Yates 202
Briefe von und an Friedrich Kaiser, ed. Jeanne Benay

H. M. Scott 203
Miriam J. Levy, *Governance and Grievance: Habsburg Policy and Italian Tyrol in the Eighteenth Century*

Lothar Höbelt 205
Lawrence Sondhaus, *The Habsburg Empire and the Sea: Austrian Naval Policy, 1797–1866*

Steven Beller 206
Alan Sked, *The Decline and Fall of the Habsburg Empire*

R. J. W. Evans 207
Otto Dahinten, *Geschichte der Stadt Bistritz in Siebenbürgen*; Franz Greszl, *Ofen-Buda: Entwicklungsgeschichte der königlichen Residenzstadt Ungarns im 18. Jahrhundert*; Carl Göllner (ed.), *Die Siebenbürger Sachsen in den Jahren 1848–1918*; Hans Rothe (ed.), *Deutsche in der Habsburger Monarchie*

Gilbert J. Carr 210
Karl Kraus, *Frühe Schriften*, I, II, and *Erläuterungen*; Rainer Dittrich, *Die literarische Moderne der Jahrhundertwende im Urteil der österreichischen Kritik*

Brian Keith-Smith 212
Friedrich Schröder, *Die Gestalt des Verführers im Drama Hugo von Hofmannsthals*; Margit Resch (ed.), *Seltene Augenblicke: Interpretations of Poems by Hugo von Hofmannsthal*

Leo A. Lensing 215
Stefan Zweig, *Briefwechsel mit Hermann Bahr, Sigmund*

Contents

Freud, Rainer Maria Rilke und Arthur Schnitzler, ed. Jeffrey B. Berlin, Hans-Ulrich Lindken and Donald A. Prater

Hanni Mittelmann   218
Texte des Expressionismus: Der Beitrag jüdischer Autoren zur österreichischen Avantgarde, ed. Armin A. Wallas

Elizabeth Boa   220
Stanley Corngold, *Franz Kafka: The Necessity of Form*; Detlev Kremer, *Die Erotik der Schrift*

Andrew Barker   221
Lothar Huber (ed.), *Franz Werfel: An Austrian Writer Reassessed*

John Warren   223
Harald Klauhs, *Franz Theodor Csokor: Leben und Werk bis 1938 im Überblick*

Marc A. Weiner   224
Heinz Steinert, *Adorno in Wien: Über die (Un-)Möglichkeit von Kunst, Kultur und Befreiung*

Robert Knight   226
Gernot Heiss (ed.), *Willfährige Wissenschaft: Die Universität Wien 1938 bis 1945*; Christian Brunner and Helmut Konrad (eds.), *Die Universität und 1938*

Elisabeth Stopp   229
Theodor Haecker, *Tag- und Nachtbücher 1939–1945*, ed. Hinrich Siefken

Austrian Studies   232

List of illustrations

1. On the Steamship Maria Anna (1837) by Rudolf von Alt
2. The Steamship Journey (1845) by Leander Russ
3. View of Dornbach from the Studio Window (1836) by Jakob Alt
4. Domestic Garden in Vienna (1829–30) by Erasmus Engert

Notes on contributors

ANDREW BARKER is Senior Lecturer in German at Edinburgh University. He is working on a book on Peter Altenberg.

DEREK BEALES is Professor of European History at Cambridge University. Volume I of his biography of Joseph II was published by Cambridge University Press in 1987.

STEVEN BELLER lives in New York and is the author of *Vienna and the Jews, 1867–1938: A Cultural History* (Cambridge University Press, 1989) and *Herzl* (Peter Halban, 1991).

ELIZABETH BOA is Senior Lecturer in German at the University of Nottingham. She is author of *The Sexual Circus: Wedekind's Theatre of Subversion* (Blackwell, 1987) and is now working on a feminist study of Kafka for Oxford University Press.

LESLIE BODI is Emeritus Professor of German at Monash University, Melbourne, and the author of *Tauwetter in Wien: Zur Prosa der österreichischen Aufklärung 1781–1795* (S. Fischer Verlag, 1977).

PETER BRANSCOMBE is Professor of Austrian Studies at St Andrews University. He edited (with E. Badura-Skoda) *Schubert Studies: Problems of Style and Chronology* (Cambridge University Press, 1982).

GEOFFREY BUTLER, who has a special interest in English translations of German fiction, has recently retired from the Chair of German at the University of Bath.

GILBERT J. CARR is Lecturer in Germanic Studies at Trinity College, Dublin, and the author of numerous articles on Kraus and his contemporaries.

R. J. W. EVANS is Reader in the Modern History of East-Central Europe at Oxford University, and the author of *Rudolf II and his World: A Study in Intellectual History, 1576–1612* (Oxford University Press, 1973) and *The Making of the Habsburg Monarchy, 1550–1750* (Oxford University Press, 1979).

SANDER L. GILMAN is Goldwin Smith Professor of Humane Studies at Cornell University. Besides teaching in the Departments of German and Near Eastern Studies there, he is Professor of the History of Psychiatry at Cornell Medical College in New York. The most recent of his numerous books are *Jewish Self-Hatred: Anti-Semitism and the Hidden Language of the Jews* (Johns Hopkins University Press, 1986) and *Disease and Representation: Images of Illness from*

Notes on contributors

Madness to AIDS (Cornell University Press, 1988).

LOTHAR HÖBELT is 'Assistent' in the Institute for History at Vienna University and author of *Die britische Appeasement-Politik 1937–1939: Entspannung und Nachrüstung* (1983) and the forthcoming *Kornblume und Kaiseradler: Die deutschfreiheitlichen Parteien Altösterreichs 1882–1918*.

PETER HORWATH is Professor in the Department of Foreign Languages at Arizona State University and the author of *Der Kampf gegen die religiöse Tradition: Die Kulturkampfliteratur Österreichs, 1780–1918* (Peter Lang, 1978), and of numerous articles on the Austrian Enlightenment.

ROBERT KNIGHT teaches in the Department of European Studies at Loughborough University, and is the author of *'Ich bin dafür, die Sache in die Länge zu ziehen'*.

LEO A. LENSING is Professor of German at Wesleyan University, Middletown, Connecticut, and author of a study of Wilhelm Raabe. He is at work on a biography of Karl Kraus.

EVE MASON has recently retired as Fellow in German at Newnham College, Cambridge. She is the author of a book on *Bunte Steine* (Grant & Cutler, 1986) and numerous articles on Stifter.

HANNI MITTELMANN teaches German at the Hebrew University of Jerusalem. She is currently editing the complete works of Albert Ehrenstein.

ROGER PAULIN is Schröder Professor of German at Cambridge University. His books include *The Brief Compass: The Nineteenth-Century German Novelle* and *Ludwig Tieck: A Literary Biography* (both published by Oxford University Press in 1985); a German translation of the latter has recently appeared from C. H. Beck.

RITCHIE ROBERTSON is Fellow and Tutor in German at St John's College, Oxford, and author of *Kafka: Judaism, Politics, and Literature* (Oxford University Press, 1985; German translation published by Metzler, 1988).

EDA SAGARRA is Professor of Germanic Studies at Trinity College, Dublin. Her many books include *A Social History of Germany* (1977) and studies of Fontane and Ebner-Eschenbach.

H. M. SCOTT is Lecturer in History at St Andrews University. He has recently edited *Enlightened Absolutism* (Macmillan, 1990) and published *British Foreign Policy in the Age of the American Revolution* (Oxford University Press, 1990).

HARTMUT STEINECKE is Professor of German at the University of Paderborn and the author of many studies of the German and Austrian novel, including *Hermann Broch und der polyhistorische Roman* (1968), *Romantheorie und Romankritik in Deutschland* (1975–6), and most recently *Romanpoetik von Goethe bis Thomas Mann* (Wilhelm Fink Verlag, 1987).

ELISABETH STOPP was formerly Fellow in German at Girton College, Cambridge. She has published many articles on German Romanticism, Robert Musil, and Catholic devotional literature.

JOSEPH P. STRELKA is Professor of German at the State University of New York at Albany. His many books include studies of Austrian literature, literary theory, Goethe, and the esoteric tradition.

Notes on contributors

JOHN WARREN teaches German at Oxford Polytechnic. He is co-editor, with Kenneth Segar, of *Austria in the Thirties: Culture and Politics* (Ariadne Press, 1990).

MARC A. WEINER is Professor of German at Indiana University and author of *Arthur Schnitzler and the Crisis of Musical Culture* (Carl Winter, 1986).

EWAN WEST is Research Fellow in Music at Mansfield College, Oxford. He is working on a study of the Viennese *Lied*.

W. E. YATES is Professor of German at the University of Exeter. His books include *Grillparzer* and *Nestroy* (both published by Cambridge University Press in 1972), and he is one of the editors of the new edition of Nestroy.

Preface

This second volume of *Austrian Studies* focuses chiefly on Austrian culture between two crucial dates: 1780 and 1848. In 1780 the Empress Maria Theresa died and her son, Joseph II, who had shared power with her for the previous fifteen years, became sole ruler of the Habsburg domains and initiated the reform programme known as Josephinism. The ten years of Joseph's sole reign are the main period of the Austrian Enlightenment. In 1848 revolution broke out in Vienna, as in many other European cities. What had begun as a 'revolution of the intellectuals', in Namier's phrase, moved rapidly leftwards as industrial workers came to dominate it. It was brought to an end in October with the siege and capture of Vienna by Imperial troops.

Our main purpose in this volume has been to trace the continuities between 1780 and 1848, by investigating the survival, partly underground, of the Austrian Enlightenment. Joseph's accession to sole power marked a break with the past. Unlike his mother, he did not regard himself as a ruler by divine right, but as the chief administrator of a secular and, so far as possible, homogeneous state. His most famous reforms, the Toleration Patents of 1781 and 1782, extended freedom of worship to Protestant and Orthodox Christians, and sharply reduced the social and educational restrictions on the Jews, in an attempt to make his non-Catholic subjects into fully active members of the state. Yet Joseph also established a political police force that kept his subjects under close surveillance. Despite his undoubted benevolence towards his people, there are good reasons, as his biographer Derek Beales demonstrates, for calling him an enlightened despot. The tensions between benevolence and control also appear in Ritchie Robertson's article on Joseph Rohrer, which explores the imaginative world of a Josephinist bureaucrat. Josephinism also promoted a patriotic cult which long survived Joseph's death in 1790; one of its most curious expressions, the novel *Dya-Na-Sore*, is examined here by Peter Horwath.

Joseph's liberalisation of the censorship laws began to create a 'public sphere' of intellectual debate. This was conducted in a luxuriant pamphlet literature and in the Masonic lodges to which most Josephinist intellectuals belonged. One of them, Gottlieb von Leon, is here the subject of a study by Joseph Strelka. Freemasonry also encouraged musical culture, both to assist its conviviality and to accompany the expression of its humane ideals, as Ewan West describes. The outspokenness of Masonic intellectuals led in 1785 to the subjection of the lodges to police control. Thereafter, especially after the accession of the cautious and conservative Franz I in 1792, open discussion was stifled. Fear of the French Revolution, the discovery of a supposed Jacobin conspiracy in 1794 and Austria's defeat at the hands of Napoleon, strengthened the conservatism of its rulers. Metternich, who became Austria's Foreign Minister in 1809 and its Chancellor in 1821, and who led the way in repressing revolutionary or even constitutional aspirations in post-Napoleonic Europe, used censorship to restrict the public sphere to apolitical matters.

Under Metternich, Vienna became famous as a centre of that preoccupation with individual, domestic and aesthetic concerns which is known as 'Biedermeier'. The term has often been used disparagingly, and the Biedermeier period (1815–48), both in Austria and Germany, has too readily been dismissed as provincial. Yet, as Roger Paulin shows in his survey of the literature, art and music of the Austrian Biedermeier, the period was full of complexities and even contradictions. Though its artistic achievements were for the most part conservative, they also articulated a response to rapid technological changes. Rudolf von Alt's 'On the Steamship Maria Anna', which is featured on our jacket, expresses this contrast by juxtaposing the steamer against the baroque tower of a castle or monastery.

The complexity of the Austrian Biedermeier arose not least from the survival of various currents of Enlightenment and especially Josephinist thinking, which are examined in the next group of articles. Eve Mason shows how Austria's greatest nineteenth-century prose writer, Adalbert Stifter, strove but never quite managed to reconcile the Leibnizian optimism and Christian providentialism of his upbringing with the seeming arbitrariness of life and with the disasters of 1848. Eda Sagarra demonstrates how the tradition of the Catholic Enlightenment survived in the fiction of Marie von Ebner-Eschenbach, whose stature as a major woman writer is only now being recognised. And Hartmut Steinecke, discussing the runaway monk and adoptive American Karl Postl, alias Charles Sealsfield, shows that his exotic novels were written not only to entertain but also to promote humane and democratic values. Finally, R. J. W. Evans argues that the revolution of 1848 resulted in part from the survival of Josephinist ideals among the liberals who thought their hour had come at last. These articles are supplemented by a biographical directory providing concise information about the many writers, from Alxinger to Zedlitz, who are mentioned in passing in this volume and whose names are in many cases unfamiliar even to Austrian specialists.

One of the aims of *Austrian Studies* is to make the results of specialist research available to a wider audience, by reviews and review articles. In Part II, Leslie Bodi surveys the scholarly work on the Austrian Enlightenment that has appeared since the publication in 1977 of his study *Tauwetter in Wien*. Peter Branscombe looks at a selection of Mozart studies published in anticipation of the bicentenary of the composer's death. And Sander L. Gilman considers the recent spate of publications on the history of the Jews of Vienna. The short reviews that follow monitor a wide range of literary, musical, and historical

Preface

publications, extending beyond the main theme of this volume to indicate the variety of topics currently being treated in the field of Austrian studies.

All German quotations in the text have been translated, except for some short phrases whose meaning is apparent from the context. When a passage quoted is of literary or historical significance, the original is provided as well.

Part One

Was Joseph II an Enlightened Despot?

Derek Beales

Joseph II died just over two centuries ago, on 20 February 1790. He was buried in the Kapuzinergruft with much of the usual pomp, but in a sarcophagus totally unlike any of his predecessors'. Absolutely plain, it silently continues, in death, the protest he made all his life against the Baroque ostentation of his parents, still opulently relaxing on their overpowering tomb-chest nearby.[1]

As he himself said, it is difficult to imagine a more unhappy death. Twice a week, his desperate letters followed each other across the Alps to his brother Leopold in Tuscany. In pain and scarcely able to breathe, he believes himself 'the unhappiest mortal alive'; he has sacrificed everything to his 'fanaticism ... for the good of the state' and now sees his reputation in tatters and the Monarchy going to rack and ruin; his is a worse fate than that of the martyrs – living 'to suffer, and dishonoured':

> seeing that I am unfortunate in everything I undertake, the appalling ingratitude with which my good arrangements are received and I am treated – for there is now no conceivable insolence or curse that people do not allow themselves to utter about me publicly – all this makes me doubt myself, I no longer dare to have an opinion and put it into effect, I allow myself to be ruled by the advice of the ministers even when I don't think it's the best, since I dare not hold out for my own view and indeed I haven't the strength to impose it and argue for it.

Thus he renounced, under extreme duress, his absolutism – or should one call it despotism?[2]

Everyone, even the savagely critical Prussian envoys, had to admire the dignity, courage and fortitude Joseph displayed during his final illness, and the strength of will which enabled him to write generous farewell letters to friends and ministers in his last hours. But many people had longed for his death, which some thought a necessary condition of the very survival of the Monarchy. His rule had been widely regarded as a despotic aberration, and there were many, including most Belgians and Hungarians, who wanted it relegated – as Chancellor Kohl has consigned the German Democratic Republic – to the footnotes of history.[3]

Was Joseph II an Enlightened Despot?

In fact, historians have remained fascinated by Joseph II and his experiment in government. I want to pursue the question most often asked about him: 'Was Joseph II an enlightened despot?' In writing the first volume of my biography of Joseph II, which ends with the death of his mother Maria Theresa in 1780, I had no doubt that the question needed answering; but I had decided to leave a proper consideration of it to volume II, when I should have completed my work on the reforms of his sole reign during the 1780s. This I have not finished, and so I can give only a preliminary answer to the question. What has really provoked me to prepare such an answer is a review of my book by Professor William Doyle. In the course of the review (which was entirely fair, not to say generous) he wrote that I hedged on the question whether Joseph was an enlightened despot. He gave his own answer to the question: that the whole notion of enlightened despotism was 'rusty', that to add the word 'enlightened' in front of despotism 'now impedes more than it promotes historical understanding' and that in any case Maria Theresa was the greater revolutionary.[4] To the stimulus of these remarks should be added the recent appearance of a number of studies which breathe new life into the theme.[5]

I shall argue that the notion of enlightened despotism or absolutism – and I think the use of 'despotism' is, on balance, preferable to that of 'absolutism' – is meaningful and valuable, and that Joseph's rule clearly belongs to this category. I do not have space here to consider adequately the question whether Maria Theresa was the greater revolutionary. But it may put her activity in perspective to recall that her annual output of laws (excluding those for Hungary) averaged less than a hundred, while Joseph's averaged 690.[6]

I am going to assume that when we speak of enlightened absolutism or despotism we are thinking of a regime in which the ruler possesses or assumes the right to enact legislation without consent, exercises the right extensively and, in doing so, is influenced by 'the Enlightenment' as the term is used by historians of the eighteenth century – not by enlightenment in some more general sense. I am also going to assume that Enlightenment so used is itself a meaningful concept, a term denoting critical, rationalist, reformist opinion in the eighteenth century.

Problems of definition

It seems necessary first to deal with some general difficulties raised by the concept of enlightened despotism. The first is the claim that the very notion of an enlightened despot, or an enlightened absolute monarch, is a contradiction in terms. This view derives support from a tradition of thought epitomised by Lord Acton's dictum: 'Power tends to corrupt, and absolute power corrupts absolutely.'[7] How could a necessarily corrupt despot possibly be enlightened? Further, most American historians, Peter Gay at their head, and many historians from other English-speaking countries, nurtured as they are in a tradition of representative government unbroken since the Middle Ages, and aware that the American Revolution ranks as an aspect and achievement of the Enlightenment, see the movement as inherently associated with political liberty and parliamentary rule. Among great thinkers of the Enlightenment some, like Montesquieu and Rousseau, always agreed, and others like Diderot came to agree, that Enlightenment and despotism or absolutism were incompatible.[8]

My first response to this line of thinking would be that many examples can be found of absolute rulers who manifestly were not absolutely corrupt, such as Frederick the Great and Catherine the Great. Secondly I should reply that the Enlightenment was very various. Not infinitely various: I think all its representatives were critical of the more extreme claims of Christian churches and in favour of some measure of religious toleration, condemned some aspects of what were called superstition or fanaticism, supported some legal reform tending to greater uniformity, greater rationality or utility and greater fairness – similarly with economic reform – and also supported some mitigation of censorship. But economic policy, for example, was much debated among the Enlightened, some writers like the Physiocrats favouring free trade, others still adhering to forms of mercantilism. What was acceptable in the way of monarchical rule to the great majority of German representatives of the *Aufklärung* went far beyond what was acceptable to Montesquieu, Rousseau and Diderot and to English and American thinkers in general.[9] I would not maintain – and no sensible person would – that all Enlightened thinkers were ready to accept, still less justify, absolute monarchy. That would be absurd. But I would maintain that many were, and I shall shortly give chapter and verse.

The second principal objection is that the terms enlightened despotism and despot, or their variant, enlightened absolutism, were not used in the period to which they are supposed to apply. Betty Behrens was particularly strict on this point.[10] My first answer to this point would be: So what? The fact that the term *ancien régime* cannot be found before 1788 quite rightly doesn't stop Doyle – any more than it stopped Behrens – from writing books with that title which are almost entirely devoted to periods before 1788.[11] Many indestructible historical concepts were invented after the period to which they refer, for example the Industrial Revolution, the Middle Ages – or indeed the Enlightenment itself, except in reference to Germany.

However, I should take as a second line of defence that the term 'enlightened despot' – and, once, 'enlightened despotism' – can be found in eighteenth-century writing. Incidentally, though the word 'absolute' had long been used to mean more or less 'untrammelled', the word 'absolutism' itself was not invented until the nineteenth century.[12] Further, I should argue that the *notion* of enlightened despotism, as opposed to the precise term, was widespread in the eighteenth century.

This seems the appropriate place to consider a subsidiary difficulty, the significance of 'despotisme légal'. This is an important concept in Le Mercier de la Rivière's *L'ordre naturel et essentiel des sociétés politiques*, published in 1767. The notion has been taken to correspond with enlightened despotism – or at least, according to Behrens, to be the only eighteenth-century usage that approximated to it.[13] Le Mercier's book was the collectively-agreed political manifesto of the physiocrats, whose main concern, of course, was with economics. It is one of those books that are much mentioned but little read. It claims that government, society and especially the economy are subject to laws which, like the laws of geometry, are indisputable and self-evident. They are the laws of the free market, but with agriculture treated as the only true productive activity. It is the business of the good ruler to put these laws into effect, or – according to one formulation – to get rid of the existing counter-productive laws and then sit back, do nothing and let the new laws operate. These laws may, by a play on words, be described, like Euclid's laws, as despotic. The concept 'despotisme légal' therefore does not imply, as is sometimes supposed, the vindication as lawful of what is normally understood by despotism. Far from acting wilfully or individually, the ruler who enacts Le Mercier's laws will have no discretion; he will be doing the self-evidently right thing, not what he likes but what is natural and essential.[14] True, there are certain affinities with the notion and practice of enlightened despotism. On Diderot's recommendation, Catherine the Great summoned Le Mercier to St Petersburg to give her advice.[15] Some rulers, including Joseph II, showed their susceptibility to enlightened theory by declaring their conviction that one or more of the physiocrats' economic principles, such as the encouragement of private property in land, was ineluctably right.[16] The Natural Law on which German rulers relied as a justification for making the laws of their provinces uniform and more rational is not wholly unlike Le Mercier's geometric laws.[17] But the concept of enlightened despotism, as normally understood, involves rulers exerting themselves to impose on their states, not an immutable set of laws, but a particular brand of Enlightenment, and admits that each state has specific problems in some ways different from those of other states. So 'despotisme légal' cannot be identified with enlightened despotism.

In an invaluable article, François Bluche has marshalled some of the best and earliest French instances of the usage 'enlightened despot'. This is the most striking. In 1767, when discussing Le Mercier de la Rivière's notion of *despotisme légal*, Baron Grimm, editor of the *Correspondance littéraire*, wrote:

> On a dit que le gouvernement d'un DESPOTE ÉCLAIRÉ, actif, vigilant, sage et ferme, était de tous les gouvernements le plus désirable et le plus parfait, et l'on a dit une vérité; mais il ne fallait pas l'outrer. Moi aussi j'aime de tels despotes à la passion.[18]
>
> [It has been said that the rule of an ENLIGHTENED DESPOT, active, vigilant, wise and firm, was of all regimes the most desirable and most perfect, and this is a true saying; but it was important not to take it too far. I too passionately love such despots.]

Even more notable is this quotation from the third edition of Raynal's *Histoire philosophique et politique du commerce et des établissements des Européens dans les deux Indes*, dated 1780: 'However you will hear it said that the most satisfactory government would be that of a just, firm, enlightened despot. What a wild view!'[19] We now know that these are the words of Diderot. Coming from such a source, this remark would seem sufficient by itself to establish that a theory of enlightened despotism was significant in French thought of the period. Moreover, he goes on to argue that the first enlightened despot in a line of rulers is a great evil, the second worse still, and the third a terrible scourge. In other words, however much he condemns them, he accepts that enlightened despots may exist. Indeed, it is clear that, earlier, Diderot had himself believed in the possibility of beneficent enlightened despots. He denounced Frederick the Great, whom he had previously admired, in the unpublished *Pages contre un tyran* of 1771; but that he had not entirely abandoned hope is shown by his journey to Russia in 1773, undertaken with the idea of converting Catherine II, whom he considered to be unquestionably a despot, into a more enlightened ruler.[20]

Apart from the admittedly infrequent use of the phrase 'enlightened despot' in the eighteenth century, there seems to me abundant evidence that many enlightened thinkers had hopes of a ruler of this kind. The best-known Enlightenment writer, Voltaire, did not put all his eggs in one basket. He much admired the English constitution, where law was sovereign, and where the king was restricted (Voltaire claimed) to the point that he could do only good. He even showed sympathy with the democratic movement in Geneva. He at first welcomed the embrace of Frederick the Great, then escaped, disillusioned, from his clutches, but after an interval resumed a flattering correspondence with him. He was made historiographer royal by Louis XV in 1745 and supported the *thèse royale* against the *parlements*. He eventually wrote what may be called the first social or not purely political and religious history, the *Essai sur les mœurs* (first edition, 1756). But he still maintained that great men had brought about most of the great changes of history, and wrote eulogistic biographies of Charles XII of Sweden, Louis XIV of France and (after the appearance of the *Essai*) Peter the Great. In the last years of his life he became the uncritical admirer and correspondent of Catherine II. He refused to accept what he considered Montesquieu's laboured distinction between despot and monarch, and much of what he wrote assumed the possibility of beneficent change from above by fiat of an enlightened ruler. Lortholary's *Le mirage russe* mordantly catalogues the credulous expectations inspired by Catherine's rule in one *philosophe* after another.[21]

A less well-known author who addressed the problem directly was Giuseppe Gorani (1740–1819), an associate of the Verri brothers and Beccaria in Milan. In his book *Il vero dispotismo,* published in 1769, he pinned all his hopes of reform and improvement on a monarch possessed of despotic power, who would use it to abolish feudal and ecclesiastical abuses, vested interests, even property rights, and to introduce a rational economic system, freedom of expression and so on.[22] Here we have a dream of Utopia to be achieved through enlightened despotism. The efforts and visits of Joseph II helped to keep such attitudes alive in Lombardy. Pietro Verri himself wrote as late as 1781:

> In my opinion, subjects ought never to fear the power of the sovereign when he himself exercises it and doesn't surrender any essential part of it into other hands ... Only intermediate power is to be feared, and I think

and feel that the best of all political systems will always be despotism, provided that the sovereign is active and in overall control and doesn't give up any portion of his sovereignty.[23]

More generally, it has to be remembered that the American dream had scarcely been invented by the time Voltaire died and had not come to fruition by the time Joseph succeeded his mother; that until the American colonies won their independence, no country had been the product of a revolution since the Dutch Republic; and that no country at all had a full-blown rational written constitution until the American revolt. Such republics as there were before then seemed backward and doomed, and such constitutions as existed seemed to make beneficent change almost impossible, as for example in Venice, Belgium and Hungary. The effective reforming lawgivers of Europe were in fact the monarchs.

The third main difficulty lies in distinguishing the concepts 'despotism' and 'absolutism'.[24] Virtually everyone writing with awareness of serious political thinking – as opposed to just tossing off abusive remarks – regarded a despot as a ruler who possessed untrammelled power. At least in the second half of the eighteenth century, the word 'despot' was generally pejorative and connoted the exercise of untrammelled power according to the whim and caprice of the ruler, perhaps as opposed to its exercise for the general good. Usage was much influenced by Montesquieu's novel distinction in *De l'esprit des loix* of 1748 between despotism and monarchy, a classification to which he attached great importance and which soon became almost universally known and widely, though not universally, accepted among writers and statesmen. In a monarchy, as he defined it, there must be a constitution of sorts, embodying both a law of succession and intermediary bodies like *parlements* that the ruler had to consult over legislation. If these conditions were not satisfied, the state was a despotism. Hence, according to Montesquieu, Russia was a despotism and France a monarchy. However, Montesquieu recognised that examples of pure despotism or pure monarchy were hard to find. What we call, but Montesquieu was very careful not to call, the pretensions of the French Crown to absolute power, for example to legislate without the consent of the *parlements*, were to be regarded as steps towards despotism. It is important to grasp that for Montesquieu despotism is a form of government characterised both by the nature of the constitution in the state concerned and by the behaviour of the ruler, which will necessarily be dictatorial, cruel and capricious; and that he deliberately avoided the word and concept 'absolu' applied to power and government, no doubt wishing to identify it with despotic rule and thus discredit it.[25]

Jaucourt's article 'Monarchie' in the *Encyclopédie* avowedly follows Montesquieu, but his article 'Monarchie absolue' introduces – or, better, revives – an intermediate stage between monarchy and despotism:

> l'origine et la nature de la *monarchie* absolue est limitée, par sa nature même, par l'intention de ceux de qui le monarque le tient et par les lois fondamentales de son état.[26]

[the origin and nature of absolute monarchy is limited by its very nature, by the intentions of those from whom the monarch derives it and by the fundamental laws of his state.]

Jaucourt's classification is close to that of Roger Mettam in his recent book, *Power and Faction in Louis XIV's France*. Mettam emphasises the limitations on Louis's power, both in practice and in theory, maintaining that the contemporary expression *la monarchie absolue* 'did not describe the system as it was presently constituted. It was rather a direction in which the royal ministers were hoping to proceed.' Even so, he contends, it was understood to mean the exercise of royal power 'for the greater good of the kingdom. Otherwise it was *monarchie arbitraire*.' *Monarchie arbitraire* corresponds with despotism.[27]

Montesquieu's distinction remains important in modern writing, although his notion of 'monarchy' has fallen into disuse. Some modern historians like Mousnier have used 'absolutism' in virtually the same sense as Montesquieu used 'monarchy', contrasting it with despotism. It must be recognised that most of these usages – of 'monarchy' by Montesquieu, of 'absolutism' among historians of France and even of *la monarchie absolue* in the *Encyclopédie* – fall short of other established notions of 'absolute monarchy' and 'absolutism'. Jean Bodin in his *Republic* of 1576 stated categorically: 'The principal mark of sovereign majesty and absolute power is the right to impose laws generally on all subjects regardless of their consent.'[28] This was what the Stuarts and Louis XIV were thought by many of their opponents to stand for. It is also more or less the position adopted in eighteenth-century Germany by many rulers and by the large body of writers who justified absolute government. The subjects, it was maintained, had surrendered all their rights to their ruler, who therefore had the right and power to make such laws as he thought proper without consent. It was held to be by far the best arrangement that sovereignty should be placed straightforwardly in the hands of the prince: he was much more likely than any group of people, or than all the people, to govern in the interests of the whole state and of all its population. It was his moral and Christian duty to act for the general good rather than for his private advantage. But his power was to be in no sense formally restricted. It was admitted that, if he acted arbitrarily, his absolute power degenerated into despotism. But absolutism as used by historians of Germany to describe this sort of government and the theory behind it, though still differentiated from despotism, clearly means something much nearer to it than Montesquieu's monarchy or Mousnier's absolutism, and as such reflects the differences between German and French reality.[29]

So there is a broad range or spectrum of meaning covered by the term 'absolutism'. The normal German usage of the word is compatible with the sort of conduct we have in mind when we speak of 'enlightened despotism', the imposition of an enlightened programme of reform by the ruler from above, on his own legislative authority, for the general good. Such activity is plainly quite irreconcilable with Montesquieu's monarchy and Mousnier's absolutism, both of which are conceived to be limited by intermediate powers, by fundamental laws and by ancient liberties and privileges varying from province to province, town to town and corporation to corporation. Under such a constitution, radical reform from above is inconceivable. As Jaucourt said, '*Monarchy* is lost when a prince believes that he demonstrates his power better by changing the order of things than by accepting it.'[30]

To use the term 'enlightened absolutism', then, does not make everything plain. Nor is despotism so clear-cut a concept as is often assumed. Bodin was not the only writer to distinguish between despotism and the still worse condition of tyranny.[31] Hobbes, on the contrary, maintained that sovereign, absolute, despotic and tyrannical all meant the same thing: 'for they that are discontented under *monarchy*, call it *tyranny*'.[32] Montesquieu's insistence that despotism is characterised both by the ruler's legislative sovereignty and by his capriciousness confuses the issue. But I still find it more satisfactory to use 'Enlightened despotism' for five reasons: because despotism unequivocally refers to a situation in which the ruler possesses the power to legislate without consent; because what needs to be expressed is something more drastic than French (and Stuart) absolutism as now commonly understood by historians; because it is a long-standing usage, especially in English but also in other languages; because, unlike absolutism, the term despotism was current in the eighteenth century and the usage 'enlightened despot' has some eighteenth-century warrant; and because, whereas there is no personal noun cognate with absolutism, despot is cognate with despotism. But I employ the word despot, as did writers like Hobbes, Grimm, Gorani and Verri, with the understanding that he may use his untrammelled power not for his personal advantage but for the public good.

Joseph as despot

I come now to the Austrian Monarchy and Joseph II. His education was firmly based on the theory of Natural Rights and Natural Laws, especially as taught by the German school, particularly Pufendorf. They cherished the idea of a wise and rational sovereign who would work for 'das allgemeine Beste', that is, to strengthen his state as against other states, to make its laws more rational and homogeneous, to promote the welfare of his subjects, perhaps to grant them all the same civil rights and to accord a certain measure of religious toleration. But the young prince was also firmly told that he must respect the various constitutions of the Monarchy's diverse provinces.[33]

Joseph said with Rousseau that education is everything. His own case goes far to disprove the claim. While he drank in the despotic aspects and implications of what he was taught, he rejected the constitutionalism. In his *Rêveries* of 1763 he horrified his mother by the intentions he revealed. His first basic aim was to secure 'the absolute power to be in a position to do all possible good for the state'. To this end he would seek to 'humble and impoverish the grandees'.

> This smacks of despotism, but without an absolute power ... to be in a position to do all the good which one is prevented from doing by the rules, statutes and oaths which the provinces believe to be their *palladium*, and

which, sanely considered, turn only to their disadvantage, it is not possible for a state to be happy or for a sovereign to be able to do great things ... God keep me from wanting to break sworn oaths, but I believe we must work to convert the provinces and make them see how useful the *despotisme lié*, which I propose, would be to them. To this end I should aim to make an agreement with the provinces, asking them [to yield to me] for ten years full power to do everything, without consulting them, for their good.

While it is true that he talks in this passage of persuading rather than compelling the provinces to grant him despotic power for ten years, it seems clear that the only force of the word *lié* is to restrict the period of the despotism, not its scope.[34]

He appears to have remained faithful to this plan, at least in respect of Hungary. When he succeeded his mother in 1780, he refused to be crowned King of Hungary, which would have involved his swearing to uphold its constitution. Almost until he died, for over nine years, he acted as though he could exercise unlimited power there, introducing a welter of enactments which most Hungarians considered illegitimate because he was uncrowned and declined to summon a diet. In the preface to a collection of his Hungarian laws published in 1788 the editor, Joseph Keresztury, stated that the Emperor would soon be calling a diet and would submit all his ordinances to it.[35] This was plainly not his intention all along. When in 1784 his officials suggested that the decree making German, instead of Latin, the language of administration in Hungary needed the approval of the diet, Joseph responded:

The chancellery could have saved itself the trouble of making the recent representation in which it urges the necessity of putting off until a diet [meets] the abolition of the Latin language in official business, because it's only a matter of language not of substance and I am the last man to make soap bubbles into bullets.[36]

Only rebellion, his need for war supplies and finance, and his desperate illness, brought him to recognise the necessity of calling a diet and submitting to a coronation – though he died before either could happen.[37]

In Belgium, for reasons I do not understand, Joseph allowed deputies to take the necessary constitutional oaths on his behalf when he succeeded his mother. Nevertheless, he introduced reforms that flouted the old constitutions. Rebellion in Brabant compelled him in 1787 to withdraw some of his measures; but, when his troops had restored order, he claimed the right to treat the country as a conquered land, completely at his mercy. He then swept away the entire old constitution, informing the Estates of Brabant a month before the fall of the Bastille: 'I do not need your consent for doing good.' No wonder that Belgian publicists compared him to Tiberius, Caligula, Nero, Caracalla, Alaric, Attila, Mahomet, Amurath, Machiavelli, Alva and Cromwell. By the time he renounced his personal rule, his armies had been driven out of nearly all his Belgian lands.[38]

On the spectrum of monarchical pretensions, his rule in Hungary and Belgium must plainly be located at the despotic end. It would be hard to claim and exercise more personal power than he did. We have seen that he did not scruple, in private, to argue explicitly that the Monarchy needed a period of despotism. On another occasion he suggested that he be made dictator.[39] All that was lacking to qualify him unequivocally as a despot by Montesquieu's definition was that his actions were evidently inspired by a conception of the public good rather than by mere caprice.

It is instructive to read what is said about Joseph's rule and the constitution of the Monarchy in a comprehensive *Essai sur la Monarchie Autrichienne et son état actuel*, prepared for the Neapolitan government just after his death.[40] This document specifically addresses the question whether the Habsburgs are absolute or despotic rulers in the Monarchy. The answer given is: absolute, in every province. Admittedly the legislative power as well as the executive lies with the sovereign.

> It is necessary nevertheless to grasp that there is a great distance between the absolute monarch and the despotic monarch. [The latter is] a designation which is in no way appropriate to the sovereign of the hereditary lands, which these sovereigns would never wish to have, and which they have always held in horror.
>
> Despotic government recognises no laws but the mere will, and often the mere caprice, of the sovereign; while in monarchical government, even if absolute, the sovereign's will is subjected to councils, formalities, to privileges of Estates, peoples, corporations and even individuals, and caprice can have no place.

Great stress is laid on the ruler's wise practice of consulting with trusted ministers, respected by the people, who can 'enlighten him about so many things' and 'who countersign the laws after him'.

The *Essai*, however, betrays embarrassment on several fronts, two of which are of special interest here. On Hungary it describes the articles of the constitution 'tending to limit monarchical power' as being 'insufficiently clear' and alleges that the diet meets only for a coronation, while admitting that the country has to be governed 'in accordance with the laws established by His Majesty and the general Diet'. On the reign of Joseph II, it does its best to associate as many of his policies as possible with his mother's and with the influence of 'this enlightened minister', Prince Kaunitz. But the writer has to acknowledge that Joseph did not always observe formalities and that:

> After the death of the Empress Queen, Prince Kaunitz stood out against several reforms that the late Emperor projected, and so strong was his opposition that the monarch used to consult him only rarely.

I have not yet discovered who wrote this treatise nor in precisely what circumstances. It is obviously related to the visit of the Neapolitan Court to Vienna and to current plans for an alliance between Vienna and Naples; it must, to put it at its lowest, owe much to Austrian sources close to Kaunitz; it clearly owes something to the Neapolitan minister, Sir John Acton, and also to the Marquis de Gallo, the Neapolitan ambassador in Vienna and the confidant of the Queen of Naples. It is by way of being a eulogy of Kaunitz's successes and an apology for his role under Joseph II, and it does its best to minimise the latter's autocracy. No doubt its constitutionalism is designed to ape or gratify Leopold II, whose manifesto to the Belgians commending representative government was published in March 1790.[41] But what strikes the modern reader is that the *Essai*, even while underplaying the pretensions of Joseph, gives a surprisingly high estimate of the powers possessed by the Habsburgs, making it hard to distinguish their absolutism from despotism. As for Joseph, he made it clear that he regarded his officials as servants rather than advisers. He constantly complained that they were slow, incompetent and obstructive and that he had to draft despatches himself.[42] He was prepared to humiliate even the great Kaunitz. The Emperor was in Russia during the earlier stages of the Brabant revolution in 1787. He had left Kaunitz to mind the shop in Vienna, but when the chancellor wrote recommending him to approve a document involving a concession to the rebels, Joseph returned it 'torn in pieces', with orders that it should be passed on to the administration in Brussels in that state.

> I am surprised [he wrote] that the people of Brussels and the fanatics who stir them up haven't yet asked for my *culottes*, and that the government hasn't meanwhile given them assurances that I will send them on.

So much for consultation of ministers and observance of formalities by an absolute, not despotic, ruler! [43]

Joseph's Enlightenment

Finally, were Joseph and his rule Enlightened? I have myself contributed a little to make it more difficult to answer this question. My description of Joseph's education, based on the work of other scholars, shows it to have been relatively unenlightened, innocent of almost all the great works of the French Enlightenment except Voltaire's *Henriade* and carefully selected portions of Montesquieu's *De l'esprit des loix*, and apparently innocent too of Maria Theresa's own practical plans for quite radical administrative and ecclesiastical reform.[44] I have also shown, or rediscovered, that many of the most famous quotations attributed to Joseph were not in fact his. He did not say – most notorious of all – 'I have made philosophy the legislator of my empire.' He meant by philosophy, when he used it, metaphysics or stoicism; he did not accept the redefinition of the word by such men as Voltaire which gave it a radical, anti-Catholic, critical sense. He once said that he followed neither the ancient Greeks nor the modern French.[45] He lacked two characteristics which, according to Birtsch, are essential to ideal enlightened rulers: he wrote no theoretical tracts and he conducted no correspondences with *philosophes*. But Birtsch's ideal type is manifestly tailor-made to fit Frederick the Great.[46] It is certainly wrong to suppose that Joseph was a disciple of the *philosophes*, who should in any case be regarded as only one small, if very influential, group within the diversity of the Enlightenment. But he was unquestionably associated with many other aspects of the movement.

Many of Joseph's contemporaries thought him an exemplar and promoter of the Enlightenment, quite radically understood; and his behaviour, pronouncements and enactments often supported this view. Voltaire was informed in 1769, on the authority of Grimm, that the Emperor was 'one of us'. In 1774 appeared *Le monarque accompli* by the Swiss Protestant publicist, Lanjuinais, three volumes of unmitigated and indiscriminate praise of Joseph as an ideal ruler who resembled not only the most notable kings of France, especially Henry IV, but also the most celebrated Roman emperors like Trajan and Marcus Aurelius, who favoured toleration and understood *l'esprit philosophique*. Voltaire docketed this effusion 'monarque rôti'. In 1777 Joseph visited France, as was claimed, *en philosophe*; he spoke well of Diderot and Raynal, and met D'Alembert, Lavoisier, Marmontel, Turgot and La Harpe. In 1781 he dined at Spa with Grimm and Raynal.[47]

More important, after succeeding his mother he embarked on his well-known programme of reforms, introducing measures of religious toleration for Protestants and Jews, some personal liberties for serfs, a much looser censorship, the suppression of all purely contemplative monasteries, mendicant orders and religious brotherhoods, and so forth. One of his most active supporters, Gebler, a member of the Staatsrat, dared to tell Nicolai, the creator of the *Allgemeine deutsche Bibliothek*, the principal organ of the North German Protestant Enlightenment:

> But for a man who thinks philosophically there is no more remarkable period than that which opened in 1781. Such a rapid change in the general way of thinking, reaching down to the common people, who put to shame many still obscurantist persons of higher classes, is to my knowledge without parallel. The just recently effected abolition of brotherhoods, of most so-called *Andachten* and all *Klosterpredigten* has finally given the last blow to superstition ... The freedom of the press, and still more the *freedom of reading* (for there is virtually no book that is not publicly on sale) bring with them much else ... Our intrepid monarch meanwhile pursues his way undeterred.[48]

In 1782 was published an authentic correspondence the Emperor had been conducting with the Elector of Trier, who had written to him complaining about his religious reforms. In these letters Joseph displayed a mocking knowledge of theology, scoffed at the infallibility of the Pope, rejected some of his other claims, urged the futility of discussing the bull *Unigenitus* and defended the relaxation of the censorship.[49]

At the end of 1783 the Emperor issued to all his officials what became known as his *Hirtenbrief* or 'pastoral letter', originally written in his own hand in French and soon published in several languages. These were some of the assertions in the German version:

> Ich habe die von Vorurtheilen und eingewurzelten alten Gewohnheiten entsprungene Umstände durch Aufklärung geschwächet, und mit Beweisen bestritten;
> Ich habe die Liebe, so Ich fürs allgemeine Beste empfinde, und den Eifer

für dessen Dienst jedem Staatsbeamten einzuflößen gesucht.
Hieraus folgt nothwendig, daß vor sich selbsten anzufangen, man keine andere Absicht in seinen Handlungen haben müsse, als den Nutzen und das Beste der grössern Zahl.
Da das Gute nur eines seyn kann, nämlich jenes, so das Allgemeine und die größte Zahl betrifft, und ebenfalls alle Provinzen der Monarchie nur ein Ganzes ausmachen, und also nur ein Absehen haben können; ... Nation, Religion muß in allen diesen keinen Unterschied machen, und als Brüder in einer Monarchie müßten alle sich gleich verwenden, um einander nutzbar zu sein ...

[I have reduced the conditions resulting from prejudices and old, deep-rooted habits by means of Enlightenment, and disputed them by means of proofs;
I have tried to imbue every official of the state with the love I feel for the general weal and with zeal to serve it.
Hence it necessarily follows that in order to act on one's own account one should have no other purpose in one's actions save the utility and the good of the majority.
Since the good can only be one, namely that which concerns the whole and the greatest number, and likewise all the provinces of the monarchy only form a single whole, and thus can have only one purpose; ... in all of them nationality and religion must make no difference, and as brothers in one Monarchy all should set to work equally in order to be useful to one another ...]

The monarch has been chosen by Providence ('die Vorsicht') 'für den Dienst dieser Millionen zu diesem Platz' ('to serve these millions in this place') and 'ist dem allgemeinen und jedem Individuo Rechenschaft zu geben schuldig' ('must account to the state as a whole and to each individual') for his use of taxes. This document, Joseph's most elaborate public statement of his views and aims, embodies many of the commonplaces of radical Enlightenment: the desire to weaken ingrained prejudices through *Aufklärung*; the zeal for the service of the state and its millions, for the *allgemeine Beste* and the good of the greatest number; the intention to treat all provinces, nations and religions equally; the acknowledgment of the monarch's responsibility to every individual; and the substitution of Providence for God as the justification of the monarch's position.[50] It received universal praise and was the inspiration, through its insistence that officials be thoroughly acquainted with his ordinances, of the numerous collections of his laws published during the latter part of his reign.[51]

In the same year as the pastoral letter there appeared the most elaborate and effective panegyric of his work, the philosophical novel, *Faustin oder das philosophische Jahrhundert*, by Johann Pezzl. It achieved the distinction, rare for a book written in German, of being translated into French and published in France. The hero, Faustin, undergoes experiences very reminiscent of Candide's. But it is not the philosophy of Leibniz that plays Faustin false. It is the conviction instilled into him by his teacher, represented as a priest, that beneficent enlightenment was now – since 1763, that is – advancing unstoppably. For

> eifert ein Monarch den andern vor, Toleranz, Erleuchtung und Denkensfreiheit in seinen Staaten zu befördern; Aberglauben, Barbarei, Fanatismus, Dummheit, Schikane und Elend ferner von seinen Völkern zu verbannen.
>
> [Each monarch vies with the others to promote tolerance, enlightenment and freedom of thought in his states, and to expel superstition, barbarism, fanaticism, stupidity, chicanery and misery from his peoples.]

This is the 'allgemeiner Sieg von Vernunft und Menschheit, ist's aufgeklärtes, philosophisches Jahrhundert' ('the universal victory of reason and humanity, it is the enlightened, philosophical century'). But, when Faustin and his tutor put this happy conviction to the test, it is proved false in one country after another in Europe and America, with disastrous results. One or other or both of them are beaten up by workers who resent the abolition of feast-days; imprisoned for possessing works by Voltaire, Helvetius, Bayle, Montesquieu, Frederick the Great and so on; attacked by a crowd which had gathered to watch the antics of the notorious exorcist, Gaßner; for criticising South German monasticism, driven to take refuge in Venice; there set on by bandits and banished for criticising the constitution; faced with a variety of similar problems in other parts of Italy, Spain and Portugal; disillusioned in France by the government's treatment of Voltaire's body; appalled by the Gordon riots and general intolerance in England; after having fled to America, sold as slaves. Hope rises again only when Faustin, after endless adventures, all of them based on genuine events of the period, reaches Prussia. There at last is to be found a 'gekrönter Philosoph'. But even in Berlin a *Liederkrieg* is in progress about the right of a congregation to sing Paul Gerhardt's hymn 'Nun ruhen alle Wälder'. Only when Faustin finally gets to Vienna does he discover a place where Enlightenment is in full cry. Joseph's letters to the elector of Trier Faustin considers the most notable contribution made to the debate between Church and State, or Empire and Papacy, since the days of Hildebrand. The Emperor's opening of the Augarten park to the entire public in 1775 is described as 'ein Denkmal der Philosophie auf dem Thron' (a monument to philosophy on the throne). 'Joseph der Große' (Joseph the Great), who is to be compared to Sesostris, to the first Chinese emperor, to Orpheus, Titus and Marcus Aurelius, has inaugurated 'die Ära des aufgeklärten südlichen Deutschlandes' (the era of enlightened Southern Germany). 1780 is 'das Jahr des Heils' (the year of salvation), opening 'die Josephische Ära' (the era of Joseph). So, unlike Candide's, Faustin's philosophy is ultimately vindicated – in Joseph's Vienna.[52]

Soon after this effusion appeared, the Emperor began to get a worse press. No doubt this had much to do with his involvement in wars and attempted annexations, with his legislation placing some limitations on Freemasonry in his dominions, and with signs of his withdrawal from the fullest implications of other measures like the toleration edicts. But it is common to exaggerate the extent of the disillusionment felt by men of the Enlightenment at the end of

Joseph's reign.[53] On his death, Beethoven in Bonn set to music an Ode about it, which contained these sentiments:

> *Recitative*: Ein Ungeheuer, sein Name Fanatismus, stieg aus den Tiefen der Hölle, dehnte zwischen Erd' und Sonne, und es ward Nacht.
> *Aria*: Da kam Joseph, mit Gottes Stärke
> riss das tobende Ungeheuer weg ...
> und trat ihm auf's Haupt.
> Da stiegen die Menschen in's Licht.[54]
>
> [A monster, its name Fanaticism, arose from the depths of hell, stretched itself out between the earth and the sun, and all became night.
> Then Joseph came, and with God's strength he tore the raging monster away ... and trod on its head. Then mankind arose into the light.]

If Joseph's public pronouncements and recognition by Enlightened writers are insufficient justification for calling him Enlightened, more can be adduced from his private utterances. In the *Rêveries*, written in 1763, he advocated making all official appointments on the sole ground of 'personal merit. If this principle is inviolably observed, what geniuses will not emerge, who are now lost in obscurity either through laziness or because they are oppressed by nobles!'[55] In the next year, even before the appearance of Beccaria's *Dei delitti e delle pene* (*Crimes and Punishments*), he cast doubt on the utility of the death penalty.[56] As soon as he became co-regent, he urged on his mother in a famous document a massive programme of change including the end of the censorship, wide religious toleration, and the raising of the minimum legal age at which binding monastic vows could be taken to twenty-four. This last proposal, of course, was designed in the long run to reduce drastically the number of monks and nuns. He had much to do with the enactment of a similar measure in 1770, and it was not his fault that the other reforms were delayed until after her death.[57]

He was no great reader, but it is clear that once he was free – or as free as his mother would let him be – to go into society, he became acquainted with up-to-date radical writings ignored in his education. His knowledge of Voltaire passed the acid test of conversation with Frederick the Great. He is known to have read a physiocratic periodical. He justified not seeking out the great *philosophes* during his visit to France on the ground that, once you had read them, to meet them would be disappointing. One of the women who knew him best claimed that he followed the doctrines of Holbach and Helvetius. This is plainly untrue, but could hardly have been said if he had been wholly ignorant of these authors.[58]

Two major difficulties stand in the way of his acceptance as an enlightened ruler by anglophone historiography. First, he was not anti-Catholic. He told his mother, in the midst of denouncing her refusal to tolerate Protestants, that he would give all he possessed if that would make all his subjects Catholic. He was convinced, and he persuaded the Pope, that he was a faithful son of the Church.[59] But it was possible to be a Catholic by the standards of the late eighteenth century, if not by those of the first Vatican Council, while holding views highly critical of the claims of the Pope and the state of the Church. From one point of view, a Catholic and enlightened ruler had much more to do than a Protestant and enlightened ruler. Frederick the Great inherited a measure of toleration; there were so few monasteries in his dominions that he could afford to leave them alone. On the other hand, Joseph's edict of toleration of 1781 went far beyond that of any Catholic state and stirred envy in many Protestant communities, like the city of Hamburg. His toleration of the Jews, inspired though it was by ideas of assimilating them, was uniquely generous in its day. His relaxation of the censorship was considered astonishingly liberal.[60]

Secondly, many historians have felt uneasy because his reforms may be said to be primarily directed towards obtaining more taxes and more soldiers to support a bigger army for the purpose of gaining more territory. The problems of defence certainly obsessed Joseph. But it was the business of every ruler to preserve his territories, and the Monarchy was exposed to attack on several fronts. Joseph could not, like his brother in Tuscany, assume the status of a neutral. True, Joseph also worked hard to win Bavaria for the Monarchy, whether by inheritance or exchange, and sought aggrandisement in the East. But, for what it is worth, his most secret document, the *Rêveries*, is concerned with internal reform and defence, whereas Frederick's under the same title is full of schemes for aggrandisement. Joseph wrote in 1768, as though in reply to the very criticism that modern historians make:

> I am no more attached to the military than to finance. If I could be persuaded that the reduction of the army would be a real advantage, I would disband them this very day and make them labourers. But our circumstances are very far from permitting us to do anything like that. We must try always to combine the necessary security with the country's welfare.[61]

When he was reluctantly fighting the Turks in 1788, unsuccessfully leading his own troops in the inhospitable climates around the Danube, he wrote home to Kaunitz:

> Nothing is so easy as to propose that we should get together a couple of great armies, pass into enemy territory, provoke some important and decisive events by battles or sieges...
> But ... in Serbia or Bosnia, provinces in any case without resources and devastated, we would have 20 leagues of the finest country behind us, with the best agriculture and substantial population, which have cost immense sums to establish, ruined in a moment: neither the risk nor the advantage would be worth it. And by what right may even a sovereign, whom his subjects pay to defend them, allow their lives to be lost and their possessions taken away, and abandon them purely to go and make some insignificant conquests or to obtain futile advantages which resound only in the newspapers and in the opinion of the mass, while he would be diminishing the true capital of his state and weakening all its resources for years to come?[62]

Belgium is a striking case, a province (or group of provinces) that Joseph wanted to exchange with Bavaria. It has often been claimed that this foreign policy aim dominated his approach to domestic reform in Belgium. But his programme proceeded on very similar lines to his programme in Lombardy, which he had no idea of giving up. When he decided to have a second try at exchanging Belgium for Bavaria in 1784 – surely a scheme of such overwhelming strategic advantage to the Monarchy that it should have been pursued regardless of financial benefit – he wasted precious weeks enquiring how the revenues of the two provinces compared and, learning that Belgium was supposed to yield more than Bavaria, made his task even more difficult by demanding more than just Bavaria in exchange for it. Further, so little did he appreciate the risks associated with domestic reform that his drastic measures of 1787 to remodel the Belgian administration were promulgated when only a handful of troops were stationed in the province. In all these cases he allowed the pursuit of internal reform and fiscal advantage to take precedence over considerations of foreign policy.[63]

Joseph, then, was both despotic and in many respects enlightened. He would have liked to wield yet more despotic power and impose still more measures of an enlightened character. When in the last months of his life he conceded the failure of his attempt at personal rule, he was surrendering also the hope of carrying further his programme of enlightened reform in the Monarchy.

Notes

This is an expanded version of a lecture given in the Juridicum of the University of Vienna on 27 March 1990. I am grateful to Professor Grete Klingenstein and Professor Wilhelm Brauneder for making that occasion possible. Other organisations have heard variants of the piece and provided helpful comments on it, especially the Austrian Studies Conference of April 1989 at the University of Minnesota. I also owe thanks to Dr T. C. W. Blanning, Prof. P. G. M. Dickson, Mr S. M. Dixon, Dr T. J. Hochstrasser, Prof. S. E. Lehmberg, Dr L. Péter, Dr H. M. Scott, Dr S. J. C. Taylor and Dr R. L. Wokler, but I should emphasise that they are not to be taken to agree with every part of my argument.

1. M. Hawlik-van de Water, *Die Kapuzinergruft. Begräbnisstätte der Habsburger in Wien* (Vienna, 1987) gives details of the monuments, but does not explain why Joseph's is such a new departure.
2. A. von Arneth (ed.), *Joseph II. und Leopold von Toscana. Ihr Briefwechsel von 1781 bis 1790* (2 vols, Vienna, 1872), vol. II, pp. 303 (21 Dec. 1789), 304 (24 Dec.), 310 (14 Jan. 1790), 312 (21 Jan.).
3. The reports of the two Prussian envoys, Podewils and Jacobi, in Zentrales Staatsarchiv, Merseburg, esp. 20 and 24 Feb. 1790 (Rep.96.154.J). Cf. F. Engel-Jánosi, 'Josephs II. Tod im Urteil der Zeitgenossen', *Mitteilungen des österreichischen Instituts für Geschichtsforschung*, 44 (1930), 324–46.
4. W. Doyle, *London Review of Books*, 19 May 1988, pp. 19–20. Cf. his more recent remarks in *Times Higher Education Supplement*, 29 June 1990, reviewing Scott's collection (see next n.), in which he declares that Catherine II was the only enlightened *despot* and Joseph II 'the most celebrated practitioner of Enlightened absolutism'.

5. Among the most important are: F. Venturi, *Settecento riformatore* (Turin, 5 vols [7 tomes] to date, 1969–), esp. vol. IV, tome 2, section VIII (pp. 615–779), on Joseph II generally, and vol. V, tome 1, section III (pp. 425–834), on Lombard reformers; C. Capra, 'Il Settecento' in D. Sella and C. Capra, *Il Ducato di Milano dal 1535 al 1796* (Turin, 1984, vol. XI of *Storia d'Italia*, ed. G. Galasso), pp. 153–684; M. Bazzoli, *Il pensiero politico dell'assolutismo illuminato* (Florence, 1986); B. Köpeczi, A. Soboul, E. H. Balázs and D. Kosáry, *L'absolutisme éclairé* (Budapest, 1985); P. G. M. Dickson, *Finance and Government under Maria Theresa* (2 vols, Oxford, 1987); H. M. Scott (ed.), *Enlightened Absolutism* (London, 1990); G. Birtsch, 'Der Idealtyp des aufgeklärten Herrschers. Friedrich der Große, Karl Friedrich von Baden und Joseph II. im Vergleich', *Aufklärung* II, 9–47; V. Press, 'Kaiser Joseph II. – Reformer oder Despot?' in G. Vogler (ed.), *Europäische Herrscher. Ihre Rolle bei der Gestaltung von Politik und Gesellschaft vom 16. bis zum 18. Jahrhundert* (Weimar, 1988). I owe thanks to Professors Bazzoli, Dickson and Venturi, and to the editors of *L'absolutisme éclairé* for generously sending me copies of the volumes cited, and to Professor Sir Geoffrey Elton for lending me Press's article.
6. Dickson, *Finance and Government*, vol. I, pp. 318–19.
7. In Acton to Creighton, Apr. 1887 (L. Creighton, *Life and Letters of Mandell Creighton* (2 vols, London, 1906), vol. I, p. 372), with reference to popes and kings and in a sixteenth-century context.
8. It is perhaps sufficient to cite P. Gay, *The Enlightenment: An Interpretation* (2 vols, London, 1967–70), esp. vol. II, pp. 461–96.
9. To give references for the whole paragraph would mean providing a bibliography of the Enlightenment. For the differences in political outlook between Germans and others see esp. T. C. W. Blanning, *Reform and Revolution in Mainz, 1743–1803* (Cambridge, 1974), pp. 1–38.
10. B. Behrens, 'Enlightened despotism', *Historical Journal*, 18 (1975), 401–8.
11. W. Doyle, *The Ancien Régime* (London, 1986); C. B. A. Behrens, *The Ancien Régime* (London, 1967).
12. So it is universally stated. Dr Wokler has generously drawn my attention to Diderot's use of 'despotisme ... éclairé': *Œuvres politiques*, ed. P. Vernière (Paris, 1963), p. 272.
13. Behrens, *Historical Journal* (1975), 401. Cf. K. O. von Aretin (ed.), *Der aufgeklärte Absolutismus* (Cologne, 1974), p. 11, and M. Cranston, *Philosophers and Pamphleteers: Political Theorists of the Enlightenment* (Oxford, 1986), pp. 112, 114. These authors all seem to me to have misunderstood Le Mercier's argument, as, I think, in a different way has Gay (*Enlightenment*, vol. II, pp. 494–6).
14. The best treatment remains G. Weulersse, *Le mouvement physiocratique en France* (2 vols, Paris, 1910). For other valuable discussions see H. Holldack, 'Der Physiokratismus und die absolute Monarchie' in Aretin, *Aufgeklärte Absolutismus*, pp. 137–62; Bazzoli, *Pensiero politico*, esp. ch. X.
15. I. de Madariaga, *Russia in the Age of Catherine the Great* (London, 1981), pp. 337, 627.
16. E.g. Joseph II to the Duke of Courland, 2 Feb. 1781: 'les Terres ne fructifient jamais plus qu'entre les mains des Particuliers' (Vienna, Haus-, Hof- und Staatsarchiv, Handbilletenprotokolle, tom. V).
17. On the role of geometry in the thinking of German *Aufklärer*, especially Kaunitz, see G. Klingenstein, *Der Aufstieg des Hauses Kaunitz* (Göttingen, 1975), 168–70, and H. Klueting, *Die Lehre von der Macht der Staaten* (Berlin, 1986), esp. pp. 26, 172, 228. Professor Klingenstein generously sent me a copy of Klueting's book.
18. F. Bluche, 'Sémantique du despotisme éclairé', *Revue historique du droit français et étranger*, 4th series, vol. 56 (1978), 79–87, quotation from p. 86.
19. The third edition of Raynal's book seems to have become available only in 1781: Y. Benot, *Diderot, de l'Athéisme à l'Anticolonialisme* (Paris, 1981), p. 163. The quotation

is from vol. X of the Peuchet edition of 1820, p. 52.
20. On the part played by Diderot in the composition of Raynal's book, and on the development of his political attitudes, see Benot, *Diderot*; H. Wolpe, *Raynal et sa Machine de Guerre* (Stanford, 1957); Denis Diderot, *Pensées détachées* (2 vols, ed. G. Goggi, Siena, 1976–7); A. Strugnell, *Diderot's Politics* (The Hague, 1973); and the characteristically elusive discussion in L. Krieger, *An Essay on the Theory of Enlightened Despotism* (Chicago, 1975), pp. 20–2, 86–7.
21. The classic account is P. Gay, *Voltaire's Politics* (London, 1959), from which I differ in emphasis. See Voltaire on Montesquieu's distinction in *L'A.B.C* (1768) and A. Lortholary, *Le mirage russe en France au XVIIIe siècle* (Paris, 1951).
22. On Gorani and his book Venturi, *Settecento riformatore*, vol. V, tome 1, esp. pp. 500–11; Bazzoli, *Pensiero politico*, pp. 95–9; C. Capra introducing G. Gorani, *Storia di Milano (1700–1796)* (ed. A. Tarchetti, Bari, 1989), esp. pp. ix-xi. Prof. Capra kindly gave me a copy of this book, as also of his article cited in the next n.
23. Quoted in C. Capra, 'Alle origini del moderatismo e del giacobinismo in Lombardia: Pietro Verri e Pietro Custodi', *Studi storici* (1989), pp. 876–7.
24. Among treatments of this distinction I have found especially useful Krieger, *Enlightened Despotism*; Bazzoli, *Pensiero politico*, esp. ch. III.
25. Uses of 'absolu' in *De l'esprit des loix* are at least very rare. Montesquieu does refer to 'les monarchies extrêmement absolues' in Book XIX, ch. XXVI. For interpretation of the work see M. Richter, *The Political Theory of Montesquieu* (Cambridge, 1977); R. Shackleton, *Montesquieu* (Oxford, 1961), esp. ch. XII.
26. The articles are conveniently reprinted in J. Lough (ed.), *The Encyclopédie of Diderot and D'Alembert: Selected Articles* (Cambridge, 1954), pp. 160–4.
27. R. Mettam, *Power and Faction in Louis XIV's France* (London, 1988), pp. 34–5.
28. J. Bodin, *Six Books of the Commonwealth*, ed. M. J. Tooley (Oxford, n.d.), p. 32. Cf. Q. Skinner, *The Foundations of Modern Political Thought* (2 vols, Cambridge, 1978), vol. II, pp. 284–9.
29. A valuable discussion of the issues raised in this paragraph is to be found in F. Hartung and R. Mousnier, 'Quelques problèmes concernant la monarchie absolue' in the proceedings of the X Congresso Internazionale di scienze storiche (Rome, 1955), *Relazioni*, vol. IV, pp. 1–55. Cf. for Germany E. Parry, 'Enlightened Government and its Critics in Eighteenth Century Germany', *Historical Journal*, 6 (1963), 178–92; T. J. Reed, 'Talking to Tyrants: Dialogues with Power in Eighteenth-Century Germany', *ibid.* 33 (1990), 63–79.
30. Lough, *Encyclopédie: Selected Articles*, p. 163. I should add that Montesquieu's writings were found useful in certain respects by enlightened despots. See Bazzoli, *Pensiero politico*, esp. pp. 54–8; P. Dukes (ed.), *Catherine The Great's Instruction (NAKAZ) to the Legislative Commission, 1767* (Newtonville, 1977), Introduction.
31. Bodin, *Six Books*, pp. 56–9.
32. T. Hobbes, *Leviathan*, ed. M. Oakeshott (Oxford, n.d.), pp. 121, 132–3. A further range of semantic problems arises in Russian: see I. de Madariaga, 'Autocracy and Sovereignty', *Canadian-American Slavic Studies*, 16 (1982), 369–87.
33. See my *Joseph II. I: In the Shadow of Maria Theresa, 1741–1780* (Cambridge, 1987), pp. 43–68 and the sources cited there.
34. D. Beales, 'Joseph II's "Rêveries"', *Mitteilungen des österreichischen Staatsarchivs*, 33 (1980), esp. pp. 155–6. See my *Joseph II*, pp. 97–106.
35. J. Keresztury, *Introductio in opus collectionis normalium constitutorum. quae regnante ... Josepho II. pro regno Hungariae ... condita sunt* (Vienna, 1788), pt.2, p. 96.
36. Haus-, Hof- und Staatsarchiv, Vienna, Staatsrataktenprotokollen 1784, vol. III, no. 3602.
37. There is no entirely satisfactory account of his Hungarian policies and his

renunciation of them. The best guide in English is C. A. Macartney, *The Habsburg Empire 1790–1918* (London, 1968), chs 1–3. For a valuable recent contribution see H. Haselsteiner, *Joseph II. und die Komitate Ungarns* (Vienna, 1983).
38. For Joseph and the Brabant revolution the best treatments available in English are W. W. Davis, *Joseph II: An Imperial Reformer for the Austrian Netherlands* (The Hague, 1974) and J. L. Polasky, *Revolution in Brussels, 1787–1793* (London, 1987), but neither has gone beyond the published sources on the emperor himself. Cf. Beales, *Joseph II*, p. 5.
39. Beales, *Joseph II*, p. 215.
40. I first encountered this striking document in the Austrian collection of the library of the University of Minnesota in Minneapolis (MS Z943.6 fEs 73) (pp. 528). I later found another copy, apparently identical in text though not in pagination, in the Acton MSS, University Library, Cambridge. My quotations come from pp. 67–9, 73, 89, 216, 508 in the Minneapolis version.
41. I have as yet found no reference of any kind, contemporary or subsequent, to this not inconspicuous document. The fact that there is a copy in the Acton MSS clearly links it to the Acton family. On p. 479 of the MS it is coyly stated: 'Je ne dirai rien du Marquis de Gallo ..., parceque je suis partial.' Cf. A. Wandruszka, *Leopold II*. (2 vols, Vienna, 1963–5), vol. II, pp. 213–19, 297-301.
42. E.g. Joseph to Leopold, 7 Aug. 1782; 6 July 1787 (Arneth, *Joseph und Leopold*, vol. I, pp. 128–9; vol. II, p. 83).
43. Joseph to Kaunitz, 23-24 June 1787, from Leopol (Haus-, Hof- und Staatsarchiv, Vienna, Handbilletenprotokollen, vol. XI).
44. Beales, *Joseph II*, pp. 55-63.
45. D. Beales, 'The False Joseph II', *Historical Journal*, 18 (1975), 467–95; id. 'Christians and *philosophes*: the case of the Austrian Enlightenment' in D. Beales and G. Best (eds), *History, Society and the Churches: Essays in honour of Owen Chadwick* (Cambridge, 1985), pp. 169–194.
46. Birtsch, *Aufklärung*, II (1987), 9–47.
47. Beales, *Joseph II*, pp. 377–8, 393. H. Wagner, 'Die Reise Josephs II. nach Frankreich 1777 und die Reformen in Österreich' in *Österreich und Europa. Festgabe für Hugo Hantsch zum 70. Geburtstag* (Vienna, 1965), pp. 221–46.
48. Gebler to Nicolai, 16 Nov. 1783: R. M. Werner (ed.), *Aus dem josephinischen Wien* (Berlin, 1888), p. 112.
49. They were republished in D. G. Mohnike, 'Briefwechsel Kaiser Josephs II. mit Clemens Wenzel, Churfürst von Trier', *Zeitschrift für die historische Theologie*, 4 (1834), 263–90.
50. One contemporary German version was *Joseph des Zweyten Erinnerung an seine Staatsbeamten, am Schlusse des 1783ten Jahres* (Vienna, [1784]). The original French MS is in Haus-, Hof- und Staatsarchiv, Vienna, Staatskanzleivorträge 138 (1783).
51. Its inspiration is acknowledged by Keresztury, *Introductio*, Pt. I, p.iv; in [J. Kropatschek,] *Handbuch aller unter der Regierung des Kaiser Joseph des II. für die KK Erbländer ergangenen Verordnungen und Gesetze ... 1780 bis 1784*, vol. I (Vienna, 1785), p. (i); and in J. N. von Hempel-Kürsinger (ed.), *Alphabetisch=chronologische Übersicht der k.k. Gesetze und Verordnungen vom Jahre 1740 bis zum Jahre 1821*, vol. I (1825), p. (vii).
52. On *Faustin* see L. Bodi, *Tauwetter in Wien: Zur Prosa der österreichischen Aufklärung 1781–1795* (Vienna, 1977), pp. 184–91; M. Delon, 'Candide au service de Joseph II' in E. Bene (ed.), *Les Lumières en Hongrie, en Europe centrale et en Europe orientale. Actes du 4me Colloque de Mátrafüred, 1978*, pp. 61–6.
53. This seems to me true both of Bodi and of E. Wangermann, for example in *The Austrian Achievement, 1700–1800* (London, 1973), pp. 142–7, 157–66.

54. *Ludwig van Beethoven's Werke. Serie 25: Supplement* (Leipzig, 1887), pp. 1–54.
55. Beales, *Mitteilungen des österreichischen Staatsarchivs*, 33 (1980), p. 156.
56. Beales, *Joseph II*, p. 237.
57. Ibid. pp. 164–76, 445–55.
58. Ibid. pp. 154–5, 317–18.
59. Ibid. p. 469. E. Kovacs, *Der Pabst in Teutschland* (Munich, 1983), p. 101.
60. J. Whaley, *Religious Toleration and Social Change in Hamburg, 1529–1819* (Cambridge, 1985), p. 146; J. Karniel, *Die Toleranzpolitik Kaiser Josephs II.* (Gerlingen, 1986); P. von Mitrofanov, *Joseph II. Seine politische und kulturelle Tätigkeit* (2 vols, Vienna, 1910), pp. 841–2.
61. Beales, *Joseph II*, p. 189 and chs 9 and 13.
62. Joseph to Kaunitz, 26 Aug. 1788: A. Beer (ed.), *Joseph II., Leopold II. und Kaunitz* (Vienna, 1873), pp. 307–08.
63. For a chronology of Italian church legislation see F. Valsecchi, *L'assolutismo illuminato in Austria e in Lombardia* (2 vols, Bologna, 1931–4), vol. II, p. 238n. On the attempted exchange of 1784, P. P. Bernard, *Joseph II and Bavaria* (The Hague, 1965), chs X and XI. For the Belgian reforms, Davis, *Joseph II*, esp. ch. VII.

Joseph Rohrer and the Bureaucratic Enlightenment

Ritchie Robertson

Our understanding of the Enlightenment has recently changed in emphasis. Sixty years ago, Ernst Cassirer's influential *The Philosophy of the Enlightenment* described a purely intellectual movement.[1] He did not inquire how the ideas of the *philosophes* affected the practice of eighteenth-century absolute monarchs. In fact, eighteenth-century rulers were largely hostile to theorising. Maria Theresa frequently denounced the *philosophes*. Her son Joseph II maintained the ban on the writings of Voltaire and Hume, ostentatiously refrained from visiting Voltaire when passing through Ferney, and brusquely rebuffed offers of advice from Joseph von Sonnenfels, the most prominent intellectual of the Austrian Enlightenment.[2] Scarcely any of the reforms introduced under enlightened absolutism can be shown to have been directly inspired by specific doctrines of the *philosophes*. They are due rather to the spread of enlightened thinking among the vast numbers of bureaucrats who ran the eighteenth-century 'police states'.[3] The importance of these university-trained and reform-minded administrators as bearers of the Enlightenment has been demonstrated above all by the historian Franco Venturi.[4] If Cassirer presented the philosophical Enlightenment, Venturi has transferred attention to the bureaucratic Enlightenment.

This is the context in which to see the work of Joseph Rohrer (1769-1828), a member of the new class of enlightened bureaucrats, who was also a cultivated man and an entertaining and idiosyncratic writer. His major literary project was an ethnographic study of all the peoples of the Habsburg domains, three volumes of which were completed. And he upheld the ideals of Josephinism long after the anti-Josephinian reaction of the 1790s. The virtually complete neglect of his work by modern historians is difficult to understand.[5] He deserves to be rescued from oblivion.

Although born in Vienna, Joseph Rohrer was brought up in the Tyrol, where he attended the Haupt-Gymnasium at Innsbruck.[6] After attending the University of Vienna, where his studies included mathematics, he entered the civil service in 1791, initially as a book-keeper at Bregenz. Soon, however, he was transferred to Vienna, where he evidently mixed in literary circles: he knew Johann Baptist von Alxinger personally, and some of his early essays were published in the *Österreichische Monatsschrift* (1793-4), a short-lived periodical edited first by Alxinger and then by Gottlieb Leon and Joseph Schreyvogel.[7] He also published two books: *Uiber die Tiroler* (1796), a first effort at ethnographic writing, and *Neuestes Gemählde von Wien* (1797), intended as an updated successor to Johann Pezzl's *Skizze von Wien* (1789). By 1797 he must already have moved into the police service, for his second book goes into detail about the functioning of the police and includes much sociological information about the behaviour of thieves and prostitutes. In 1800 he went as a commissioner of police to Lemberg (now Lvov), capital of Galicia, the province which had been added to the Habsburg domains in 1772 by the first partition of Poland.[8] Commissioners of police had extensive powers. They were supposed not only to forestall and punish crime, but to prevent people from being idle or making a noise in public. From 1801 they were also in charge of censorship.[9] Even with wide powers, however, Rohrer's job cannot have been easy. A travel account of the 1780s describes Lemberg as full of brothels which the police, at that time, made no attempt to control; another, from the early 1790s, denounces the town's administration as exceptionally slow and inefficient.[10]

Rohrer's ethnographic project probably antedates his move to Lemberg. He mentions (B 146) that one of his books, the *Versuch über die slawischen Bewohner der österreichischen Monarchie,* was completed in 1801 and delivered to the Court Censorship, which evidently took three years to deal with it. The oddities of Habsburg bureaucracy presumably account for his publishing five books in a single year (1804). These included a statistical account of the Tyrol and neighbouring regions, concentrating on physical rather than human geography, and an account in letter form of a journey from Moldavia, just across the south-eastern frontier of the Habsburg territories, via the Bukovina to Galicia, and from there through Silesia and Moravia to Vienna. The journey was begun on 20 November 1802 and ended in Vienna in April 1803. More important, however, are the three ethnographic works dealing respectively with the Germans, the Slavs, and the Jews. These three books, amounting together to more than a thousand pages, give evidence not only of extensive travel, but also of wide reading and remarkable industry.

In 1806, no doubt thanks to his publications, Rohrer was appointed professor of statistics at the University of Lemberg. After repeated requests for a transfer, he received a similar post in Olmütz (Olomouc in Moravia) in 1816, but returned to his position in Lemberg two years later. He knew the playwright Franz Kratter, who was living in rural retirement outside Lemberg and was the leading figure in its German-language literature. Rohrer's own writing seems to have been hindered by his teaching duties, for he published nothing more until 1827, when the first volume of a planned statistical account of the entire Habsburg dominions appeared. Ill-health, particularly an illness of the chest, obliged him to retire prematurely in 1822, and his statistical project was cut short by his death on 21 September 1828.

Throughout his life Rohrer travelled extensively within the Habsburg domains. By 1804, when he published his major ethnographic works, he had travelled widely in the German-speaking lands, Bohemia, Moravia, Carniola, Silesia, and of course Galicia. From his last book it appears that by 1827 he had also become familiar with Hungary, which is seldom mentioned in the earlier books. However, he seems scarcely ever to have been outside Habsburg territory. He tells us that he had visited Regensburg (D i.114), but despite his enthusiasm for English life and literature, only one reference suggests that he had actually visited Britain. In *Uiber die Tiroler* he tells how Tyrolean canary-sellers travel as far as London, where 'in the City, in the handsome square Moorfields, [they] have a special booth to sell their birds; since this booth stands between two madhouses, St Luke's Hospital and Goldbedlam [sic], it makes a strange impression on the feelings of the onlooker' (T 44). This could, however, be a second-hand account.

To read systematically through Rohrer's works is to become aware of a tension between his bureaucratic calling and his imagination. With part of his mind he enthusiastically appreciates the human diversity of the Habsburg domains. Another part of his mind, however, wants to judge that diversity by the single standard of progress towards enlightenment, and to substitute uniformity and discipline. In propagating enlightenment, he comes close to regarding people, not as Kantian ends in themselves, but as objects of administration who must, if necessary, be disciplined into happiness.

Similar tensions are obvious in the career of Rohrer's hero, the other Joseph. In his enthusiasm for enlightened reform, Joseph II failed to realise that rational arguments were not sufficient to win people for his reforms. Though sincerely devoted to his conception of his people's good, he was also a friendless workaholic, tactless and often wounding in dealing with relatives, associates, and subjects.[11] He showed his insensitivity when in 1784 he ordained that the Hungarian Crown of St Stephen should be transferred from Pressburg (Bratislava) to Vienna, thus arousing a storm of protest from the Hungarians whom Maria Theresa had worked so hard to conciliate; and when he ordained that, because of the timber shortage in Vienna, corpses should be sewn into linen sacks instead of being buried in coffins – an edict which aroused such fury that it had to be withdrawn.[12] Hence his subjects felt no affection for him, as a contemporary pamphleteer pointed out.[13] Rohrer's writings, like Joseph's career, illustrate the tensions generated by the Enlightenment with its promise of happiness under the rule of reason.

Unlike the Emperor, Rohrer was a highly cultivated man. He had a remarkable knowledge of languages, being familiar not only with Latin and Greek but with English, French, Italian, Polish, and at least one South Slavonic language. In Galicia he was able to communicate with servants and peasants in Ukrainian. In later life he appears also to have mastered Hungarian. His reading in classical and modern languages was extensive, though his taste was conservative. He speaks familiarly of the literature of the Austrian Enlightenment, praising Alxinger, Blumauer, Denis and Mastalier, and though he considers Austrian literature to be in decline, he commends the writings of Gabriele von Baumberg and Karoline Pichler (D ii. 9–10). Although he praises the good taste of Schiller's periodical *Die Horen* and knows the Schlegels' *Athenäum*, he never mentions Goethe. His heroes among German writers are Lessing and Kant; he also refers appreciatively to the idylls of Salomon Gessner. In the theatre he praises Lessing's *Minna von Barnhelm* and the domestic comedies of Iffland and Kratter. He dislikes the vulgarity of Viennese popular comedy, complaining:

> daß unsere Damen und Fräulein in den vorstädtischen Theatern die zottenhaften Reden, Gebärdenspiele und Gassenlieder in dem Fagottisten, den Nymphen der Silberquelle, den Waldmännern u. m. s. mit vollen Händen beklatschen, und immer noch lieber als eine Minna von Barnhelm im Nazional-Theater besuchen (G 179).[14]

> [Our married and unmarried ladies clap their hands vigorously at the obscene speeches, gestures and popular songs in *The Fagottist, The Nymph of the Silver Spring, The Woodmen*, etc., and would still far rather see them than go to *Minna von Barnhelm* in the National Theatre.]

Shakespeare is never mentioned: the mutilated versions of *Hamlet* and *Macbeth* performed on the eighteenth-century Viennese stage would hardly arouse enthusiasm. Rohrer's preferences in English literature are those usual in Vienna in the 1780s: he likes Pope, who provides epigraphs to two of his books, and Macpherson's 'Ossian', which had been translated into German by the Austrian poet Denis.[15] He also quotes Gibbon, Hume, and Sterne's *Tristram Shandy*, while the drunkenness in Galicia reminds him of Hogarth's punch-drinkers.

A large proportion of Rohrer's extensive reading, especially in English, consists of political and statistical works. Like many contemporaries, from Voltaire and Diderot to the Italian nobleman Alberto Radicati and the Bavarian-born novelist Johann Pezzl, he saw Britain as the birthplace of enlightenment.[16] His reading ranges from Adam Smith and the zoologist Thomas Pennant to William Marshall's *Rural Economy* (1788) and James Robertson's *View of the Agriculture in the County of Perth* (1799). His favourite periodical was evidently the *Staatsanzeigen* edited by the Göttingen historian A. L. Schlözer; this enjoyed such favour among the enlightened that Blumauer, in his anticlerical travesty of the *Aeneid*, has it read by the sanctified philosophers inhabiting his enlightened heaven.[17] Schlözer's studies of Russia are themselves important early contributions to ethnography or 'Völkerkunde', a word which Schlözer apparently coined.[18] Rohrer also kept up with travel writing, including not only well-known accounts of Pacific voyages by Cook and Forster, but even such an obscure work as Martin Martin's *A Late Voyage to St Kilda* (1698; often reprinted), which Rohrer quotes in order to compare the St Kildans to the isolated, eagle-hunting inhabitants of Plangross in the Tyrol.

Rohrer also enjoyed the other arts. He proclaims his love of music, especially that of Haydn and Mozart, and tells us: 'It is my own playing of several stringed instruments that has enabled me to forget many unmerited slights' (D ii. 12). He took a guitar on his journey to Moldavia and back, and at an inn near Vienna was glad to be able to dispel his low spirits by playing a piano. His love of music is evident also from the account he gives of the musical gifts of the Czechs (S ii. 24). In *Statistik des österreichischen Kaiserthums* he enthusiastically praises the architecture of Palladio and others, and lists the buildings to be seen in and near Vicenza, including the Villa Rotonda and the tomb of Canova. *Uiber die Tiroler* includes a long list of painters born in or near the Tyrol, notably the famous Angelika Kauffmann, who is mentioned with great pride (T 69). His taste in landscape runs to romantic mountain scenery and the picturesque disorder of English gardens. 'Romantisch' and 'mahlerisch' ('picturesque') are terms of praise. He had even read theorists of the picturesque, for he recommends Addison and Home (D ii. 45).[19]

In discussing Rohrer's writings, I shall say little about the *Abriß der westlichen Provinzen des österreichischen Staates* and the *Statistik des österreichischen Kaiserthums*, since these are dryly factual books which can interest only the economic historian. His travel narrative also consists largely of information about geography and agriculture, interspersed with brief references to the hospitality he receives and the discomforts of his journey. I shall concentrate on the ethnographic works, which most deserve attention for their informational and literary value.

Since Rohrer's was the first attempt in Austria to compose ethnography, in his preface to his study of the German-speaking subjects of the Habsburgs he is at pains to define his undertaking. It is not a history, he insists, but a descriptive account (not 'Völkergeschichte' but 'Völkerbeschreibung', D i. 13). He usually describes his work as 'Völkerkunde'. Its purpose, he explains, is to inform patriots about the resources and present state of their country and indicate how people's material and moral condition may be improved. Elsewhere, he defends his discursive and personal style by explaining that he is not writing simply for scholars, but has in mind a wide readership, in whom he wants to inculcate an appreciation of beauty and sublimity and an interest in the size and resources of their fatherland.[20] Each of his three ethnographic books is divided into eight sections. The first four describe in turn the physical character, the diet, the dress, and the occupations of the people in question; the next four deal with cultural and moral matters, namely their aesthetic sense ('Kunstsinn'), their mentality ('Denkart'), their religion, and their moral character. He tells us that, having found very few written sources of any value, his knowledge is drawn mainly from observation.

Despite his reliance on first-hand experience, Rohrer still needed literary models to organise his material. Very few books were of direct use. His closest model appears to be the survey of non-Slavic peoples of the Russian Empire by Johann Gottlieb Georgi.[21] Georgi's book systematically and informatively examines the material and cultural life of numerous peoples, but is much more concise and impersonal than Rohrer's. Rohrer explains that his task is harder, since the peoples surveyed by Georgi were all at a primitive level, whereas those in Austria are at many different points along the scale running from 'savagery' via 'civilization' to 'sophistication' (D i. 7).

Rohrer's ethnographic works are a bold and sometimes uneasy hybrid of two forms of writing: the travel narrative and the statistical account. Travel narrative is a familiar genre. It foregrounds personal experience, mediated to us by the voice of the narrator. It narrates direct encounters between the traveller and other people. The statistical account originated from the desire to impose method on travel-writing. In the early modern period, travellers were encouraged to make their observations systematic. Manuals called apodemics told them what to look for and what questions to ask.[22] The apodemic developed into the statistical account, which is severely impersonal and factual. Although it does not consist solely of figures (as the modern sense of 'statistics' might suggest), it does present information as far as possible in quantitative and tabular form. Where a persona can be discerned, it is that of the dispassionate scientific enquirer or the public-spirited civil servant. Statistical accounts of the Habsburg domains, in which short accounts of various peoples are squeezed between lists of geographical and agricultural data, were already available in Rohrer's day, the best-known being by J. A. Demian.[23] Rohrer's ethnographic project was original in trying to combine factual and personal modes of writing.

On the one hand, Rohrer is writing as a traveller. His experiences in the Tyrol and Galicia, like Forster's in the Pacific, have appealed to his imagination, and he uses his literary talent to record them vividly. Hence his ethnographic works contain numerous anecdotes and personal reflections, especially in the footnotes. These interfere with his other intention, which is to provide a methodical survey of the human resources of the Habsburg domains. While Georgi's book is his main ethnographical model, his principal model of statistical writing, if a single one can be isolated, is the *Statistical Account of Scotland* edited by Sir John Sinclair.[24] This massive project surveys the material and cultural state of every parish, the entries being written in each case by the parish minister. Rohrer refers admiringly to this work, but adds mournfully: 'Where, save in Scotland and Bohemia, is the clergy so far advanced in the love of sciences as to include not only theological but also profane knowledge (as it is called) among its intellectual interests?' (D ii. 107). Another model which is frequently apparent is the moral essays of the popular philosophers, which were widely read in eighteenth-century Germany and helped considerably to diffuse enlightened ideas. Rohrer had evidently read many of these, and refers admiringly to the best known of the popular philosophers, Christian Garve, whose knowledge of human nature he praises (D i.224; G 191). That he is writing in part as a moralist is signalled by the epigraph to his *Versuch über die deutschen Bewohner der österreichischen Monarchie*, which comes from Book 1 of Pope's *Essay on Man:*

> Eye Nature's walks, shoot Folly as it flies,
> And catch the Manners living as they rise;
> Laugh where we must, be candid where we can—

Rohrer's literary talents are best displayed in some lyrical descriptive passages, especially the descriptions of female beauty which figure prominently in his sections on the physical character of the various peoples, and his account of the festivities held on the first Sunday in August on the Brigittenau near Vienna. These passages bring us to the centre of his imaginative world. His ideal landscape, his *locus amoenus*, is a meadow surrounded by water. The Brigittenau is a 'romantic island', a 'meadow embraced by the double arm of the Danube' (D ii. 159), while the Linz area, whose girls Rohrer particularly admires, is 'this romantic landscape embraced by two rivers' (D i. 51). In this setting culture and nature are reconciled. The Viennese enjoy themselves in a manner which is 'relaxed, natural and cordial' (D ii. 59) while deer graze unafraid in their presence. The repeated word 'embraced' ('umschlungen'), with its sexual connotation, gently eroticises the landscape. The union of nature and culture is embodied in female beauty: the Bregenzerwald girl is 'this untroubled daughter of Nature' (D i. 64). Natural beauty surpasses art: Linz girls have 'cheeks whose rosy colour shifts with their changing emotions through all possible shades, now into darker, now into lighter tones, so charmingly that no painter can imitate it' (D i. 52), while the Bregenzerwald girl has 'features which only Angelika Kauffmann, who was born here, contrived to express in her painting of Elisa as a nun' (D i. 64). Literature, however, can convey these suggestions: the description of Linz girls ends by alluding to Rousseau's *La nouvelle Héloise* (D i. 52), and the charms of Viennese girls invite the reflection: 'but O Montaigne! it is the cats who play with us, not we with them' (G 173).[25] Here the literary reference reintroduces animal imagery as the expression of nature at one with culture. In such passages we see Rohrer's share in the late eighteenth-century sensibility which gave a heartfelt response to natural beauty: the sensibility of Rousseau and the young Goethe.

The literary persona Rohrer usually adopts is that of an unprejudiced friend of humanity ('unbefangener Menschenfreund', D i. 100), who combines reason and feeling in the service of his country. Although a Catholic, he considers the essence of Christianity to lie in toleration and right action ('Rechthandeln', D ii. 119). He shares, in other words, the Enlightenment ideal of undogmatic, practical religion most famously expressed in Lessing's *Nathan der Weise* (1779).

Rohrer makes no secret of his Josephinism. His writings are filled with references to 'the unforgettable Joseph' (e.g. D i. 38), 'this creative monarch, at whose urn, sunk in profound reverence, I silently mourn' (S i. 52). Maria Theresa is also mentioned with respect, as is Joseph's successor Leopold II and even the enlightened Portuguese minister Pombal, but references to Franz I, who ruled Austria from 1792 to 1835, are few and lukewarm.

In the aftermath of the Jacobin trials, however, a profession of Josephinist ideals could risk being misinterpreted. In 1794 Jacobin conspiracies were uncovered in Vienna, Graz, and Budapest. Eight of the principal accused were executed the following year, while numerous others received long prison sentences. Accordingly, in *Neuestes Gemählde von Wien* Rohrer declares his Josephinism in a manner which, while unmistakable, is also inoffensive. Early in the book he describes the inscription which has been placed, with (as he emphasises) official permission, on the house of a wealthy Greek in the Fleischmarkt. Beneath a likeness of Joseph II the following verse is inscribed in golden letters:

> Vergänglich ist dies Haus
> Doch Josephs Nachruhm nie
> Er gab uns Toleranz
> Unsterblichkeit gibt sie.
>
> [This house will pass away, but Joseph's fame never will: he gave us toleration, and that gives immortality.] (G 12)

Later in *Neuestes Gemählde von Wien* Rohrer forthrightly blames the censorship for the poor state of contemporary literature. He shows some discomfort over the reintroduction of capital punishment, half-heartedly justifying it by reference to the troubled times and 'the turbulent will of the people' which has clamoured for it (G 137). He notes a general change in the Viennese character in the 1790s: they have become unsociable and suspicious of foreigners. This he attributes to 'the events in France and the intensified vigilance of the government which these have rendered necessary' (G 171): again, his defence is so lame as to imply a criticism. At the end of the book Rohrer firmly asserts his own patriotism and comments cautiously on the political disposition of the Viennese. All want peace and order, but want to achieve these by different means: 'some pay traditional reverence to the legal and monarchical constitution, others want to establish and strengthen it by better understanding' (G 203–4). This is a plea for an intelligent patriotism.

In all his works, Rohrer's patriotism is that of a state official concerned for the public weal. He holds the economic assumptions of cameralism: that it is important for a state to be wealthy, that wealth depends on the happiness and prosperity of its subjects, and that the state should therefore regulate its subjects' lives in considerable detail.[26] He also takes for granted the mercantilist principle that a state should as far as possible be economically self-sufficient. His writing follows the tradition founded by the Habsburg bureaucrat Philipp Wilhelm von Hörnigk, author of *Österreich über alles, wenn es nur will* ('Austria above all others, if only it wants to be', 1684). A more immediate model, praised as an 'ardent patriot' (G 112), is the reformer Sonnenfels, who in 1763 was appointed by Maria Theresa to the newly founded chair of government ('Polizeiwissenschaft') at Vienna. Besides a standard textbook on the principles of administration, which Rohrer would undoubtedly have read, Sonnenfels wrote an influential moral weekly, *Der Mann ohne Vorurteil* ('The Man Without Prejudice', 1765–7). The two enterprises were linked by the conviction, which Rohrer also held, that private morality is essential to public welfare.[27]

In both public and private life, Rohrer is concerned to describe and promote the progress of enlightenment. For him, as usually in eighteenth-century German usage, enlightenment is not the name of a period but denotes a process of intellectual, moral and cultural advance. Like his mentor Kant, Rohrer emphasises the spread of intellectual autonomy, the development of the ability to think for oneself.[28] 'Selbstdenken' ('intellectual autonomy') is one of Rohrer's favourite words. His enlightenment is also, by implication, politically radical. This appears from the definition of 'true enlightenment' that Rohrer quotes from an anonymous work, the *Geschichte der Vervollkommnung des menschlichen Geschlechts* ('History of the Perfecting of the Human Race', 1788): 'Where true enlightenment rules, no one demands more than his due; there is a true estimation of property and merit. A person's inner worth decides everything; appearance gives nothing' (S ii. 49–50n).

Rohrer is convinced that the world is governed by Providence, and perceives its workings in the discovery of the potato, which nourishes the poor, and in the propensity even of animals to put sociability above self-preservation. Although writing during the Napoleonic wars, he maintains a Panglossian conviction that we live in 'the best of worlds' (D ii. 97). The cultivated shores of Lake Constance support his belief in history as progress:

> Einst erschienen den gebildeten Römischen Kriegern, als sie zum ersten Mahle in diese Gegenden vordrangen, die streifenden Allemannischen Horden, welche hier ihnen aufstießen, wahrscheinlich in eben jenem Bilde, in welchem wir Deutsche vor nicht langer Zeit die nordamerikanischen Wilden ansahen (D i. 197).
>
> [When the civilised Roman warriors first penetrated into these regions, the wandering Alemannic hordes which encountered them probably presented the same image as we Germans, not long ago, beheld in the North American savages.][29]

Disasters still happen, but people's increased readiness to help one another demonstrates the spread of humanity and confutes the 'disparagement of enlightenment' practised by those 'watchers for Zion ('Zions-Wächter') who threaten us with the Last Judgement' (D ii. 169–70). This is a shallow conception of progress: it compares poorly with Herder's remark that the progress of civilisation resembles a mountain torrent rather than a gently flowing river, or Kant's conception of the progress of society through the mutual antagonism of its members.[30]

Though unimpressive as an amateur philosopher, Rohrer deserves respect when he deals with the diffusion of enlightenment among ordinary people ('Volksaufklärung', D ii. 78). This interest distinguishes him from many proponents of enlightenment who thought that ordinary people could not benefit from it.[31] He gives credit to individuals who work for the enlightenment of the people, like the South Tyrolean Abbate Tartarotti with his campaign against belief in witchcraft, and the Lutheran clergyman Magliarik who introduced cotton-spinning among the Slovaks (S i. 108).[32]

In Rohrer's ethnographic treatises, the chapters on 'Kunstsinn' deal principally with popular culture. A people's aesthetic sense, he says, cannot be judged by their knowledge of great artists, of whom they have seldom heard, but by the construction of their houses, furniture, and domestic utensils. Music and dancing are also discussed: Carniolan dances, for example, are praised as 'no less lively than skilful' (S ii. 12). For Rohrer, aesthetic culture also includes activities like the mechanical ingenuity of the Tyroleans. As an example of their ingenuity, Rohrer describes a cradle being rocked by remote control:

> So traff ich zufällig einmahl in einer Alpenhütte des Zillerthales eine sanft und gleichförmig geschaukelte Wiege, ohne in der ganzen Wohnung außer dem schlummernden Kinde und einer heimischen Dohle eine andere Seele zu entdecken. Dies brachte mich auf den Einfall, die Schnur, welche hinaus ins Freye ging, zu verfolgen. In einer Entfernung von etwa 50 Schritten fand ich dann dieselbe mit einer kleinen Verrichtung, welche das Gepräge der simplen Natur trug, an einem Rade festgemacht, welches von einer Felsenquelle herumgetrieben wurde (T 60–1).

[Thus I once, in an Alpine cottage in the Zillerthal, came upon a cradle rocking gently and regularly, although there was not another soul to be found in the entire house besides the sleeping baby and a pet jackdaw. This made me think of following the string which led out of doors. At a distance of some fifty paces I then found the string attached by a small device, which bore the mark of simple nature, to a wheel which was turned by a rocky brook.]

Rohrer's literary skill is shown by the delightful though strictly unnecessary detail of the pet jackdaw, which brings the little episode to life.

An important aspect of popular enlightenment is the attack on superstition. Rohrer rejects the idea that popular superstitions should be tolerated. He deplores the Tyroleans' fondness for going on pilgrimages to Venice, Einsiedeln in Switzerland, the Wieskirche in Bavaria, and Weingarten in Swabia (T 82). He reports with horror that even within the last half-century an alleged witch was burnt at Würzburg (T 84).[33] Such superstitions have been adequately explained, Rohrer considers, by the popular philosopher Zimmermann in his account of the hallucinations arising from solitude.[34] As for more primitive peoples, the belief in vampires still held by the Morlaks of Dalmatia proves to Rohrer that they are at a rudimentary stage of development (S ii. 30).

For Rohrer, enlightenment extends beyond religious belief into personal morality. 'The treatment of the female sex, of servants in general, and of strangers is practically the correct standard by which to judge a nation's degree of moral culture' (S ii. 6). This idea underlies Rohrer's sharp criticism of the Polish nobility, who display a veneer of French culture but no genuine enlightenment. Although they are servile when paying formal calls on officials, they treat the same officials rudely when they pass them in the street (S ii. 130): Rohrer no doubt speaks from personal experience. He castigates their habits of idleness and luxury, and their brutality towards their servants.

More generally, enlightenment means, as it did for the French Encyclopaedists and for the classical Goethe, the diffusion of useful knowledge.[35] Rohrer takes a keen interest in industrial and agricultural methods, deploring the backward state of Styrian mining (D ii. 70) and the primitive agricultural implements used in Dalmatia (S i. 91). He offers many suggestions about how the Galicians could exploit their land by planting grass on the sandy banks of the Vistula, extracting oil from sunflowers, and growing hops and cherries (S i. 131-8). He proposes a vast system of canals, connecting the Elbe with the Vltava and the March (east of Vienna) with the Oder, and extending into Lower Austria and Hungary (D i. 239). He complains that human excrement pollutes streams and rivers, when it might be used to manure fields, as is done by the peasants around Linz (D i. 147). A sign that Galicians are 'unenlightened' ('unaufgeklärt') is that they do not know what precautions to take against cattle disease (S ii. 43-4). Humans, too, require medical precautions: Rohrer repeatedly advocates inoculation for smallpox and cowpox.

Rohrer's advocacy of popular enlightenment of course has political implications. It is incompatible with serfdom: people can hardly think for themselves if they cannot work for themselves. In describing the Galician peasants Rohrer points out how the compulsion to labour for their feudal lord makes the peasants careless, lazy, and prone to do wanton damage (S i. 125–7). He praises Joseph II for granting peasants civil rights and reducing their compulsory labour. And he makes much of the happiness of the Tyroleans, clearly his favourites, who had managed to retain their ancient freedom when the rest of central Europe was reduced to a second serfdom:

> Patriarch auf seinem sonnigen Hügel oder im Thalschrunde führt der tirolische Bauer eine abgesonderte Wirtschaft, und weiß von Hörigkeit nichts. [...] Bey solch einem Grad politischer und bürgerlicher Freyheit, welchen diese Bergbewohner unstreitig größtentheils der Humanität ihrer Oesterreichischen Beherrscher zu verdanken haben, ergiebt sich von selbst der Schluß, daß die Tiroler – wenn anders Glückseligkeit hienieden unter dem Monde gesucht werden kann, ein glückliches Volk in ihrem Felsenrund sind (T 136, 139).

> [Patriarch on his sunny hill or in the deep valley, the Tyrolean peasant manages an independent household and knows nothing of feudal servitude. [...] With such a degree of political and civil freedom, which these mountain-dwellers unquestionably owe in large part to the humanity of their Austrian rulers, it is natural to conclude that, if indeed happiness can be sought in this sublunary world, the Tyroleans are a happy nation within their rocky circle.]

This makes manifest one of the tensions in Rohrer's commitment to enlightenment. Although he is strongly attached to the Tyroleans, he has to admit that they have not been receptive to enlightened influences. Their widespread illiteracy and their inability to speak High German have debarred them from high culture. Many of them display what Rohrer tactfully calls 'ein gewisser mit vieler Behaglichkeit verbundener Ideenstillstand' ('a certain comfortable fixity of ideas', T 77). They do not even know their own history. One curious instance he gives of their backwardness in civilisation is that in certain districts children address their parents by the familiar pronoun 'du' (T 104).

Moreover, the Tyroleans were not sympathetic to Joseph II's reforms. As devout Catholics, they objected to the dissolution of contemplative monasteries (23 were dissolved in the German Tyrol alone). They resented the sharp diminution in the powers of their provincial Estates. Having been exempt from compulsory military service, they resented Joseph II's introduction of a uniform conscription throughout his domains. On Joseph II's death, the Tyroleans successfully appealed to Leopold II to restore their former constitution and their exemption from conscription.[36]

Rohrer gives an instance in which Joseph II's reforms threatened to cause serious harm. Since all Tyroleans expect to marry, the priests can ensure that a young man who gets a girl pregnant will marry her once he is able to support her. Here a diminution in priestly authority would have caused great unhappiness, had not the older custom been firmly enough rooted to prevail (T 117). As a proponent of enlightenment, however, Rohrer ought consistently to oppose the irrational force of tradition. It is strange to find him admitting that tradition can be a valuable safeguard against imprudent enlightenment.

When Rohrer writes about the Tyrol, he is close to another author he admires, Justus Möser (T 58–9), whose *Patriotische Phantasien* (1774–8), dealing with the laws and customs of Osnabrück, defended traditional communities as repositories of national feeling and political wisdom, superior to the abstract uniformity which academic theorists wished to impose. Rohrer's attachment to the Tyrol has much in common with Möser's to Osnabrück. He is, for example, fascinated by Tyrolean customs. In *Uiber die Tiroler* he gives detailed descriptions of the sports practised in the Tyrol, such as wrestling, racing up mountains, ball-games, and shooting. Elsewhere he describes tobogganing and yodelling. A long and vivid footnote in *Uiber die Tiroler* deals with transhumance and describes how the inhabitants of Vorarlberg move in processions to the mountain pastures where they spend the summer (T 24–6). In his love of ancient customs, Rohrer aligns himself with the Counter-Enlightenment represented by such writers as Möser and Herder; and he provides support for the argument, recently advanced by Jonathan Knudsen, that the Counter-Enlightenment should not be seen as a distinct movement but as a reaction proceeding dialectically from within the Enlightenment itself.[37]

Elsewhere, too, Rohrer has to acknowledge that the methods of enlightenment may do harm, and that its aims may conflict with one another. The decline of superstition does not necessarily promote the advance of morality. 'The level of intellectual autonomy ('Selbstdenken') on which the Italian Tyroleans are at present is not the most favourable for morality' (T 90): the decline of traditional belief has encouraged frivolous impiety and weakened the sanctions against perjury, theft, and gambling. Similar objections were raised by opponents of Joseph II's Edict of Toleration, who accepted that freedom of thought was suitable for the nobility and urban middle classes, but thought it could only harm 'rude and uncivilised peasants in the country' by filling their minds with doctrines they could not understand.[38] Dealing with more primitive people, Rohrer admits to having been much moved by a Serbian funeral ceremony, and describes the keeners ('Klagefrauen') still found among the Morlaks and in Istria and Friuli. This is one superstition which Rohrer respects, even at the price of inconsistency. 'Let the wit deride the superstition of simple nations. The psychological inquirer ('Seelenforscher') thinks and feels more than he laughs and sneers; and therefore sees nothing more in the conduct of the Slavs than still unspoiled human nature, seeking to give relief to its oppressed heart' (S ii. 74).

A similar tension is apparent when Rohrer writes as a moralist. He reveals a conservatism which makes him defend the old and criticise anything newfangled. Dignified old men among the Saxon colonists in Transylvania put him in mind of the semi-mythical past, populated by 'honourable German knights' (D i. 73) – the era evoked by Goethe in *Götz von Berlichingen* (1773). Rohrer also praises the traditional character of the 'Austrian of the old stamp' (D ii 159), and compares traditional hospitality in Upper Austria to that of the ancient Germans recorded by Tacitus, deeming it much superior to the ascetic primitivism of Rousseau.

Rohrer the moralist tends to locate virtue in the country and vice in Vienna, which is the home of luxury, affectation, and worse. Rohrer gives a detailed account of how young women drift into prostitution (G 186–91) which throws valuable light on the social type celebrated in literature as the 'Mädel aus der Vorstadt' or the 'süßes Mädel'. More typically, however, he denounces Viennese gormandising ('Schwelgerey', G 163), especially the habit of eating a three-course breakfast. The greatest best-seller in the city's history is a cookery book which went through 22 impressions in 25 years. Yet Viennese girls, he says, starve themselves in order to be fashionably slender:

> Sie tanzen so federleicht selbst in Orten, deren Inneres Ehrfurcht gebietet, von einem Stuhle zum andern, als kaum eine Wassersumpfspinne von einer Pflanze zur andern flattert (D i. 49–50).
>
> [They dance from one chair to another with even more feathery lightness, even in places whose interior commands reverence, than a water-spider fluttering from one plant to another.]

The Viennese spend too much time indoors and suffer from pallor, shortsightedness, rheumatism, and haemorrhoids. Young women spend their time reading horror stories and romances set in the Middle Ages (a familiar complaint at the end of the eighteenth century). They injure their health by dancing, especially by waltzing, which, Rohrer claims, causes coughs, stitches, haemorrhages and consumption. Rohrer dismisses ballet as 'erotic hopping about' and recounts at second hand an anecdote about Lessing praising Joseph II for abolishing ballet in Vienna (D ii. 18n). And yet elsewhere he warmly defends dance-halls as a recreation for artisans (D ii. 4 n).

To counter luxury, Rohrer offers the Viennese a drastic austerity programme. They are to take swimming lessons and mountain walks. Girls should learn to spin flax instead of playing the piano. Education should also change: instead of Latin rhetoric, schoolboys should study agriculture and domestic economy; instead of mythology, they should study the science of fruit-growing ('anstatt der Mythologie die Pomologie', D ii. 54).

Rohrer's criticisms and recommendations result in part from his mercantilism. He disapproves of the Viennese because they consume without producing, and because their luxurious tastes have to be satisfied by costly imports. Hence he recommends that, to save importing sugar, a native species of grass should be found which can serve to flavour food (D i. 85). His attacks on luxury, along with his emphasis on useful skills, are close to the doctrines professed a few years earlier by the Austrian Jacobins. The alleged ringleader of the 'Jacobin Conspiracy', Andreas Riedel, who in 1795 was sentenced to sixty years' imprisonment, went further in desiring the abolition of the nobility; and he sounds like Rohrer when he declares that the true noble is someone 'who goes forth into the wild plains of the Banat [...] and of Podolia to teach its primitive inhabitants the blessings of civilisation [...] and how to till the soil'. [39]

Another theme in Rohrer's criticism of luxury is his stress on disciplining the body. His attacks on excessive eating and unconstrained dancing are linked: in both, the body is being released from control. Instead, Rohrer recommends English dances, because they have 'more method' (D ii. 16). He contrasts the constant changes of fashion in Vienna with the uniformity of country clothing. Uniformity symbolises control and discipline, the repression of individuality. Rohrer's ideal is represented by a Tyrolean mining colony where there is no over-indulgence in food and drink, no quarrelling or fighting: 'One day passes like the next in the sweat of one's brow. Here or nowhere is found a confirmation of the doctrine that only work and moderation can preserve mankind's original goodness' (D i. 96). It sounds as though Rohrer is, inconsistently, advocating a Rousseauian asceticism. But the truth is rather that this inconsistency results from the high value he sets on hard work and therefore on discipline, which he sees as an instrument of civilization. Discipline can be exercised as part of communal living: he notes that Slavonians used to live in isolated houses, but were ordered to live in villages, 'where one neighbour, as it were, naturally observes the other, and the Slavonian is gradually elevated from his rude state by greater vigilance' (S ii. 4). All this strongly recalls Foucault's account of the exercise of discipline through surveillance and the production of 'docile bodies'.[40]

Rohrer often points to Britain as a country whose prosperity is founded on hard work and on the full exploitation of natural resources. He admires the agricultural improvements in Britain, and wishes that Austrian noblemen would import some shepherds from Lincolnshire or Leicestershire, along with their flocks, instead of 'Jokeys' (D i. 111), or that some English farmers would settle in Austria, as some Scottish farmers have settled near Copenhagen. He praises the enterprise of the colonists from southern and western Germany who settled in Transylvania, and commends the mechanical skills practised in the Tyrol, the Black Forest, and by German emigrants to Galicia. Such skills, he notes, deserve every encouragement, for machinery has proved the basis of Britain's wealth. Once again, the Tyroleans are his model: he describes how their cottage industries (spinning and lace-making) were encouraged by Joseph II; and he devotes much attention to their skill as mechanics, and to the enterprising spirit which takes them all over Europe to sell their wares. The Slovaks are similarly praised for being industrious, spinning cotton and travelling around the Empire as pedlars.

Rohrer not only commends hard work but wants it to be maximised. He advises that after working in the fields, farmers and their families should occupy the evening by spinning or knitting, giving the example of the Hessian peasant who 'would feel intolerable tedium on coming home from his ploughing, if he could not occupy himself in knitting' (D i. 169). Instead of idly minding cattle, children should be set to work – thus Rohrer carries out a pre-emptive strike against the later Romantic pastorals of Eichendorff and Heine. One reason he gives for deploring the Tyroleans' habit of going on pilgrimages is the loss of working time; he calculates how much they might have earned by spinning cotton during the eighteen days devoted annually to 'pious idleness' (T 82n.). He describes with pleasure how the Schottenfeld, formerly an empty space used for cavalry exercises, is now a 'dainty little factory town':

> Es zählt nicht weniger als 394 Häuser, wovon jedes mit einem Garten versehen ist. Diese Häuser sind fast alle lediglich von Seidenzeug- Band- Düntuch- und Flormachern bewohnt, und haben grosse geräumige Säle, in welchen viele hundert Kehlen der an ihren Stühlen arbeitenden Mädchen deutsche Opernlieder singen, und sich hierdurch zur Arbeit wechselweise ermuntern. Wenn man bey heiteren Sommertagen des Morgens um 6 Uhr auf diesen Strassen wandelt, so wird man umgeben von dem Schalle dieser singenden Chöre, und seines Lebens doppelt froh (G 8).

> [It numbers no less than 394 houses, each of which is provided with a garden. These houses are almost all occupied solely by makers of silk, ribbons, gauze and crape, and have large, spacious rooms in which a hundred throats of the girls working at their chairs sing songs from German operas, and thus stimulate one another to work. When one passes along these streets at six o'clock on bright summer mornings, one is surrounded by the sound of these choirs, and feels twice as glad to be alive.]

This piece of urban georgic[41] makes one wonder how the girls felt about being hard at work at six o'clock on a summer morning. Rohrer is so convinced of the virtue of industry, however, that he does not raise such questions.

His high valuation of hard work colours Rohrer's attitude to the Jews, who are the subject of one of his ethnographic treatises. Throughout his writings there are casual and gratuitous anti-Jewish remarks. The commerce of Jewish innkeepers in Galicia is dismissed as 'the busy idleness of the dirty Jews' (S i. 141). In *Statistik des österreichischen Kaiserthums* Rohrer recommends to his readers a Viennese coffee-house which is not frequented by Jewish 'Stockjobler' (i.e. stock-jobbers).[42] The Armenians, a number of whom lived in Galicia, also annoy him by their alleged 'selfish profit-seeking' (D ii. 149). He seems not to have liked the large Jewish presence in Lemberg, which contained some 15,000 Jews in a total population of 40,000.[43] After describing the Jews' costume, he says:

> Denkt man sich nun noch zu dieser düstern und schwerfälligen Kleidungsart ein verstörtes Gesicht hinzu, in welcher Furcht, Neid und Schadenfreude ihre Züge eingruben; so kann man sich beyläufig einen Begriff machen, wie dem empfindsamen Deutschen durch die ersten Jahre seines Aufenthaltes in einem Lande zu Muthe seyn muß, in welchem ein solches, sich selbst verunstaltendes Volk mitten zwischen lachenden, grünen Fluren die Meisterrolle spielt! (J 52)

> [If, in addition to this gloomy and heavy garb, one imagines a distraught face in which fear, envy and malice have etched their signs, then one can form some notion of how the sensitive German must feel during the first

years of his residence in a country where such a self-disfiguring people plays the leading role amid smiling green meadows!]

Although Rohrer's study of the Jews later provided material for at least one anti-Semitic pamphleteer,[44] it is not itself an anti-Semitic tirade. For the most part, it is an unusually cool and descriptive work with much detail about the Galician Jews' physical appearance, their dress, their characteristic ailments, and their occupations. He corrects the stereotyped notion that Jews are all innkeepers or procurers (the impression given by Kratter's *Briefe über den itzigen Zustand von Galizien*, for instance) by noting that many are tailors, money-lenders, or dealers in small goods, while in the Bukovina (though nowhere else) a number practise agriculture (J 59). Some animus is apparent in his condemnation of the Talmud as 'enthusiastic nonsense' (J 123) and of 'Kassidim', i.e. Hasidim, as 'proud fanatics' (J 150). He knew little about either, and relied for his information largely on the autobiography of the Polish Jew Salomon Maimon.[45] He thinks highly of the Karaites, who reject the Talmud, and in his travel book he records a long conversation with a Karaite Rabbi. Although disappointed to find that this man retained some superstitions, like avoiding contact with a dying person, Rohrer expresses great esteem for him.

Rohrer's distance from anti-Semitism becomes clear if one compares his account of the Jews with that given by the naturalist Belsazar Hacquet. Hacquet, generally bilious when he turns from botany and geology to human affairs, descends to senseless rantings against the Jews as 'filthy', 'stinking' 'parasites', 'scum of the human race', oppressors of Christians and adherents of 'Talmud-mishmash'.[46] Rohrer's criticism of the Jews is based not on insensate hatred but on the rational and cameralistic argument that they are not useful to the state. They are for the most part employed unproductively; their health is too poor for them to provide useful soldiers; and their religion separates them from the rest of society and disqualifies them from their civic duties. Since the Talmud is said to contain a 'casuistry which flies in the face of all the requirements of sound reason' (J 123), Rohrer evidently regards it as a form of clerical obscurantism.

Rohrer declares his admiration for Moses Mendelssohn and associates himself with the Berlin philosemite Christian Wilhelm von Dohm, author of *Über die bürgerliche Verbesserung der Juden* ('On the Civil Improvement of the Jews', 1781).[47] Dohm argued that the Jews' character had been degraded by isolation, and that it would be improved by their admission to civil society. Rohrer differs from Dohm in thinking it more difficult to reform the Jews' character. He points out that in Galicia not all are innkeepers or businessmen: many are manual workers, and yet their character shows no signs of improvement. His own proposals for the reform of the Jews are at least better than Hacquet's, who thinks they should be extirpated by being forbidden to marry till after the age of child-bearing; but perhaps not much better. Jews prepared to take up productive work should be placed in forced labour institutions ('Zwangs-Arbeitsanstalten', J 101) modelled on English work-houses or the Philadelphia penitentiary. 'Immoral' Jews should be sent abroad to settlements resembling those at Sydney Cove and Norfolk Island, which Rohrer greatly admires; he proposes that Austria should enter into an agreement with a colonial power like Britain or Holland to establish penal settlements overseas. Alternatively, they should be confined in prisons using the Philadelphia system of solitary confinement; if they have to work with other prisoners, these should be forbidden to speak to them.

These proposals reveal the inhumanity of which enlightened reformers were capable. The Australian penal settlements were in fact a fair anticipation of the Soviet gulag.[48] The Philadelphia penitentiary was denounced by Dickens and used by Schopenhauer to illustrate the tortures induced by boredom; and an extract from its regulations forms part of the arresting introduction to Foucault's *Discipline and Punish*.[49] In Rohrer we see a friend of humanity proposing, in all good faith, to transform people into happy and useful citizens by placing them in concentration camps and forced-labour battalions.

We have now reached the far end of Rohrer's imaginative world. If his world has at its centre the paradisal union of culture and nature, at its outer rim there is an archipelago of penal settlements where recalcitrant nature is being civilised through discipline. His emphasis on discipline derives largely from the cameralist assumption of responsibility for regulating people's lives in order to increase their happiness. The dangers attending that assumption are apparent in Rohrer's limited tolerance for other people, his assumption that they do not know what is good for them, and that, if necessary, they must be forced to be happy. This assumption was consistent with the principles of cameralism and was common in enlightened absolutism. As an anonymous writer puts it in the *Journal Général de l'Europe* in 1785: 'It is not surprising that reforms meet with contradiction and give rise to complaints. But an enlightened and firm government places itself above complaints and continues to do good to people despite themselves.'[50]

Books published by Rohrer

Uiber die Tiroler. Ein Beytrag zur österreichischen Völkerkunde (Vienna, 1796). Cited as T.
Neuestes Gemählde von Wien (Vienna, 1797). Cited as G.
Abriß der westlichen Provinzen der österreichischen Monarchie (Vienna, 1804).
Bemerkungen auf einer Reise von der Türkischen Gränze über die Bukowina durch Ost- und Westgalizien, Schlesien und Mähren nach Wien (Vienna, 1804). Cited as B.
Versuch über die deutschen Bewohner der österreichischen Monarchie, 2 vols (Vienna, 1804). Cited as D.
Versuch über die jüdischen Bewohner der österreichischen Monarchie (Vienna, 1804). Cited as J.
Versuch über die slawischen Bewohner der österreichischen Monarchie, 2 vols (Vienna, 1804). Cited as S.
Statistik des österreichischen Kaiserthums, vol. I (Vienna, 1827); no more published.

Notes

1. Ernst Cassirer, *The Philosophy of the Enlightenment*, tr. F. C. A. Koelln and J. P. Pettegrove (Princeton, 1951); originally *Die Philosophie der Aufklärung* (Tübingen, 1932).
2. See Paul von Mitrofanov, *Joseph II: Seine politische und kulturelle Tätigkeit*, tr. V. von Demelic (Vienna, 1910), pp. 90–3, and Derek Beales, 'Christians and *philosophes*: the case of the Austrian Enlightenment', in Derek Beales and Geoffrey Best (eds), *History, Society and the Churches: Essays in Honour of Owen Chadwick* (Cambridge, 1985), pp. 169–94, who argues that the *philosophes* exercised very little influence on the Enlightenment in Austria.
3. On the eighteenth-century meaning of 'Polizei' and 'Polizeistaat', see Keith Tribe, *Governing Economy: The Reformation of German Economic Discourse 1750–1840* (Cambridge, 1988), pp. 32–4. 'The *Polizeistaat* is a state in which the good of the ruler is indistinguishable from the good of the populace; the administrative apparatus is devoted to the increase of the ruler's wealth through the optimization of the happiness of his subjects' (p. 34).
4. See Franco Venturi, *Utopia and Reform in the Enlightenment* (Cambridge, 1971); H. M. Scott, 'The Problem of Enlightened Absolutism', in id. (ed.), *Enlightened Absolutism: Reform and Reformers in Later Eighteenth-Century Europe* (London, 1990), pp. 1–35.
5. The only extended account of Rohrer I have found in any modern work is in Wolfgang Häusler, *Das galizische Judentum in der Habsburgermonarchie im Lichte der zeitgenössischen Publizistik und Reiseliteratur von 1772–1848* (Vienna, 1979), where Rohrer's attitude to the Jews is discussed on pp. 53–60.
6. Besides incidental references scattered throughout Rohrer's works, this biographical information comes from Constant von Wurzbach, *Biographisches Lexikon des Kaiserthums Österreich*, 60 vols (Vienna, 1856–91), XXVI, p. 284, and Ludwik Finkel and Stanislaw Starzynski, *Historya uniwersytetu lwowskiego* (Lwów, 1894); I am grateful to Dr Andrzej Olechnowicz for translating the passage about Rohrer for me. Wurzbach, by a strange oversight, attributes to Rohrer a catalogue of the Imperial collection of paintings, which he elsewhere correctly ascribes to Johann Rosa.
7. Rohrer's contributions to the *Österreichische Monatsschrift* were: 'Über die Wanderungen der Tiroler', *Österreichische Monatsschrift*, 1 (March 1793), 221–50; 'Über die Industrie in Vorarlberg', *Österreichische Monatsschrift*, 2 (June 1794), 251–6; 'Von der Denkart in den Wälschen Confinen', ib., 257–62.
8. On Galicia, see Wasyl Gawlitsch, *Ostgalizien im Spiegel der deutschen Reiseliteratur am Ende des 18. Jahrhunderts* (diss., Vienna, 1943); Horst Glassl, *Das österreichische Einrichtungswerk in Galizien 1772–1790* (Wiesbaden, 1975); Maria Klanska, 'Erkundungen der neuen österreichischen Provinz Galizien im deutschsprachigen Schrifttum der letzten Dezennien des 18. Jahrhunderts', in Fridrun Rinner and Klaus Zerinschek (eds), *Galizien als gemeinsame Literaturlandschaft* (Innsbruck, 1988), pp. 35–48.
9. Mitrofanov, *Joseph II*, p. 270; Ernst Wangermann, *From Joseph II to the Jacobin Trials*, 2nd edn (Oxford, 1969), p. 175.
10. Franz Kratter, *Briefe über den itzigen Zustand von Galizien*, 2 vols (Leipzig, 1786), vol. II, p. 191; Belsazar Hacquet, *Hacquet's neueste physikalisch-politische Reisen durch die Dacischen und Sarmatischen oder Nördlichen Karpathen*, 4 vols (Nuremberg, 1790–6), vol. III, pp. 178–80.
11. See the character sketches in Mitrofanov, *Joseph II*, pp. 97–112; Derek Beales, *Joseph II*, vol. I (Cambridge, 1987), pp. 306–37.
12. See Leslie Bodi, *Tauwetter in Wien: Zur Prosa der österreichischen Aufklärung* (Frankfurt, 1977), p. 245.

13. Joseph Richter, 'Warum wird Kaiser Joseph von seinem Volke nicht geliebt?' reprinted in *Literatur der Aufklärung 1765–1800*, ed. Edith Rosenstrauch-Königsberg (Vienna, 1988), pp. 69–81.
14. Two of these plays, Perinet's *Kaspar der Fagottist* and Schikaneder's *Die Waldmänner*, are discussed in Otto Rommel, *Die Alt-Wiener Volkskomödie* (Vienna, 1952), but he does not mention *Die Nymphe der Silberquelle*. Was this perhaps an alternative title for Hensler's popular *Das Donauweibchen*?
15. See William Steedman, *Die Aufnahme der englischen Lieratur im 18. Jahrhundert in Österreich* (diss., Vienna, 1938).
16. See Roy Porter, 'The Enlightenment in England', in Roy Porter and Mikulás Teich (eds), *The Enlightenment in National Context* (Cambridge, 1981), pp. 1–18; for Germany, Michael Maurer, *Aufklärung und Anglophilie in Deutschland* (Göttingen, 1987); Johann Pezzl, *Faustin oder das philosophische Jahrhundert* (Zürich, 1783), p. 292: 'Es sind dort [in England] die ehrwürdigen Grabstätten des Kerns der neuern Philosophie, sagte er; die Grabstätte eines Bacon, Newton, Steele, Addison, Loke [sic], Swift, Bolingbroke, und unsers unvergleichlichen Pope.'
17. Hier schmauchten Solon, Wilhelm Penn,
    Confuz und Zoroaster,
    Und Montesquieu beim himmlischen
    Bierkrug ihr Pfeifchen Knaster,
    Und lesen dann, wenn ihnen sehr
    Die Zeit lang wird, den Erlanger,
    Und Schlözers Staatsanzeigen.
    Virgil's Aeneis, travestirt, in *Aloys Blumauer's gesammelte Schriften* (Stuttgart, 1871), part I, p. 161.
18. See Justin Stagl, 'Der wohl unterwiesene Passagier. Reisekunst und Gesellschaftsbeschreibung vom 16. bis zum 18. Jahrhundert', in B. I. Krasnobaev, Gert Robel and Herbert Zeman (eds), *Reisen und Reisebeschreibungen im 18. und 19. Jahrhundert als Quellen der Kulturbeziehungsforschung* (Berlin, 1980), pp. 353–84 (p. 375).
19. 'Home' is Henry Home, Lord Kames (1696–1782), author of *Elements of Criticism* (1762). Rohrer also mentions 'Whentley', presumably a mistake for Thomas Whateley, author of *Observations on Modern Gardening* (1770).
20. Rohrer, *Abriß*, pp. iv–v.
21. Johann Gottlieb Georgi, *Beschreibung aller Nationen des Rußischen Reichs, ihrer Lebensart, Religion, Gebräuche, Wohnungen, Kleidungen und übrigen Merkwürdigkeiten* (St Petersburg, 1776).
22. See Justin Stagl, 'Die Apodemik oder "Reisekunst" als Methodik der Sozialforschung vom Humanismus bis zur Aufklärung', in Mohammed Rassem and Justin Stagl (eds), *Statistik und Staatsbeschreibung in der Neuzeit* (Paderborn, 1980), pp. 131–87.
23. Johann Andreas Demian, *Darstellung der österreichischen Monarchie nach den neuesten statistischen Beziehungen*, 4 vols (Vienna, 1804–7).
24. Sir John Sinclair (ed.), *The Statistical Account of Scotland drawn up from the communications of the ministers of the different Parishes*, 21 vols (Edinburgh, 1791–9).
25. 'Quand je me joue à ma chatte, qui sait si elle passe son temps de moi plus que je ne fais d'elle?' – Michel de Montaigne, *Apologie de Raymond Sébond*, in *Œuvres complètes*, ed. Robert Barral (Paris, 1967), p. 188.
26. See Scott, 'The Problem of Enlightened Absolutism', p. 18; Tribe, *Governing Economy*.
27. See James J. Sheehan, *German History 1770–1866* (Oxford, 1989), p. 196, where Sonnenfels's periodical is wrongly called *Der Mann ohne Vorteil;* Tribe, *Governing Economy*, pp. 78–90.

28. See 'Beantwortung der Frage: Was ist Aufklärung?' (1784) in Immanuel Kant, *Aufsätze zur Geschichte und Philosophie* (Göttingen, 1975), pp. 55–61; H. B. Nisbet, '"Was ist Aufklärung?": The Concept of Enlightenment in Eighteenth-Century Germany', *Journal of European Studies*, 12 (1982), 77–95.
29. Cf. the comparison between ancient Germans and present-day primitives in Schiller's 'Was heißt und zu welchem Ende studiert man Universalgeschichte?' (Friedrich Schiller, *Werke*, 3 vols [Munich, 1966], vol. II, pp. 13–14).
30. Johann Gottfried Herder, *Ideen zur Philosophie der Geschichte der Menschheit* (Frankfurt, 1989), p. 655; Kant, 'Idee zu einer allgemeinen Geschichte in weltbürgerlicher Absicht' (1784), in *Aufsätze zur Geschichte und Philosophie*, pp. 40–54.
31. Examples from Germany in Sheehan, *German History*, pp. 203–4; from elsewhere in Harvey Chisick, *The Limits of Reform in the Enlightenment: Attitudes towards the Education of the Lower Classes in Eighteenth-Century France* (Princeton, 1981); id., 'David Hume and the common people', in Peter Jones (ed.), *The 'Science of Man' in the Scottish Enlightenment* (Edinburgh, 1989), pp. 5–32.
32. On Girolamo Tartarotti and his book *Del congresso notturno delle lammie* (1749), see Franco Venturi, *Settecento riformatore: Da Muratori a Beccaria* (Turin, 1969), pp. 359–63.
33. This occurred in 1749. It is mentioned in Pezzl, *Faustin*, p. 45; for details, see the reprint edited by Wolfgang Griep (Hildesheim, 1982), p. 28*.
34. Johann Georg Zimmermann, *Über die Einsamkeit*, 4 vols (Leipzig, 1784–5). This immensely popular work was also translated into French and English. Rohrer cites it at D ii. 96. Much of it is a scurrilous attack on monasticism, which would appeal to an adherent of Joseph II.
35. See John Lough, *The 'Encyclopédie'* (London 1971); Johann Wolfgang Goethe, *Wilhelm Meisters Lehrjahre*, V, xvi: 'so hatte er in Zeit von zwanzig Jahren sehr viel im stillen zur Kultur mancher Zweige der Landwirtschaft beigetragen und alles, was dem Felde, Tieren und Menschen ersprießlich ist, in Bewegung gebracht und so die wahrste Aufklärung befördert' (*Werke*, ed. Erich Trunz, 14 vols [Hamburg, 1948–60], vol. VII, p. 348).
36. See Mitrofanov, *Joseph II*, pp. 363–5 and 588; Helmut Reinalter, *Aufklärung – Absolutismus – Reaktion: Die Geschichte Tirols in der 2. Hälfte des 18. Jahrhunderts* (Vienna, 1974), pp. 75–137.
37. See Isaiah Berlin, 'The Counter-Enlightenment', in his *Against the Current: Essays in the History of Ideas* (Oxford, 1989), pp. 1–24; Jonathan B. Knudsen, *Justus Möser and the German Enlightenment* (Cambridge, 1986), esp. p. 148.
38. Mitrofanov, *Joseph II*, p. 770.
39. Quoted in Wangermann, *From Joseph II to the Jacobin Trials*, p. 13.
40. Michel Foucault, *Discipline and Punish*, tr. Alan Sheridan (London, 1977).
41. On the late eighteenth-century shift from pastoral (portrayal of rural leisure) to georgic (portrayal of rural industry), see John Barrell, *The Dark Side of the Landscape* (Cambridge, 1980).
42. Rohrer, *Statistik*, p. 279n.
43. *Hacquets neueste physikalisch-politische Reisen*, vol. III, p. 176.
44. Friedrich Rühs, *Über die Ansprüche der Juden an das deutsche Bürgerrecht*, 2nd edn (Berlin, 1816).
45. *Salomon Maimons Lebensgeschichte von ihm selbst geschrieben* (Berlin, 1792–3); Salomon Maimon, *An Autobiography*, tr. J. Clark Murray (Paisley and London, 1888).
46. *Hacquets neueste physikalisch-politische Reisen*, vol. III, pp. 204–34.
47. Christian Wilhelm von Dohm, *Über die bürgerliche Verbesserung der Juden* (Berlin, 1781). See Jacob Katz, *Out of the Ghetto: The Social Background of Jewish*

Emancipation, 1770–1870 (Cambridge, Mass., 1973).
48. See Robert Hughes, *The Fatal Shore* (London, 1987).
49. Charles Dickens, *American Notes* (London, 1957), esp. p. 99: 'I hold this slow and daily tampering with the mysteries of the brain, to be immeasurably worse than any torture of the body'; Arthur Schopenhauer, *Die Welt als Wille und Vorstellung,* ed. Julius Frauenstädt, 2 vols (Leipzig, 1923), vol. I, pp. 369–70; Foucault, *Discipline and Punish,* pp. 6–7; Michael Ignatieff, *A Just Measure of Pain: The Penitentiary in the Industrial Revolution 1750–1850* (New York, 1978). For further examples of well-meant alternatives to capital punishment, including life imprisonment, forced labour, and vivisection, see Venturi, *Utopia and Reform,* p. 113; John McManners, *Death and the Enlightenment* (Oxford, 1981), pp. 399–401.
50. 'Il n'est pas étonnant que les reformes éprouvent des contradictions et causent des murmures. Mais un gouvernement éclairé et ferme se met au dessus des murmures et continue de faire le bien au peuple malgré lui.' Quoted in Mitrofanov, *Joseph II*, p. 292, n. 2.

The Altar of the Fatherland
Wilhelm Friedrich von Meyern's Utopian Novel *Dya-Na-Sore*

Peter Horwath

In 1787, two years before the outbreak of the French Revolution, there appeared the first volume of a sensational and highly provocative novel, *Dya-Na-Sore, oder Die Wanderer. Eine Geschichte aus dem Sam-skritt übersezt* ('Dya-Na-Sore or The Wanderers. A story translated from Sanskrit'). The second volume was published in the first revolutionary year, and the third and last volume appeared in 1791, as did the extensively re-worked first volume.[1] The original intent of the anonymous author seems to have been to write an educational novel (Bildungsroman). The final product, however, was a political novel (Staatsroman) that called for the transformation of the monarchic state into a republic, offered the constitutional framework for such a state, and developed models for the kind of citizen-aristocrat the new state needed in order to constitute and to maintain itself. Because of its political content, nobody can have been surprised when the Crown suppressed the work (1791?).

The novel's setting is Northern India and Tibet several centuries earlier. Its esoteric title, *Dya-Na-Sore*, seems to betray the author's original intention to write a novel of character development in which the hero was suspended between contemplation and love: while *'Sore'* appears as an anagram of Eros, *'Dya-Na'* may be derived from the Sanskrit *dhyāna* (meditation). The title thus means: Eros reversed leads to insight.[2] Meyern was a polyglot who seems to have been also acquainted with Sanskrit.[3]

Biographical background

Wilhelm Friedrich von Meyern (1759-1829), the novel's anonymous author, was 28 years old when the first volume of his novel was published. We know little about his private life, firstly because he was a very private person who led a Spartan existence, but also because in his later years Meyern, a bachelor all his life, had ample reason to hide his social background and his political agitations as a young man. The author of *Dya-Na-Sore* was born as Johann Wilhelm Friedrich Meyer (not Meyern/Mayern) in 1759 in the Franconian hamlet of Frauenthal an der Steinach near Creglingen.[4] There was little, if any, vanity in him; his great obsession was to form public opinion, to do something for many, to create, individually and collectively, an active human organism that was imbued with the highest feelings and principles.

As a youth Meyern had come under the spell of Johann G. Schnabel's Utopian novel *Wunderliche Fata einiger Seefahrer* (better known as *Insel Felsenburg;* 1731-43). Around 1780, he enrolled in Leibniz's alma mater, the University of Altdorf near Nuremberg, where he studied law, mathematics, history, and geography, as well as languages. (It was probably at this time that he read Montesquieu and Rousseau.) While in Altdorf he became a member of a secret student society, the 'Bund der schwarzen Brüder', which agitated for political freedom. Next we know that on 23 December 1783 he joined an Austrian artillery unit in which he served until 31 July 1786. Even while in the army, he continued his studies, and it is quite possible that he started his novel while in the service. Meyern had great admiration for English sailors and for a while toyed with the idea of joining the British navy, or even emigrating to America. As his novel indicates, he must have been intimately acquainted with Masonic and Rosicrucian 'work' and 'wandering' (ritual and trials); we also know that he was a member of the Prague Lodge *Zur Wahrheit und Einigkeit* ('Truth and Unity') (Pauscher, 36). In 1792 Meyern was in London, where he wrote a preface for his pro-Masonic pamphlet *Ruinen am Bergsee: Gerettete Bruchstücke aus der Geschichte des Bundes für Wahrheit und Würde. Nach dem Englischen* ('Ruins by the Mountain Lake: Fragments Rescued from the History of the Society for Truth and Dignity. Translated from English') (published anonymously, 1795). In the following year, 1793, he published a five-act tragedy, *Die Regentschaft* ('The Regency'), which was again alleged to be a translatlon from English.

In the face of Napoleon's direct threat to Austria in 1796, for two consecutive years Meyern organised a volunteer corps ('Freikorps') along the lines of his 'nation-in-arms' concept, promulgated in *Dya-Na-Sore*. It was at this time that 'Herr von Meyern' surfaced. This shift in political perception is reflected in the 1800 edition of *Dya-Na-Sore* (which had grown from 933 to 2399 pages). In the same year he visited Prague and Dresden, and in 1802 he set out in the company of two young aristocrats for the south. He visited Italy, Greece, and Turkey, and spent seven months in Sicily, where he proposed to improve Sicilian living conditions by settling 30,000 industrious German farmers there. The Austrians did not buy his idea, nor did the English who had occupied the island. In 1805 he wrote his last publication entitled *Über die Dichtkunst*, which Varnhagen von Ense found 'unpalatable' ('ungenießbar').[5]

Meyern's finest hour as a military reformer came with a renewed threat by Napoleon, now the French Emperor. Meyern joined the 'Landwehr' (militia, second reserve) which he had reorganised along with the 'Landsturm' (last reserve). Varnhagen von Ense observed that if the military authorities had listened to Meyern, the Battle of Wagram (1809) would never have taken place, or, if it had, the Austrians would have been victorious.[6] The court and illustrious aristocrats were now willing to listen to Meyern in the hour of the greatest national need. Meyern was entrusted with important tasks that dealt with military reforms. In the years 1813-15 he was a member of the staff of Field-

Marshal Prince Schwarzenberg. At the Battle of Leipzig, Meyern was decorated for bravery; and in 1815 he was also decorated by the Pope to whom he, along with the sculptor Antonio Canova, had returned artwork that Napoleon had carried off from Italy. Before being attached to the Austrian military Commission to the Federal Diet in Frankfurt am Main, 1825-28, he served a stint with the Austrian Embassy in Madrid. He died in Frankfurt in 1829 at the age of 70 and was buried in Mainz.

Little is known about the formative intellectual influences on Meyern. His having studied law indicates that he must have been exposed to the most important works on political, social, and linguistic matters. As a product of German secondary education, he would have been well grounded in languages and the humanities. Later, living in Imperial Vienna during the heyday of Josephinism must have given him the opportunity to observe economic, ecclesiastic, and socio-political reforms undertaken by the Crown. As a Freemason, he must have wanted to influence the course of events. As a Freemason he would have also resisted agitation by women for full membership in the lodges. As an Anglophile he most definitely must have admired the British political system. Mirabeau, also a Freemason, had apparently made personal and ideological impressions on him (Pauscher, 24-35). Like Mirabeau, Meyern called for placing the entire population under arms.

There are indications that Meyern was aware of the heroic past of Greek antiquity (III, pp. 855, 876). And there are so many parallels to the rites and concepts of Freemasonry and Rosicrucians that an investigation into Meyern's relationship with secret societies would be profitable. It might also be fruitful to investigate further his indebtedness to Rousseau (*Lettre à D'Alembert sur les spectacles*, 1758), especially as regards the feminization of men. Concerning Meyern's view of women, it might be worthwhile to consider Theodor G. von Hippel's study of marriage (*Über die Ehe*, 1774); also, some of Meyern's views of women find themselves in agreement with the anti-feminist views of the *philosophes* (Diderot, Montesquieu, Helvétius, Holbach, and Voltaire). Yet Meyern emancipates the female far beyond the wildest dreams of the *philosophes*, inasmuch as he has them crown their lives by dying on the battlefield defending the man they love and admire. Not even Hitler envisioned female soldiers.

Technically, *Dya-Na-Sore* stands at the beginning of a series of German novels in which, as in Goethe's *Wilhelm Meister* (1795-96), Schiller's *Der Geisterseher*, Tieck's *William Lovell*, and Jean Paul's *Die unsichtbare Loge, Hesperus,* and *Titan*, secret societies play an important part in the development of the hero. In these novels, the hero must undergo dangerous trials and blindly trust the leadership of unknown superiors and powers. However, it is not so much the idea of the formative process of the hero that gives Meyern's novel its special place in German literature, but rather its radical political doctrine.

Dya-Na-Sore can hardly be called a standard novel, for its plot, largely undiscernible, is submerged in a sea of exhortations, declamations, maxims, as well as aphorisms about social, political, and philosophical issues. It is especially the first volume which betrays the novel's source in Masonic and Rosicrucian thought (wandering, trials by water, fire, and air, a secret society, all-knowing unknown superiors, degrees of initiation, and so on). By and large, the ideas expressed are either in harmony with Joseph II's enlightened socio-political reforms, or they run totally counter to the doctrines of enlightened monarchic absolutism. Some of Meyern's notions are original to him; others he seems to have appropriated from Montesquieu, Rousseau, and Mirabeau (Pauscher, 17-18). As the first edition progressed, it came to reflect quite strongly the events taking place in France. In the rewritten Volume 1, the four heroes are no longer destined to make a 'Bildungsreise' ('educational journey') from sage to sage and from natural cataclysm to natural cataclysm, but rather to the capital to witness the oppression of the people. Also in this volume, the reader realises right away that the king of the country is to be deposed.[7] However, it is only toward the end of Volume 2 that there is a parallelism between fiction and reality, between Tibet and France (de Bruyn, 955). Volume 3 begins with an event that resembles the convening of the French Estates on 5 May 1789, and King Ilwend may be a reflection of the hapless Louis XVI, as the hero Tibar is said to stand for Count Honoré de Mirabeau.[8]

When the 1800 edition of *Dya-Na-Sore* appeared,[9] the French Revolution had lost its steam, the Parisian bloodbaths had changed the initial European enthusiasm into disappointment, fear, and hatred. At the same time there was often a strong spontaneous upsurge of monarchic sentiment, and it was not long before France's military genius Napoleon had himself crowned Emperor (1804). Meyern, now 41 years old, had brought lasting impressions from his trip to England and Scotland in 1791. All of this caused a shift in emphasis in the new edition. Patriotism is emphasised, the role women are to play in the scheme of things is presented in far greater detail, and the original revolutionary enthusiasm is de-emphasised; at the same time there is much stress laid on the need to liberate the people from the yoke of a foreign oppressor.

The nation is now adjudged to be in need of wise leadership; the word 'freedom' is frequently replaced by less conspicuous words, and the term 'king' is avoided when something unfavourable is said about the monarch (see de Bruyn, 966). While many of the changes resulted from a change in political perspective, Meyern must also have thought of the censors on whom the publication of the work depended.

Contemporary Reception

The *Allgemeine Literaturzeitung* (Jena) in its April 1788 edition (No. 103) printed an anonymous review of Volume 1 by Friedrich Schiller.[10] Schiller observed that the story could also take place in Egypt or China, and he wondered why the author chose to use a historical costume since the customs and the atmosphere of India were grossly violated on almost every page. Four sons, Schiller informs his readers, bid farewell to their father and their homeland and set out on a journey to the 'Sanctuary of Primeval Times', a country where truth and happiness are found. The brothers traverse desolate wastelands, pass chasms, climb over steep mountains, and venture across turbulent streams. This allows the novelist, observes Schiller, to pile one horrendous description of nature onto another. He finds the monotony indescribably fatiguing but admits to seeing in the descriptions themselves the touch of a poet. Schiller mentions the excruciatingly painful journey of the brothers, who are now assisted by a barely decipherable inscription, at one point by a hermit, and later by an old man, who in turn directs the brothers to another old man. The four or five old men encountered, says Schiller, are all of the same mould, saying more or less the same thing. According to Schiller, the extremely poor story serves as a vehicle for 'eine reine und schöne Sittenlehre' ('a pure and beautiful treatise on morality'); yet it produces obscurity rather than enlightenment. Schiller complains of the barbarous intermingling of abstract elements with symbolic ones, and allegory with philosophy. He concludes:

> Es fällt in die Augen, daß es dem Vf. überhaupt nur um ein Vehikel für seine Philosophie zu tun war; ob es paßte oder nicht, galt ihm gleich; und so entstand denn dieser Zwitter von Abhandlung und Erzählung, der durch eine fast durchaus metrische Prosa womöglich noch ermüdender wird.

> [It is obvious that the author was only interested in finding a vehicle for his philosophy. Whether it was appropriate or not did not matter. Thus there arose this hybrid of treatise and story, rendered even more tiring by almost uninterrupted metric prose.]

A more positive review of Volume 1 was written in the same year by the dramatist Johann Friedrich Schink (1755-1835).[11] Schink informs his readers that no one will regret buying this book. But he warns that it is not a novel. The young author, he observes, offers food for thought. The book's purpose is to form noble, active, and free human beings. Its aim is to return mankind to the simplicity of nature, to an age where a virtuous and truthful society was a confraternity with equal rights for all. On the basis of these rights, says Schink, a free, brave, and virtuous people acted in the spirit of brotherly love, enjoyed life wisely, and strove for truth and wisdom. By emulating their ancestors in a distant past they gained the necessary strength to struggle against the tyranny of human passions and of men.

Shortly after its appearance, Volume 2 was reviewed by NM (=Walch von Schleusingen).[12] This reviewer observes that Volume 2 consists largely of dialogue and declamation about the value of life, patriotism, love of freedom, hatred of tyrants, and the heroic virtues, of which contempt of death is one. There are endless repetitions, says the reviewer, of what should and could happen, yet never happens; and there are also endless reproaches and encouragements. The heroes, he reports, are outside their country, which is oppressed by tyrants. Consequently, the tenor of this volume, he contends, deals with the liberation of their country. There is criticism of inactivity and discussion about the disregard for life. Schleusingen says it is impossible to say anything about the book's plan, content, or coherence. Only those who seek food for thought, who love great and powerful ideas and maxims, and who have cause to be dissatisfied with the general affairs of men, or who have become contemptuous of life and indifferent to death, will find here rich food for the cravings of their soul. The reviewer proceeds thereupon to offer his readers almost a page and a half of maxims that strike him as particularly elevating: for example, 'Moral ist nichts anders als das auf Regeln gebrachte Gefühl edlerer Menschen zum Gebrauch für Schwache' ('Morality is nothing but the feeling of nobler persons moulded into rules for the use of the weak'); 'Liebe und Spiel sind ein Bedürfniß für mindere Geister, für bessere – Ersatz beym Mangel an Thätigkeit, ein Schauplatz wo man die Rolle im Kleinen übt, die man im Großen spielt' ('Love and play are needs for lesser spirits; for better ones, they are a substitute when activity is lacking, [or] a stage where one practises on a small scale the role that one will play on a large scale').

A contemporary reviewer ('Tb.') of Volume 3 remains unidentifiable.[13] This volume, says the reviewer, contains as many strongly phrased ideas about freedom, patriotism, despotism, the sins of the rulers, etc., as the previous volumes. The reviewer proceeds thereupon with the almost impossible task of outlining the basics of the plot: by means of heroic deeds, the wanderers and brothers Terglud, Tibar, Dya, Altai, and others finally succeed in attaining their goal of liberating a people that had been suffering under a weak king. The king becomes their prisoner and they are intent on having him executed. However, some of the people want him merely deposed or his rights and privileges curtailed. Others have become accustomed to the presence of royal dignity, while others want a king because the life of a courtier is profitable. The royalists and opportunists lead an army against the republican patriots (who, to their undoing, have started quarrelling among themselves) and defeat them. The freedom-loving heroes remain on the battlefield. It seems, says the anonymous reviewer, that the unknown author wanted to say that it was easier to throw off a monarchist yoke than to preserve the newly-won freedom; a people must be prepared for freedom through education, customs, and principles. This reviewer, likewise, concludes his review by quoting a series of maxims:

> Man schätzt sich, wo man sich nothwendig findet. Wechselseitige allgemeine Achtung ist die erste Stufe des Patriotismus, der seiner Natur nach nichts ist als das veredelte Gefühl unsrer selbst bey dem Anblick eines Ganzen, dessen würdiger Theil zu seyn unser höchster Stolz ist.
>
> [One esteems oneself where one finds oneself necessary. General mutual respect is the first step towards patriotism, which, by its very nature, is nothing but the ennobled feeling of ourselves when contemplating the whole of which it is our greatest pride to be a worthy part.]

An interesting review of Meyern's *Dya-Na-Sore* appeared in 1798 in the *Oberdeutsche allgemeine Litteraturzeitung* (Salzburg, II, 435-6). The reviewer finds much that is attractive in Meyern's style. He is especially impressed by Meyern's skill in describing horrendous natural cataclysms. The reviewer is in full agreement with the book's attacks on domineering women and effeminate men. The reviewer, however, is upset by the book's positive attitude toward war, and he is amazed that the Viennese censor would pass such a work.[14]

Patriots and Citizens

As these reviews show, *Dya-Na-Sore* is a philosophical novel, and its philosophy can best be understood against the background of the socio-political and ecclesiastical reforms initiated by Empress Maria Theresa (1717-80) and accelerated, intensified, and extended by her son Joseph II (1741-90; 1765-80 Co-Regent), which were propelled by an increase in the efficiency and productivity of the civilian sector. Besides might, security, and prestige for the country, the Crown also aimed at prosperity for its citizens. The reforms rested on mercantilistic and physiocratic principles. As a scheme of political economy, physiocracy advocated the supremacy of the natural order and stressed agriculture, free trade, and private property.[15] At the same time legal and constitutional reforms were instituted for the purpose of creating a 'Rechtsstaat', a state based on law, within the framework of enlightened absolutist rule. By necessity, education moved away from humanistic and metaphysical concerns, stressing increasingly practical and profitable matters. All education, including religious education and instruction, aimed at instilling those virtues that produced hard-working and responsible citizens. Eternal human concerns were relegated to the background. In church religiosity, attempts were made to suppress emotional and contemplative piety and concentrate entirely on moralistic and utilitarian aspects of religion. Ties with Rome were severely limited, and the foundations for a dynastic-territorial church were strengthened. Patriotism became the secular ideology, and for some the surrogate religion, of the bureaucracy.

The influential Professor of Law Joseph von Sonnenfels reflected the nascent spirit of patriotism in his famous essay *Über die Liebe des Vaterlandes* ('On the Love of the Fatherland') (1771). His social and political Utopianism anticipated by a generation Meyern's dream of turning every citizen by means of education into a citizen-aristocrat. Sonnenfels demanded that patriotic scholars, historians, and artists should serve their country by means of their skills, research, and talents, and he conjured up role-models from Roman antiquity to support his idea of finding a higher unity for the nation in the concept of the Fatherland.[16] Some twelve years later Joseph II considered upgrading the social position of his officials by claiming in return their total commitment to the State. Referring to Joseph's *Hirtenbrief* ('Pastoral Letter') of 1783, the standard history of Austrian literature speaks of 'der kategorische Imperativ, der in Josephs II. Staatsprincip enthalten ist, wie in Kant's Philosophie, der "keine Verbindung, kein persönliches Geschäft, keine Unterhaltung" kennt, welche den "Staatsdiener" von seinem "Hauptgeschäft" abziehen dürfte' ('the categorical imperative, contained in Joseph II's political principle as in Kant's philosophy, which knows "no connection, no personal business, no relationship" that would distract the "state servant" from his "principal business"').[17] Sonnenfels saw in the army more than an instrument of the dynastic state. He was most probably influenced by the philosophical writer Thomas Abbt (1738-66), who had stated in his *Vom Tod fürs Vaterland* ('Of Death for the Fatherland') (1761) that every citizen should be a soldier, and every aristocrat both a soldier and a citizen. And it was under Joseph II that the soldier became a citizen, and the army a manifestation of the strength of the people.

To further the reforms, the state also incorporated useful tenets and doctrines of the rationalist Enlightenment. Among a relatively small segment of the Austrian bureaucracy 'Enlightenment' also signified deism, anti-Christianity, or secularism. Sonnenfels came to add a religious dimension to the love of one's country by declaring in *Über die Liebe des Vaterlandes* that there was no happiness outside the 'Vaterland' (pp. 35-6). This is actually a secular version of St Augustine's dictum that there is no salvation outside the Church. His aims as regards Church and religion went far beyond the establishment of a state church (Gallicanism; *Staatskirchentum*) and an 'enlightened' moralistic Catholicism. Sonnenfels came close to deifying the state: he described the Church as a political institution which must serve the aims of the state until popular enlightenment permits its replacement by a secular organisation. However, only a few Austrians of the time, notably Aloys Blumauer, Hebenstreit and Johann Pezzl, seemed willing to see either the institutional form or the supernatural content of Christianity disappear.[18]

With the Enlightenment and the improvement in social and economic conditions also came the secular belief in human perfectibility. And yet, this belief had as one of its roots the Baroque-Catholic notion that man was moving forward victoriously on the path of moral and spiritual perfection before a retreating evil, in a world that had attained almost full redemption in the here and now. The greatest of the Josephinist dramatists, Heinrich Joseph Edler von Collin, aptly placed at the core of his historical drama *Balboa* (1806) the dictum: 'Der Mensch ist gut' ('Man is good').[19]

At the beginning of the reform period, authors consciously used their art as a medium for furthering imperial reforms. Political reformers and literati alike were almost without exception members of secret societies (Freemasons, Rosicrucians, Illuminati, Asian Brethren, etc.). Since Catholicism and Masonry were compatible at that time, most Masons practised their Catholicism, often fervently. The didactic tendency normally present in Josephinist literature was often combined with a mild strain of Utopianism; thus exemplary characters were drawn who set out to raise every sphere of social, political, and religious life to a state of perfection through the power of the human mind, nurturing industriousness and incorruptible virtue on the basis of an unqualified good will. The authors who created the literary image of the *homo novus* included Alxinger, Pezzl, and many lesser-known figures. The image of the new *Austriacus Perfectus* was diverse, ranging from the progressive manufacturer, whose industriousness makes him an equal of any nobleman, to the modest bureaucrat, whose fearlessness in the face of corruption causes him to become a martyr for truth.[20] They all congregate around what Meyern calls the 'Altar des Vaterlands' ('the Altar of the Fatherland', *Dya-Na-Sore*, III, 853). Heinrich von Collin, who uses a similar phrase, wrote very much in the spirit of Josephinism when he made the hero of his Roman tragedy *Regulus* (1802) solemnly declare: 'Der Tod wird Pflicht, wenn er dem Staate frommt' ('Death becomes a duty when it benefits the State').[21]

The major issues of Josephinist Austria are also present in Meyern's *Dya-Na-Sore*. They are: 1) the quest for a state of citizens ruled by law and order, 2) the need for an effective army, 3) the longing for economic prosperity, 4) the striving to make the Church an instrument of the state, and 5) the desire to produce a national spirit. Josephinist literature neglected to grapple with man's need for religious-mystical experiences and metaphysical answers. Meyern's response to these needs and concerns was, as we shall see, to deify the state as a democratic republic to an unheard-of extent.

The Religion of the Fatherland

Meyern's characters are spokespersons for certain human attitudes and views. Through them we get a multifarious picture of the possibilities Meyern envisioned in the creation of ennobled individuals. He looks at the issues he presents from many angles, filtered through the mind and temperament of the novel's heroes and villains, all for the benefit of the reader, who is told what it takes to establish, maintain, and defend, nay, even to destroy a republic of ennobled citizens. Meyern's characters receive their sharply outlined profiles and *raison d'être* from the myriad of frequently provocative and at times memorable maxims they utter; and, since space does not allow printing them, the following character-sketches must remain woefully inadequate and bloodless. The major mouthpieces of Meyern are the following: Athor, the Priest, and his four sons Dya, Tibar, Altai and Hamor. Also important are Terglud, the General and leader of the secret society, Elkanar, the evil courtier, and Meatoa, who speaks for ennobled womanhood. Other characters of importance are Irgud, Eringpat, Deminarad, Oglar, Perkund, and King Ilwend. The major theme of the book is stated very early when the Hermit declares that the individual owes his life to the 'Vaterland', and that it is his duty to die for it (I, 94).

Dya is the most philosophically and idealistically individual of the brothers. Sex, beauty, and marriage do not tempt him. Woman's purpose in life is to obey, beautify a man's more peaceful days, and smooth the male's rough nature. Dya is the opposite of his pleasure-loving, inactive, and weak-willed brother Hamor. In Dya's opinion, natural cataclysms, including war, are beneficial to man's mind and soul. He considers his task in life to be selflessly and sacrificially active in the 'großen Werk der allgemeinen Freiheit' ('great work of universal freedom') (I, 237). Emotionally, Dya is on the side of Altai, while idealistically, he feels drawn to Tibar's philosophy of life. Altai is a man of duty and realism. Essentially, his ideal is a life without struggle. In his eyes, 'Das beste Weib ist [...] ein zu unwichtiger Gegenstand für die Würde eines Mannes' ('the best woman [...] is too unimportant an object for the dignity of a man') (I, 187). But woman, he believes, has the power to improve the male, or to corrupt him. She should cherish the beauty of her body and develop her intellect. Altai declares that good laws not only make good people but also good kings. Tibar is a man of practicality. He suffers in his knowledge of the misery war causes. While he is duty-conscious, he takes no joy in doing his duty. To him, the family breeds tyranny, but he admires the sailor for his freedom and open-mindedness. 'Das Schwerd gegen Tirannen ist Gottes Schwerd,' he declares ('The sword against tyrants is God's sword', II, 370). To him, death is a blessing, for it leads to glory. Without a belief in God, man lacks individuality. Tibar strengthens the power of the middle class by encouraging trade and founding banks. As a lover of refined social life and the arts, he creates centres where all ranks meet for pleasure, entertainment, and refinement. As a committed republican he is for a National Assembly and a constitution anchored in the law. In order to protect freedom, Tibar establishes a physically and ideologically well-trained citizens' army, and he decrees that the citizen must be educated from childhood on to despise death. Until the day a thoroughly democratic people exist, Tibar opts for retaining the monarchy in which the king is elected (III, 891).

Terglud is the man of action *par excellence* who knows that there is more than one way of doing things. His motto is: 'Last uns leben um nie mehr zu leben, last uns sterben um nie mehr wiederzukehren' ('Let us live in order never to live again, let us die in order never to return again', II, 400). He believes that God instituted war to shake man and to develop his better self. 'Das Schlachtfeld,' he says, 'ist ein Land, das tausendfältige Früchte trägt. Kein guter Mann ging noch ins Treffen, der nicht besser heraus kam' ('The battlefield is a land that brings forth a thousand fruits. No good man ever went into battle without coming out of it a better man', III, 660). In the last analysis, patriotism is his religion. Even though he is a hater of kings, he finds a constitutional monarchy acceptable for the time being. Public schools, he believes, are the places where democracy can be taught to everyone, regardless of social background. The army, being also an educational institution, has a similar purpose. Irgud is the novel's heroic nihilist who (similarly to the Hermit) views the belief in a life after death as the invention of weaklings. Dya listens with rapture as Irgud describes his ideal man, a superior person who will not hope for anything and yet act (II, 259). Eringpat rejects both monarchy and despotism. According to him people are slaves of religion, partisans of luxury, and worshippers of power. But power corrupts, and freedom may be used to tyrannize others (III, 839). Before being given a constitution, man needs to be brought up in the spirit of liberty from childhood on, otherwise man will live in a state worse than slavery. And Eringpat cautions that not too much can be expected of people. The law is supreme, and the king, he says, must become the servant of the people. Deminarad believes that through trade and commerce people become open-minded and independent (II, 407), and that commerce and trade create the material basis for man's education and ennoblement. Oglar is a *Realpolitiker*. In his view, people as a group tend to follow their urges, drives, and illusions; they are not created for sacrifice and freedom. History has taught him that all republics will go under, which is cause enough for him to opt for a monarchy.

The end of the novel, which deals with the defeat of the republicans, seems to belie the original rather brutal praise of war by the Hermit, who saw in it the most creative force in men's life: want awakens man, hunger makes him use his intelligence and danger brings forth virtue. An earth without destruction, the Hermit declares, a nation without war would be a calamity that one should avert through prayer (I, 111).

Meyern addresses the reader in a memorable passage close to the end of the novel. His thoughts, a further elaboration of those expressed initially by the Hermit, are concerned with the relationship of patriotism and religious belief, e.g. Christianity. The heroes who have proven themselves in the struggle for freedom he calls the Immortal Ones (III, 880), because fulfilling one's patriotic duties bestows immortality in the memory of successive generations. Thus 'Der Mensch ist nur groß durch den Begrif eines Vaterlandes' ('Man is only great through the concept of a fatherland', III, 881). Man should discard the 'stumpfe Frömmigkeit, die nur im Himmel auf Seligkeit zielt' ('the musty piety which aims only at bliss in heaven', II, 882). This world, too, has its rewards, even if death brings only an eternal sleep. For the indolent and cowardly ones it is easier to expect help from a god, rather than rewarding themselves by means of personal effort and strength. God became a God for weaklings. When one stopped loving God in one's Fatherland, the chains were imperceptibly forged. When religion became separated from the state, priests started to rule and kings arose. God, placed between the two, became a distorted tool which was used to stigmatise man. This dishonouring of life was considered a gain in terms of the future, and egotism, extended, came to include life in heaven (III, 883). A nation which accepts that God can be reached outside the temples of the Fatherland is doomed to be unhappy, disordered, immoral, and to constitute a multitude of scoundrels, hypocrites and fools. Meyer writes:

> Ich ehre Gott. Aber dienen kan ich ihm nur durch *ein* Vaterland. Er machte mich zum Wesen, zum Menschen kan er mich nur durch *ein* Vaterland machen. Ich verachte eine Zukunft, die mir ohne Verdienst um dasselbe zu Theil würde. Ich will nicht fortdauern, ich will nicht glüklich seyn, wenn ichs nicht durch dasselbe werde. Die Würde meines Karakters besteht in diesem Gefül, das mir heiliger ist, als iede erträumte Seligkeit. Ich begnüge mich, unerkant zu sterben, wenn ich nur das Bewustseyn rette, nach Iahrhunderten einst den Samen reifen zu sehen, den ich iezt zu säen wünsche.

> [I honour God. But I can only serve him through a fatherland. He has made me into a being, but he can make me into a human being only through a fatherland. I despise a future that I gain without merit. I do not want to become eternal, I do not want to be happy, if I cannot become so by merit. The dignity of my character consists in this feeling, which is more sacred to me than any dreamed-of bliss in a hereafter. I am satisfied to die unknown so long as I retain the awareness that the seeds I wish to sow now will ripen centuries hence.] (III, 884).

Enlightened Totalitarianism?

Dya-Na-Sore had an electrifying effect on its contemporary readers.[22] The radical German nationalist, Friedrich Ludwig Jahn, confessed that he had received the first stimulus for his essay *Über die Beförderung des Patriotismus im Deutschen Reiche* ('On the Promotion of Patriotism in the German Empire') from this novel. He remained a devotee of Meyern, whom he also met personally, for the rest of his life. Jahn found in *Dya-Na-Sore* not only the idea of physical exercise as para-military training but also certain notions about the rights of people that would lend themselves to post-Herderian definitions of 'Volk'. Like Jahn, Clausewitz was also a student of Meyern (de Bruyn, 970). Having read *Dya-Na-Sore* shortly after its appearance in 1791, Jean Paul recalled it years later in his *Vorschule der Ästhetik* ('Primer of Aesthetics') (1804). The plot of his *Hesperus* (1795) is indebted to *Dye-Na-Sore*, and probably also his 'noble' characters who like Meyern's heroes crave to be politically active. Friedrich de la Motte Fouqué's *Vier Brüder von der Weserburg* (1820) likewise is indebted to Meyern's novel, as are perhaps the novels of Karl May and Nietzsche's *Thus Spoke Zarathustra* (1883-85) and *The Will to Power* (1901).[23] Strangely enough, *Dya-Na-Sore* had no impact on German authors just before and during the Hitler period.

It was only after World War II that Meyern's *Dya-Na-Sore* found critical rejection: Arno Schmidt, writing under the impact of the devastating effects of war, offers something that is close to a diatribe, and Günter de Bruyn, the East German writer (and editor of *Dya-Na-Sore*), writes as if he was criticising the political condition of the GDR. Even though Meyern made it clear that war was only justified when defending or regaining freedom,[24] both critics harp on Meyern's alleged war-mongering and warped elitism. Schmidt describes *Dya-Na-Sore* as a manifesto hailing the 'blondeste aller Bestien' ('blondest of all beasts'), and sees nothing in the novel but elitism, militarism and glorification of war. In a letter to Alfred Andersch he writes as follows about his planned essay on the novel:

> 'Dya-Na-Sore' – im Jahre 1787 erschien der 5bändige Riesenroman zuerst; in jener Zeit der Geheimbündelei und Erziehungstheorien begeistert begrüßt (sein Einfluß auf Goethes 'Meister' ist bemerkenswert!). Es ist eines der fürchterlichsten Bücher unserer Sprache – vielleicht gebe ich ihm den Untertitel 'oder der SS-Staat' – und es ist ein wahres Wunder zu nennen (nur erklärbar durch die braune Unwissenheit), daß er nach 1933 nicht noch einmal aufgelegt wurde. Der einzig mögliche literarische Vergleich ist mit Platons 'Politeia': nur dort schlagen abstrakte politische Grausamkeit und kalte Wahnwitz die gleichen rollenden Irrsinnsaugen auf!

> [*Dya-Na-Sore* – the five-volume novel first appeared in the year 1787; enthusiastically welcomed in that age of secret societies and pedagogical theories (its influence on Goethe's *Meister* is noteworthy!). It is one of the most horrendous books in our language – perhaps I will give it [his essay] the subtitle 'or the SS state' – and it is a real wonder (only explicable by

brown ignorance) that it was not reissued again after 1933. The only possible literary comparison is with Plato's *Republic*: only there do abstract political cruelty and cold absurdity open the same rolling eyes of madness!]

Ironically, it is the same Schmidt who, having rejected the notion that war may also develop nobler qualities in man, declares that the contemporary Swiss have no right to venture an opinion because they had not experienced a war in the course of the past 100 years. And yet, there is not the slightest ethnic, national, or racial bias present in the novel, and perhaps the strongest statement concerning a sort of nationalist or rather neo-tribalist thinking is found in volume III, where there is a brief mention of 'Brüder durch die Gemeinschaft eines gleichen Stammes' ('brothers through membership of the same stock,' III, 832). Meyern cannot be accused of being a racist, nor of having advocated a state like Hitler's. If there was any racism at the time, then it was in revolutionary France, where blond and blue-eyed aristocrats were regarded as foreigners on Gallic soil.[26] Meyern's concept of 'Volk' and 'Vaterland' leave room for multi-ethnic and multi-linguistic bodies. Customs and constitutions are essential to produce a nation (III, 736), and citizens are found where freedom prevails (I, 147).

Objecting to Meyern's emphasis on the state, Schmidt argues that a free person has the controlling factor within rather than outside himself. If viewed through the Nazi prism, a dictum like Irgud's 'Der einzelne Mensch ist nichts für dich. Das Ganze ist ein Augenmerk' ('The individual person is nothing to you. Your gaze should be fixed on the whole,' II, 264) is indeed objectionable. But Meyern sees man as primarily a social being who needs his peers to prosper. Meyern has a total view of the needs of the community. The same applies to the observation made by Terglud that nature teaches us that the soft will not survive, and that man often attains rejuvenation by passing through a cataclysm (II, 681).

De Bruyn juxtaposes Meyern's notion of a democracy with the notions held presently by the Americans and French, without realising that originally the American and British democracies were also democracies 'of the rich', and that the French National Assembly decreed in 1792 that altars be created everywhere bearing the inscription: 'The citizen is born, lives, and dies for *la Patrie*.'[27] Meyern's cult of ancestors is also misunderstood by de Bruyn because the novel's ancestors are role models for teaching self-esteem, awareness of the needs of others, and patriotism of a free people. They have nothing to do with privileges based either on inheritance or on biological values. It is not true that Meyern argues in favour of retaining a useless aristocracy.

De Bruyn is indignant over Meyern's ideal man who is both merchant and soldier. Yet Meyern seems to betray here again his admiration of the British who had at that time developed the merchant-soldier in the tradition of Lord Clive. Moreover, de Bruyn overlooks that there is plenty of room in the soldier for individual patterns of behaviour. Above all, there is no mindless execution of orders. 'Duty', not obedience, is the watchword. He objects also to the term 'Haufen' for the mass of people, not realising that mass-instinct is a social reality and that the novel's character who has so little esteem of humans is Oglar, the novel's anti-individualist. (Moreover, 'Haufen' did not have the strong derogatory meaning it has today.) De Bruyn makes much of the *Bund's* principle of subordination which, after all, operates legitimately in any free democratic society (Freemasonry, industry, the military). He would be on safer ground if Meyern had called for blind obedience. *Dya-Na-Sore* does not propound a 'Führerprinzip' (dictatorship) nor do the novel's heroes enjoy special privileges, or tenure in office. Meyern insists that a change of attitude must come from education and through example, not by command. De Bruyn objects strongly to Meyern's view that a nation must be continuously ideologised to adhere to the principles of democracy. In the USA this process from kindergarten on would be called 'citizenship training'. Meyern's patriotic celebrations in a landscape dotted with public monuments remind one, for example, of American Fourth of July celebrations with Washington, D.C., as their background (the Capitol, Lincoln and Jefferson memorials).

Under the influence of Arno Schmidt, Kindler's *Literatur-Lexikon* talks about a 'blood-thirsty militarism' as the centre of the novel (II, 1749). This is not so; at no point does Meyern call for wars of conquest, nor does he call for revenge on the defeated enemy. As a matter of fact, he strongly reproves the killing of civilians, especially of babies and children. If De Bruyn objects to Meyern's realisation that in war (as in any other dangerous situation) a good person may develop hitherto unknown strengths of character, then he objects to reality itself. No one would call Schiller a proto-fascist or militarist for his 'Reiterlied', nor would anyone take E. M. Arndt to task for his poem 'Der Gott, der Eisen wachsen ließ', which celebrates the idea of a justified uprising against a tyrant. De Bruyn makes the impossible claim that the people do not know why they are armed. (Naturally, if one plans a revolution one needs to be careful what and how much one says and to whom.) The answer, given on almost every page, is simple and clear: To defend freedom against internal and external oppressors. In Switzerland the free citizen is armed to this very day. It is a fact that freedom, like any other good, must be defended and regained every day.

One may make too much of Dya's Spartanism if one overlooks the fact that he personifies the counterpart to the extreme epicureanism and indolence of his brother Hamor. Spineless *Weltschmerz* and incessant pleasure-seeking are dangerous for a free society since man becomes enslaved to an inner tyrant. The logical outcome of Rococo society was artificiality, effeminacy, and egocentricity. For the enlightened bureaucracy, Spartanism was an antidote to decadence, injustice and national catastrophe.

Notes

1. Subsequently, this became Volume 1 of the revised and enlarged second edition of 1800 (5 vols). I shall limit my discussion to the first edition of 1787-91. All translations are mine.
2. See Peter Horwath, 'Friedrich Wilhelm von Meyern's *Dya-Na-Sore* (1787–91): The Meaning of the Novel's Title and Proper Names: A Linguistic Contrast', in *Contrastes* (Sorbonne, Paris), Dec. 1989, pp. 77–9.
3. See Josef Pauscher, *Dya-Na-Sore: Ein Staatsroman von Friedrich Wilhelm von*

Meyern, XXXIV. Jahresbericht der K. K. Staatsrealschule Jägerndorf (Jägerndorf, 1911), pp. 24-5. Pauscher uses the middle name as the first name.

4. For further details about Meyern's life, see Wilhelm Friedrich von Meyern, *Dya-Na-Sore, oder Die Wanderer: Eine Geschichte aus dem Sam-skritt übersezt* (3 vols, Vienna and Leipzig, 1787-91), reprinted by Zweitausendeins (Frankfurt, 1979) with an afterword by Günter de Bruyn, pp. 935-49. See also Constant von Wurzbach, *Biographisches Lexikon des Kaiserthums Österreich* (60 vols, Vienna, 1856-91), vol. XVII, pp. 179-85, and Reinhold Lorenz, *Volksbewaffnung und Staatsidee in Österreich, 1792-97* (Vienna and Leipzig, 1926), pp. 33-43, 72-6, 128, and 166-9.
5 Karl August Varnhagen von Ense, *Aus dem Nachlaß: Tagebücher* (14 vols, Leipzig, 1861-70), VIII (Zürich, 1865), p. 204.
6. Varnhagen von Ense, *Denkwürdigkeiten und Vermischte Schriften* (2 vols, Mannheim, 1837), vol. I, pp. 304-12, also 124 and 357, as well as vol. II, p. 83. See also Wurzbach, vol. XVII, p. 182.
7. *Dya-Na-Sore, oder Die Wanderer: Eine Geschichte aus dem Sam-skritt übersezt*, 2nd, improved edn, vol. I (Vienna and Leipzig, 1791).
8. See Edith Narath, *Fr. W. v. Meyerns dichterisches Lebenswerk: Unter Berücksichtigung des Romans 'Dya-Na-Sore'* (diss., Vienna, 1934), pp. 68-9 and 95. See also Pauscher, pp. 24-35.
9. *Dya-Na-Sore, oder Die Wanderer*, new edn (5 vols. Leipzig: Schaumburg, 1800), 2399 pp. The poet and physician Ernst von Feuchtersleben (he did not know Meyern personally) re-issued this edition in 1840-41 to fortify his contemporaries whom he considered to be weak and devoid of ideals. The publisher Ignaz Klang appended to vol. 5 Meyern's recently discovered Nachlass.
10. Anonym. review by Friedrich Schiller in the *Allgemeine Literaturzeitung*, 103 (April 1788); also in *Schillers Werke, Nationalausgabe* (Weimar, 1938), vol. XXII, pp. 196-7. Reprinted in G. de Bruyn, pp. 976-7.
11. In J. F. Schink, *Ausstellungen* (Vienna, 1788), pp. 378-83. Reprinted in G. de Bruyn, pp. 974-6.
12. In *Allgemeine deutsche Bibliothek* (Berlin-Stettin, 1790), 95/1, pp. 171-3. Reprinted by G. de Bruyn, pp. 977-9.
13. In *Allgemeine deutsche Bibliothek* (Kiel, 1792), 107/1, pp. 445-6. Reprinted by G. de Bruyn, pp. 979-81.– De Bruyn reprints also four sonnets in praise of *Dya-Na-Sore* by Captain Karl von Lohbauer, a patriot from Württemberg, pp. 981-3.
14. See Eduard Beutner, 'Die Rezeption der josephinischen Literatur in der *Oberdeutschen allgemeinen Litteraturzeitung*' in H. Zeman (ed.), *Die österreichische Literatur: Ihr Profil an der Wende vom 18. zum 19. Jahrhundert, 1750-1830*, 2 vols (Graz, 1979), vol. I, p. 251.
15. See e.g. Helen Liebel-Weckowitz, 'The physiocrat tax reform of Joseph II: the challenge of modernisation in the Habsburg Empire, 1780-1790', in *Transactions of the Sixth International Congress on the Enlightenment*, Studies on Voltaire and the Eighteenth Century, 216 (Oxford, 1983), pp. 287-9.
16. See Sonnenfels, *Über die Liebe des Vaterlandes* (Vienna, 1771), esp. pp. 128-9, and Dolf Lindner, *Der Mann ohne Vorurteil: Joseph von Sonnenfels, 1733-1817* (Vienna, 1983), esp. p. 87.
17. J. W. Nagl, Jakob Zeidler, and Eduard Castle, *Deutsch-Österreichische Literaturgeschichte*, 4 vols (Vienna and Leipzig, 1914-37), vol. II, p. 264.
18. See Peter Horwath, *Der Kampf gegen die religiöse Tradition: Die Kulturkampfliteratur Österreichs, 1780-1918*, German Studies in America, 28 (Berne, 1978), pp. 50-1; id., 'Literature in the service of enlightened absolutism: the age of Joseph II (1780-1790)', in *Transactions of the Second International Congress on the Enlightenment*, Studies on Voltaire and the Eighteenth Century, 56 (Geneva, 1967), pp. 707-34.
19. *Balboa, Trauerspiel in fünf Aufzügen* in Heinrich von Collin, *Auswahl aus dem Werk*,

ed. Kurt Adel (Vienna, 1967), p. 60.
20. See Peter Horwath, '*Austriacus perfectus:* the ideal man of the Austrian literature of the Enlightenment', in *Transactions of the Sixth International Congress on the Enlightenment*, pp. 59-61. Meyern (*Dya-Na-Sore*, III, 607) and Johann Pezzl (*Faustin oder das philosophische Jarhrhundert* [Zürich, 1783], p. 185) were probably the only literati of the period who glorified the military at the expense of the clergy.
21. Collin, *Regulus* (Frankfurt, 1802), line 1104. Cf. Regulus' vision of his nation's past in lines 1120-2: 'Nun rollte sich dem Blick die Vorwelt auf, / Ich sah – ein jeder Fleck des Vaterbodens / War ein Altar, auf dem ein Edler fiel' ('Now the past was exposed to view; I saw that every spot of paternal soil was an altar on which a noble-minded man had fallen').
22. Schikaneder, the librettist of *The Magic Flute* (1791), may have been influenced by *Dya-Na-Sore*. See Peter Horwath, 'Friedrich Wilhelm von Meyern's Utopian novel *Dya-Na-Sore*', in *Transactions of the Seventh International Congress on the Enlightenment* (Budapest, 1988), pp. 1380-4.
23. *Kindlers Literatur-Lexikon*, vol. II (Zürich, 1964), pp. 1747-9.
24. At the Congress of Vienna Meyern told Varnhagen von Ense that wars could easily be prevented if there were a universal law that mandated that diplomats were the first to be ordered to the battlefield (*Denkwürdigkeiten*, II, p. 83).
25. In a letter to Alfred Andersch (Darmstadt, 15 November 1957), reprinted in *Der Spiegel*, 45 (1985), p. 269.
See also Schmidt, '*Dya-Na-Sore*: blondeste der Bestien', in his *Dya-Na-Sore: Gespräche in einer Bibliothek* (Karlsruhe, 1958), pp. 14-53.
26. French aristocrats were seen as 'descendants of barbarous Germans, while French commoners were descendants of civilized Gauls and Romans' (Crane Brinton, *The Anatomy of Revolution* [New York, 1938], p. 62).
27. As quoted by Carlton J. H. Hayes, *Essays on Nationalism* (New York, 1926), p. 103.

Gottlieb von Leon and his *Rabbinische Legenden*

Joseph P. Strelka

The *Rabbinische Legenden* ('Rabbinical Legends') of the underrated Austrian Josephinist writer Gottlieb von Leon cannot be fully understood without some knowledge of his personal background and of the background of his time. Gottlieb von Leon was born on April 16, 1757 in Vienna[1] and together with another Josephinist writer, Joseph Franz Ratschky, attended the Jesuit school 'am Hof'. Like Ratschky, he studied at the University of Vienna.

In 1780 he became a private tutor in the house of Hofrat Franz von Greiner. The young Greiner whom he had to educate happened to be the brother of Karoline Pichler, who later became famous and in whose literary salon, in addition to other celebrities, Grillparzer was often seen. It was Leon who introduced Karoline to German literature.[2]

In 1782 Leon became 'Scriptor', and in 1816 'Custos' at the K. K. Hofbibliothek (Imperial Library, now known as Österreichische Nationalbibliothek). He remained unmarried, devoted his life almost entirely to scholarship and literature, and possessed astonishing erudition. The tall, lean, even skinny Leon, who dressed strangely,[3] was said to be shy and clumsy in his dealings with ladies.

About Leon's serious devotion to literature Castelli reported an anecdote: Once a man came into the Imperial Library and asked for 'Castelli's poems'. Leon replied: 'Castelli's poems? Where did they appear?' The man answered: 'Here in Vienna, under the title "Castelli's poetic trifles".' Leon raised his eyebrows and said in a stern voice: 'Trifles are no poems and poems are no trifles.'

Leon spent his spare time with friends, either privately in their homes or in the café 'zum Kramer' (or: 'Kramersches Kaffeehaus'), which was located in the Schlossergässchen at Nr. 604. This alley, which no longer exists, led off the Graben. The café was an eighteenth-century predecessor of the famous literary 'Café Griensteidl', and though there was scarcely space for twenty people, the clientele included many distinguished customers. Here Leon met other Josephinist authors like the wealthy Alxinger, General Ayrenhoff, the censor and later bookseller Blumauer, the moody Haschka, his own boyhood friend Ratschky, the court agent Rautenstrauch and the Voltaire-admirer Retzer. But it was not only writers that Leon counted among his friends. There were also such different persons as the Austrian field-marshal (Feldzeugmeister) Carl Friedrich von Lindenau, a native Prussian who used to say that he preferred Austrian disgrace to Prussian grace, or the merchant Benedikt David Arnstein, who had also written minor plays.[4]

Leon found in Freemasonry a combination of everything he loved, friendship, literature, music, the arts and erudition. His lodge was 'Zur wahren Eintracht' ('True Harmony'), which was chaired from 1782 to 1786 by the famous Ignaz von Born, the real-life model for Sarastro in the *Magic Flute*.[5] Through Masonry Leon also became acquainted with Mozart. Not only was Mozart often a visitor at Leon's lodge and received his second degree here by way of delegation, but Leon wrote two poems for Mozart's lodge, 'Zur neu gekrönten Hoffnung' ('Newly Crowned Hope'). These two poems, 'Zur Eröffnung der Meisterloge' and 'Zum Schluß der Meisterloge', according to masonic records, were set to music by Mozart but were unfortunately lost.[6] Leon's friends from the 'Kramersche Kaffeehaus', Alxinger, Ayrenhoff, Blumauer, Haschka, Ratschky and Retzer, were brothers of the 'True Harmony', as were other Josephinist authors like Friedrich, Pezzl, Prandstetter, Sonnenfels and others.[7] Most of Leon's literary activities, like his involvement with the *Wiener Musenalmanach*, were directly or indirectly related to Masonry.

Together with Ratschky, Leon founded the *Wiener Musenalmanach* in 1777,[8] doubtless after the model of the *Göttinger Musenalmanach*.[9] He regularly contributed poetry to the *Wiener Musenalmanach*, and when this poetic yearbook was threatened with closure in 1795 he took over the editorship and was able to save it for a further year in 1796.[10]

It was not by accident that Leon's first contribution to the Austrian *Journal für Freymaurer* was his speech 'Von der Geistes–Duldsamkeit des Freimaurers' ('On the Spiritual Tolerance of the Freemason').[11] In 1783 his Lodge 'True Harmony' celebrated the Emperor Joseph II's nameday and Leon was one of the four poets of the group who contributed an ode to the monarch.[12]

The time of Josephinism, of the flowering of Austrian Freemasonry, and of the *Wiener Musenalmanach*, was for Gottlieb Leon a time of hope and activity, of happiness and fulfilment. In 1808, looking back at the seventies and eighties of the former century, he called it the 'golden age of Josephinism'.[13]

Although his early poetry is often clumsy, sometimes even ridiculous, although he seemed constantly lost in a realm of fantasy and imagination, and although in his beginnings there are epigonal imitations of German Anacreontic poetry, of Klopstock's tones, and of medieval poetry, it is with good reason that a critic of the calibre of Otto Rommel has claimed that Leon was one of the most interesting personalities of Austrian literary life and that full presentation of his works and achievements would enrich literary history in general and the history of Romanticism in particular.[14]

When Leon published his first and only volume of poetry in 1788 he made the mistake of including in it his earliest poems, thirty of which had already appeared in the *Wiener Musenalmanach*. He wanted to save for the second volume at least thirty others, mostly later and better poems, which had also appeared in the *Musenalmanach*. However, probably because of the negative review of the first volume in the *Allgemeine Deutsche Bibliothek*, he was discouraged from publishing the already planned second volume. Anyone who wants to read Leon's poems has to consult the later volumes of the *Wiener Musenalmanach* and other later journals and collections. This is hardly ever done and therefore even one of the most perceptive histories of Austrian literature concludes that his poems are generally weak and that his only interesting works were his *Rabbinische Legenden*.[15]

The playfulness of the Rococo in Leon's early poems was very natural to him, though an occasional heavy sentimentality or an overdone, artificial simplicity are disturbing. Of more substance and quality are the poems he wrote under the influence of Wieland, and also the poem 'An Gott', which refers to Jacobi's novel *Aus Ed. Allwills Papieren* in Wieland's journal *Der Teutsche Merkur*. It was also through Wieland that the *Wiener Musenalmanach* and the *Österreichische Monatsschrift* – of which Leon edited one issue – became known in Germany.[16] The influence of Hölty and Goethe is sometimes visible and later Leon did more translating. Instead of his own weak imitations of Middle High German love songs, he translated original poems as well as Petrarch and Spanish poets.

Leon published some of his poems under the pen-names Lödl and W–g. While it was Bürger and Gleim who first stimulated his interest in Middle High German poetry, he soon became deeply impressed by the original old poems, a fact which demonstrates his literary taste, as does his devotion to Goethe. Occasionally, as for example in his poem 'Meisterschwank an den Aerzkünstler Herrn Gabriel Fiessinger', he struck genuinely Goethe-like notes.

It was certainly a shock for Leon when the Berlin critic Friedrich Nicolai, who had recently sent him a letter of friendship and praise, had Leon's first volume of poetry practically destroyed by a critic in his *Allgemeine Deutsche Bibliothek*.[17] However, it was not only this rejection that ended his lyrical production. It was, first, the political climate which created more and more outer and inner hindrances to his poetic creation. As early as 1786, two years before the appearance of his first volume, he complained to his friend and Masonic brother Reinhold, Wieland's son-in-law and co-editor of the *Teutsche Merkur*, about the oppressed, gloomy, and 'marshy' climate of the times,[18] and his complaints increased in the following year.

Joseph II, with his 'Freimaurerpatent' of 1785,[19] had already ordered strict government control of Masonry, and brought about the end of Leon's lodge, 'True Harmony'. True Harmony no longer seemed either literally or symbolically feasible. Most of the members of the lodge, including the master of the chair, Ignaz von Born, had left by the end of 1786. After Joseph II's death the persecution of Masonry began with the Emperor Leopold II. Although Leon started to visit Born privately even more often, and their relationship intensified after 1786, neither of them was able to stem the increasing suppression of literary and intellectual activity.[20]

Under the impact of the news of the French Revolution and its atrocities on the one hand and of the increasing suppression of freedom inside the country on the other hand, the Masonic writers (and not the writers only) started to split into three groups. First a polarisation took place. Some of them joined a democratic, anti-government oriented group, which tried to organise a political opposition to the absolutism which had ceased to be enlightened and benevolent. They discussed French politics, smuggled foreign newspapers into Austria, and read Thomas Paine's *Rights of Man* in a French translation. Their leaders were finally accused of a 'conspiracy of Jacobins', arrested and eliminated.[21] The Josephinist writers belonging to this group were Prandstetter, Riedel and Hebenstreit.

On the opposite end of the spectrum, representing an even more radical position, were writers who, partly from fear of the cruelties of the French Revolution, partly out of opportunism, and partly out of true loyalty to the new government, took a truly reactionary approach; some of them separated themselves radically from their own Josephinist past. The two most important writers of this group were Leopold Alois Hoffmann and Haschka.

The largest group finally tried to hold a middle line and to keep the old ideals by passing them on secretly or in coded form. They believed in the possibility of an evolution which finally would lead to freedom. Members of this group were Alxinger, Retzer, Leon's old friend Ratschky and Leon himself.

Even after the total suppression of Masonry Leon remained a stern and upright defender and representative of the brotherhood, not only in his personal beliefs but also in his literary activities. He was, for example, involved in editing the journal *Österreichische Monatsschrift* which appeared from 1793 to 1794 and tried to combat the slander by Leopold Alois Hoffmann, the former Mason who later attempted to justify persecution and the suppression of freedom.[22] While he wrote a seemingly neutral essay 'Die Weihen der Tanzkunst' ('The Sacraments of the Art of Dance') for the July issue of 1793, we find him as the editor of the April issue of 1794. The unsigned, long and harmless but charming poem 'Das Problem' in this issue, about an uncle and a nephew who visit the same young lady at night, was probably written by Leon himself. The 'problem' is whether to marry or not.

An unquestionable though indirect Masonic allusion, however, is the text of Leon's serenade for Karl Count Dietrichstein, K. K. Kämmerer and a close relative of the former Grandmaster of the Grand Lodge of Austria. The serenade, set to music by Ignatz Wenzel Raphael, is sung in the name of the corps of volunteers on horseback. It starts with the words 'Auf Brüder, auf! Vereinigt euch zum Feste', so that the members of the corps addressed each other as the Masonic brothers had done.[23]

Together with his friends and former Masonic brothers Ratschky and Kreil, Leon edited *Apollonion. Ein Taschenbuch zum Vergnügen und Unterricht*, from 1807 to 1811. Poems and translations of Leon's appeared in the Taschenbuch *Aglaja*, edited by Joseph Sonnleithner. We find contributions by Leon in the years 1815, 1816, 1817, 1818, 1819 and 1821. Between 1820 and 1830 he also contributed to the *Wiener Zeitschrift für Kunst, Litteratur und Mode*.

When in 1821 Leon's *Rabbinische Legenden* appeared, they expressed a specific form of Romanticism into which his writing had developed and which is also seen in his personal literary relationships. Unlike Ratschky, who never outgrew his first literary idols and models Gleim and Bürger, Leon underwent a significant development. He started out under the influence of 'Anakreontik' and 'Göttinger Hain' and later he was one of the few, perhaps the only, Josephinist writer who fell under the spell of the 'Sturm und Drang'. However, it was a special mild Austrian form of 'storm and stress' which shunned empty revolutionary phrases and oriented itself only after certain works of Goethe, Jacobi, and Rousseau. Indeed Leon translated Rousseau's *Pygmalion*. Then he turned in a pre-Romantic way to the great German poems of the Middle Ages, but again he lacked the enthusiasm of some of the early German Romantics for the French Revolution. He also lacked the anti-Semitism of the late Romantics.

It was no accident that it was Leon who resolved the misunderstanding between Schreyvogel and the young Grillparzer in 1816 and brought the two together.[24] All three, Leon, Grillparzer, and Schreyvogel, had little use for the German Romantics, although their own works were full of Romantic elements and traits. All three were in a certain way admirers of Goethe, and all three had their roots in Josephinism.

Leon dedicated his *Rabbinische Legenden* to three late friends of his, and this dedication too sheds light on his position at the time, and the status of the work. The three were Michael Denis, Johann Gottfried Herder, and Johannes von Müller. It was Denis who was, of all his former Masonic brothers, especially close to Leon, so close that Leon published separately a special poem on the occasion of Denis' death and also edited his last poem.[25] Denis on the other hand developed among his poetic reminiscences an evocation of Klopstock's verses which used images of Greek and Roman antiquity as well as images of the Old Testament:

> Schön wie der Jüngling David, wenn er an Bethlehems Quelle
> Saß, und entzückt in der Quelle den großen Allmächtigen hörte.[26]
>
> [Fair as the youth David, when he sat at Bethlehem's fountain, and heard in the fountain with rapture the great Almighty.]

Just as Leon wrote a poem about the death of Joseph II,[27] his 'brother' Herder included a 'Gespräch nach dem Tode des Kaisers Joseph's II' ('Dialogue after the Death of the Emperor Joseph II') in the first series of his *Briefe zur Beförderung der Humanität* ('Letters on the Advancement of Humanity').[28] In his *Ideen zur Philosophie der Geschichte der Menschheit* ('Ideas on the Philosophy of the History of Mankind') Herder wrote of the spiritual heritage of the Jews: 'gewissermaßen sind sie sowohl durch das Christentum als durch den Mohammedanismus eine Unterlage des größten Teils der Weltaufklärung geworden' ('in a sense they are through Christianity as well as through Islam a basis of most of the world's enlightenment'). He also expressed here the thought: 'so ist der Vorzug der hebräischen Schriften vor allen alten Religionsbüchern der Völker unverkennbar'[30] ('thus the superiority of the Hebrew writings to all the old books of religion of the nations is clearly evident').

Finally Leon befriended Johannes von Müller when the famous German historian arrived in Vienna as 'Wirklicher Hofrat' at the 'Geheime Hof- und

Staatskanzlei' in 1793. After Herder's death Müller participated in the editing of his collected works; Müller himself returned to Germany in 1804, since for a Protestant in these years any higher career in the Austrian state hierarchy was closed. Müller was, like Denis and Herder, filled with enthusiasm for a supranational humanism and in his *Vierundzwanzig Bücher allgemeiner Geschichte besonders der europäischen Menschheit*[31] ('Twenty-four Books of Universal History, particularly of European Mankind') granted the Jewish religious and spiritual tradition a place as important as had Herder.

This means that the dedication of Leon's *Rabbinische Legenden* already signalled the significance the book had for him, namely, among other things, the evocation of the bygone days of Josephinism, that 'golden age' in which intellectual freedom and religious tolerance were dominant.

Although some of the most learned and objective authorities in the field of Austrian history hold that Joseph II disdained the Jews,[32] his protection of their minority rights is undisputed. This alone sufficed to win him the minds and the hearts of the long persecuted Jews, and it is no accident that the figure of the Emperor appears in a most positive if not legendary light throughout the nineteenth century in the works of such notable fiction writers as the Austrian Jewish liberal authors Leopold Kompert or Karl Emil Franzos.

On the other hand, the Emperor Franz I, during whose reign Leon's *Rabbinische Legenden* appeared, was labelled, for good reasons, as 'judenfeindlich'.[33] Leon's intention with his book was to fight the old and the new prejudices against the Jews and their traditions, prejudices which had for a few years been revoked by Joseph II's 'Toleranzpatent' (Edict of Toleration). Doubtless Leon knew of Joseph II's refusal of Ignaz Aurelius Fessler's request to suppress Rashi's commentary on the Torah. Fessler, a former Capuchin monk, and a Masonic brother of Leon, had been appointed by the Emperor as professor of Oriental languages and the Old Testament at the University of Lemberg and a censor of all Jewish books in the Empire. He wanted to forbid the Hebrew text of Rashi and have it replaced by Moses Mendelssohn's German translation. Joseph II, who read Hebrew, did not allow this change but wanted the original Hebrew tradition to be continued.[34]

There is no question that an important goal of Leon's *Rabbinische Legenden*, besides other considerations, was the underground continuation of the spirit of Josephinism during the reign of Franz I. If the dedication to his three late friends already gave a clear signal of this, his introduction to the book was even more outspoken. He entitled it 'Vorerinnerung' ('Pre-remembrance'), which has a double meaning: on the one hand it refers to the remembering of the original meaning of distorted Jewish stories, and on the other hand it refers to the remembering of the time of Josephinism when the pejorative distortions began to be put right.

Leon tells us in his introduction that in most cases he found the subject of these legends not in Jewish sources but in Christian polemics against the Jews. He places them symbolically in a secluded and abandoned territory, where – thank God – no person of intelligence and of heart would any longer wish to travel. It is the typical Enlightenment desire to educate and to improve through expressing noble thoughts in books.

The method underlying most of the legends is very interesting. Leon turned upside down the distorted old stories which he found shaped by the enemies of the Jews and arrived at the genuine meaning of original Jewish legends. One of the best examples is the sixth legend of the first part of the collection, which Leon has entitled 'Lohn der Wohltätigkeit' ('Reward of Charity').[35] This is the story of a man who has been egotistic and pitiless throughout his entire life. When he is dying he asks for a hard-boiled egg. At the moment the egg is brought to him a poor man knocks at the door and asks for alms. The sick man requests his friend to give the egg to the poor man, and this is the only good deed he has ever done. However, it wins him the grace of the Lord and opens for him the door of paradise. It is almost literally the same story in the original, undistorted Jewish tradition as it can best be found today in Micha bin Gorion's collection of Jewish legends, fairy tales, and stories under the title 'Auf dem Sterbebette' ('On the Death-Bed').[36] Leon's only 'change' consists of a kind of frame within which he has put the story. The frame consists of just one verse of Proverbs at the beginning of the story and one verse of Jesus Sirach at the end. Perhaps he could not resist the temptation to display his erudition; perhaps the references to the Bible were meant to make the story more legitimate and acceptable at the time; but perhaps there was another reason, which will be mentioned later.

Five or six of the legends in the book, Leon claims in his introduction, can be counted as his own original creations. He lists six.[37] Even these, however, are not totally free inventions but are stories based on single Rabbinical images and topoi in connection with characters or stories of the Bible or Jewish religious tradition. Leon followed the example of his 'teacher and friend' Herder in shaping all the legends in a literary way which made them acceptable and relevant to his own time.

If one looks at the six legends which Leon has thus singled out, one finds the following stories. The first, 'Die Erschaffung des Menschen' ('The Creation of Man') paints a picture of man between heaven and earth as positive and optimistic as that of eighteenth-century Masonry.

The second story, 'Das erste Grab' ('The First Grave'), shows a disconsolate Eve mourning over the corpse of her son Abel; she is finally taught by an angel of the Lord to accept fate, a story of actual symbolic meaning for the suppressed and surviving Masons. The third legend, 'Der Stab Mosis' ('The Staff of Moses'), tells the story of Moses' staff, which gave him and his followers the wisdom and power of the Lord. After the destruction of the Temple of Solomon by the Romans, the Lord took the staff away and hid it until the day of judgement. However, the staff has still, though invisible, the same effect in the hands of those who are just and pious judges and teachers of their 'brothers'. It might be helpful to remember that the Masonic temple is built symbolically after the model of the Temple of Solomon and that this temple was destroyed in Austria by Leopold II and Franz I, although the wisdom connected with it survived unseen.

Leon's fourth story, 'Die Kraft des Gebets' ('The Power of Prayer'),

Rabbinische Legenden

describes the power of true faith in a prayer which turns vinegar into oil and lets it burn in the temple. The implication is obvious: there are no actual candles lit any longer in a Masonic temple in Austria, but true faith in the Masonic ideals will turn anything into burning lights. The fifth story, 'Der Traum des Propheten' ('The Dream of the Prophet'), evokes again the place of the destroyed city of Jerusalem and the destroyed temple. The prophet Jeremiah in his lament has a vision of Rachel, the mother of all Jews, and of her bitter complaints. However, the Lord appears to Rachel and announces that a time will come when he will free his people of Israel again and lead them back to the land of their fathers. Jeremiah arises newly strengthened and proclaims the same message to the people. This message is of course not less valid for the people of Leon's time.

In the sixth and last story 'Der Tod des Gerechten' ('The Death of the Just Man') it is Munbes, king and high priest of Jerusalem, the city of the temple, who in a time of hunger and despair rejects the opportunistic temptations of his relatives and advisers. He gives away the treasures of his ancestors in order to feed his hungry people and is of course rewarded in the hour of his death by Gabriel, the angel of death who appears to the chosen ones. Here is the message of Munbes which is also significant for Leon's time: 'The just man will flourish like a palm tree, he will grow like a cedar in Lebanon.'

Rudolf Kalmar, an Austrian journalist, in his memoirs, *Zeit ohne Gnade* ('Time without Grace'), described his sufferings in the Nazi concentration camp of Dachau. During a short period of better treatment the inmates were not only permitted but encouraged to perform a play. The play was written, rehearsed, and performed by the inmates under the suspicious eyes of the SS guards. The play turned out to be a parody of Hitler and an attack against Nazism. There was not one inmate who did not understand it and there was no guard who understood. Similarly, Leon's Masonic brothers had learned to understand symbols and allusions even during the time of Josephinism. The period of suppression under Franz I had sharpened their awareness. Leon knew how to fool the toughest censor. Not only did he attack anti-Semitism in the guise of Old Testament religiosity, but he also indirectly evoked memories of Masonic life in the early eighties.

It is astonishing what one can detect by taking a closer look. The above-mentioned legend 'Lob der Wohltätigkeit', for example, turned into a classical, unchanged Jewish legend. Leon's only change, in addition to restoring it to the original version, was putting the little frame around it. This little frame consisted of one short Bible sentence at the beginning and one at the end. And since he was a learned man he did not abstain from quoting his source.

If one checks the sources one finds that they are not correct. In the first half of the frame at the beginning of the story, we read the text (in English translation): 'He that hath pity upon the poor lendeth unto the Lord; and that which he hath given will he pay him again.' That makes perfect sense as a frame to this story. The note to this sentence says: Proverbs 19, 11. If one checks, this sentence is in Proverbs 19, 17 while the real verse 11 of chapter 19 reads: 'The discretion of a man deferreth his anger; and it is his glory to pass over transgression.'

This might be a printing error. But what of the second half of the frame at the end of the story? The 'quotation' in the text of Leon's story reads: 'As the water extinguishes the fire, alms extinguish sin.' This again would make perfect sense in connection with the legend itself. In his note Leon refers to Jesus Sirach 4, 33. If one checks Jesus Sirach 4, 33 one finds: '... but defend the truth to your death, then the Lord will fight for you.' The first quotation cannot be found in the entire chapter, indeed in the entire book of Jesus Sirach.

The real quotation about defending the truth has little relevance to the hard-boiled egg which the dying man gave to the beggar, but it has a lot to do with the intention of Leon's *Rabbinische Legenden* to pass on a second hidden meaning bearing on the suppression of Masonry. Sometimes we have to forget the sentences 'quoted' in the text which were meant for the censor and to replace them by the real text of the quotations which reveals the intended meaning.

Sometimes the quotation is correct and really belongs to the story, as in 'Der Opferstein des Baal' ('The Altar of Baal') or in 'Die Macht der Zunge' ('The Power of the Tongue'). In the case of 'Aristoteles and der Jüngling' ('Aristotle and the Youth') the numbering of the second quotation is really a printing error: instead of Psalms 118, 72 it should read Psalms 119, 72.

The longest and most remarkable note is to be found in connection with the legend 'Das Gastmahl' ('The Feast'), in which Leon evokes the legendary Simeon ben Jochai, supposedly author of the first kabbalistic book, the *Zohar*, who was born shortly after the destruction of the temple. Contrary to the general view according to which Simeon hid himself in a cave from the Romans for thirteen years,[38] Leon has him banished by his own people into a desert for thirteen years. This describes much better the Masonic situation of Leon's own time. But there is the further message that this Jewish mystic transcended the 'limited arid presence' of his time after the destruction of the temple and taught that everyone thirteen years old or older had in himself the potential to reach enlightenment and to receive God's grace.

There is no question that this legend reminded many readers who were former masons of the 'Hebrew Mysteries' which Leon's friend and brother, Reinhold, had published in the *Journal für Freymaurer*.[39]

The legend 'Elieser und Joseph' ('Eliezer and Joseph') ends with a vision of guardian angels around the two men and with the intention of the two to announce this welcome fact of the angels' presence to their 'brothers' in faith in order to comfort them.

In the case of the legend 'Chyah und Josi' ('Chyah and Josi') we find again two deliberately changed quotations. First, Leon printed in his story-text: 'I am the one who sinned and did evil; what have these sheep done to you'. The note refers to Chronicles, book I, 22, 17. If we consult the real quotation we find: 'David also commanded all the princes of Israel to help Solomon his son.' He deliberately chose a quotation which did not reveal how they should help him, because every Masonic reader knew it: by rebuilding the temple. This is not the only time that Leon carefully avoids the catchword 'temple'. The second quotation Leon gives correctly in the text according to Psalms 29, 9, with the exception of one word. Leon has printed: In the Lord's '*room* doth every one speak of his glory.' The real text reads: 'in his *temple* doth every one speak of his glory.'

It is not only the word 'temple' which Leon tries to avoid but even the seemingly less suspicious catchword of Austrian Masonry, 'wisdom'. When – in the legend 'Abbah' – he quotes Proverbs 3, 21 and 23 rather freely as 'He who walks the way of *piety*, his foot shall not stumble,' instead of 'He who walks the way of *wisdom* ... ', it might still be mere carelessness, or it might be chance. But a few pages later, in the last legend, 'Der Todesengel' ('The Angel of Death'), the same quotation occurs again and now Leon changes it even more drastically, again avoiding the word 'wisdom': 'The law of the Lord was the life of his soul.' The true quotation of Proverbs 3, 21 and 23 would have been: 'My son, let not them depart from thine eyes: keep sound *wisdom and discretion* ... Then shalt thou walk in thy way safely, and thy foot shall not stumble.'

A certain group of Leon's readers at this time, who had known him earlier and who knew who he was, understood well how to read these 'legends'. But even in our times, readers who miss entirely the second level of meaning referring to the specific Masonic situation in the reign of Franz I can enjoy these legends because of their first level of meaning alone: that is, because they are in themselves filled with general religious wisdom and beauty.

Leon died on 30 September 1830 in his apartment in the 'Tiefe Graben, Nr. 223 an der Gestätte'. Because of the strict censorship laws a so-called 'Sperr-Relation' had to be filled out with a report to the 'K. K. Bücher-Revisions-Amt'. Therefore we find attached to his death certificate a list of the books he owned. This was done in the form of a 'Schätzungsprotokoll' on 6 October 1830. A closer look shows that the list gives only the titles of books which he had 'officially' owned, since it can hardly be believed that he owned only *Erwin and Elmire* by Goethe. There are other discrepancies.[40]

Leon was a reliable and faithful friend not only in literary and political matters but also in his personal relations. The Wiener Stadtbibliothek keeps letters of his to Karoline Pichler '*neé* de Greiner' from as late as 1822 in which he gives the sister of his former pupil information about books. In another letter, of 1828, he promises an acquaintance in Jena to send him the manuscript of the biography of his friend Blumauer who had died 30 years before.[41] In a letter of 1825 he is trying to help the playwright Johann Ludwig von Deinhardstein to find a way to the Archduke Carl when Deinhardstein wanted to dedicate his play to Carl's wife.[42]

Leon was not only a kindhearted and helpful person and friend, he was as a writer a man of freedom, of peace, and of good will. He deserves credit for the persistence with which he sustained these qualities in a hostile climate.

Notes

1. See Taufbuch der Dompfarre St Stephan, Wien I, Tom. 82/1757, fol. 284.
2. See Caroline Pichler, *Denkwürdigkeiten aus meinem Leben*, ed. Emil Karl Blümml (Munich, 1914), pp. 49, 75, 82, 83.
3. I. F. Castelli, *Memoiren meines Lebens*, ed. Joseph Bindtner (Munich, n.d.), p. 258.

4. See Franz Gräffer, *Kleine Wiener Memoiren und Dosenstücke*, ed. Anton Schlosser and Gustav Gugitz, vol. I (Munich, 1918), pp. 38–46, 182, 200-1; also Alfred Meissner, *Rokokobilder* (Gunnbinden, 1871).
5. Edwin Zellwecker, *Das Urbild des Sarastro* (Vienna, 1953).
6. See Otto Erich Deutsch, *Mozart and die Wiener Logen* (Vienna, 1932), p. 15; Paul Nettl, *Mozart and Masonry* (New York, 1937), p. 48.
7. Protokoll der St Johannis Loge genannt zur wahren Eintracht, in Vertrauliche Akten der Kabinettskanzlei (Wiener Haus- Hof- und Staatsarchiv), Karton 91, pp. 8–14.
8. See Wynfried Kriegleder, 'Joseph von Retzers Briefe an Friedrich Nicolai', *Jahrbuch des Wiener Goethevereins*, 89-91 (1985-7), p. 262. See also Robert Keil, *Wiener Freunde* (Vienna, 1883), p. 61.
9. The young Leon was an admirer of Gottfried August Bürger (1747-94), whose most famous poem, the ballad *Lenore*, was published in the *Göttinger Musenalmanach* in 1774.
10. See Otto Rommel, 'Der Wiener Musenalmanach 1776-96', *Euphorion*, 6, Ergänzungsheft (1906); Maria Gräfin Lanckoronska and Arthur Rüman, *Geschichte der deutschen Taschenbücher und Almanache* (Munich, 1954).
11. Vol III, no 3. Leon's contributions are listed by Ludwig Abafi, *Geschichte der Freimaurerei in Österreich-Ungarn*, vol. IV (Vienna, 1893), p. 295.
12. Ibid., p. 287.
13. Letter to an unnamed friend, dated 5 May 1808, in the Manuscript Collection of the Österreichische Nationalbibliothek.
14. Otto Rommel, *Der Wiener Musenalmanach* (Leipzig and Vienna, 1906), p. 191.
15. J. W. Nagl, Jacob Zeidler and Eduard Castle, *Deutsch-Österreichische Literaturgeschichte*, 4 vols (Vienna, 1899-1937), vol. II, pp. 318-19.
16. Friedrich Rosenthal, 'Wieland und Österreich', *Jahrbuch der Grillparzer-Gesellschaft*, 24 (1913), p. 102.
17. Keil, *Wiener Freunde*, p. 71.
18. Ibid., p. 60.
19. Hans Wagner, 'Die politische und kulturelle Bedeutung der Freimaurerei im 18. Jahrhundert', in Eva H. Balazs et al. (eds), *Beförderer der Aufklärung in Mittel- und Osteuropa* (Berlin, 1979), pp. 69-86.
20. See Keil, *Wiener Freunde*, p. 71.
21. See Ernst Wangermann, *From Joseph II to the Jacobin Trials* (Oxford, 1959), and Joseph Strelka, 'Ein aufrechter Josephiner', in *Brücke zu vielen Ufern* (Vienna, Frankfurt, Zürich, 1966), pp. 45-53.
22. See E. V. Zenker, *Geschichte der Wiener Journalistik* (Vienna and Leipzig, 1892), pp. 99–100.
23. The text of the serenade appeared in print separately on two leaves of quarto format.
24. See Franz Grillparzer, *Sämtliche Werke*, ed. Peter Frank and Karl Pörnbacher, 4 vols (Munich, 1960-5), vol. IV, pp. 70-1.
25. Gottlieb von Leon, *Auf Denis Tod* (Vienna, 1801), and id. (ed.), *Sineds letztes Gedicht May 1801* (Vienna, 1801).
26. Michael Denis, *Zurückerinnerungen* (Vienna, 1794), p. 107.
27. *Über Joseph II. Tod an Eulogius Schneider* (Vienna, 1790).
28. *Herders Werke*, ed. Heinrich Kurz (Leipzig and Vienna, n. d.), vol. IV, pp. 41-53.
29. Ibid., vol. III, p. 378.
30. Ibid., vol. III, p. 382.
31. 3 vols. (Tübingen, 1810).
32. See Robert A. Kann, *A History of the Habsburg Empire 1526-1918* (Berkeley, Los Angeles, London, 1974), p. 186.
33. See Hermann Broch, *Dichten und Erkennen*, ed. Hannah Arendt (Zürich, 1955), p. 107.

34. See *Dr Fessler's Rückblicke auf seine siebzigjährige Pilgerschaft* (Breslau, 1824), p. 204.
35. Gottlieb von Leon, *Rabbinische Legenden*, reprinted (Vienna and Berlin, 1919), pp. 21-2.
36. *Der Born Judas. Legenden, Märchen, Erzählungen. Gesammelt von Micha bin Gorion*, ed. Emanuel bin Gorion (Wiesbaden, 1959), p. 289.
37. Nos. 1, 2, 3, 4, and 8 of Part I, and no. 7 of Part II.
38. See *Philo-Lexikon. Handbuch des jüdischen Wissens* (Berlin and Amsterdam, 1937), col. 692.
39. Keil, *Wiener Freunde*, p. 58.
40. The 'Sperr-Relation' dealing with the 'Todtenfall' is kept in the archives of the Magistratisches Zivilgericht Wien, Z. 1917/1830 in the Wiener Stadt- und Landesbibliothek.
41. These letters are kept in the Manuscript Collection of the Wiener Stadt- und Landesbibliothek.
42. This letter is kept in the Manuscript Collection of the Österreichische Nationalbibliothek.

Masonic Song and the Development of the *Kunstlied* in Enlightenment Vienna

Ewan West

Although German song was cultivated elsewhere with considerable vigour and enthusiasm from the middle of the eighteenth century, it was not until 1778 that the first collection appeared in Vienna. Composed largely in response to the current popularity of Italian and French song, the twenty-four songs of the first part of Joseph Anton Steffan's *Sammlung Deutscher Lieder für das Klavier* had few pretensions. The preface to the collection, even allowing for false reticence, makes only modest claims on behalf of the composer:

> Herr Steffan, der diese Lieder bloß einigen seiner Freunde zu gefallen, und keineswegs zur öffentlichen Bekanntmachung geschrieben hat, war sehr verlegen, als er das erste dieser Lieder im Drucke erschienen gesehen, und hat uns gebeten, die Liebhaber deutscher Lieder ... aus eben der Ursache, daß er diese kleinen Gesänge nie für die Welt zu schreiben gemeint habe, um Nachsicht für dieselben ... zu ersuchen.

> [Herr Steffan, who simply wrote these songs in order to please some of his friends and in no way intended them for publication, was very embarrassed when he saw the first of them in print and has asked us to crave the indulgence of connoisseurs of German song ... because he never intended to write these little pieces for the whole world.]

Little can Steffan have known that his collection was to begin a long tradition of Viennese song composition, culminating early in the next century in the masterpieces of Schubert. After 1778 new collections, as well as individual songs, were published every year: this was a period of considerable expansion for the Viennese music publishing houses, and song composers were a significant beneficiary of their frenetic activities.

But from the outset, the style of German song nurtured by the Viennese differed sharply from that current in Berlin, Leipzig, Hamburg, and other song centres. For earlier composers of German song, a new musical approach had emerged only after an extensive engagement with aesthetics.[1] Both the style and structure of such song publications as Görner's three volumes of *Neue Oden und Lieder* (Hamburg, 1742, 1744 and 1752) and Krause's two volumes of *Oden mit*

Melodien (Berlin, 1753 and 1755) would have been unthinkable without the preparation of Gottsched's *Versuch einer critischen Dichtkunst* (Leipzig, 1730) or Krause's own *Von der musikalischen Poesie* (Berlin, 1752). But Viennese composers began without any such foundation and remained largely aloof from the ideals of *Volkstümlichkeit*, which had been propounded by Gottsched, Krause, and their disciples. For the Viennese, 'song' simply implied a setting to music of German verse, the style of which was determined not by some abstract, aesthetic formula, but largely in imitation of the most popular pre-existing type of vocal music. Given Vienna's importance as a centre of opera composition in the 1770s and 1780s, it is thus not surprising that the models of Italian opera and German Singspiel should have played such a crucial role in the emergence of the new genre. Neither is it coincidence that the rise of song composition in Vienna was paralleled by the appearance of an increasing number of publications of individual numbers from popular stage works, arranged for voice and keyboard.[2]

To view Viennese song as simply forming a part of the wider eighteenth-century German repertory is thus mistaken. On the basis of available evidence, it is certainly clear that the dissemination of Viennese song to other centres was limited, as was the circulation within Vienna of song not published in the city (West, I, 54–64). More importantly, Viennese song did not begin from the same aesthetic basis as German song generally, it differed considerably in its musical approach, and it drew inspiration from a rather different corpus of lyric poetry. In this respect it was critically influenced by Austria's cultural isolation under the reign of Empress Maria Theresa, resulting in a literary taste which lagged well behind that of Germany. Hence the anacreontic movement, largely a spent force in German music by the 1780s, still exerted a noticeable influence during the early years of Viennese song, while the use of Goethe's verse by Viennese composers was very sporadic until the model of Reichardt's collection *Göthe's Lieder, Oden, Balladen und Romanzen* appeared in the city early in the next century. However, despite the insight which it lends to Schubert's activities in the next century, the Viennese song tradition of the late eighteenth century has been a relatively neglected area of both musicological and literary scholarship.[3]

Of the many aspects which still require careful examination, that of the relationship between genuine *Kunstlied* and Masonic song is perhaps the most undervalued. The general importance of Freemasonry for the political and cultural life of Austria during this period has, of course, long been recognised and need not be repeated here.[4] Suffice it to say that because of Maria Theresa's stance, it was only on Joseph II's accession in 1780 that Freemasonry began to flourish in an overt fashion. Hence the rise of song composition in Vienna coincided exactly with the golden years of Freemasonry, which lasted until 1785, when its activities began to be strictly curtailed under the shadow of revolutionary activity in France.

Although Freemasons were members of a supposedly secret society, the Craft was so widely practised in the 1780s that there was little need for circumspection. As Karoline Pichler says, when describing her youth, 'Der Orden der Freimaurer trieb sein Wesen mit einer fast lächerlichen Öffentlichkeit und

Ostentation. Freimaurerlieder wurden gedruckt, komponiert und allgemein gesungen. Man trug Freimaurerzeichen als joujoux an den Uhren ... Damen empfingen weiße Handschuhe von Lehrlingen und Gesellen.' ('The Order of Freemasons carried on its affairs with a publicity and ostentation that was almost ridiculous. Freemasons' songs were printed, composed, and universally sung. Masonic insignia were worn as pendants on watches ... ladies received white gloves from apprentices and craftsmen.')[5] (The wearing of white gloves was a common Masonic practice, commemorated in several poems of the period, including one by Blumauer, set to music by Johann Holzer in the *Wienerischer Musenalmanach* for 1785: 'An ***. Bey Überreichung eines Paars weißer Handschuhe'.) But it is indeed ironic that throughout history Masonic activities were so widely recorded. For Vienna in the 1780s police reports, as well as membership lists and other records, have permitted the reconstruction of Lodge activities in surprising detail. And from such documentary evidence two main points emerge: first, that many of the most significant writers, poets, and musicians were active Freemasons, and second, that music played an extremely important role in Lodge meetings.

A comprehensive examination of the links between Freemasonry and music has yet to be written. Most studies have concentrated on Haydn and Mozart and, if not purely biographical, are invariably concerned with suggesting Masonic allegories for stage, or less frequently instrumental, music.[6] Mozart's *Die Zauberflöte* has, of course, been the classic subject for such treatment,[7] although both *Die Entführung aus dem Serail* and *La clemenza di Tito* have been dealt with similarly.[8] But such studies are inevitably speculative and subjective. Certainly, when the music of Beethoven or Schubert is subjected to similar analysis, such interpretation is even more questionable, if only because neither composer can be proved to have been an active Freemason.[9]

Masonic song specifically has attracted even less scholarly attention, despite the important ceremonial role which it played in Lodge activities. Probably the clearest indication of its significance is shown by its inclusion in the famous *Journal für Freymaurer*. This periodical, in which many artistically talented Freemasons turned their gifts to the service of the Craft, was published at quarterly intervals by Christian Friedrich Wappler between 1784 and 1787. By undertaking to distribute the *Journal* only among the Brotherhood, Wappler, whose other Masonic publications included Ignaz von Born's influential *Physikalische Arbeiten der einträchtigen Freunde in Wien,* managed to evade the watchful eye of the censor. As well as essays and other prose pieces, many of the issues of the *Journal für Freymaurer* also contained poems, some of which were clearly intended to be set to music, and songs. Following a practice also common in many non-Masonic publications, both the text and music of these songs were unsigned, although a cipher (such as 'von Br. H**r.') usually provides a clue to the poet or composer. Few of these ciphers present any problem to the modern scholar armed with an adequate knowledge of the main artistic personalities active in the Masonic community.

In essence, the function of Masonic song may best be compared to that of the hymn in Church worship, for it was performed at the beginning and end of Lodge meetings, as a prelude to important events within a Masonic ceremony, and on festive days of Masonic significance. Such an example is provided by the three songs written by Wranitzky to celebrate the Feast of St. John at the lodge 'Zur gekrönten Hoffnung' ('Crowned Hope') in 1785 (Nettl, p. 62). A distinction may be drawn between songs intended for the actual Masonic rites, and those designed for the more convivial celebrations which followed, although these two parts of the Lodge meeting were perhaps then more closely linked than they are today. Both kinds of song are represented in the pages of the *Journal für Freymaurer*: in the first quarterly issue for 1785 is a song entitled 'Zur Gesellenreise', a setting by 'Br H**r' (i.e. Johann Holzer) of a poem by 'Br. J.F. R**y' (i.e. Ratschky) for those passing to the degree of 'Entered Apprentice' (*Journal für Freymaurer*, 1785, pp. 117–8), while in the third quarterly issue there is the text of a 'Tafellied' by 'Br. B***r' (i.e. Blumauer) which was clearly intended to be set to music (*Journal für Freymaurer*, 1785, pp. 119–20).

So many composers were active Freemasons that there was always a sufficiency of talent to provide the musical settings, with some Lodges even appointing an official composer (Nettl, pp. 60–6). Many songs were not written as independent pieces, however, but set new Masonic words to a pre-existing melody. Such melodies were frequently taken from well-known stage works, and it is not surprising that Mozart's operas provided material for a number of such treatments, as for example in the collection *Gesänge für Frey-Maurer* (Leipzig, 1798; copy in British Library) which makes extensive use of three melodies from *Die Zauberflöte*: 'Ein Mädchen oder Weibchen', 'Bei Männern, welche Liebe fühlen', and 'In diesen heil'gen Hallen'. Finally, it should be recognised that Masonic song was also connected to the many political songs in circulation at the time. The latter, which functioned as a public expression of political aims, were so ephemeral that few have survived. But it is clear from surviving police reports and the transcripts of trial proceedings that songs were circulated much like political pamphlets, the dissemination of seditious songs being an offence with which various Jacobins were charged (Wangermann, p. 159).

Although not as ephemeral as political song, Masonic song has also survived in only limited quantities. This is largely because, by their very nature, collections have survived not in public libraries, but in the archives of the Lodges for which they were written. Lodge amalgamations, disbandments, and the ravages of two world wars have resulted in the loss of many collections, while the frequent practice of omitting both place and date of publication from the music, not to mention details of composer and poet, has created insuperable problems of identification. This is seen most clearly in Wolfstieg's Masonic bibliography. For its compilation, the author and his assistants were given access to many private lodges and archives in Germany, which resulted in a list of song collections running to almost one hundred pages. Yet since so many items, particularly the individual songs, lack any geographical identification, it is impossible to establish with any certainty the repertory of particular localities.[10]

Previous treatment of Masonic song has focused upon it as an isolated genre, rather than relating it to the wider German context. Indeed many studies have been written by Freemasons who possess only a limited knowledge of the general field, which has inevitably hindered their perception of cross-currents, though in Vienna it is precisely these relationships which make Masonic song so important. Comments such as the following by Roger Cotte are commonplace: 'En Autriche, il est évident que circulèrent dans les Loges ces volumes allemands et français, mais une important production locale de chansons maçonniques allait se répandre, dont les conséquences pour l'histoire de la musique seraient considérables.' ('In Austria it is clear that these German and French volumes were in circulation, although an important local production of Masonic song was going to spread, the consequences of which would be considerable for the history of music.')[11] To date nobody has undertaken the important task of cataloguing and analysing this tradition in detail, and although Masonic collections have often featured in exhibitions, and hence in exhibition catalogues, there has not even been any conspicuous attempt to describe their contents or style. The only exceptions are such isolated cases as Ballin's monograph on 'O Heiliges Band', where one collection has formed the object of exhaustive study.[12]

The very fact that Masonic songbooks from Germany and Austria were circulating in Vienna at a time when it stood apart from the general tradition of song composition provides one important reason for undertaking a more wide-ranging treatment than has hitherto been attempted. This is not the only justification for such a study, however. In three quite crucial and distinct ways even a cursory examination of the evidence suggests that a deeper study of Masonic song would throw fresh light on Viennese song of the late eighteenth century.

First, the Masonic collections may be examined as a purely musical phenomenon, as a means of highlighting the diverse nature of the general Viennese song repertory of which they form a part. A consideration of the Masonic lyric, and a comparison of it with that of the *Kunstlied*, provides the second justification for our study, since a similarity of language and imagery suggests a possible connection between the two genres. Finally, fresh evidence suggests that the patterns of circulation of Masonic song and *Kunstlied* were not as independent as has usually been supposed.

Since so many song composers of the day were active within the sphere of the Lodges, collections of Masonic song do indeed have a fair claim to be considered part of the general Viennese repertory, although they have usually escaped such treatment. They are, for example, completely ignored in the studies of Pollak-Schlaffenberg and Alberti-Radanowicz. Naturally, the role which Masonic song had to fulfil shaped it differently from pure *Kunstlied*, but there are many points of contact. These, and the general nature of Viennese Masonic song, can best be demonstrated by examining one of the most important collections to appear in the city, the *Lieder zum Gebrauch der Loge zur wahren Eintracht* (Vienna: Archiv der Gesellschaft der Musikfreunde, Q 10508 [VI 19110]). This work, which has been included in several catalogues although never adequately described, has the superficial appearance of a typical late-eighteenth-century Viennese song collection, with no publisher or year of publication given. On the title-page the composer is described simply as 'Br. B—j.', although one song was apparently provided by 'Kapellmeister

Sarti', i.e. Giuseppe Sarti, who passed through Vienna in 1785 on his way from Milan to St Petersburg, where he was to be Kapellmeister to Catherine II. The identity of 'Br. B—j.' (who is possibly also the composer 'B.J.B.' whose cipher appears on some song inserts in the *Wienerischer Musenalmanach*) cannot be established with certainty, although two suggestions have been proffered. Wolfstieg attributes the songs to Bruder B[emernjöpel], otherwise Joseph Bauernjöpl, a Government official (Wolfstieg, II, 795), and this identification has been accepted without question by such later authorities as Nettl, who incorrectly states that some of the pieces were already known (Nettl, p. 65). However, Otto Biba has recently pointed out certain flaws in this attribution and suggested Joseph Anton von Bianchi as an alternative to Bauernjöpl. He points out that Bauernjöpl was not a member of the Lodge 'Zur wahren Eintracht', but of first 'Zur Beständigkeit' and later 'Zur neugekrönten Hoffnung', where he was 'Erster Aufseher' (Mraz, p. 560). Bianchi, however, was Secretary of 'Zur wahren Eintracht' and unlike Bauernjöpl wrote other Masonic music under his full name (Mraz, p. 441).

The title-page is followed by a note entitled 'Erinnerung für die Melodien':

> Bey den Liedern, wo die Melodie zwey Theile hat und der Gesang einstimmig gesezt ist, wird der erste Theil von einem Br. vorgesungen, und ebenderselbe von den sämtl. Brüdern nach dem Gehör wiederholt: alsdann singt den zweyten Theil wieder ein Br. allein vor, und die übrigen wiederholen ihn. Da selten viele musikalische Sänger in einer Loge zusammenkommen, so war es überflüssig, die Wiederholungen insbesondere und vollstimmig zu schreiben, hingegen um so mehr nothwendig, die Melodien so leicht zu setzen, daß die sämtl. BB. sie nicht alsogleich nachsingen, sondern sie sogar, bloß nach dem Gehör choralisch ausfüllen können.
>
> Bey den vollstimmigen Liedern, oder bey jenen, wo die Chöre ganz angesetzt sind – sollten sie in irgend einer anderen Loge gesungen werden – so wäre es zu wünschen, daß sich, so wie in der unseren, nur musikalische BB. damit beschäftigten.

> [In the case of songs where the melody is in two sections and the song is set for one voice, the first part will be sung by one Brother, and the same will then be repeated by all the Brothers: the second part is then once again sung by one Brother alone, while the others repeat it. As a large number of musical singers seldom come together in one Lodge, it was unnecessary to write out the repetition completely, but even more vital to set the melody in an easy fashion, so that all of the Brothers might not only sing it again straight away, but after simply hearing it, might be able to fill it out chorally.
>
> In the part-songs, or those where the chorus is completely written out, should they be performed in any other Lodge, it is to be wished that, as in our Lodge, only musical Brothers will take part.]

From the suggestions of the first part of this preface, and the cautionary words with which it ends, it is clear that the standard of musicality possessed by an average Lodge member was not high. Support for this view is provided by a little-known document written by Johann Holzmeister, Konzipist (i.e. Chief Clerk) at the Imperial War Ministry and a member of the lodge 'Zur wahren Eintracht'. Remembered mainly as the author of the speech read at Haydn's admittance to the Lodge on 11 February 1785, Holzmeister was a noted Masonic writer, who contributed to the *Journal für Freymaurer*.[13] His 'Vorschlag über die Pflege der Musik in der Loge zur wahren Eintracht', a manuscript document preserved like most such Viennese Masonic material as part of the 'Vertrauliche Akten' in the Haus-, Hof- und Staatsarchiv, provides useful details of the forces which might be employed at a Lodge ceremony. But most interestingly, it suggests that even in the most prestigious Lodges, performance standards were not very high.[14] From Holzmeister's proposals, it would seem that the prevailing approach was improvisatory rather than rehearsed, and that the standard of execution was generally uneven. Indeed, while criticism is levelled at the performers, Holzmeister praises the efforts of the composers.

From the titles of the twelve songs and their organization within the volume, it seems that the *Lieder zum Gebrauch der Loge zur wahren Eintracht* was intended for regular use. The first six songs refer to the three degrees of Freemasonry and relate to the ceremonial part of the meeting, viz.: 'Bey Eröffnung der Lehrling Loge', 'Zum Schluß der Lehrling Loge', 'Bey Eröffnung der Gesellen Loge', 'Zum Schluß der Gesellen Loge', 'Bey Eröffnung der Meister Loge' and 'Zum Schluß der Meister Loge'. Of the next six songs, the first three are clearly intended for the convivial conclusion of the meeting: indeed, the first is entitled 'Bey Eröffnung der Tafelloge' and makes explicit reference to the ending of the ceremony. This is followed by a 'Tafellied', sung during the social gathering, and the concluding song, 'Zum Schluß der Tafelloge'. The final three songs are intended for special occasions: 'Kettenlied am St. Johannisfeste', 'Kettenlied gesungen bey einer Schwestertafel' and 'An die Rosennähterinn'.

The title 'Kettenlied' ('Chain-song') refers to the practice whereby the Brothers stood at the end of a meeting in a circle with their hands linked like a chain. In the collection of Masonic songs produced by Naumann in Dresden in 1782 (*Vierzig Freimaurerlieder*) there is an instrumental piece entitled 'Die Kette', in which chain-like suspensions feature prominently.[15] The 'Rosennähterinn' ('Seamstress of the Rose') to whom the final song is addressed was Maria, Countess Bassegli, daughter of the Master of the Lodge 'Zur wahren Eintracht', Ignaz von Born. She was an accomplished pianist who often performed at her father's house (Robbins Landon, *Haydn: Chronicle*, II, 474). It has been suggested that it may have been Maria's musical talents which attracted Haydn to the Born household and that it was here that he was first invited to become a Freemason (Hurwitz, pp. 34–5). In the poetic source (see below) precise details are included for the ritual of the 'Rosennähterinn', who apparently circulated among the Brothers distributing rose-bedecked ribbons in return for a garlanded hat. Of her popularity amongst members of the Lodge there can be doubt: in the *Wienerischer Musenalmanach auf das Jahr 1785* (pp.

16–17) there is a poem by Blumauer clearly addressed to Maria Born, entitled 'Dem Fräulein M** v. B* ... '.

A date of publication for the collection may be ascertained with some accuracy. In 1783 the printer Christian Friedrich Wappler, himself a member of the Lodge 'Zur neugekrönten Hoffnung', published a collection entitled *Gedichte und Lieder verfaßt von den Brüdern der Loge zur wahren Eintracht*. This work, although likewise mentioned in several exhibition catalogues and bibliographies, has so far never been accurately identified, namely as the poetic source for the Bauernjöpl/Bianchi collection. With the exception of one poem, the whole of the section described as 'Lieder' in Wappler's collection was set to music. (In the poetry collection there is one item inserted between the two songs for the Meisterloge, a 'Gegenstück zu vorstehenden Liedern' by 'Br. J.G. S***' [i.e. Sauter]). Like the preceding section of 'Gedichte', which consists of longer pieces in honour of Joseph II, invocations to Masonic observance, and occasional odes, each of the poems is signed with a cipher. The main contributors are Leon, Ratschky, and Blumauer, although Sauter, Schittlersberg, and Pauer also feature (Wolfstieg, II, 795). All of the poems set to music were the work of either Blumauer or Ratschky.

In the preface the editors of the collection provide a justification for their endeavours and include some valuable comments on the state of contemporary Masonic song-publication:

> Schon der selige Lessing machte die Bemerkung, daß die Reden und Lieder der Freymaurer meistentheils schöner gedruckt als gedacht and gesagt seyn. (*Ernst und Falk. Gespräche für Freymaurer. Seite 20) Wir kennen itzt bereits an die verschiedene Sammlungen von Freymaurerliedern, und noch scheint diese Beobachtung wenig oder nichts von ihrer Wahrheit verloren zu haben. Warum die Dichtkunst auf maurerischem Grund und Boden, dem es für sie gewiß weder an Urbarkeit noch Ergiebigkeit fehlt, so wenig gedeihen wolle, ist eben so schwer zu bestimmen, als warum unsere besten Dichter sich so wenig mit Erzeugung solcher Produkte abgeben, die doch für die ganze Maurergesellschaft zu einer Art von Hausbedürfnis geworden sind. Man kann sich dieses sonderbare Phönomen [sic] nicht anders erklären, als wenn man annimmt, die maurerische Muse habe sich durch Gleichgültigkeit an einem Orden rächen wollen, der ihr Geschlecht von seinen Geheimnissen ausschließt. Nicht mit der stolzen Miene, als hätten wir von der Gunst, mit der sie gegen die Sänger unsers Bundes so sehr zu kargen scheint, mehr als andere errungen, sondern mit dem zuversichtlichen Bewußtsein, gemeinschaftlich mit unsern Brüdern nach selber gerungen zu haben, theilen wir gegenwärtige, zum Gebrauch unserer Loge bestimmte, Versuche dem maurerischen Publikum mit, und hoffen von demselben um so mehr Nachsicht, da diese Sammlung keine aus anderen Sammlungen entlehnte oder fremde Gedichte sondern lauter noch ungedruckte Versuche von Brüdern einer einzigen Loge enthält. Auch die Melodien sind ganz neu, und wir hoffen unsern Brüdern damit ein nicht unwillkommenes Geschenk zu machen. Die Gesundheiten

komischer Art, wodurch wir in das Einförmige der bisherigen Gesundheitsformeln mehr Mannichfaltigkeit und Leben zu bringen suchten, werden keinem der Würde der Maurerey zuwider scheinen, der weiß, daß sie nur dahin gehören, wo der Maurer nach vollendetem Tagewerk berechtiget ist, nur Scherz und Freude zu erwarten.

[The late Lessing has already made the observation that the speeches and poems of Freemasons are for the most part better printed than they are conceived or delivered [*Ernst und Falk. Gespräche für Freymaurer*, p. 20]. We are already acquainted with various collections of Masonic poetry, yet this observation appears to have lost little or none of its truth. Since Freemasonry certainly offers a bounteous and fertile pasture for the art of poetry, the reasons why such poetry has flourished so little are just as difficult to determine as why our best poets will not bother themselves with the production of such artefacts, though they have become a kind of domestic need for the whole Masonic community. This strange phenomenon can only be understood if one presumes that, through indifference, the Masonic Muse has wanted to take revenge on an Order that excludes her sex from its secrets. We present our present endeavours to the Masonic public not with a proud countenance, as though we had achieved more than others by means of that kindness which the Muse appears to restrict so much when she looks on the singers of our society, but rather with the confident awareness that we have striven together with our brothers towards that goal. We also hope for all the more indulgence from the public in that this collection contains no poems by outsiders or poems borrowed from other collections, but is taken from the unprinted efforts of the Brothers of a single Lodge. The melodies are also completely new and we hope thereby to make a not unwelcome present to our Brothers. The toasts, in which we have sought to impart more variety and life into the uniformity of previous items of this kind, will not appear contrary to the dignity of Freemasonry to anyone who knows that they are only appropriate after a completed day's work, when the Mason is entitled to expect amusement and pleasure.]

Compared to contemporary Viennese song, the *Lieder zum Gebrauch der Loge zur wahren Eintracht* exhibit a number of small, yet significant differences. Most importantly, the style of the accompaniment is often more advanced, owing to its independence from the vocal line. Although the accompaniment doubles the voice, it does more than simply provide a filled-out harmonisation. In the first song, for example, it has some genuinely independent musical interest, both by means of flourishes in the bass part and through the filling-out of the treble part with semiquavers. The third song, 'Stral der Klugheit', shows a similar practice: although the vocal part is contained within the accompaniment, which elaborates the melody with semiquavers, there is a quite independent interlude between the two halves of the stanza and a closing epilogue. More independence of accompaniment from vocal line is provided in the song for the closing of the Meisterloge, whose brilliant writing suggests an operatic influence. Much use is made initially of a tonic pedal, over which the right hand performs an elaborate semiquaver pattern, a technique also employed in the song to close the Tafelloge. The roots of this accompanimental independence may lie in the possibility that the song collection actually presents a keyboard reduction of an instrumental accompaniment, for there is evidence that 'Zur wahren Eintracht' maintained a small instrumental band (Chailley, *Magic Flute*, p. 91).

Certainly, the sonorities of the Meisterloge song would be appropriate for a wind band: equally important is that some of the songs bear performance indications appropriate to instrumental music, for example 'March' and 'Tempo di Minuetto'. In addition, the ambiguous indication 'solo' before the two instrumental interludes in 'Stral der Klugheit' suggests that the keyboard player was perhaps accompanied by other instrumentalists. But the nature of this keyboard accompaniment itself is unclear (Morehen, p. 217). The rise of Freemasonry in the late eighteenth century corresponds to the rise in supremacy of the piano over the harpsichord: however, accompaniment on the organ would have been equally possible. This problem is highlighted by a comparison of the autograph of Mozart's Masonic song 'Lied zur Gesellenreise' (K. 468), where an organ accompaniment is specified, with the entry for the work in his own *Werkverzeichnis*, which states 'Clavier'.[16] Some later Masonic collections explicitly required the accompaniment of a piano: for example, *Maurer-Gesänge mit Begleitung des Piano-Forte* (Frankfurt, 1809) (Wolfstieg, II, 803) .

The preface makes clear the structure of the songs, most of which are strophic in design, with an internal bipartite structure. In the ceremonial items the verse consists mainly of invocations of Masonic wisdom. See, for example, the first stanza of the first song:

> Brüder, laßt mit frohem Muth,
> Uns die Arbeit nun beginnen!
> Denn der Zeiten schnellen Fluth
> Soll uns nicht umsonst verrinnen.
> Singt mit freudigem Gefühl:
> Arbeit ist des Maurers Ziel.

[Brothers, let us now begin work with a cheerful spirit! For we should not let the quick passage of time elapse in vain. Sing enthusiastically: Work is the goal of the Mason.]

For the celebratory items the words are equally appropriate, as in this passage from the song 'Bey Eröffnung der Tafelloge':

> Legt für heut das Werkzeug nieder,
> Laßt die blanken Kellen ruhn,
> Denn der Hammer ruft, ihr Brüder,
> Euch zum frohen Mahle nun.
> Sehet! manche süße Gabe,
> Die den Körper neu erfrischt,
> Hat aus ihrem reichen Habe,
> Mutter Erd' uns aufgetischt.

[Put down your tools for today, and let the shiny trowels be silent, for Brothers, the hammer now calls you to the joyful feast. Look! From her rich bounty Mother Earth has regaled us with many sweet gifts to refresh the body.]

Some measure of the circulation of this collection may be gleaned from the fact that it was noted by the copyist Johann Elssler in his catalogue of Haydn's music library, although against his entry the ambiguous word 'unbrauchbar' (unusable) was later added (Robbins Landon, *Haydn: Chronicle*, V, 299–316). Once mistakenly attributed to Haydn himself, the collection was removed from the composer's effects after his death by the censor (Hurwitz, p. 53). Even comparatively recently the myth that a copy of these songs is no longer extant has continued to be propagated.[17]

By offering a brief glimpse into the music of a typical Lodge meeting in eighteenth-century Vienna, the *Lieder zum Gebrauch der Loge zur wahren Eintracht* are of considerable importance. In general, however, it is regrettable that although Lodge meetings were widely documented, there is usually little mention of the musical activities which took place under their auspices. One of the few complete accounts is of a musical evening which Mozart's Lodge 'Zur neugekrönten Hoffnung' was to host for the other Viennese Lodges. The handwritten invitation (Vienna: Haus-, Hof- und Staatsarchiv, Vertrauliche Akten, f. 103) lists the works to be performed, which include two symphonies by Wranitzky, a cantata and piano concerto by Mozart, and a suite for wind by Stadler. But it must be remembered, however, that this was no ordinary Lodge meeting, but a special Masonic occasion.[18]

In some senses, of course, the performance of song under the aegis of a Masonic Lodge was not so very different from any gathering which featured music. Often a Lodge meeting and a domestic soirée would attract a broadly comparable attendance, and while the ceremonial part of the Lodge meeting had an obvious mystical connotation, the concluding Tafelloge consisted more of musical entertainment. But in a Masonic meeting the main *raison d'être* for singing was clearly to engender a feeling of community and brotherhood. As Nettl says, 'Es hat die maurerische Musik keinen anderen Zweck, oder soll keinen anderen Zweck haben, als eine geistige Gemeinschaft der Brüder vorzubereiten, durch Erziehung eines gleichartigen psychischen Zustandes.' ('Masonic music has no other purpose, or ought to have no other purpose, than to prepare a spiritual community of Brothers through the attainment of a homogeneous psychic condition.') (Nettl, pp. 33–4). This levelling effect was, of course, an important element in the striving for a kind of social equality which was always a feature of the Craft. For a Freemason, attainment of the correct spiritual condition was in no way dependent on the social standing of the individual, as the following lines from Gottlieb Leon's 'Ordenspflichten der Maurerritter', included in Wappler's 1783 collection discussed above, explain:

In der Maurer Zunftgemeine
Gilt der König wie der Knecht:

Tugendliche Sitt' alleine
Giebt zu Vorrang hier das Recht.

[In the communal guild of Freemasons the slave is as worthy as the king: here precedence is justified only by virtuous conduct.] (*Gedichte*, p. 23)

A poem by Aloys Blumauer, also included in this collection, makes the same point even more strongly:

Ja, wär' er eines Fürsten Sohn,
Und fand er sich an seinem Prüfungstage
Nur um ein Gran zu leicht auf deiner Wage
So muß er fort von deinem Thron!

[Yes, were he the son of a prince and found on his day of trial to be only one grain too light on your scales, he would have to depart from your throne!] (*Gedichte*, p. 3).

The importance of song for achieving these feelings of brotherhood and equality cannot be underestimated, yet it follows as a consequence that composers of Masonic song were in general perhaps less concerned about the intimate relationship of words and music, than with ensuring that words and music together created an overall mood appropriate to its main function. This is not to deny that in individual cases it is possible to show that both the melodic material and overall structure of a song were shaped by Masonic influences. The use of chain-like suspensions as a prominent feature of the 'Kettenlied' in Naumann's collection of 1782 has already been alluded to above (Nettl, pp. 52–60). Another particularly interesting case is provided by Mozart's overtly Masonic song 'Lied zur Gesellenreise' (K. 468), another setting of the Ratschky poem from the first quarterly issue of the *Journal für Freymaurer* for 1785. Dated 26 March 1785, this was written by Mozart for the occasion of his father's passing to the degree of 'Entered Apprentice' in the following month. An apparently straightforward strophic setting with a relatively lengthy keyboard introduction to the first stanza, it shows the clear influence of Italian opera in the shaping of its melismas, despite invoking a sombre and serious mood. As Ballin has pointed out in his seminal monograph on Mozart's songs, the musical material includes many Masonic motifs, such as the falling and rising melisma at the opening of the stanza to represent the 'chain' of brothers with linked hands.[19] Despite the presence of these Masonic features, the song survives quite easily without the listener needing to be aware of them, although there can be no doubt about the purpose of Ratschky's text:

Die ihr einem neuen Grade
Der Erkenntnis nun euch naht,
Wandert fest auf eurem Pfade,
Wißt, es ist der Weisheit Pfad.
Nur der unverdroßne Mann
Mag dem Quell des Lichts sich nahn.

[You who now would approach a new degree of understanding, walk steadfastly on your path, knowing that it is the path of Wisdom. Only the man who perseveres may approach the source of Light.]

The most interesting aspect of the 'Lied zur Gesellenreise' concerns the history of its publication. For Breitkopf & Härtel's collected edition of 1799 it was furnished with different words by Daniel Jäger and given a new title, 'Lebensreise'. The texts of several other songs received similar 'improvement', although none for the same reason. In the 'Lied zur Gesellenreise' the Masonic sentiments were clearly deemed inappropriate and were replaced by a more general exhortation to overcome the tribulations of life. Accordingly, the final stanza, with its typical Masonic image:

Rauh ist zwar des Lebens Reise,
Aber süß ist auch der Preis,
Der des Wand'rers harrt, der weise
Seine Fahrt zu nützen weiß.
Glücklich, wer einst sagen kann:
Es ist Licht auf meiner Bahn!

[Life's pathway is indeed rugged, but sweet is the prize which awaits the wanderer, the wise man who knows how to use his journey. Happy is he who can say one day, 'There is Light over my path!']

is replaced by the more neutral:

Ach! der ganze Weg durchs Leben
Würde rauh und traurig geh'n!
Sehet, was ihn macht so eben,
Freunde, was ihn macht so schön!
Seht und fühlt es jeden Schritt:
Menschen, Menschen gehen mit!

[Ah! the whole of our journey through life would be rough and sad! See, friends, what makes it so smooth, what makes it so beautiful! See and feel it at every step: Mortals, mortals, accompany you!]

Only with the appearance of a critical edition of the songs as part of the *Neue Mozart-Ausgabe* in 1963 were the original words and title restored to the song, which had hitherto been known, and appreciated, exclusively through Jäger's bowdlerised version, which had reversed the more common practice of setting new Masonic words to a preexisting melody, by providing a Masonic melody for quite innocent words.[20]

Consideration of the text suggests a second point of contact between Masonic song and the *Kunstlied*. If Masonic songs merit inclusion in the general repertory of Viennese song because of musical similarity, it is equally possible to postulate an influence in the opposite direction through the style of lyric poetry set. Even the most cursory acquaintance with the Austrian lyric of the late eighteenth century reveals the strong influence of a Masonic *Weltanschauung*, which has been commented upon, if only briefly, by the few writers who have been drawn to this area of research.[21] Admittedly, there is a certain overlap between many overtly Masonic ideas and those of both anacreontic poetry and fashionable liberalism, so that a precise identification of what is, and what is not, Masonic often cannot be made, as is shown by the standard work on the *topoi* of Masonic verse.[22] Certain clear Masonic motifs (such as the 'Licht auf meiner Bahn' in the 'Lied zur Gesellenreise') may be identified, but much of the poetic contact is to be found in a similarity of outlook. It is, for example, precisely this similarity which allows the non-Mason to empathise with the opening stanza of Mozart's 'Lied der Freiheit' (K 506) while not possessing the particular insight of a Freemason:

> Wer unter eines Mädchens Hand
> Sich als ein Sklave schmiegt
> Und, von der Liebe festgebannt,
> In schnöden Fesseln liegt,
> Weh dem! der ist ein armer Wicht,
> Er kennt die gold'ne Freiheit nicht.

> [Whoever bends under a maiden's hand like a slave, and lies firmly bound by the contemptible bonds of love, woe to him! for he is a poor wretch who does not know golden Freedom].

This poem by Blumauer was published in the *Wienerischer* (later *Wiener*) *Musenalmanach*, which for much of its existence was under the editorship of active Freemasons, and served as a source of texts for many Viennese song composers. Many contributions carried only thinly-veiled Masonic references, but this example from the 1786 issue (which included Mozart's setting as an insert) is one of the more explicit. The second stanza contains the Masonic message at its clearest:

> Wer sich um Fürstengut und Rang
> Mit saurem Schweiß bemüht
> Und, eingespannt sein Leben lang,
> Am Pflug des Staates zieht,
> Weh dem! der ist ein armer Wicht,
> Er kennt die gold'ne Freiheit nicht.

> [Whoever sweats and strives for the possessions and rank of a prince, and remains yoked to the plough of the State for his whole life, woe to him! for he is a poor wretch who does not know golden Freedom]

Clearly, the 'Lied der Freiheit', which was innocently published as an insert to an almanac in general circulation, conveyed a message readily discernible by the many Freemasons who subscribed to the publication.

Although many other examples of possible Masonic references in the lyrics of Viennese song could be suggested, it is perhaps the third point of contact which has the widest implications. This is illustrated by an examination of another apparently Masonic collection, a manuscript entitled *Musikalische Unterhaltungen der eintraechtigen Freunde in Wien. Erstes Werk enthaltend zwölf Lieder auf das Piano-Forte* (Vienna: Haus-, Hof- und Staatsarchiv, f. 317–18). From the title-page, which indicates the location for a vignette, this would appear to be the printer's copy of another songbook for 'Zur wahren Eintracht' although there is no extant printed source. It is, however, significant that none of the twelve songs makes any explicit reference to Freemasonry: as the titlepage suggests, the songs appear to be intended purely for entertainment. In fact, this title-page *Musikalische Unterhaltungen* was clearly the second which the compilation received, for it is written in a different hand to the rest of the collection. The original title-page, which has been crossed through, describes the songs more accurately as *Romanzen und Schäferlieder auf das Piano-Forte*. Another manuscript copy bearing only this title is located in the archives of the Gesellschaft der Musikfreunde in Vienna (Mraz, pp. 441–2).

As with so many collections of this period which were advertised but which have apparently not survived, it is impossible to know whether the *Romanzen und Schäferlieder* were ever published, although the *Wiener Zeitung* for 4 April 1781 carried the following advertisement by the firm of Christoph Torricella: 'Schäferlieder auf das Fortepiano. Auserlesene Gedichte von beeden Grafen Stolberg, Weisse und Jacobi. Stich von dem berühmten Huberty. Pränumerationsanzeige.'[23] Not only does the description accord with the collection *Romanzen und Schäferlieder*: the very word 'Schäferlieder' appears extremely rarely on the title-pages of other song collections.

Even harder to ascertain, however, is the connection between the *Romanzen und Schäferlieder* and the new title *Musikalische Unterhaltung*. The most plausible explanation is that this elegant collection, which is entirely typical of Viennese song at the time, was simply taken over either to provide material for the concluding celebrations of a Masonic meeting, or as a suitable source of private entertainment for individual Freemasons. Within the context of a meeting these twelve strophic songs would only be appropriate for the concluding Tafelloge: they deal mostly with Arcadian love, and are couched in a variety of contrasting moods. The poets represented include Weisse and Hagedorn and of especial interest is the third song, 'Die Verschweigung', a setting of a Weisse poem also selected by Mozart in 1787 (K. 518). A total of four of the poems set in this collection were culled from Christian Felix Weisse's *Scherzhafte Lieder* (Leipzig, 1758; facs. ed. Alfred Anger, Stuttgart, 1965). This collection, one of the most influential anacreontic publications, was reprinted and plagiarised throughout the latter part of the eighteenth century: Weisse himself issued a revised edition in 1759 (reprinted 1760) and a third edition in 1763. But the many minor textual variants in the four Weisse poems included in *Musikalische Unterhaltungen* indicate that the composer probably did not use one of the poet's own editions, but rather one of the plagiarised versions.

This interpretation of the purpose behind the collection opens up much wider implications for the role of Masonic song in the period. Crucially, it suggests that closer performance links may exist between it and the genuine *Kunstlied* than are generally recognised. If one totally non-Masonic collection could be employed by a Lodge in this way, for whatever particular purpose, is it not reasonable to assume that other superficially innocent publications may also have entered Masonic circles? Certainly, almost every other collection of the period contains items of the kind represented in *Musikalische Unterhaltung* and appropriate to the convivial ending of a Lodge meeting.

The evidence would thus seem to suggest that links between Masonic song and *Kunstlied* were closer in Vienna during the 1780s than has generally been recognised. Yet the problems this presents for the historian of song are considerable. Whatever a collection may purport to be from its title-page, an examination of its contents from this viewpoint may now well open it to more than one interpretation. But in this respect the model of poetry is very instructive. Blumauer, Ratschky, Leon, and others often published verses in volumes with such overtly Masonic titles as *Freymaurergedichte*, yet the very same pieces would surface only a short time later in a collection with a more general title. Until Viennese Masonic song has been thoroughly researched and chronicled, we would do well to approach all song of the period bearing in mind the possibility that such a similar duality of purpose existed in the mind of the composer.

Notes

For the provision of photocopies and microfilms of material I am indebted to the staff of the following Viennese libraries: Archiv der Gesellschaft der Musikfreunde; Haus-, Hof- und Staatsarchiv; Österreichische Nationalbibliothek; Stadt- und Landesbibliothek.

1. The aesthetic basis of eighteenth-century German song is discussed most fully in Heinrich Schwab, *Sangbarkeit, Popularität und Kunstlied: Studien zu Lied und Liedästhetik der mittleren Goethezeit 1770–1814* (Regensburg, 1965).
2. The publication of individual numbers from stage works is analysed in detail in Ewan West, 'Schubert's Lieder in Context: Aspects of Song in Vienna 1778–1828', unpubl. diss. (3 vols, University of Oxford, 1989), I, 117–32.
3. For earlier treatments of Viennese song see Irene Pollak-Schlaffenberg, 'Die Wiener Liedmusik von 1778 bis 1789', *Studien zur Musikwissenschaft*, 5 (1918), 97–151; Editha Alberti-Radanowicz, 'Das Wiener Lied: 1789–1815', *Studien zur Musikwissenschaft*, 10 (1923), 37–78; Herbert Zeman, 'Dichtung und Musik: zur Entwicklung des österreichischen Kunstliedes vom 18. zum 19. Jahrhundert', in id. (ed.), *Musik und Dichtung: Festschrift Anton Dermota zum 70. Geburtstag* (Vienna, 1980), pp. 20–34; Robert Schollum, *'Gelebt-Geschaffen-Vergessen?': das österreichische Lied des 18. Jahrhunderts* (Vienna, 1985); West, *op. cit.*
4. See especially Ludwig Abafi, *Geschichte der Freimaurerei in Österreich-Ungarn* (5 vols, Budapest, 1890–99); Robert Freke Gould, *The History of Freemasonry* (London, 1903); Paul von Mitrofanov, *Joseph II: seine politische und kulturelle Tätigkeit*, trans. V. von Demelic (2 vols, Vienna and Leipzig, 1910); Ernst Wangermann, *From Joseph II to the Jacobin Trials: Government Policy and Public Opinion in the Habsburg Dominions in the Period of the French Revolution*, 2nd edn (Oxford, 1969).
5. Caroline Pichler, *Denkwürdigkeiten aus meinem Leben*, ed. Emil Karl Blümml (Munich, 1914), I, 94.
6. See especially Otto Erich Deutsch, *Mozart und die Wiener Logen: zur Geschichte seiner Freimaurer-Kompositionen* (Vienna, 1932); Paul Nettl, *Mozart und die königliche Kunst*

(Berlin and Prague, 1932); Jacques Chailley, 'Haydn and the Freemasons', in H. C. Robbins Landon (ed.), *Studies in Eighteenth Century Music* (London, 1970), pp. 117–24; Alexander Giese, 'Einige Bemerkungen über Joseph Haydn als Freimaurer und die Freimaurerei seiner Zeit', in Gerda Mraz and others (ed.), *Joseph Haydn in seiner Zeit: Eisenstadt, 20. Mai – 26. Oktober 1982* (Eisenstadt, 1982), pp. 168–71; H. C. Robbins Landon, *Mozart and the Masons: New Light on the Lodge 'Crowned Hope'* (London, 1982); Philippe A. Autexier, *Mozart et Liszt sub. Rosa* (Poitiers, 1984); Joachim Hurwitz, 'Haydn and Freemasonry', *Haydn Yearbook*, 14 (1985), 5–98; H. C. Robbins Landon, *1791: Mozart's Last Year* (London, 1988), pp. 55–64.

7. See especially Edgar Istel, 'Mozart's "Magic Flute" and Freemasonry', *The Musical Quarterly*, 13 (1927), 510–27; id., *Die Freimaurerei in Mozarts Zauberflöte* (Berlin, 1928); Jacques Chailley, *The Magic Flute: Masonic Opera*, trans. H. Weinstock (London, 1972).
8. See for example Daniel Heartz, 'La clemenza di Sarastro: Masonic benevolence in Mozart's last operas', *Musical Times*, 124 (1983), 152–7.
9. A classic example of such a study is Jacques Chailley, 'Le "Winterreise" de Schubert: est-il un œuvre ésotérique?', *Revue d'esthétique* 1965, 113–24.
10. See August Wolfstieg, *Bibliographie der freimaurerischen Literatur*, 2nd edn (3 vols, Leipzig, 1923–6), I, 675–9 and II, 785–869. Other important bibliographical studies are Georg Franz B. Kloss, *Bibliographie der Freimaurerei und der mit ihr in Verbindung gesetzten geheimen Gesellschaften* (Frankfurt, 1844); Reinhold Traute, *Maurerische Bücherkunde: ein Wegweiser durch die Literatur der Freimaurerei* (Leipzig, 1886/reprinted Graz, 1971).
11. Roger Cotte, *La musique maçonnique et ses musiciens*, 2nd edn (Paris, 1987), p. 27.
12. Ernst August Ballin, *Der Dichter von Mozarts Freimaurerlied »O Heiliges Band« und das erste erhaltene deutsche Freimaurerliederbuch* (Tutzing, 1960).
13. H.C. Robbins Landon, *Haydn: Chronicle and Works* (5 vols, London, 1976–82), II, 506–8.
14. See West, 'Schubert's Lieder in Context', vol. I, pp. 140–1. I am grateful to Dr Edward Olleson for his help in transcribing this document.
15. See further John Morehen, 'Masonic and Instrumental Music of the Eighteenth Century', *The Music Review*, 42 (1981), 215–24 and Nettl, pp. 53–5.
16. See Ludwig Ritter von Köchel, *Chronologisch-thematisches Verzeichnis*, 6th edn (Wiesbaden, 1964), pp. 506–7.
17. See for example John Webb, 'Joseph Haydn – Freemason and Musician', *Ars Quatuor Coronatorum*, 94 (1981), 61–82.
18. Otto Erich Deutsch (ed.), *Mozart: die Dokumente seines Lebens*, 2nd edn (Kassel, 1966), p. 226; cf. Deutsch, *Mozart: A Documentary Biography*, trans. E. Blom and others, pp. 256–7.
19. Ernst August Ballin, *Das Wort-Ton Verhältnis in den klavierbegleiteten Liedern W.A. Mozarts* (Kassel, 1984), p. 50.
20. Wolfgang Amadeus Mozart, *Lieder, mehrstimmige Gesänge, Kanons*, Neue Ausgabe sämtlicher Werke, series 8 vol. 3, ed. Ernst August Ballin (Kassel, 1963).
21. See especially Herbert Zeman, 'Die österreichische Lyrik des ausgehenden 18. und des frühen 19. Jahrhunderts – eine stil- und gattungsgeschichtliche Charakteristik', in id. (ed.), *Die österreichische Literatur: ihr Profil im 19. Jahrhundert (1830–1880)* (Graz, 1982), pp. 513–47.
22. Olga Antoni, *Der Wortschatz der deutschen Freimaurerlyrik des 18. Jahrhunderts in seiner geistesgeschichtlichen Bedeutung* (Munich, 1968).
23. See also Alexander Weinmann, *Kataloge Anton Huberty (Wien) und Christoph Torricella* (Vienna, 1962), p. 46.

The Biedermeier Anomaly
Cultural Conservatism and Technological Progress
Roger Paulin

The term 'Biedermeier', for the literature and culture of the German-speaking countries between 1815 and roughly 1848, has gone through a succession of changes. From being a satirical and disrespectful term for the 'Spießbürgerlichkeit' of an age, it has taken on a dignity accorded it by literary historians and art historians alike, and now it is with us to stay. Since the series of articles in the *Deutsche Vierteljahrsschrift* in 1934 and 1935, notably Paul Kluckhohn's, and Friedrich Sengle's in the same periodical in 1956,[2] there can be no doubting its status. Those who do not like it can of course talk of the Restoration period, and that would not be wrong either, but it seems to me too backward-looking a term to encompass so much that was very new and very different from what went before.

I say all this because attempts to divide up German literature and culture according to chronological periods have a difficulty that, say, English and French culture do not have: for they appear to have a definable period called, say, eighteenth century, that holds itself within – or very roughly within – the confines of the dates concerned, and comes to a natural end in terms of all the major manifestations of its culture. German (I use this in its widest sense) is in this regard a difficulty: rarely do its literature, music and painting overlap and determine each other in style and mood and texture to produce a homogeneous 'century' as they seem to elsewhere. Take 1815 to 1848 and just spread out a few names of people still active, and there are the late Goethe and the late Beethoven, a good part of the active career of Caspar David Friedrich, and most of the active years of Franz Schubert, Robert Schumann, and Felix Mendelssohn-Bartholdy. I choose examples from music because one immediately senses some disjunction between the relative importance of these names and the term 'Biedermeier', especially as very few literary figures of the period (Heine, Büchner, perhaps) are commensurate in relative quality and distinction. If the dates are applied too rigidly, they will take in most of later Romantic writing (Eichendorff, for instance, did not die until 1857, Schelling until 1854), nearly all of Romantic music (at least what is so called by musicologists) and the beginnings of that highly experimental phase that starts in the 1830s and ends in Viennese Modernism; the same can be done with Romantic painting (with the major, and almost sole, exception of Philipp Otto Runge). Thus if we wish to get the feel of an age, its literature, thought, and history, the one-sided concentration on a single manifestation of culture, like literature, is inevitably going to be lop-sided and possibly misleading. Perhaps some of the old popularising books, like Max von Boehn's,[3] treated dismissively in the early scholarly Biedermeier discussion, do still have their part to play in the dissemination process.

For all that, chronology does come to our aid: there are important careers that begin and end in this confined period of time and some – a brief incandescence – do inform our understanding of it in a crucial way: the composers mentioned already, the architect Schinkel and the painter Blechen. Very few of the major writers of the period actually managed to get past the great psychological or chronological hurdle of 1848 unscathed: Büchner and Annette von Droste-Hülshoff were already dead; Lenau was insane; Grillparzer, Mörike, Gotthelf and Heine were either about to give up writing effectively or their years as active writers were numbered; Stifter and Hebbel had but a short lease of life. When Grillparzer died in 1872, the year after the final division of Germany and Austria into separate empires, he had been silent for nearly twenty-five years. And so despite overlaps – the older Romantic generation surviving sometimes well beyond 1848, a new generation trying out its paces around the same time – some sense of cohesion does emerge.

The exhibition that prompts my remarks in the first place is concerned with Austrian Biedermeier.[1] A mere *tour d'horizon* of the chronological period will not convey why Austria in the period had a special flavour and tenor of its own. Reproductions of paintings and prints from the period will produce affinities rather than differences: in landscape and genre scenes, in *vedute*, you find the same urban scenes, interiors, family poses, whether your examples are from Berlin or Munich or Vienna. Biedermeier in that sense transcends inner-German borders in its emphasis on order, family values,[4] its predilection for the idyllic and the rural, its seeming disinclination towards change, its horror of disorder and disjunction, its harking back to continuities that may never have existed, yet are willed consciously into existence and become satisfying verities. And yet there are local differences. Scenes of Munich and Berlin, closer to 1815 than to 1848, would reveal how relatively smaller they were than Vienna and how they were in the process of a massive acquisition of architectural landscape and street pattern (Munich not knocking down its old gates until quite late in the previous century). Vienna, by contrast, was still the imperial capital and centre of the German confederation, older, more venerable, a great baroque city, perhaps not quite like Naples, but more like Milan, a 'Großstadt' as the nineteenth century was beginning to understand it. We receive that impression of a great pulsating city in Adalbert Stifter's account of 1841, *Wien und die Wiener* (not that Stifter liked cities, far from it), even though by then brash and pushy Berlin was catching up fast. And Grillparzer may, as Ferdinand von Saar observed, have been 'solitary amid the turmoil of the city streets' ('einsam in dem Straßengewühl der Stadt');[5] but he produced one of the few authentic pieces of Biedermeier 'Großstadtliteratur' in his story *Der arme Spielmann*. The colossal expansion of both cities and the influx of population from the ethnic hinterland did not take place until well after 1850, but its beginnings were there. And so inevitably Vienna was in the forefront, with its place as a cultural capital and still *the* only German capital city without a rival in most branches of cultural life, especially music, the literary salon, and the theatre.

Above all, this was an imperial capital city, the centre of a much-aggrandised state that kept its borders – with the exception of its Tuscan archduchy – until the collapse of 1918. It is right that the exhibition should give a place of prominence to two figures, in this order: Prince Metternich and Emperor Franz I.

The first of these was architect of the post-Napoleon settlement at the congresses of Vienna; the chancellor of the German confederation, which Austria still dominated, with Prussia (also much enlarged) still in easy alliance; the man who held on to the system that bore his name until its ignominious collapse in 1848; the man who signed the Carlsbad Decrees of 1819 and the ban on the Young Germans in 1835; who had his network of spies in every capital and the low-down on all the political, social and literary gossip and scandal; who presided over a vigilant system of censorship (Nikolaus Lenau, for instance, was summoned into the presence in 1836 to account for his having published his *Faust* in Württemberg). For when local states allowed constitutional liberties not permissible in Austria, Metternich had his way of bringing pressure to bear there, too, as in Weimar in the years 1816–19. Here, in a painting by Johann Ender, is Metternich in his robes as knight of the Golden Fleece, the highest order of chivalry of the old and new empires. They suit him rather better than do the crown and imperial mantle the Emperor Franz I wears in Friedrich Amerling's well-known portrait from the Kunsthistorisches Museum.

Franz I was the nephew of the short-lived reforming emperor Joseph II, whose ideals and administration were the 'Josephinism' after which Grillparzer and Stifter still hankered. A man of simple tastes, on whose head rested rather heavily the 'Hauskrone' made by Rudolf II to symbolize Austrian Habsburg authority, he was not really cut out to be the 'Volkskaiser' with Josephinist leanings that Grillparzer postulated in his Shakespearean-style historical drama *König Ottokars Glück und Ende*. Nor would the spate of pro-Habsburg historical writings (Joseph von Hormayr) or even verse epics (Johann Ladislaus Pyrker) bring back the Holy Roman Empire, still less Anastasius Grün's verse romance on Emperor Maximilian, *Der letzte Ritter*, much admired by Metternich, yet written to get round his censorship.

If the Holy Alliance that so caught the imagination of conservative circles around 1814 came to nothing, there was still a philosopher, alive until 1829, whose sense of imperial and Catholic historical mission owed much to that earlier initiative: Friedrich Schlegel. His name chimed nicely with Hegel's, as his brother's satirical rhymes made clear, but he was in reality Hegel's most bitter opponent. In his *Philosophie der Geschichte* of 1829, he enunciates the Austrian, Catholic, Habsburg notion of restoration.

> Die religiöse Hoffnung einer wahrhaft so zu nennenden und vollen Wiederherstellung des Zeitalters in dem christlichen Staat und in der

christlichen Wissenschaft bildet den Schluß dieser Philosophie der Geschichte. Das feste Band des innern religiösen Zusammenhanges zwischen allen europäischen Staaten wird um so stärker werden, um so entwickelter hervortreten, je mehr jeder einzelne Staat in der eignen religiösen Wiederherstellung in seinem Innern fortschreitet, und je sorgfältiger jeder Rückfall in die falschen Idole einer täuschenden Freiheit oder trügerischen Ruhmsucht als die Überbleibsel des ehemaligen Revolutionsgeistes vermieden, und auch jede andere Art oder neue Form von politischer Abgötterei weggeräumt wird.[...] Vielmehr ist es gerade die zum Grunde liegende religiöse Gesinnung und Denkart in dem vereint zusammenwirkenden historischen Forschen und philosophischen Streben, was diese neueste Epoche der bessern europäischen Geistesbildung charakterisiert, [...] das erste Stadium der Rückkehr in diesem Stufengange der großen Wiederherstellung bezeichnet.

[The religious hope of a true and complete regeneration of the age, by a Christian system of government, and a Christian system of science, forms the conclusion of this Philosophy of History. The bond of a religious union between all the European states will be more closely knit, and be more comprehensive, in proportion as each nation advances in the work of its own religious regeneration, and carefully avoids all relapse to the old revolutionary spirit – all worship of the false idols of mistaken freedom or illusive glory, and rejects every other new form or species of political idolatry [...] It is the religious spirit and views already pervading the combined efforts of historical learning and philosophic speculation, that chiefly distinguish this new era of a better intellectual culture, [...] this first stage of a return to the great religious restoration.][6]

This statement, with its roots as much in German idealism and German Romanticism as any pronouncement by Hegel, was not necessarily the court philosophy of the Metternich system (it had too little relation to reality), but it was tolerated, and it reminds us of how Romanticism and Catholic reaction hang together and provide an interesting counter to the view of the state being advanced in Berlin.

What was this imperial state that called itself 'Österreich' (still without Hungary)? It had always been – as the heartland of the old Holy Roman Empire – a polyglot confederation based on three crowns: the archducal Austrian, the royal Bohemian and the Hungarian. We should not forget in the context of Austrian Biedermeier that in the pre-1848 settlement it was officially assumed that Germans and Magyars and Slavs got on excellently together under the Habsburg crown. Many of the notable centres of administration and culture actually lay outside the German-speaking part of Austria (Prague, for instance). They were crucial to the Habsburg power-base. One example, Olmütz, the ecclesiastical capital of Moravia, was an imperial see; it was for the enthronement of Archduke Rudolf, the Emperor's brother, as Archbishop of Olmütz, that Beethoven wrote his famous *Missa Solemnis*. If there were tensions in the non-German states (and 1848 makes that clear), the German literature of the period gives another impression. Grillparzer's vision of Bohemia under Habsburg rule, with its crucial symbolism of crowns and imperial regalia, is one example.[7] Stifter's historical novel *Witiko* (1865–7), with its vision of a bi-cultural Bohemia, is another. Clemens Brentano's unwieldy drama, *Die Gründung Prags*, published in Pest in 1815, was a genuinely Romantic attempt to present the clash of mythologies, which August Wilhelm Schlegel had advocated. The story of Libussa, which occupies the whole of *Die Gründung Prags*, was planned as merely the first part of a trilogy in which the Slavic deities would give way to the new Christian order. Stifter's 'mythology' in *Witiko* is less concerned with change than with order, continuity, and integration within a framework where *imperium* and *ecclesia* exert their primacy over two peacefully co-existing peoples. Even Lenau's romantic view of the Hungarian *puszta* in the *Heidebilder*, his insistence on being regarded as of Hungarian nationality (akin to Stifter's Bohemian identity), or his annexation of Žiska and Hus as models in the revolutionary poetry at which Metternich showed such displeasure (*Johannes Žiska, Die Albigenser*), can be read as signs of the same historical awareness.

It is the same with the new technology, as large a threat to the old order as potential restiveness among its various subject peoples. For if railways and steamships brought the various parts of the empire closer together, they also penetrated into parts previously remote and unchanged and carried the values of the urban world into rural and semi-feudal areas. In Stifter's novel *Der Nachsommer* (1857), the age is described as scientific, one of transition;[8] communications, and the responsibility of further, wholly unprecedented technological advances, hold out the prospect of a material progress never before contemplated. But will matter not triumph over the spirit? What values will emerge? Only the hope of man's gradual and systematic progression towards higher things provides grounds for a vision of the future that is not chaos and disorder. This clash of values is also evident in paintings of the Biedermeier period: in the landscape depictions, nature in its unspoilt form dominates, as in Waldmüller's view of the Dachstein near Ischl with its mountain huts and peasant costumes, but also a considerable degree of topographical and geological detail. Here we are not far from the landscapes of Stifter, not only Austria's greatest nineteenth-century prose writer, but also an accomplished painter of such scenes where nature in its various manifestations represents an order. It is not a moral or spiritual order consonant with those commanding human affairs, but one resting nevertheless in a sense of cosmic interaction as expressed by Alexander von Humboldt's *Cosmos*, the most informative work on nature at the time. And yet Stifter's finest collection of stories, *Bunte Steine* (1853), was published around the same time as Austrian railway engineers were completing that wonder of technology, the Semmering railway, which would eventually make its way down to the port of Trieste. Stifter only mentions railways when he has to (as in *Wien und die Wiener*); one has the feeling in his stories that the railways will never intrude into the remote mountain villages where can be found the true values of humanity, care, love of tradition, the stoic virtues of that 'sanftes Gesetz' ('gentle law') of which the preface speaks. And yet we know that at this very time railways were radiating out in every direction from Vienna and

Figure 1. On the Steamship Maria Anna (1837) by Rudolf von Alt (Bavarian State Collection, Munich)

were an inescapable fact of life.

This is expressed iconographically in two remarkable paintings: 'Auf dem Dampfschiff Maria Anna' ('On the Steamship Maria Anna', 1837) by Rudolf von Alt and 'Die Dampfschiffahrt' ('The Steamship Journey', 1845) by Leander Russ. The careers of Rudolf von Alt and his father Jakob span the years 1789 to 1905 and provide an interesting model against which to measure the changes in interior and landscape painting during the nineteenth century. Their careers are in a way analogous to that of the great Berlin painter, Adolph Menzel. The 'Maria Anna' (Figure 1) has considerable symbolic value for anyone concerned to establish the feel of Biedermeier. It was painted only seven years after the Donaudampfschiffahrtsgesellschaft had, in 1830, begun its service on the Danube, as far as the river's mouth in one direction and Regensburg in the other. And we may also be reminded that only fifteen years before that date Eichendorff had published the great opening passage to his novel *Ahnung und Gegenwart* (1815), where the river Danube and its course and eddies can still be seen as the symbol of perils and moral enmeshments, the cross high above the bank standing for the grace this present age of turmoil needs. Here in this picture we have a reminder that the Austrian Empire now uses this watercourse for the newest technology and the fastest transport, the Danube becoming, like the Clyde, the Rhine, and the Hudson, an important commercial artery. By contrast the painting by Russ (Figure 2) portrays a highly-stylized impression of a steamboat – I take it just launched – surrounded by flags and crowds, the whole thing set up to convey the sense of occasion. Alt's watercolour is different: he is using to artistic effect the central object of the steamer's funnel, deck, paddleboxes, mast and rigging. The passengers are suitably draped as in a genre painting. The smoke contrasts with the blue of the sky until it merges into an indefinite reddish-brown in the upper right corner of the picture. A baroque castle (possibly Schloss Wallsee in Lower Austria) looms up above the foreground linking past and present in one symbolic whole. It is interesting to find this subject and such motifs, at the time largely associated with the name of Turner, right in the centre of Biedermeier Austria. And yet this watercolour is quite different in technique and use of motif from Turner's, above all in the use of the human figure and in the concentration on the relationship between groups of figures on the deck and their surroundings, something that Turner rarely succeeded in doing satisfactorily.

From this quite remarkable portrayal we turn to two rather more traditional ones, one by Rudolf Alt's father Jakob, 'Blick aus dem Atelierfenster auf Dornbach' ('View of Dornbach from the Studio Window', 1836), the other by the lesser-known Erasmus Engert: 'Wiener Hausgarten' ('Domestic Garden in Vienna', 1829–30). Views of artists' studios, with accompanying extension of the eye out into the landscape, are sufficiently well-known and well-tried for me to refrain from further comment, did we not associate them especially in German painting with two of its greatest nineteenth-century representatives, Caspar David Friedrich and Adolph Menzel. We know it from literature (as in the 'Klopstock' section of *Werther*) and recognize there its function as leading over from the more restrained feelings associated with the mode of the beautiful (in both Burke's and Kant's terminology) into the realm of the infinite, the sublime. There is again the famous passage in a letter of Wackenroder's from his Franconian journey of 1793, where the window of a castle ruin serves just that

Figure 2. The Steamship Journey (1845) by Leander Russ (Historical Museum of the City of Vienna)

Figure 3. View of Dornbach from the Studio Window (1836) by Jakob Alt (Albertina, Vienna)

very function as a frame for the endless spectacle of nature.⁹ This is present in Jakob Alt's picture (Figure 3), but in a very restrained fashion. It is also the artist's record of his own work, of how the watercolourist and the oil painter alike need a source of light. The studio is not the bare and austere barn-like space we know from Kersting's portrait of Friedrich at his easel, but a domestic interior, a living space. The eye is drawn beyond tamed and controlled nature (flower pots, gardens) over fields to more houses and thus beyond to the rolling hills – the outskirts of Vienna itself. It is *rus in urbe*, a reminder of how city and landscape merge harmoniously at their edges – not the scene presented later in the century in so many of Ferdinand von Saar's stories, where the break-up of old villages and suburban communities is depicted, as the 'Großstadt' inexorably pushes its way out and still further out. This view of nature that we see in Alt's carefully-measured painting is typical of its period – in both literature and painting – in that the reference to human proportion and human dwelling is reassuringly there during the contemplation of the seeming endlessness of nature. The mode of the sublime – again both in painting and literature – is very much there in the period, either as a supplier of images or in straight description. By contrast, how often man alone in nature is a symbol of *Weltschmerz* (as for Chateaubriand a generation earlier). There are Lenau's poems and letters from America about the loneliness of the landscape, with no human warmth and no sustaining culture; so many of Stifter's landscapes, the greatest in nineteenth-century German prose, are related, like his own landscape paintings, to the reassuring measure of the human figure or the human dwelling, lest we lose all proportion and are overwhelmed by the sublime. For the elemental in all its forms is more often a source of terror and inner turmoil than one of uplift, the 'eternal note of sadness', in Arnold's words, that informs so much of German nature poetry until melancholy turns into the reassurance given by faith or society or convention.

Erasmus Engert's picture (Figure 4) reinforces that link between nature and domesticity, but with a further interesting variation. For the picture really consists of two elements: the lady enjoying what may be ease, but also edification, in the garden (the book looks like the Bible or a hymnbook – it is certainly not the latest poetry almanac); the sunflowers add a note of colour and 'realism', until we remember that they are also traditionally associated with fidelity. In the background – behind a wicket gate – is a timber yard and workshop; garden and place of work are typical of the outlying suburbs (which also supply the domestic labour). The connection between work and leisure and craft is important: it informs Stifter's great novel *Der Nachsommer*, where the dignity of manual work is upheld despite a clear sense of social distinctions and hierarchy. It is still the age of the master craftsman whose social status admits him into the bourgeoisie. Grillparzer may not be very flattering towards the master butcher and his wife – and their social pretensions – in his story *Der arme Spielmann*; but I think also of a novel from the period, one all-too-little read, Tieck's *Der junge Tischlermeister* (1836), where work, achievement, getting there, proving one's worth, is the condition of an aberration of the emotions – in the aristocratic sphere of the country house and the private theatre – until a wiser and chastened hero returns to the kind of suburban garden and workshop that Erasmus Engert is here depicting.

If we come further inside, into the drawing room, we will be reminded of how much musical and literary culture was intended for the domestic sphere. The almanac, the most popular form of literary presentation of the time, was

Figure 4. Domestic Garden in Vienna (1829–30) by Erasmus Engert (National Gallery, Berlin)

intended for reading aloud in the domestic circle (hence all those Novellen, but also those verse epics that today seem so tiresome, until you actually sit down and read them aloud). And if we are in Vienna, we shall wish for an opportunity to visit the house of Joseph von Spaun, the friend and helper of Franz Schubert. Schubert's *Lieder*, the ultimate expression of the fusion of words and music, are not originally conceived for the concert platform but for the soirée, and, as other illustrations of Schubert's circle make clear, the tone will not always be one of high seriousness. Yet somehow that setting of Matthias Claudius' poem 'Death and the Maiden', and its further realisation in string quartet form, bring the reality of death to all the 'Schubertiaden' and their innocent conviviality.

Death and the frivolous – here conjoined in the most harmless of fashions – are however, two of the themes without which Vienna – and Viennese Biedermeier – would not be complete. The age of course liked its stories and its paintings to have the frisson of horror and violent death. Painters and writers obliged, like Moritz von Schwind with his absurdly melodramatic painting of entwined lovers leaping to their deaths, but also Lenau in his chillingly detailed account of torture and massacre in his verse epics *Savonarola* or *Die Albigenser*. There is, however, more to it than that.

Let us be taken on a tour of Vienna in 1841. Our cicerone, who is only doing it because he was commissioned to do so, is Stifter – not noted for writing about cities, indeed positively renowned for not writing about them. Perhaps, though, the city-hater can sum up better the sense of his age than the man whose life is bound up with the very stones – like Grillparzer, whose great story about the world's very worst violinist, *Der arme Spielmann*, is inspired by what he calls his 'anthropological ardour' to depict his fellow-men in their houses and streets and places of concourse.[10] But Stifter does his duty by his readers and also unfolds before us the great organism of a city that spreads out in its arteries of communication, but is sustained by the flow into it of those who work and supply and sustain. He does not neglect the salons, either, because the writer knows that there his works will be discussed and received or rejected. But I find it somehow symptomatic that Stifter devotes three large sections of *Wien und die Wiener* to the catacombs, Easter week, and to the Prater. The section on the catacombs is prefaced by the awareness of the fragility and transience of human civilisation and self-education ('Bildung') and industrial progress. For from underneath the veneer of that civilisation can break forth 'Gräßlichkeit und Ausschweifung',[11] atrocity and excess. The 'Zeitgeist' is concerned with practical achievement and gratification of the senses. How little concern for the eternal things and how little awareness of the brevity of existence! Stifter is here reproducing in accessible form the philosophical occasionalism of his Benedictine teachers in Kremsmünster, the disharmony of body and soul, the lack of interaction between the two spheres. It is essentially from the baroque moral theology of his teachers that Stifter, too, saw in the avoidance of the passions the key to a law of life that would transcend the incursions of violence and upheaval. And that would find its classic formulation in a work that was published five years after the 1848 revolution: *Bunte Steine*.

As yet, however, we are not at the barricades, but in the bowels of the earth and amid the charnel-house of a city. We emerge into the bright sunlight to make our way with the crowds to the Prater on the first of May, where words expressing colour and allurement of the senses, movement, outward show, dominate: 'glänzend', 'schimmernd', 'Pracht', 'Reiz'.[12] The whole of society is there, from the imperial couple to gipsy musicians – a 'brodelnde Hexenküche' ('seething cauldron')[13] which ends when the cicerone bids us good-night and returns to domestic bliss in a small suburban garden. The section on Holy Week has the same dualism as the contrast between the catacombs and the Prater, and it is a dualism that Stifter wants us to remark: how both industry and the frivolous things of life ('Leichtsinn')[14] clash with the sombreness and melancholy of suffering and death. We should not gain the impression that Stifter is a reluctant spectator of the people's simple enjoyments. He seems to me, however, to have that typically Austrian dichotomy that is rooted in their Catholic and baroque culture: the appeal to the senses, in splendid facades, grand vistas, theatrical gestures (on and off stage), hedonistic, seemingly carefree abandon, wit and disrespect, and also those catacombs and other mementos of death that few other northern capitals have. There is no need for Schopenhauer here if the native theatrical tradition has stressed for centuries the instability of all things earthly, the ultimate inability (except for the very few and only rarely in human history) of men and women to fulfil the moment that is theirs to make or unmake, caught as they are between duty and inclination (Grillparzer). But even when the theatre seems all spectacle and dance and song and *féerie*, with the Viennese dialect adding its own note of free expression to the satire on human affairs – as with Raimund and Nestroy – underlying all is the awareness of human frailty and the need to be confronted with the ultimate realities behind the facade, the *desengaño* that links the Spanish theatre with the Viennese.

Our cicerone in 1841 gave us this conspectus of human affairs, not, say, as a Capuchin friar, but as a creative writer not indifferent to any of these manifestations of human life. But he was conservative, traditionalist, afraid of disorder, an upholder of social structures as they exist and, for him, must exist. Not all his readers by any means would have wished to preserve the status quo of 1841 or any other year. With the year 1848, the Biedermeier certainties of which Stifter and so many of his contemporaries speak gave way for the moment to the revolution that many feared and few wanted in this form. And with that year, the Biedermeier age was at an end.

Notes

1. This paper is based on a talk originally given to the Cambridge Austrian Study Group in May 1990 on the occasion of the exhibition 'Biedermeier in Austria'. See the catalogue *Biedermeier in Österreich*, ed. Victoria Lunzer-Talos and Heinz Lunzer (Vienna, 1988).
2. See esp. Paul Kluckhohn, 'Biedermeier als literarische Epochenbezeichnung', *DVjs*, 13 (1935), 1–43; id., 'Zur Biedermeier-Diskussion', *DVjs*, 14 (1936), 495–504. Both of these numbers of the *DVjs* contain important articles on various aspects of Biedermeier. See also Friedrich Sengle, 'Voraussetzungen und Erscheinungsformen der deutschen Restaurationsliteratur', *DVjs*, 30 (1956), 268–294, also in *Arbeiten zur deutschen Literatur 1750–1850* (Stuttgart, 1965), pp. 118–154.
3. Max von Boehn, *Biedermeier. Deutschland von 1815–1847* (Berlin, n.d.=1923).
4. See Angelika Lorenz, *Das deutsche Familienbild in der Malerei des 19. Jahrhunderts* (Darmstadt, 1985).
5. Ferdinand von Saar, *Sämtliche Werke*, ed. Anton Bettelheim and Jakob Minor, 12 vols (Leipzig n.d. = 1908), I, 184.
6. Friedrich Schlegel, *Philosophie der Geschichte. Kritische Friedrich Schlegel–Ausgabe*, ed. Ernst Behler et al., 23 vols (Munich, Paderborn, Vienna, Zürich, 1959) I. ix, 419f. Translation of passage from Frederick von Schlegel, *The Philosophy of History, in a Course of Lectures, Delivered at Vienna*, trans. James Baron Robertson, second edition, Bohn's Standard Library (London, 1846), pp. 468–9.

7. See Eda Sagarra, 'Sinnbilder der Monarchie. Herrschersymbolik und Staatsidee in Grillparzer's "König Ottokars Glück und Ende" und Shakespeares "Richard II", *Jahrbuch der Grillparzer-Gesellschaft*, 3. Folge, 16 (1984–6), 57–67.
8. See Adalbert Stifter, *Der Nachsommer*, ed. Max Stefl (Darmstadt, 1963), pp. 520–1.
9. Wilhelm Heinrich Wackenroder, *Werke und Briefe*, ed. Lambert Schneider (Heidelberg, 1967), pp. 466–7.
10. Franz Grillparzer, *Sämtliche Werke*, ed. Peter Frank and Karl Pörnbacher, 4 vols (Munich, 1960–5), vol. III, p. 150.
11. Adalbert Stifter, *Die Mappe meines Urgroßvaters, Die Sonnenfinsternis, Aus dem alten Wien*, ed. Max Stefl (Basel, 1957), pp. 340–1.
12. Ibid., p. 362.
13. Ibid., p. 368.
14. Ibid., p. 437.

Stifter and the Enlightenment

Eve Mason

In an attempt to define his own attitude as a writer toward our times Peter Handke makes some perceptive remarks about Stifter which, I think, sum up Stifter's peculiar situation and go to the essence of his writing. With reference to the pot-holes in the flooded fields that threaten the children on their way to school in *Kalkstein*, Handke writes:

> Für diese Wende der Dinge zum Unheimlichen sind Erklärungen in der Person des Verfassers gesucht und gefunden worden. Doch ist das sanfte über eine Wiese rieselnde Wasser wohl auch durch das zeitverordnete Erzählen mit den lebensgefährlichen Gruben ausgestattet worden – in die zudem niemand endgültig einsinkt.[1]

> [Critics have sought and have found an explanation of this strange turn towards the uncanny in the author's own character. However, it was rather the effect of contemporary conditions on his narrative art which accounts for the fact that the waterlogged meadow under the gently trickling water was given pot-holes where people could have lost their lives, though nobody in fact was drowned.]

The phrase 'das zeitverordnete Erzählen' (the effect of contemporary conditions on his art) which Handke uses to describe Stifter's unique mode of story-telling seems to me of especial interest. For Stifter's attitude to his times is difficult to pin down. Not only was he claimed as an adherent and attacked as a renegade by both political camps, the Liberals and the Conservatives, before, during and after the Revolution of 1848, but this battle to identify his political stance still continues among modern critics, whose research is characterised by a polarisation of judgments. While some critics, stressing Stifter's debt to the Enlightenment concepts of reason and humanity, have hailed him as an upholder of tradition, others have seen him as expressing an awareness of the relentless development of bourgeois society. His novel *Der Nachsommer* (*Indian Summer*) is respectively described as a model for a society worthy of humanity, and interpreted, often using the same textual references, as representing an absolutist ideology, or again, in more recent criticism, as a critique of the aristocracy and of bourgeois capitalism.

This continuing debate suggests that Stifter in this respect cannot easily be categorised, that any all-too-systematised approach is ultimately bound to overstate. The violence unleashed during the 1848 Revolution revealed to Stifter man's innate aggressiveness and power-hunger, and forced him to become an isolated and disappointed observer of events. In August 1848 he wrote to his publisher that he was planning a historical novel, 'da mir aus der Stimmung der ganzen Welt und der meines Innern klar war, daß Dichtungen in jetziger Zeit ganz andere Motive bringen müssen, wenn sie hinreißen sollen, als vor den Märztagen'.[2] ('It was plain to me, judging by the mood of the whole world and my own state of mind, that the themes of modern literature must be quite different from what they were before March 1848 if they were to carry the public with them.') However, the development of events overtook him. 'Diese fürchterliche Wendung der Dinge'[3] ('This fearful turn of events'), as he called the failure of the Revolution, forced him into a state of entrenchment. He responded to the political situation by first publishing in 1853 *Bunte Steine*, a collection of short stories, designed to educate young minds to a more enlightened understanding of the real values in life, and in 1857 an educative novel, *Der Nachsommer*, which celebrates the Indian Summer of a summer that never existed.

Both works are deeply 'zeitverordnet'. Not only do they display his disappointment with the Revolution, but both are also, in different ways, extraordinarily purposeful and single-minded artistic attempts to convey an alternative set of values to those of his own time. Seeing the present largely as a period of moral decline, he formulated his alternative values as follows: 'Ein ganzes Leben voll Gerechtigkeit, Einfachheit, Bezwingung seiner selbst, Verstandesgemäßheit, Wirksamkeit in seinem Kreise, Bewunderung des Schönen, verbunden mit einem heiteren gelassenen Sterben, halte ich für groß'.[4] ('What I regard as grand about humanity is a man's life-long devotion to justice, simplicity, self-control, reasonableness, effective action in his own world, admiration of the beautiful, ending in a serene and happy death.') This statement of personal beliefs is taken from the 'Vorrede' to *Bunte Steine*. The tales of the collection, with one exception, circle round the lives of cottagers, poor country priests and the minor gentry recently risen from the class of humble farmers, but in a suitably elevated register its main tenets also underwrite the ideals of selected members of the higher middle class who inhabit the quasi-feudal landed estates in *Der Nachsommer*.

It is not difficult to recognise that these articles of faith have their roots in the instruction in the ideas of enlightened humanism which Stifter received at Kremsmünster, the Benedictine monastery where he spent his most formative years and received his education. There he was taught to see the hand of Providence working for the ultimate good of mankind and the problem of evil correspondingly transformed. Man was shown to be capable of developing his inborn gifts and progressing to eventual perfection. Implicit in this process was the belief that reason and morality went hand in hand. The pupils were encouraged to entertain high ideals of the worth of human nature. It was these ideas, supplemented by his reading of Herder, Kant and Humboldt, which also informed a series of newspaper articles Stifter wrote between 1848 and 1850 on topics of the day, such as the reforms envisaged for government and education. The decline in his expectations in the months that followed the Revolution is obvious. After the proclamation of the Stadion Constitution, maintaining the ultimate authority of the Emperor, Stifter reacted lamely by pointing to the virtue of moderation based on rational behaviour, and distinguishing between mere licence and a more positive, ethical conception of freedom as 'der leere Raum, den die Menschen mit sittlichen Taten erfüllen sollen'[5] ('that empty space which people should fill up with their good deeds'). This weak response was characteristic of the loss of heart among well-meaning, decent, but essentially apolitical liberals when confronted by violence.

Like many of his middle-class contemporaries who felt threatened from both sides, Stifter put his hope in reforms rather than in a revolution. On 26 May 1849 he calls for calm and restraint: 'Daher ist die heiligste Lehre der Geschichte: Suche eher auf unermüdliche, aber ruhige Weise die Abhilfe deiner Übel, wenn es selbst Jahre dauert, ehe du dich in die Verwirrung und in das Elend einer Revolution stürzest'.[6] ('The most precious lesson of history is rather to seek tirelessly but calmly to remove evil even if it takes years to do it before you plunge into the chaos and misery of a revolution.')

The need to educate the public to a greater comprehension of these ideas was urgent, and in 1848 and 1849 Stifter contributed a series of articles on the reform of schools and the reorganisation of the educational system to the *Wiener Bote*, a newspaper founded expressly for circulation among the lower classes, to prevent them falling victim to extremists and to teach them enlightened concepts of reasonable conduct and the practical virtues. Since the articles were meant for people unused to thinking about the main principles and purposes of education, Stifter tried to strengthen his readers' self-confidence. He suggested that the will to seek enlightenment was of paramount importance: 'Der Mensch hat Vernunft und Erkennen, [...] er kann lernen bis an das Ende seines Lebens und das Gelernte seinen Nachfolgern hinterlassen.'[7] ('Man possesses reason and the power of learning from experience. He is capable of going on learning throughout his life and can bequeath what he has learned to those who come after him.')

The influence of Herder and Humboldt on Stifter's larger ideas is unmistakable, but many go back further to the kind of enlightened instruction he himself had received at Kremsmünster. Although couched in the language of idealism, his ideas are not as divorced from reality as they may sound. Up to 1848 the sole object of general education had been to make a boy 'bonus homo, fidelis subditus et pius Christianus' ('a good man, a loyal subject and a pious Christian'). Even Joseph II had only been interested in educating the poor in order to provide his army with literate soldiers. Nor does Stifter neglect the more practical aspects of educational reform. His articles make clear that a better general education requires the support of the guilds and corporations and other representatives of the various classes. Above all – and this has an all-too familiar ring about it – he demands that the status of the teachers must be raised, their pay and living conditions improved and their training taken in hand. He takes the state to task for its disregard of education and sees this as a sign of a far-reaching moral decline, ultimately affecting the very foundations of the state itself. Yet in his concluding article he expresses optimism that man is capable of shaping his future for the good:

> Kein Weltgeist, kein Dämon regiert die Welt: *Was je Gutes oder Böses über die Menschen gekommen ist, haben die Menschen gemacht.* Gott hat ihnen den freien Willen und die Vernunft gegeben und hat ihr Schicksal in ihre Hand gelegt. Dies ist unser Rang, dies ist unsere Größe. Daher müssen wir Vernunft und freien Willen, die uns nur als Keime gegeben werden, ausbilden; *es gibt keinen andern Weg zum Glücke der Menschheit,* weil Vernunft und freier Wille dem Menschen allein als seine höchste Eigenschaften gegeben sind, und weil sie immerfort bis zu einer Grenze, die wir jetzt noch gar nicht zu ahnen vermögen, ausgebildet werden können. Wer andere Wege zum Glück vorschlägt, wer die Bildung und Entwicklung unseres Geistes für verwerflich hält, der lästert Gott in seinem Werke.[8]

> [This world is not dominated by any cosmic spirit or demonic power. *All the good or evil that happens to men is the work of their own hands.* God has given them free will and reason and put their destiny in their own hands. This is our special position and our greatness. That is why we must try and develop the seeds of reason and free will which are in us. *There is no other way open for human happiness* because reason and free will were given to men alone as their noblest properties and because they are capable of being developed to a pitch which we can barely conceive today. Anyone who treats education and the development of our spirit as not worth pursuing and reprehensible, blasphemes against God's creation.]

It is only when we come to the epilogue to this last article in the series that we suddenly begin to wonder whether all this enthusiasm is not built on sand, whether, in fact, Stifter assesses the events of the time realistically enough to justify the tone of a high priest of Enlightened humanism. For in this epilogue the other Stifter comes to the fore, the man who is suddenly jolted out from his vision of a better future for mankind and is brought face to face with a reality he does not like. The change is so sudden that it would almost be comic if it were not such a clear example of the liberals' loss of heart and nerve. For what irks Stifter now is the running wild of the children during the months of unrest, the foul language they use and, most of all, that instead of covering the walls with innocent graffiti of stags, horses and little people as they used to do, they now adorn them with pictures of gallows and Death the Great Reaper. 'Sollen solche Vorstellungen Wurzel in den jungen Herzen fassen?'[9] ('Do such ideas have to take root in the hearts of our children?') he asks pathetically, blaming the bad example of the parents who allowed their passions to run riot in front of the children.

Yet in his tales and novels Stifter does not shrink from evoking the darker forces in man's life that severely call into question his ability to approach harmony by means of reason. In wonderfully varied imaginative conceptions Stifter again and again faces this fundamental dilemma in the human condition. It is, of course, a vain undertaking to try to analyse in a short article Stifter's attitude to this radical disjunction in man's existence as it found artistic expression in his works. All that can be attempted is a sketchy outline based on the analysis of two or three works. For this purpose I have chosen *Abdias* and *Turmalin* from among his tales and the novel *Der Nachsommer*. By their publication dates they span the years 1847–57, although they all go back to earlier versions and drafts. What is striking about all three works is that in spite of their very different artistic formulations, they circle round the question of the possibility of Enlightened thought giving meaning to life, and it seems to me that by the different answers Stifter suggests in them his responses to his times can be deduced, at least in some measure.

Abdias and *Turmalin* are linked by the abrupt way Stifter juxtaposes in the opening paragraphs an enlightened view of man as a reasonable being whose actions can be defined as a chain of cause and effect with one where man is the helpless victim of external forces and inner delusions.

Abdias first appeared, in an earlier version, in 1843 in the *Österreichischer Novellenalmanach*. The final version was printed as part of Stifter's collection *Studien* (volume IV, 1847). The story opens with a discussion of those aspects of human life which made the ancients adopt the concept of 'fatum' and which later generations, so the narrator puts it, turned into the 'milder' concept of 'lot, fortune, divine ordinance'. In the workings of 'fatum' Stifter includes the law of nature – a boy falls into a stream and drowns, the silvery surface of the water ripples, then closes as before; a Bedouin riding along in the desert is struck by lightning from an overcast sky, then nature is serenity as before. The word 'fatum' rings out twice from the page as 'furchtbar letzter starrer Grund des Geschehenden' ('the frightful stark final cause of all things').[10] But divine ordinance is terrible, too. The strong submit to it stoically, the weak hurl their laments against it, the common man can but stand in amazement, go mad or blaspheme.

However, this horrific description of man's subjugation to inexplicable forces is suddenly countered by the suggestion that there is hope for man to be liberated from this burden, if not in our day, then in time to come. In a poetically heightened image Stifter refers the anxious reader to the Great Chain of Being which, like an immense garland of flowers, stretches between heaven and earth, descending from the hand of God. It allows the poor mortal wretch by counting its many links to raise himself up from a state of utter incomprehension to one of enlightenment about the cause and effect of all things and to see his lot entirely in terms of crime and punishment, guilt and expiation. It is a wonderful vision of man as a rational being arriving at last at the state the serpent promised Eve: 'ye shall be as gods, knowing good and evil'.

Stifter is here adapting the *catena* allegory, the visual representation of the interconnection of all things, which was accepted in the learned world of the seventeenth and eighteenth centuries and occurs, for example, in the writings of Leibniz and Herder. It is difficult to ascertain how far Stifter was directly influenced by Enlightenment thought.[11] Certain phrases Stifter uses indicate such influence – 'und in das Haupt des Menschen ward die schönste dieser Blumen geworfen, die Vernunft, das Auge der Seele, die Kette daran anzuknüpfen'[12] – ('the most beautiful of these flowers, reason, the window of the soul, was implanted in man's head to tie up this chain') – but they do not go beyond a broad and general knowledge of the tenets of the Enlightenment. What may originally have attracted Stifter to this theory is the presence in the library of Kremsmünster of a book by Athanasius Kircher, *Magnes sive arte magnetica opus tripartitum* (Romae 1643), which on its engraved title page depicts a system of chains linking heaven and earth, attached to an eagle, the imperial eagle, hovering in the sky.[13] The double strand of influences, baroque emblematic on the one hand, enlightened optimistic thought on the other, pointing forward to and including scientific discoveries of Stifter's own age, is interesting, because it once again illustrates the forces at work in the Austria of his day. What is ultimately of greater importance, however, is how Stifter transformed these influences for his poetic purposes. He cuts short the whole elaborate reflection as suddenly as he had started it by dismissing speculations about providence and fate as insoluble, yet introducing the story of Abdias as one which insistently provokes such speculations. The tantalised reader is thus brought back to a state of utter uncertainty.

The story of Abdias which unfolds is so rich and dense in texture that it cannot easily be unravelled. It spans Abdias' whole life, from his childhood in an ancient Jewish settlement hidden among the ruins of a forgotten Roman town – a terrible memento of the vanity of human power and glory – to his lonely death in an isolated valley of the Austrian mountains. The story is punctuated by memorable scenes. We see the boy standing on top of the Roman ruins surveying the immense sky before climbing down to the Aladdin's cave, where his mother, surrounded by jewels, cashmere and silk, dresses him up in girl's clothes. We see the young man riding out, fighting his enemies in the course of amassing vast riches or cowering in sorrow beside the body of his wife who bled to death in childbirth. We watch him lovingly tending his blind daughter, with whom he has emigrated to Europe to secure a different life for her away from the scorching sun and the wrath of his enemies. We observe his joy and delight and new affirmation of life when her sight is restored by lightning and witness his collapse into madness when a second thunderbolt kills her a few years later. Much in the story seems to suggest a symbolic interpretation: the exotic setting in the biblical lands among the Atlas mountains, the cradle of mankind as Herder calls the region,[14] the daughter's blindness, the significant role lightning plays in her life. Abdias is at one and the same time mythological and real, the Wandering Jew, and a man of flesh and blood, strong, greedy, lusting for power and yet deeply vulnerable and longing for love and a higher existence which would free his soul from imprisonment in the self. There are several strands of the tale which appear to indicate a chain of cause and effect, raising the reader's hope of ultimate enlightenment, but they either do not add up or end abruptly and inconclusively. The bewildered reader soon gives up any expectation of receiving guide-lines from the narrator. The narrator makes no value judgements. What value judgements there are come from other characters in the story, whose verdict is clouded by their hatred and distrust of Abdias or their narrow, intolerant moral outlook. The reader is thus forced to conduct his own search for meaning.

Stifter is careful, in depicting the blows of fate that befall Abdias, to keep them just within the limits of the credible. This applies even to the strange 'miracles' involving the natural phenomenon of lightning: a flash of lightning restores the sight of Abdias' blind daughter and a few years later she is killed by lightning – according to Bohemian folk superstition, a sign of special divine grace. Stifter talks of a miraculous occurrence, an occurrence which will remain mysterious till man has fathomed those forces of nature by which life is encompassed. To give substance to this claim he draws on the scientific discoveries and speculations on electro–magnetism and mesmerism of his time to make every detail of these fictitious happenings realistically more acceptable. We cannot be absolutely sure whether Stifter, whose spiritual and intellectual roots seem to reach so far back into the eighteenth century, still shared that century's optimism that scientific discoveries will substantially contribute to the universal chain of cause and effect in the eventual enlightenment of man or whether he uses yet another poetic licence to keep the reader in suspense. Ultimately the question raised in the introduction, 'warum nun dieses?' ('why and wherefore?') remains unanswered.

By the time Stifter was reworking the tale 'Der Pförtner im Herrenhause', which appeared in *Libussa, Jahrbuch für 1852*, for *Bunte Steine*, published only a year later in 1853, the possibility of dealing with man's condition in such large and symbolic concepts had gone. Not that Stifter suddenly turned realist in the narrow sense, but all the stories in the collection home in on the kind of scenery his readers might know and the kind of event they might be familiar with from everyday life or from folktales forming part of their traditional cultural background. But while all the other stories are set in rural areas, *Turmalin* is set in the Vienna of Stifter's student days, among the crumbling great houses of a bygone age, soon to be replaced by new buildings. Nature, where it appears, is confined to rain-washed weeds in a shady yard or occasional glimpses of suburban gardens. *Turmalin* is also the most savage, despairing story of the collection, at times endangering the whole concept of the 'sanfte Gesetz' ('gentle law') of the preface, which is supposed to give coherence to the collection as a whole.

Turmalin is a much less ambitious story than *Abdias*, at least on the surface. The general reflective remarks in the opening paragraph are a series of simple statements:

> Der Turmalin ist dunkel, und was da erzählt wird, ist sehr dunkel. [...] Es ist darin [...] zu entnehmen, wie weit der Mensch kömmt, wenn er das Licht seiner Vernunft trübt, die Dinge nicht mehr versteht, von dem inneren Gesetze, das ihn unabwendbar zu dem Rechten führt, läßt, sich unbedingt der Innigkeit seiner Freuden und Schmerzen hingibt, den Halt

verliert und in Zustände gerät, die wir uns kaum zu enträtseln wissen.[15]

[Tourmaline is a dark stone and the story tells us of dark things, [...] of how far man gets if he dims the light of his reason to the point where he no longer understands things and abandons those inborn laws which guide him unfailingly to what is right, if he gives himself totally up to the intensity of his pleasures and pains and loses control over himself and falls into a state that we barely understand.]

Although the metaphor of light as a source of knowledge is in itself of great antiquity, it is the combination with the phrases that follow in apposition as it were as a kind of extended definition which immediately brings to mind the main tenets of the Enlightenment. The specific wording of the opening paragraph arouses the expectation in the reader that he is going to be treated to a simple illustration of what happens if and when man abandons these principles and offends against them – a moral tale, in fact, extolling the value of reason and the virtues one derives from adhering to its dictates. Only the very last remark, 'and falls into a state that we barely understand', contains the seeds of a more complex story. Yet even so, the reader is not quite prepared for what follows. For instead of choosing, as the reader would expect, an ordinary person and mapping his deviation from the path of virtue, Stifter introduces his protagonist as 'ein wunderlicher Mensch'[16] ('a strange, eccentric man').

Telling the story by two different narrators lends it a flavour of realism but also heightens the character of the enigmatic. Much of what is told is based on hearsay or subjective observations. The narrators are piecing together bits of evidence as they come across them by chance. The reader is forced to do the same, yet at the same time he has to go one better by trying to assess and take into account the narrators' characters. The story line is slight. We hear of the carefree existence of the eccentric who lives with his wife and baby daughter in a comfortable apartment in Vienna, surrounded by possessions, indulging in a dilettante way his interests in music, painting, poetry and the fashionable pursuit of making papier mâché objects. His only regular visitor is a popular actor, Dall, who shares many of the eccentric's interests. One day the wife tells her husband that she committed adultery with Dall, and soon after she disappears. After searching for her in vain, the rentier (he is never given a name) goes away from the town taking his baby daughter with him. Many years later the story of father and daughter is taken up again by a well-to-do woman, whose curiosity had been aroused by the sight of an old man guiding a young girl with a huge head through the crowded streets of Vienna. By chance she finds out where the couple live and comes into sporadic contact with them. The story takes a dramatic turn when the rentier is killed by a fall from a ladder while trying to reach the window of the dark basement flat where he and his daughter were eking out a meagre existence. The woman narrator takes the orphaned girl in and by careful, patient and enlightened effort succeeds in implanting enough knowledge in the girl's tortured mind to make it possible for her to live on her own. However, this harmonising ending is ultimately only a compromise, when we hear that the woman has moved, the houses have been pulled down and nobody knows what happened to the retarded girl.

The story is shot through by what appear at first sight as links in a chain of cause and effect only to resist such an interpretation in the end. In the case of the girl we are strongly reminded of the Biblical 'visiting the iniquity of the fathers upon the children', but this does not help us to understand the rentier's fate. As no cause is ever given for his strangeness and eccentricity, the reader, as in *Abdias*, is confronted with the question of fate. The question also arises how such a man whose relation to life is impaired from the start can be expected to exercise his reason when his eccentric but well-regulated life is suddenly shattered by his wife's adultery with his best friend and her eventual disappearance without trace. Yet Stifter does not use what appears to be an ingrained mental defect as an extenuating circumstance. On the contrary, the man's strangeness and warped attitude to life are described in their detailed manifestations, and the vanity of his efforts to escape the demands of reality by surrounding himself with belongings and indulging in dilettante pursuits is ultimately cruelly exposed by the almost baroque imagery of dust like sand trickling down from the rich curtains of the deserted flat.

As with *Abdias*, the reader is constantly forced to ponder the questions of guilt, responsibility, chance, fate and misfortune and how they relate to each other and affect human life. But while Abdias endeavoured to stand up to his trials, albeit often in a misguided fashion, and comes across as a vigorous intelligent being, capable of fighting back, the rentier strikes the reader as an inadequate being. Abdias tries to counter his daughter's blindness in the only way he knows by amassing riches to ensure a safe future for her; the rentier, although guiding his suffering and mentally deficient daughter lovingly and carefully through the crowds, forces her to write little essays about her mother roaming the world in despair and himself lying dead. While Abdias' wish to emigrate to the temperate climate of Europe and to listen to and commune with the wise men he hopes to find there appears as a rational attempt at self-help, however severely ironised by realities, the rentier's headlong flight with his young child into utter obscurity, living in caves as the gossip goes, is symbolic of his abandoning himself to emotions and deserting reason. Yet Stifter manages to arouse the reader's pity and an overwhelming feeling of 'there but for the grace of God go I'. In the case of *Abdias* the exotic background of the biblical lands contributes to a feeling in the reader that this man who, although often longing for a more spiritual life, is caught in an existence that by tradition and necessity is based on material gain, has to be seen as an awful symbolic warning to modern man bent on material ends. In *Turmalin*, on the other hand, the lack of a solid centre in the rentier and the susceptibility of his mind to confusion open up a haunting vision of an ever-widening disjunction in modern life.

Taken together, the two stories seem to present a pessimistic critique of the rationalist belief in the possibility of an enlightened world, not so much because Stifter portrays man as a victim of external circumstances as because he suggests man carries his fate within him. As a result man is unable to exercise his gift of reason when called upon to do so. Stifter refuses to present the fullness and complexity of life and the mysteries of human nature as ultimately explicable.

If anything, his general reflections in the opening of both these stories, seemingly invoking the tenets of the Enlightenment as viable possibilities to counter the vagaries of life, bring out their fragility in full relief.

When we come to *Der Nachsommer* we face an astonishingly different situation. In 1850 Stifter had been appointed inspector of schools and a member of the supervisory committee of the state schools of Upper Austria. His reports give a frightening insight into the prevailing conditions. The period of reforms immediately after the Revolution was too short-lived to make any impact. Under von Thun-Hohenstein's Ministry comparatively little was done for the primary schools, but reforms based on Prussian models of the secondary and higher establishments were carried through and remained in force till 1869. Gradually the authority of the Church in school affairs was re-established and the sole purpose of education became once again the production of obedient and efficient citizens. The emphasis in the curricula was on practical subjects and religious instruction, in the higher schools on those subjects which were necessary for entry to the state service and the Church. The monotony with which Stifter in his reports lists the presence or otherwise of a crucifix in the schoolrooms, the level of discipline, the ability of teachers to teach their subjects and to impart good German to their pupils, their appalling living conditions, the dilapidation of school buildings, the absence of a library or books for instruction,[17] is an ironic corrective to his ideals of school reform, intended in the long run to form personality and to lead towards human dignity. Even so his modest proposals for reforms found little favour with his superiors, as their sour comments in the margins of his reports show. In 1856 he was summarily dismissed from his position of inspector of the secondary school in Linz which he had helped to establish.

It is ironic that at the time Stifter should be engaged in writing an educative novel. Although often likened to the typically German genre of 'Bildungsroman' (novel of education), such a comparison is extremely tenuous, especially if one takes into account Wilhelm Dilthey's famous definition, that in such a novel the dissonances and conflicts of life appear as the necessary growth points through which the individual must pass on his way to maturity and harmony.[18] The story unfolds very gradually and to the despair of many readers nothing eventful ever happens. The emphasis is on the intellectual and spiritual development of the young narrator. Stifter involves the reader more and more in this process by the skilful manipulation of the narration, amounting at times to gentle coercion.[19] Heinrich Drendorf is predisposed for such an experiment, both by nature and upbringing. He comes from a merchant family where education is highly valued. While his father had to work hard to reach the financial and social standing that would allow him to build up a small but valuable collection of pictures and gems, Heinrich from the start is encouraged to go beyond his father by cultivating his intellectual capacities. His natural interests in botany and geology are allowed to develop as his father is confident that each man will serve society best if he is encouraged to follow the inner urge God has given him as a guide to his true vocation. On one of his expeditions exploring the Austrian countryside, Heinrich is obliged to seek shelter from a threatening storm in a house which immediately impresses him by its orderliness and harmony. The owner, Herr von Risach, welcomes him and he becomes a frequent visitor to the house and garden, where flowers and vegetables mingle to produce a feeling of domesticity and usefulness and nature is perfected by science into art. He meets Risach's friends and neighbours. The time is spent in conversation. Eventually Heinrich discovers his love for Natalie, the beautiful daughter of Mathilde, Risach's elderly female friend, who comes to stay in Risach's house when the roses covering its walls are in full bloom. There is a hint of mystery and suspense in the relationship of Risach and Mathilde. Heinrich wonders about it but never asks. However, after his engagement to Natalie he is allowed to hear the full story. To complete his education Heinrich is sent on a tour of Europe, of which the reader, however, hears next to nothing except that Heinrich, like Homer's Odysseus, saw many different peoples and learned to understand their characteristics against the natural setting of their countries. An elaborate wedding celebration closes the novel. Heinrich was deemed by all the members of the select society involved to have reached a level of culture which would enable him to fulfil a position of responsibility within his family and society at large, to pursue his scientific studies to unknown heights, and to take on responsibilities in the affairs of the State if called upon to do so.

Yet it would be wrong to see *Der Nachsommer*, because of its utopian and fairy-tale-like features, simply as a sustained exercise in escapism from the dire realities that oppressed Stifter at the time. There is a good deal more to it than that: Stifter puts his belief in the values of the Enlightenment once more to the test. The novel is an experiment in education, not merely aimed at producing *mens sana in corpore sano* but at exorcising 'fatum' itself. In *Nachsommer*, once Heinrich Drendorf, like a fairy-tale prince, has found his way into the enchanted enclave of Risach's estate, the possibility of a fateful downfall is excluded. Any potentially disturbing elements are dealt with immediately: people who show a *penchant* for passion are sent on their travels, while quarrelling robins are shot. The mentor-pupil relationship that develops between Risach and Heinrich is extraordinary. It flies in the face of the Socratic principle of education, where truth is found by means of argument and the pupil eventually overtakes his teacher in knowledge and perception. Here education is all one way. Although Risach's attitude to the young man is always benevolent paternalism, there is an element of tyranny in the way his development is channelled into well-defined, laid-down directions. The ominous ring of arrogance is unmistakable in Risach's joking remark at the wedding feast, intended to establish the family as the nucleus of society: 'Und du, Heinrich, [...] werde darum nicht stolz. Verdankst du mir nicht endlich ganz und gar alles?'[20] ('You, Henry, don't let it go to your head. After all, don't you owe me everything you are?') The awful truth is that he does. And Heinrich's pious remark that it was Providence that led him to the garden gate to seek shelter cannot blur the impression that Risach has created Heinrich in his own image, and that among the activities and pastimes with which Risach adorned his retirement 'educating Heinrich' was the most ambitious but also the most self-indulgent. All Heinrich is allowed to contribute towards the experiment is an inquisitive mind and a willingness to be instructed and guided, without any inconvenient desire to contradict.

With an amazingly sustained imaginative effort Stifter creates a world of great beauty and peacefulness. The experiment is based on values that go back even further than the ideals of Weimar classicism to the teleology of the eighteenth century. The whole of Risach's enterprise is inspired by a belief that a rational and teleologically ordered world exists and that it is up to man to discover and maintain its beauty. This beauty is not limited to natural phenomena but extends to works of art, the products of crafts, to furniture, tools, implements. Behind all of them, Heinrich is taught by Risach, is a mind and a will as the ultimate cause of all things. The acts of discovering, of bringing the hidden beauty of objects to light, are symbolic of the novel as a whole. They form part of the main educational process: to bring Heinrich to an ever deeper and clearer understanding not only of the nature of external things but of his own actions, intentions and wishes and their actual and potential consequences. Here Stifter seems to have drawn on Christian Wolff's teaching, which in one form or another significantly shaped his outlook.[21] Like Wolff, Stifter appears to have unshakeable confidence in the power of reason. For Wolff reason is the principle of principles, our guide and leader which teaches us the laws of nature. Wolff bases morality on a knowledge of good and evil. Once we have acquired this knowledge, he says, happiness will follow, though our primary aim must always be to do good to others. Man can be guided by examples and through others to greater insights. Where Stifter differs from Wolff is in neglecting the leading idea that man can learn from the consequences of his *own* actions. Stifter had included in his series of articles for the *Wiener Bote* a discussion of the value of experience in the school of life, in which, inspired by Herder's thought, he wrote:

> Die Ursache aber, weshalb die Menschen in der Schule des Lebens lernen, ist die Not [...] Und wo die Umstände am allerungünstigsten sind, dort muß er seinen Verstand am meisten anstrengen, die Mittel zu erfinden, und dort kommen gewöhnlich die außerordentlichsten Erzeugnisse des Geistes zustande.[22]

> [What makes men learn something in the school of life is dire necessity [...] the more unfavourable the conditions are, the more he must sharpen his wits to find a remedy, and here we come upon the commonest cause of the most extraordinary productions of the human spirit.]

Yet the novel steadfastly refuses Heinrich this possibility. Even his sensuality is carefully nurtured and channelled. Stifter in this novel seems to proffer the thought that moral perfection could be found by hearing of the experience of *others*.

Nevertheless, when we turn to the old man's account of all he had to go through before he acquired his serenity, and above all when we find Stifter's prose, which had been so measured and rhythmical with almost ritual cadences, change into a lively, sensuous, passionate description of Risach's love for Mathilde and the sufferings he had to go through, the whole moral outlook of the educational scheme is overturned. It becomes clear that it is only by doing and suffering, by collapsing and pulling oneself together time and time again, that one can gain moral insight and learn to distinguish between good and evil. Even Heinrich, who by then should have gained the necessary insight to recognise all the negative traits in Risach's story, is moved to ask his mentor the perfectly justified question why he did not marry Mathilde when they met again, since their love was so obviously still alive. Risach's answer testifies to his belief that all things have a purpose in life at a given moment and only then. This was a calm and wise subjugation to fate neither Abdias nor the rentier would have been capable of. But the answer cannot really convince. The reader is tempted to say to the author: 'You know perfectly well that your novel could never have been written if you had allowed a marriage of the mature couple to take place.' While listening to Risach's story with Heinrich, as it were, the reader realizes that here he is presented with a totally different form of education, one through passion, suffering and renunciation and that, in fact, the 'playful pastimes' with which Risach fills the days of his retirement are part of a long and painful process of attrition for having failed at a crucial moment in life, or – to put it more negatively – an artificial creation of a purpose for a life shattered at its roots.

Stifter was always a very self-aware writer, as his meticulous revisions to his stories show. He must have known what effect this disjunction between two different concepts of education would have on the reader. Or had he hoped that the sincerity and strength of his vision of a harmonious world of values handed down from generation to generation was convincing enough to invalidate the passion and suffering which formed its very basis and which was so much closer to the reality of his readers? There are many signs that Stifter knew all this, and that he was at a loss how to fashion convincingly Heinrich's entry into the world outside, which would have validated Risach's experiment. In the final chapter so much is merely stated that we have to take the word for the deed. Many urgent questions present themselves to the reader. What if Heinrich, coming as he does from an ideal enclave where a wholly harmonised set of values reigns, finds nothing but fragmentation outside? Risach took early retirement because he did not like what he saw. Will Heinrich's reaction, moulded as he is by Risach, be any different, or will he retire even earlier from those vague affairs of state, conveniently supported as he is by a large portfolio of stocks and shares and by landed property?

Nevertheless, we must give Stifter full credit for not trying to plaster over the fissures that appeared in the novel between the two concepts of education, one based on a deep knowledge of life and reality, the other on a pious dream or, worse than this, one we might also call a monstrous self-indulgence. Stifter, the deeply disappointed observer of his times, knew as well as anyone that the relentless march of history cannot be stopped. We can only guess at the depth of his despair when in *Der Nachsommer* he seems to repudiate so fundamentally the belief stated with such conviction in that earlier article that God, by giving man free will and reason, had put his fate in his own hands.[23]

Yet the novel realises to some extent the hope in which Stifter composed it: that men at present opposed to his views would eventually 'sich einiges andere Leben anlernen' ('learn something of a different way of life').[24] Influenced by the ideas of the Enlightenment on the place of art in life, Stifter always understood writing as a mission. It is poignant to find Stifter in 1857 still trying to put into practice some of the ideas Johann Georg Sulzer had laid down almost a hundred years earlier when he wrote:

> Sollen aber die Menschen diese herrlichen Früchte des Verstandes recht genießen, und in dem großen gesellschaftlichen Leben glüklich seyn, so müssen gesellschaftliche Tugenden, so muß Gefühl für sittliche Ordnung, für das Schöne und Gute in die Gemüther gepflanzet werden.[25]

> [If men are ever to enjoy to the full the splendid fruits of their intellect and find happiness on a large scale in their social relations, then their social virtues, a passion for the moral order and a feeling for beauty and goodness must be deeply implanted in their hearts and minds.]

Some of these ideals Stifter hoped to reawaken and keep alive in his readers, who are ultimately forced by the author to make their own choice based on the insights the novel provides.

If we look back at *Abdias*, we realise that Stifter had never been very confident of the possibility of understanding man's place in an enigmatic universe, but felt it worthwhile, even necessary, to put before the reader various interpretations of the human condition. The story seems to me to be aimed at jolting the reader out of a general state of complacency engendered by the rise of capitalism and the ever-increasing confidence placed, rightly or wrongly, in scientific discoveries as a means of ultimate enlightenment. In *Turmalin* his hopes for man ever being able to realise his highest potential had reached their nadir. His vision of a better, juster, freer world had been shown up as a mere illusion. Man, once again, had betrayed his greatest gift. The story reflects his bitter disappointment with the general decline all round him. Considering that only four years separate *Der Nachsommer* from *Turmalin*, one stands amazed at the sheer ethical effort Stifter must have expended on turning his disillusionment into such a glowing avowal of the potential goodness and eventual perfectibility of man as we find it demonstrated through his art in the novel. The price he paid, however, is an irreparable loss of his hold on reality, on things as they really are and always will be, which even his great narrative art cannot make us forget. This is what we may suppose Handke had in mind when he spoke of 'zeitverordnetes Erzählen' ('the effect of contemporary conditions on Stifter's art'). Stifter's dilemma was at the same time personal and one that he shared with many of his contemporaries.

Notes

1. Peter Handke, *Die Lehre der Sainte Victoire* (Frankfurt, 1980), p. 59.
2. Stifter to Gustav Heckenast, 8 August 1848.
3. Stifter to Gustav Heckenast, 6 March 1849.
4. Stifter, *Bunte Steine. Späte Erzählungen*, ed. Max Stefl (Augsburg, 1960), p. 8.
5. Stifter, *Kulturpolitische Aufsätze*, ed. Willi Reich (Einsiedeln/Zürich, 1948), p. 37.
6. Ibid., p. 51.

7. Ibid., p. 115.
8. Ibid., p. 145.
9. Ibid., p. 168.
10. Stifter, *Studien II*, ed. Max Stefl (Augsburg, 1956), pp. 5–6.
11. See Rudolf Jansen, 'Die Quelle des "Abdias" in den Entwürfen zur "Scientia Generalis" von G. W. Leibniz?', *Vierteljahresschrift des Adalbert Stifter-Institutes des Landes Oberösterreich*, 13 (1964), 57–69.
12. op. cit., p. 6.
13. Johann Lachinger, 'Mesmerismus und Magnetismus in Stifters Werk', *Stifter-Symposion* (Linz, 1978), pp. 16–23 (p. 22).
14. Johann Gottfried Herder, *Sämmtliche Werke*, ed. B. Suphan, 33 vols (Berlin, 1877–1913), vol. XIII, p. 33 and p. 35.
15. *Bunte Steine*, p. 122. See also the present writer's 'Stifter's *Turmalin*: a reconsideration', *Modern Language Review*, 72 (1977), 348–58.
16. *Bunte Steine*, p. 122.
17. *Die Schulakten Adalbert Stifters*, ed. Kurt Vancsa, Schriftenreihe des Adalbert Stifter-Institutes, 8 (Nürnberg, 1955), *passim*.
18. Wilhelm Dilthey, *Das Erlebnis und die Dichtung*, 15th edn (Göttingen, 1970), p. 273.
19. For a discussion of structure and style see Klaus Amann, *Adalbert Stifters 'Nachsommer': Studie zur didaktischen Struktur des Romans* (Vienna, 1977).
20. Stifter, *Der Nachsommer*, ed. Max Stefl (Augsburg, 1960), p. 822.
21. Christian Wolff, *Vernünfftige Gedanken von der Menschen Thun und Lassen* (Halle, 1743), 3rd edn, *passim*. For the transmission of Wolff's philosophy at Kremsmünster see Moriz Enzinger, *Adalbert Stifters Studienjahre 1818–1830* (Innsbruck, 1951).
22. *Kulturpolitische Aufsätze*, p. 121.
23. Ibid., p. 145.
24. Stifter to Balthasar Elischer, 14 January 1860.
25. *Allgemeine Theorie der Schonen Künste*, 1. Teil, Vorrede, 2nd edn (Leipzig, 1792), p. XII.

Marie von Ebner-Eschenbach and the Tradition of the Catholic Enlightenment

Eda Sagarra

'Als die erste Frau lesen lernte, trat die Frauenfrage in die Welt.' ('When the first woman learned to read, the women's question was born.')

Marie von Ebner-Eschenbach's best-known aphorism not infrequently serves as motto for contributions to modern feminist literary history. Yet its author, though long acclaimed as one of Germany's major women writers, has not been assigned a secure place in the growing 'canon' of feminist authors.[1] Undoubtedly women predominate as protagonists in her fiction, including many stories with a male narrator; and women are more frequently presented than men as the embodiment of a rational and enlightened mentality. Yet as far as the elaboration of a specifically female perspective in the corpus of her work is concerned, Marie Ebner, as she is now more usually styled, appears to convey a preoccupation with tactics over strategy. She seems to be content, not least in the aphorisms, the most enduringly popular of her works, with the moral victory of having established the intellectual equality of women with men while tacitly accepting the immutability of the status quo.[2]

Ebner's fiction was concentrated on the decades spanning her middle and old age, starting with the publication of the early stories by Cotta in 1875, when she was forty-five, up to the appearance of her last collection of Novellen, *Stille Welt*, in her eighty-sixth year. In the assessment of that work in her lifetime and in twentieth-century literary historiography up to the late 1970s, 'bourgeois realism' and 'Naturalism' have provided the parameters for its evaluation. Scholars have emphasised the influence of a variety of writers and thinkers on her short stories and novels, among them Turgenev,[3] to whom many of her characters explicitly refer, Schopenhauer, Nietzsche and the contemporary exponents of social ethics. The distinctive ethical impulse of her work, which constituted its appeal to critics as diverse as Julius Rodenberg, Paul Heyse, and her biographer Anton Bettelheim, as well as to the writers of doctoral theses during the Third Reich and the editors of German and Austrian school textbooks, was presented in terms of the epoch in which she wrote as characteristic of realist literature's alternative to a metaphysical world-view and/or a tribute to her 'womanly nature'. This last argument, besides raising obstacles to a proper appreciation of her contribution as a woman writer to German literature, typifies her admirers' neglect of analysis of the literary work in favour of apotheosis of the person.[4] The moral idealism which informs her fictional oeuvre, and which frequently finds expression in the harmonious resolution of conflict at the close of a story, has been variously interpreted in terms of an eclectic nineteenth-century literary tradition: as evidence of the reception of classical humanism in Austria (specifically Schiller), of German bourgeois realism's aesthetic requirement of 'poetic transfiguration' ('poetische Verklärung'), of a characteristically 'Austrian' form of 'ethical realism', of the contemporary literary market's demand for a 'happy end' or the 'unwritten' conditions for admission of women to that market.[5]

Ebner's fictional oeuvre undoubtedly belongs to the common European realist tradition of which her German contemporaries, Fontane, Keller, Ludwig, Raabe and Storm are exponents. But both by culture and education there was another dimension to her world-view which they did not share, one which, it can be argued, is amply reflected in her work and may have had a formative influence on the ethical impulse and didactic quality of her writing. Ferdinand von Saar, with whom she is often associated, might share with her, at least by virtue of his early upbringing, a common Catholic heritage. But as the daughter and stepdaughter of the high Austrian nobility and as a woman, Ebner had received a religious formation very different from that of Saar and one which had a profound impact on her self-image and her view of women. At the same time other influences caused her to question the principles on which that view was based – notably the autodidactic aspect of her reading since adolescence, the influence of her husband and the impact of the liberal debate in Austria during the 1860s and 1870s and, possibly most important of all, the Catholic Enlightenment tradition, known as Reform Catholicism.

While several critics have emphasised the importance of the Enlightenment tradition for Ebner's work,[6] a link between that and Reform Catholicism[7] was first suggested by Rainer Baasner. He disputed the received wisdom of seeing the Ethical Society and specifically the American philosopher and sociologist William M. Salter and his book *Die Religion der Moral* as a formative influence on her social thought and particularly her major long story *Das Gemeindekind* (1889).[8] Instead Baasner drew attention to the parallels between her own deep concern with the mediation between reason and faith and the exemplary exponent of Reform Catholicism in Austria, Bernard Bolzano, the Prague rationalist theologian, philosopher and mathematician, disciplined, not to say persecuted, by church and state in Metternich's Austria. Baasner disclaimed direct evidence of Bolzano's influence on Ebner – in fact many of his seminal works were not published until the twentieth century – but argued rather in terms of a specific tradition of rationalist religious culture in nineteenth-century Austria.[9] A further general argument that might be adduced in support of such a view is of course that the tradition of Catholic Enlightenment in Austria was centred on Bohemia and Moravia, where Ebner spent so much of her life. Its strongest and most influential advocates were those – often Czech – priests (and laymen) associated with the education and the pastoral care of souls. These were pupils or followers of Bolzano, and they were often themselves disciplined or relegated to rural parishes for advocating his ideas about moderation and tolerance, the role of individual conscience in matters of faith, and rational persuasion as against blind obedience to authority in matters of religious belief and practice.

However, as has already been indicated, the religious culture into which the author was born and in which she received her education was shaped by a tradition in general very different from that of Enlightenment thinking. Marie, Freifrau Dubsky, was born in 1830 at the height of the Catholic Restoration period in Austria; her adolescent years coincided with the consolidation in Austria of the radical conservative and papalist Catholic movement known as Ultramontanism, which, from one of its focal points in Bavaria, found strong institutional support in Vienna (and a vigorous representative in the Bavarian Archduchess Sophie, mother of Franz Joseph); she came of age almost exactly at the time when the last institutional vestiges of the Josephinist reform were eradicated (abolition of the Josephinist state church in 1850); the years of her early married life coincided with the period when Pope Pius IX's reforming zeal focused on the Austrian Church and when public discussion of the Concordat with the Vatican (1855), signed during the neo-absolutist regime, polarised political and religious opinion in Austria. Her own religious formation as a child, so far as we can judge from references in her autobiography, was generally in conformity with the attitudes of the Catholic establishment. True, in early childhood, as part of her preparation for first reception of the sacraments of confession and communion, she received, in her own words, 'an undogmatic form of Christianity' from the local priest in Moravia (M. K., 50). Her description is reminiscent of the traditional portrait of the idealised Enlightenment simple clergyman as the true representative of the Christian ethos.[10] For the rest, her religious formation appeared typical of her class and epoch, exemplifying in fact the ideological penetration of nineteenth-century female Catholic Europe by the French devotional tradition. Not only were the mothers, wives and daughters of the Austrian, German, French, Italian and Spanish Catholic nobility formed in its mould, but so were the daughters of merchants and well-to-do farmers from regions as different as the Rhineland, Flanders, Normandy and Ireland, and, later in the century, girls from English Catholic families. This was made possible – and promoted therein with considerable missionary zeal – through the growing impact of French religious orders and their convent boarding schools. Here the future governesses of the well-born were trained to propagate the French devotional tradition. They were often themselves young women of noble birth but straitened circumstances, or the victims of family misfortune, as, for example, the French governess, Claire Dübois, in *Wieder die Alte*, who after her parents' financial disaster is 'placed' in 'suitable' employment abroad (in Vienna) by the superior of her school: 'Mutter Niceta, die Oberin, ließ ihr ihren mächtigen Schutz angedeihen, empfahl sie, verschaffte ihr Lektionen' ('Mother Niceta, the Reverend Mother, extended her powerful patronage to her, recommended her, arranged lessons for her'). The intellectual quality of that training is scoffed at by Claire herself, who also recognises the deliberate strategy involved: 'Die Kinder lernen nichts bei mir, und das ist es, was ihre Mamas so freut' ('What pleases their mamas so much is that their children don't actually learn anything from me') (Klein, III, 107 and 108). Character formation as part of religious training began in very early childhood and was reinforced not just through ritual practice, but with a central role afforded to devotional reading. Ebner mentions as the devotional manual of her childhood the *Nouvelles heures à l'usage des enfants*, and – since the age of seven a particular favourite – Pierre Corneille's *Méditation sur la mort* (M. K., 60). The author of the *Imitation of Christ* is described by her as 'ein frommer und milder Apostel' ('a mild and pious Apostle') (M. K., 113), and his work, so favoured by the French editors of devotional reading for Catholic schoolgirls in the nineteenth century, appears also to have formed part of her religious training.

The gender difference in nineteenth-century Catholic education is striking and has been little discussed in scholarly literature on the social history of education. While religious training provided in boys' schools the context and general objectives of their Catholic education, in Austria as elsewhere in Europe[11], 'secular' subjects, such as classical rhetoric, mathematics, and natural science had a considerable degree of autonomy in the curriculum. By contrast, the focus of girls' education, regardless of subject, was on the development of appropriate qualities of character for 'their station in life', and it was generally based on a low estimation of 'knowledge' as both unsuitable for girls and women, and even inimical to their hope of salvation.[12] Central emphasis was placed on the daily 'examination of conscience', that is, on analysis, not just of one's every act as the possible occasion of committing a sin in 'thought, word and deed', but also of the motives of one's action. The daily or rather nightly examination was seen as an essential element in the training to accept wrong inflicted on oneself (as a form of 'expiation' of wrong wilfully or unconsciously inflicted on others); on recognising one's fault, one was immediately required to seek pardon from those injured. Parallels between this tradition and the tenor of several sections of the author's diary, particularly where she writes of family disapproval of her work, are not difficult to see. Obedience was the paramount virtue, as the Countess in the short story *Bettelbriefe* explains: 'Gehorsam wurde im Kloster gelehrt, Gehorsam forderte mein Onkel als mein vom Gesetz bestellter Gebieter. Gehorsam ist des Weibes Pflicht auf Erden, sagte mein angebeteter Schiller' ('Obedience was taught in the convent, my uncle as my legally constituted guardian demanded obedience. Obedience, according to my adored Schiller, is the duty of woman on this earth') (Klein III, 640); the last sentence could be read as an interpretative gloss on the tendency of Ebner scholarship to present the influence of Schiller on her as an absolute. In the dramatic scene in her memoirs where her grandmother responds angrily to the child's confidential report of her 'poetry', Ebner notes both affectionately and ironically her elder sister's firm counsel: 'Ja, es war eben anders bei uns, und ich hatte mich zu fügen' ('Yes, with us it was different, and I simply had to do as I was told') (M. K., 59) – yet even in adult life she appeared to retain her respect and admiration for her elder sister's ready submissiveness. In the short story *Das tägliche Leben* and in the fate of the elder sister, Elisabeth,[13] in *Komtesse Paula*, the authorial narrator challenges the idea that any higher purpose is achieved by the woman's submitting to the yoke of filial and marital obedience. Of course a secularised form of this type of moral training, and the sanctions associated with the infringement of the moral code it enjoined, are a characteristic theme of the eighteenth and nineteenth-century woman's novel, where the heroine gains merit in accepting injustice, often from a misguided or even brutal husband or father. In taking issue with the irrationality of such a view, by challenging the validity of the moral imperative on the woman to deny her own nature and her own sense of right and wrong, Ebner distances herself from traditional Catholic moral teaching on the subject, and at the same time from the tradition of the woman's novel in the Biedermeier period (as for example Johanna Schopenhauer or Theresa Huber) or the Christian *Tendenzroman* of her own time.[14]

There is little or no evidence to support the view that Ebner-Eschenbach, as the product of such religious formation, was a particularly pious woman. And it would of course be patently absurd to associate her oeuvre in any way with the Catholic 'subculture' being elaborated during the early years of her own literary career, as a response to the so-called *Kulturkampf*, led by liberal and state opposition to the anti-modernist stance of the Catholic Church. Ebner's friendship with Enrica Handel-Mazzetti (1871–1955), a successful exponent of Catholic literature, whose work she frequently praised, does not suggest sympathy with the younger author's ideological stance, but rather is an example of her empathy with views different from her own. Her diaries attest her regular formal observance of religious duties – mass on Sundays and certain saints' days, such as St Leopold, patron of Lower Austria, as well as the combined social duty and pious practice of attendance at commemorative masses for the dead, funeral obsequies and church weddings. That such observance did form an intrinsic part of her 'culture' is suggested by her characteristic Roman Catholic inclusion in the diary record of references to overly long sermons, arriving late at or actually missing Mass.

There is, however, ample evidence of a critical stance towards many aspects of her Catholic education, both in Ebner's autobiographical writings and in her narrative prose. In her early thirties, which coincided with the beginning of the liberal era in Vienna, she began to distance herself from the Church as an institution, not least through her reading, with her husband Moritz, of Ernest Renan's *Vie de Jésus*, David Friedrich Strauss's *Das Leben Jesu* and Buckle's *History of Civilisation* (*Tgb*. I, 20, 25, 47f.). In the same way as the exponents of the Catholic Enlightenment in eighteenth-century Germany and Austria, she too attacked in her writings the power-political aspects of traditional Catholicism, as in the portrait of the Konsistorialrat in *Glaubenslos?*, Stiftsdame Eveline in *Wieder die Alte* and, with especial force, the superior of the convent in *Das Gemeindekind*. Of particular significance in the context of current feminist debate is the way in which she takes issue in her fictional oeuvre, and more obliquely and even tentatively in her autobiographical writings, with the subjugation of women demanded by the Catholic Church; that is, the manner in which she combines her critique of traditional Catholic social and moral culture from the rational and conciliatory perspective of Reform Catholicism with a genuine feminist perspective. In her critical account of her (step)mother's attempts to 'convert' her (*Tgb*. I, 119), it is above all the challenge to her reason which evokes irritation and resistance. In her diary entry of 15 June 1865 she takes issue with the inherent illogicality of the commonly held 'Christian' view that requires women to be 'religious' and society to need to protect women against 'unbelief', while holding the actual content of that belief to be unimportant: 'Da heißt es immer, die Frauen sollen nicht erschüttert werden im Glauben und wenn es ein Köhlerglaube wäre' ('It is always said that women's faith, however ignorant, must not be shaken') (*Tgb*. I, 47). It seems clear from this and other references to the ethical postulate of obedience for women that she recognises the (ab)use of traditional Catholic (and Christian) teaching as an instrument of misogynistic social control. Similarly in *Mašlans Frau*, the new parish priest, well-meaning in his efforts to reconcile an estranged couple but deficient in his understanding of human nature, exhorts the wronged wife to make the first move by putting her under severe emotional pressure: 'Ist aber Verzeihen nicht Christenpflicht, vor allem Pflicht des christlichen Weibes?' ('But is forgiveness not the duty of the Christian, and above of the Christian woman?') (Klein I, 476), as though Catholic (Christian) morality could be differentiated according to gender. As the Baron remarks to the Countess in *Bettelbriefe:* 'Freilich – die Religion, das Corpus juris, die Ästhetik forderten Sie zum Gehorsam auf' ('You are right, religion, the legal code and aesthetics required that you obey') (Klein III, 640). In the remarkable short story *Das tägliche Leben*, she exemplifies the hidden cost, particularly to the intelligent and responsible woman, of enforced acceptance of an ideal of womanly subordination to a preordained 'role' in the name of Christian family life. Suddenly, on the occasion of her silver wedding, after years of faithful observation of that role, Frau Gertrud's pride and hatred of pretence can take no more, and she commits suicide. The family 'condemn' the model daughter, wife and mother to eternal damnation: 'Für Verdammte', remarks Gertrud's pious old mother, 'betet man nicht', as she weeps for one 'für die der Heiland umsonst gestorben ist' ('You do not pray for the damned ... [one of] those for whom the Saviour died in vain') (Klein III, 627).

Yet in contrast with most realist writers in Germany, notably Keller, Storm, or Fontane, Ebner's critical distance towards the institution of the Christian Church did not imply the reduction of religion in her work to the realm of psychology or anthropology. Christian symbolism plays a role in the presentation of her protagonists. When Lotti (*Lotti, die Uhrmacherin*) goes out to visit the Halwigs on their country estate to enjoy, as it were, the fruits of her genuinely Christian charity, and then decides, living up fully to the dictates of *agape* or selfless love, not to intrude on their idyll, she sits and rests under a stone cross (Klein II, 942). 'Ein kleiner Weihbrunnkessel und ein Zweiglein der Palmenweide an der Wand' ('A little holy water font and a sprig of palm on the wall') (Klein III, 126) of the impoverished Baroness's flat in *Wieder die Alte* convey both the suffering she endures and its quality as immolation; her strength and her realism will eventually give her young friend Claire Dübois the strength to come to terms with her betrayal by her lover Arnold Bretfeld and face the future with renewed courage and resourcefulness. The passionate love and the suffering of the protagonist, as well as the religious dimension of her experience, are conveyed in the prominent place of a 'Muttergottesbild, vor dem ein Flämmchen in einer Lampe aus rotem Glas flackerte' ('an image of Our Lady with a little flame flickering in the red glass lamp in front of it') in Frau Mašlan's house (Klein I, 484). In his analysis of the structure and form of *Das Gemeindekind* Baasner has drawn attention to the significance of Christian iconography in the work, such as the names of Pavel and his mother, Barbara, or the incident with Hanusch's ear in the latter part of the story (Baasner, 264 and 316).

The theme of *caritas* in Ebner's fiction provides further evidence of the influence of enlightened Catholic thinking. In *Lotti, die Uhrmacherin* Lotti's sacrifice of her priceless collection of clocks is, at least on the face of it, pointless and even irresponsible. She sells them – although destined for the city museum by her father – for the sake of a man who once loved her. But her deed is clearly going to be ineffectual in achieving its objectives: to 'save' Halwig from the 'damnation' of sacrificing his 'God-given' poetic gift to the writing of trashy literature for material gain; nor, as the narrator makes clear, will Halwig's marriage be saved by her sacrifice. Catholic theology of *caritas* requires both that the gift be something that the giver cherishes and also that it be made regardless of the 'deserving' nature of the recipient. There are many examples in both her fictional and her autobiographical work of Ebner's criticism of upper class 'charity' – the best known being *Der Muff*, with its abundant comedy of situation and ironic revelation of the true nature of the generosity of the General's wife: the weak-minded woman, whose low self-image is perpetuated by her role in marriage – she has no name! – seeks to enhance her self-regard by exercising the role of protectress of the poor and lowly – with disastrous, if hilarious, consequences. By contrast the old Baroness in the rather slight tale *Die Sünderin* is shown to exemplify true charity, despite her reiterated dismissive interjection: 'Ich kann solche Sachen nicht leiden' ('I simply cannot bear that sort of thing'). Although in her confrontation with the loose-living Fanka she initially exercises what she sees as her need to educate the recipients of charity in moral responsibility, the Baroness ends by deciding in Fanka's favour. Infringements of the sixth commandment have traditionally in the Christian dispensation drawn down on the transgressors – at least as far as women have been concerned – the greatest moral obloquy. It is characteristic of Ebner that the old lady sees Fanka, not as society sees her – exemplified in the title – as a 'sinner', but as the good mother she is, perennially forced (or persuading herself that she is forced!) towards various forms of prostitution in order to rear her children. Critics have often commented on the harsh judgement of her own kind in Ebner's work, by contrast with her tendency to relativise the faults of the lowborn. Such a view is of course fully in line with the Christian notion of social responsibility – the more elevated one's position, the greater one's moral responsibility – and the more severe the sanctions for those who do not fulfil their duty.

Ebner's focus on the marginalised in society has very properly been seen by scholars in both East and West as an example of socially engaged literature, though generally rather in the utopian tradition of the *Dorfgeschichte* ('village story') than as a product of contemporary European realism. It is, however, arguable that this emphasis reveals the influence of the Catholic Enlightenment tradition in Austria, with its stress on the perfectibility of humanity, its readiness to acknowledge individual worth regardless of differences of personality, class, education and culture, and its understanding of the demoralising effect of poverty. The basic equality of all before God, a central axiom of Christian doctrine, imposes an obligation on the well-born and well-to-do to succour those less favoured by society, however imperfectly this may be implemented by 'Christians' themselves, as expressed in Ebner's diary entry for 2 October 1866 during the cholera epidemic in Moravia: 'Wir ahnten nicht dass rings umher so viel Elend geherrscht – wir wollten nichts davon wissen, – u. entheben uns somit der Verpflichtung zu helfen u. zu trösten. Und wir wären beleidigt wenn Einer uns sagte, dass wir keine Christen sind' ('We were quite unaware of the misery all around us – we did not wish to know about it – and hence were free of the obligation to aid and succour. And we would have been insulted had someone told us that we were not Christians') (*Tgb.* 1, 121). The 'lowborn' become, according to this dispensation, the potential agents of salvation for 'their betters'. And, like Büchner in *Woyzeck*, Ebner perceives a greater degree of fidelity in common-law marriage (imposed, as in *Er läßt die Hand küssen*, by a patently unjust social system) than in the higher echelons of society. The Catholic Enlightenment position that the capacity for virtue is present in every human being, accessible to him (or her) through the workings of grace or of nature, may be illustrated from the brutalised young farm hand, Provi, in *Die Spitzin*, who sadistically kills a bitch and then finds himself unaccountably responsive to her expression of trust in him to care for her surviving pup, or the incident with the grouse in the fourth chapter of *Das Gemeindekind*:

> Pavel hatte über der Besorgnis um das Dasein des kleinen Wesens alle seine Selbstmordgedanken vergessen ... Unmittelbar nachdem er sich elend, verlassen und reif zum Sterben gefühlt, dämmerte etwas wie das Bewußtsein einer Macht in ihm auf, ... einer andern, höheren als der, die seine starken Arme und sein finsterer Trotz ihm oft verliehen.

> [In his concern for the life of the little creature Pavel had forgotten his own thoughts of suicide ... At one moment he had felt wretched, abandoned and ready to die, at the next he felt an awareness of a power within himself, ... different from and of a higher order than that which his strong arms and sombre obstinacy were wont to endow him with] (Baasner, 22).

The manner in which Ebner criticises the Catholic Church as an institution while emphasising its significant pastoral and social role is quite in conformity with the tradition of Reform Catholicism. As the chronicler of the daily misery of people's lives, whether as a result of poverty, loss of status, unsuitable marriage, or child abuse, she shows that the rural priest and the convent school – or rather those which live up to the Christian ideals on which the institutions were founded – play a role both as educator and as consolation and refuge. For Vroni, the principal victim of her violent crippled father in *Glaubenslos?*, the 'Arbeitsschule' (training school) run by the local nuns, was 'Paradise on earth, peace, love'. Not only did 'the good nuns' provide training in a kindly atmosphere so different from home, but they are shown to display psychological understanding of her situation and a therapeutic approach by trying to promote a positive self-image in the abused child, for whom they have 'nur Aufmunterung und Lob' ('nothing but encouragement and praise') (Klein II, 255).

An analysis of the selective references in Ebner's fiction to Catholic devotional practice is also revealing. The cult of the saints played a dominant role in the Austrian Catholic church of the baroque period; and in the nineteenth-century Restoration era it was revived and sedulously promoted with the support of the state. Josephinist reform, by contrast, had aimed to curb what was seen as emotionalist excess in reducing the number of saints' days celebrated as feasts – something that provoked widespread resentment in Austrian society at various levels. Ebner's references to saints – few in number – certainly appear to associate her with the position of the Catholic Enlightenment in seeing the saints, not as 'celestial messengers' or miracle workers, to counteract as it were the power of an ill-disposed Fortuna, but rather as role models. (And it is in terms of such a role model that Josef Breuer, friend and correspondent of her old age, clearly associates Ebner herself with two of the most intellectual and practical of female saints, Catherine of Siena, first woman doctor of the church, and Teresa of Avila, both characterised, as he puts it, by their 'Verstand, der praktische Sinn, die Energie' ('intelligence, common sense and energy').)[15] The invocation of the warrior saint Martin, who shared his cloak with the beggar, in *Der Muff*, is clearly part of the ironic strategy of the story. By contrast the reference to St Francis de Sales, Bishop of Annecy, one of the most charitable of men and rational of spiritual advisers, serves to characterise the old priest Thalberg in *Glaubenslos?*, and to underscore, by comparison with the two other priests in the story, the religious foundation of his human understanding. Thalberg, like Pfarrer Emanuel in *Unverbesserlich*, is described as having few books, but what he does possess are 'die Werke des Heiligen und Dichters Franziskus von Sales vollständig' ('the complete works of the saint and poet Francis de Sales') (Klein II, 275). And it is scarcely surprising that a lover of animals, such as Ebner was, should include a number of references to St Francis of Assisi in her work. Indeed it could be argued that *Krambambuli* and *Die Spitzin* offer each in their different way a secularised version of Franciscan spirituality, according to which animals serve to deepen humanity's understanding of the inter-relatedness of all creation. Franciscan in spirit is the healing impact of nature on tormented or depraved humanity, so often evoked in her writing – and specifically Catholic the notion that redemption may come through nature as well as through grace. The narratorial evaluation of the priest's challenge to the doctor in *Mašlans Frau:* 'Warum sagen Sie nicht einfach: durch die Gnade Gottes?' ('Why don't you just say: through the grace of God?') (Klein I, 470) appears to discount the exclusive dependence of the individual on the intervention of the Spirit. It is revealing that the reference to St Francis in

Komtesse Paula occurs via the account of the saint's life in *Poètes franciscains* by Frédéric Ozanam (1813-53), the French university professor and – with Père Lacordaire – exponent of democratic Catholicism (Klein III, p. 348). Ozanam was of course the founder of the world-wide charitable organisation, the Society of St Vincent de Paul, an eminently praxis-orientated lay organisation. It was (and is) an exemplary instance of the 'ethical postulate of charity' in its practical manifestation, which Roger Bauer has identified as a characteristic feature of the Austrian Catholic Enlightenment and which critics have long found characteristic of Ebner-Eschenbach's work.[16] And it is the tale of St Francis and 'Brother Wolf' which provides the role model for Edinek in *Unverbesserlich* which will help him develop into a useful citizen. That change is wrought, not by the miraculous intervention of the Saint, but, as Pfarrer Emanuel puts it 'Das Wunder kannst nur du selbst an dir vollbringen' ('Only you can perform the miracle on yourself') (Klein III, 199).

Given the pervasive presence of the Catholic church establishment in nineteenth-century rural Austria, relatively few of its spokesmen appear in Ebner's fiction. But it is noteworthy that the many positively drawn rural parish clergymen, as well as some nuns, conform to the Josephinist ideal of simple practical Christianity, which equips those under their care to be both pleasing to God and also good and useful citizens, making the Church 'eine Anstalt des Heiles nicht nur im Jenseits, sondern auch im Diesseits' ('an institution of salvation both for this world and for the next').[17] Both Pfarrer Thalberg and Pfarrer Emanuel, as well as the often impetuous Pater Leo, 'der Glaubenslose' ('the man without faith'), and the murdered priest in *Das Gemeindekind* exemplify the good priest or 'pastor bonus',[18] so central to Catholic Enlightenment belief, and the significant role of the parish in rural society is never denied in her work. There is a marked contrast between the benign influence of the nuns, already mentioned, on Vroni, and the primitive 'unredeemed' character here, and in many other stories, of the village community. It is symptomatic that Pinzer (in *Glaubenslos?*), the representative of the ecclesiastical establishment, wishes to take the young priest Leo away from the parish at the very moment when he begins to exercise influence for good on the community. In so doing Pinzer, in his capacity as Visitor, crassly neglects his pastoral duties – one recalls the central role of the parish visitations in the disposition of Josephinist church reform, indeed of the formative role of the visitation of Bishop Kindermann of Leitmeritz (Litomerice), reformer of the primary schools in Bohemia and Moravia, in guiding Emperor Joseph II's reform of the lower clergy.[19] Worse still, Pinzer tries to entice Leo away for motives which are seen to be purely secular – he wishes to use him as agent of the Church's imperialist ambitions: 'Trachten Sie, ein Eckstein unserer einzig wahren, heiligen Kirche zu werden, die allmählich die Weltherrschaft erringen und die Menschheit zum ewigen Heile führen wird' ('Try to become a cornerstone of our one, holy Church, which will gradually come to rule the world and to bring men to their eternal salvation') (Klein II, 314).[20] Both Emanuel and Thalberg have been 'disciplined' by the Church authorities for their excessive mildness – which, given the pastoral quality of their mission, might be said to reflect the failure of the Josephinist reform to survive in Austria, apart from a few isolated examples.

In the case of the positive representatives of the Catholic Church, goodness is invariably associated with reason, in the manner described by Roger Bauer as characteristic of Josephinist piety: 'ausgesprochen "vernünftig", jedem Mystizismus abhold, der die Gläubigen ihre Pflichten als nützliche Glieder der Gesellschaft vergessen lassen könnte' ('thoroughly "reasonable", opposed to any form of mysticism which could distract the faithful from their duties as useful members of society') (Roger Bauer, 34). By contrast, the representative of authority, with its characteristically pessimistic view of human nature, relies on irrational arguments. Pfarrer Thalberg is reprimanded by his former curate Pinzer for failing to exploit the credulity of the parishioners and pander to their superstition (Klein II, 312). A principal issue in *Glaubenslos?*, the conflict between faith and modern science, was a topical one at the time of writing, as the references to Father Leo's scientific instruments and 'library' imply; it was also one of which Ebner herself had personal experience from her studies of astronomy. But the context of the problem: idea and reality, reason and faith, nature and grace, and also its (psychologically implausible) resolution belong to the tradition of the Austrian Catholic Enlightenment. The religious conflict in Ebner's last major work of fiction, *Unsühnbar*, is presented as a study in the psychology of the main protagonist. Although Maria confesses and is absolved from her sin, and makes restitution, her subsequent position – that her sin is 'unsühnbar' ('inexpiable') – explicitly challenges a central tenet of Catholic doctrine, that there is no sin which is not forgiven to the contrite and for which atonement cannot be made. Indeed her very insistence on guilt makes Maria guilty of the 'greatest sin', despair, known as 'the sin against the Holy Spirit'. Yet even here it could be argued that in her exploration of the religious dimension of human experience, Ebner – as in *Mašlans Frau* – is concerned to show the individual nature of the struggle to find God and to challenge the topos that women are 'naturally religious'. Maria's failure to find redemption through grace is a key element in the story.

A further link between Ebner's oeuvre and the tradition of the Catholic Enlightenment in Austria, as exemplified by Bernard Bolzano, is the question of tolerance. Even at the height of his persecution by his own Church, a campaign which was often conducted with a degree of brutality by members of the Restoration establishment, Bolzano had endeavoured to represent fairly, in debate and writing, the position of his opponents. Unusually for critics of the Catholic Church from within the fold, Ebner is at pains to show how intolerant attitudes and bigotry can be the product of the individual's circumstances, of narrow lives, lack of experience, or of the barriers imposed on personal development by inadequate education – as for example in the ironic juxtaposition by the narrator of Komtesse Paula's filial devotion and her naive understanding of Luther (Klein III, 349). The social conditioning of human morality is, as has been mentioned, an important theme in her work and one which reflects contemporary thinking on the subject. However, as is clear from her treatment of Pavel Holub in her best work, *Das Gemeindekind*, neither environment nor heredity are to be seen as determinant influences (Baasner, 232ff.). In most of her work, she shares the moral optimism associated with the Catholic Enlightenment, a belief in the perfectibility of human nature co-operating with grace – though in the case of Pavel 'grace' may take the secularised form of a benefactor in the guise of the teacher, Habrecht, whose treasured copy of Lucretius moreover conveys that he is in fact an atheist. In a number of her stories, however, such as *Das Schädliche* or *Der kleine Roman*, arguably among her weaker works, which treat the theme of evil and challenge the Enlightenment view of childish 'innocence', she appears to subscribe to a pessimistic view of human nature, indeed of depraved, irredeemable humanity, as exemplified in the wife Edith and the child Anka, and one which questions the moral optimism of Catholic Enlightenment thinking.

I do not wish to claim that Marie Ebner was a conscious advocate of liberal Catholic thought in late nineteenth-century Austria nor that she was directly influenced by Bolzano. Nevertheless several thematic and formal features of her work associate her with the Catholic Enlightenment tradition which Bolzano exemplifies. Bolzano's belief, as expressed in a letter of 1831 to his pupil Fesl, in 'eine mit Vernunft vereinbarliche, der Tugend und Glückseligkeit der Menschen wahrhaft beförderliche Religion' ('a religion which is consonant with reason, and which truly promotes human virtue and happiness')[21] finds a parallel both in Ebner's portrayal of 'true' Christians and, more generally, in the ethical impulse which informs all her work. The tradition of the Catholic Enlightenment manifests itself in the central role given by her to pedagogy – usually in the form of the relationship of an older person – most frequently a woman – with a younger relation or friend. The life story acts as a kind of moral *exemplum*, from which the listener, or the reader, may draw lessons (or comfort) for him- or herself. While it is certainly arguable that Ebner's many idealised women figures derive from the traditional woman author's need to win entry into a male-dominated literary market (Schieth, 113), the fact that women are so frequently the exponents of reason links her with the Enlightenment. It is noteworthy that many of these women are also characterised by their religious piety and yet do not accept with their rational mind the notion of self-subordination as a moral imperative of the Christian woman. Ebner's reference to her early contact with a priest of the enlightened dispensation apart, she herself was the product of a religious formation which could fairly be described as anti-intellectual and, if not misogynistic, at least one designed to make women internalise their status and allegedly inferior mental powers as a meaningful part of the Divine order. The critical attitude she subsequently elaborated towards the religious culture in which she had been nurtured was both in origin and impulse consciously feminist. Only a small number of her works treat the destructive character of traditional Catholic teachings on the personal life of a woman; many, on the other hand, demonstrate its irrationality. Many women are portrayed as deriving solace or guidance from priests, but a significant number do not require or cannot profit from their mediation. One could go so far as to suggest that for a number of them religion, as described by Phillip Schäfer as characteristic of Catholic Enlightenment theology, becomes rather 'Angelegenheit der Einsicht des Verstandes und des Entschlusses zur Freiheit. Sie kennt keine Erlösung und bedarf keiner Vermittlung' ('a matter of the insight of understanding and the will to freedom. In such a view of religion salvation does not have a place nor does it require mediation').[22] And it is these women as well as those, more numerous, strong and self-reliant women in her fiction who live according to a secularised form of such enlightened religion, who, in common with the representatives of oppressed social groups – Pavel Holub, the Jewish doctor Nathaniel Rosenzweig, Edinek in *Unverbesserlich* and others – develop a reflective use of language which characterises their growth to moral autonomy. For it is an expression of the ultimate strength and logic of her feminist awareness, not a diminution of its conviction, that she values equally the claims of both sexes to personal and moral freedom.[23]

Notes

References are made where possible to the existing volumes of Karl Konrad Polheim, *Kritische Texte und Deutungen:* vol. 1, Marie von Ebner-Eschenbach, *Unsühnbar*, ed. Burkhard Bittrich (Bonn, 1978); vol. 3, Marie von Ebner-Eschenbach, *Das Gemeindekind*, ed. Rainer Baasner (Bonn, 1983), quoted as Baasner; vol. 4, Marie von Ebner-Eschenbach, *Autobiographische Schriften I. Meine Kinderjahre. Aus meinen Lehr- und Kinderjahren*, ed. Christa-Maria Schmidt (Tübingen, 1989), quoted as M. K.; Marie von Ebner-Eschenbach, *Tagebücher I. 1862-1869* ed. Karl Konrad Polheim and Rainer Baasner (Tübingen, 1989), quoted as *Tgb*.

All further references are to the three-volume edition of Marie von Ebner-Eschenbach's works by Johannes Klein: *Das Gemeindekind. Novellen. Aphorismen* (Munich, 1956), quoted as Klein I; *Kleine Romane* (Munich, 1957), quoted as Klein II; *Erzählungen. Autobiographische Schriften* (Munich, 1958), quoted as Klein III; and to *Aphorismen*, ed. Ingrid Cella (Stuttgart, 1988), quoted as Cella.

1. By contrast with the case of Ebner, contemporary feminist literary criticism recognises Annette von Droste-Hülshoff as a feminist writer – see e.g. Irmgard Röblin, 'Heraldik des Unheimlichen. Annette von Droste-Hülshoff. Auch ein Portrait', in Gisela Brinker-Gabler (ed.), *Deutsche Literatur von Frauen* (Munich, 1988), vol. II, pp. 41–68. Heidi Beutin's feminist claims for Ebner's first short novel *Božena* ('Marie von Ebner-Eschenbach: *Božena* (1876). Die wiedergekehrte "Fürstin Libussa"', in Horst Denkler [ed.], *Romane und Erzählungen des bürgerlichen Realismus. Neue Interpretationen* [Stuttgart, 1980], pp. 246–59), have not found general acceptance. Helga Harriman is one of the few scholars to devote a full-length article to Ebner's claims to feminist status in 'M. v. E.-E. in Feminist Perspective', *MAL* 18 (1985), 27–38. Konstanze Fliedl discusses her, along with Betty Paoli and Louise von François, in terms of the 'Voröffentlichkeit' or critique of their work by their friends on which these women relied to overcome the psychological obstacles imposed by the literary market on their sex, in 'Auch ein Beruf. "Realistische" Autorinnen im 19. Jahrhundert' (Brinker-Gabler, *Deutsche Literatur von Frauen* vol. II, pp. 69–85).
2. For example: 'Eine gescheite Frau hat Millionen geborener Feinde: – alle dummen Männer' ('a clever woman has millions of born enemies: all stupid men') or 'Es gibt mehr naive Männer als naive Frauen' ('there are many more naive men than naive women'), *Aphorismen*, ed. Cella, pp. 15, 22.
3. Jiří Vesely, 'Turgeniew in ungedruckten Tagebüchern M.s. v. E.-E.', *Zeitschrift für Slawistik*, 31 (1986), 273–7.

4. Baasner, p. 230.
5. Lydia Schieth, *Die Entwicklung des deutschen Frauenromans im ausgehenden 18. Jahrhundert: ein Beitrag zur Gattungsgeschichte* (Frankfurt, 1987), esp. pp. 200ff.
6. For example, Ingrid Cella, p. 66, or Ernst Alker, *Die deutsche Literatur im 19. Jahrhundert (1832–1914)* (Stuttgart, 1961), pp. 610 and 613.
7. There is considerable current scholarly interest in the neglected field of the Catholic Enlightenment, including its significance for polite literature in Austria and South Germany: cf. Carsten Zelle, 'Katholische Aufklärung – Aufklärung im katholischen Deutschland', in *Das achtzehnte Jahrhundert. Mitteilungen der Deutschen Gesellschaft für die Erforschung des 18. Jahrhunderts*, 12, nos. 1 and 2, pp. 4–8 and 127–33. On *Reformkatholizismus* see Eduard Winter, *Die Geschichte des österreichischen Reformkatholizismus 1740–1848* (Berlin, 1962), esp. pp. 175–194; Werner M. Bauer, *Fiktion and Polemik. Studien zum Roman der österreichischen Aufklärung* (Vienna, 1978).
8. In vol. 3 (1983) of *Kritische Texte and Deutungen*. Cf. also his '"Armes Gemeindekind, wirst du noch?" Die Entstehungsgeschichte der Erzählung "Das Gemeindekind" im Lichte der Tagebücher M. v. E.-E.s', *ZfdP* 104 (1985), 554–65.
9. It is conceivable that Ebner may have had some contact in her late teens or early twenties through her stepmother with Franz Schneider, confessor of Countess Thun, mother of the Austrian minister Count Leo Thun. Schneider, a pupil of Bolzano's favourite student Fesl and a warm admirer of Bolzano, was the editor of his lectures. Baasner, p. 346, points to further possible political references to him.
10. Werner M. Bauer, p. 30.
11. Georg Jäger in Karl-Ernst Jeismann and Peter Lundgren (eds), *Handbuch der deutschen Bildungsgeschichte III. 1800–1870. Von der Neuordnung Deutschlands bis zur Gründung des Deutschen Reichs* (Munich, 1987), pp. 201f.
12. 'Défaitez-vous du trop grand désir de savoir, parce qu'il s'y rencontre beaucoup de dissipation et d'illusion [...] Plus vos connaissances sont étendues et profondes, plus votre jugement sera rigoreux, si vous n'avez pas vécu saintement'. In *Imitation de Jésus-Christ. Edition abrégée avec avis pratiques et des Exemples à l'usage des Enfants de Marie et des Pensionnats de jeunes filles*, 6th edn (Lille and Gramont, 1909), pp. 29f.
13. Elisabeth is the name of the Landgravine of Thuringia, married, like Griselda, to a husband who allegedly tried her humility to an inhuman degree. Griselda, a favourite theme of mid nineteenth-century German literature, was the subject of a play by Ebner's mentor, Halm; a biography of Elisabeth by the French liberal Dominican, Lacordaire, went into 15 editions in German translation in the two decades following its first publication in France in 1847.
14. See Eda Sagarra, 'Gegen die Zeit und Revolutionsgeist. Ida Gräfin Hahn-Hahn und die christliche Tendenzliteratur im Deutschland des 19. Jahrhunderts', in Brinker-Gabler, vol. 2, pp. 105–18; ead., '"In Jerusalem": Ida von Hahn-Hahns konfessionelle Schriften im Rahmen des katholischen Buchmarkts', in E. S. (ed.), *Deutsche Literatur in sozialgeschichtlicher Perspektive* (Dublin, 1989), pp. 108–28.
15. Robert A. Kann (ed.), *M. v. E.-E. und Dr. Josef Breuer. Ein Briefwechsel, 1889–1916* (Vienna, 1969), p. 48.
16. Roger Bauer, *Die Welt als Reich Gottes. Grundlagen und Wandlungen einer österreichischen Lebensform* (Vienna, 1974), p. 34.
17. Winter, *Reformkatholizismus*, p. 103.
18. Ibid., pp. 123ff., esp. p. 134.
19. Ibid., pp. 113 and 128.
20. The conflict between church authorities and 'true' Christianity is of course a topical theme in many German novels of the 1890s, among them (in the figure of Pastor Lorenz) Fontane's *Der Stechlin*.
21. 2 February 1831 (quoted in Winter, *Reformkatholizismus*, p. 300).

22. Philipp Schäfer, *Kirche und Vernunft. Die Kirche in der katholischen Theologie der Aufklärungszeit* (Munich, 1974), p. 100.
23. The view expressed in her mature work was advanced with some diffidence in a letter of 20 December 1879 to Baron Emmerich du Mont, quoted in Anton Bettelheim, *M. v. E.-E.s Wirken und Vermächtnis* (Leipzig, 1920), pp. 277–8: 'Wie aber, wenn die Frau in erster Reihe ein menschliches und erst in zweiter ein weibliches Wesen wäre?'

Charles Sealsfield and the Novel as a Means of Enlightenment

Hartmut Steinecke

(translated by Ritchie Robertson)

When histories of the German novel deal with the half-century between Hoffmann and Fontane, they mention very few works and authors whose importance is internationally acknowledged.[1] By comparison with the fiction of Scott, Dickens, Thackeray, Balzac or Stendhal, one cannot seriously dispute Thomas Mann's judgement that mid nineteenth-century German fiction 'does not really count in European terms'.[2] Even in the more restricted context of the genre's development in German, pride of place has generally gone to works by authors like Eichendorff, Mörike, Stifter or Keller, who wrote novels only occasionally and who also practised other literary forms. They have enjoyed a higher reputation than the few genuine novelists who, unlike the mass of penny-a-liners who kept the lending libraries going, were conceded a certain literary status: Willibald Alexis with his novels taken from Prussian history, Jeremias Gotthelf with his novels of Swiss peasant life, and Charles Sealsfield with his adventure novels set in America. This form of German 'backwardness' has long been interpreted by analogy with the political concept of the 'belated nation', on the grounds that the 'epic of bourgeois life', with its close relation to society, must reflect German political and social provincialism and particularism.

This explanatory model, many versions of which are already found in nineteenth-century discussion, has something to be said for it; it is, however, too general and all-embracing to capture the variety and differentiation of the genre's rich development. Above all, it has often perpetuated the existence of outdated modes of reading and evaluation, and impeded a new, unprejudiced engagement with the subject. Since the 1970s such a discussion has got under way, examining nineteenth-century German fiction from various viewpoints, including those of poetic theory and the aesthetics of reception, a new, open conception of form, and a revaluation of the function of literature as entertainment. In particular, the work of the Austrian Charles Sealsfield has attracted increasing attention. It is no longer seen as being primarily of ethnographic and historical interest, and it has influenced arguments about literary evaluation in general.

Charles Sealsfield was the name adopted by Karl Postl, who was born in 1793 in Moravia. He was ordained a priest in 1814. In 1823, however, he ran away and emigrated to the United States, where he lived until 1832. After five years as a journalist in London and Paris, he moved to Switzerland and lived there under his assumed name until his death in 1864. His first novel, written in English, was *Tokeah; or, the White Rose* (1829). Of his later novels, the best known is *Das Cajütenbuch* (1841), an adventure story set in the south-western United States, the region which Sealsfield knew best.[3]

Sealsfield's novels, and his conception of their genre, deviate from the mainstream of the German-language novel as it developed in the first half of the nineteenth century. Many contemporary reviewers were conscious of this, recognised at least some aspects of Sealsfield's originality, and formulated these in their critiques. No other novelist writing in German at this time had so many reviews and profiles written about him as did Sealsfield. A number of these contemporary observations provide starting-points for a new study of the author. In this study, a formulation by Sealsfield himself must always be borne in mind. In the preface to his first novel in German, *Der Legitime und die Republikaner* ('The Legitimate Ruler and the Republicans', 1833), Sealsfield maintains that the novel is 'für alle Stände [...] ein weit einflußreicheres Bildungs- und Aufklärungsmittel, als bisher geglaubt wurde' ('a much more influential means of education and enlightenment for all levels of society than has hitherto been supposed', VI, pp. 6f.).[4] With this definition Sealsfield combines the tradition of the Enlightenment with that of Goethe, though admittedly education is no longer aimed at the individual personality, but at 'all levels of society'. He implies a kind of popular education, with the novel as its main instrument. Although in eighteenth- and even in nineteenth-century Germany this largely remained a wishful fantasy, abstract or semi-didactic in character, Sealsfield's experience of American democracy enabled him to give it concrete literary form. In this and numerous other important ways, he anticipated insights that Alexis de Tocqueville was to develop theoretically in his influential work *Democracy in America* (1836-40), especially in the chapters on education and culture as the basis for democracy.

Sealsfield's literary career began with two books, one about his new and the other about his old home: *Die Vereinigten Staaten von Nordamerika, nach ihren politischen, religiösen und gesellschaftlichen Verhältnissen betrachtet* ('The United States of North America as they are in their political, religious, and social relations', 1827) and *Austria As It Is* (1828). These have received little scholarly attention, having been considered, at best, as factual treatises on politics and geography. However, they are important for Sealsfield's development in general, as well as for our subject in particular. They disclose, much more directly than the later novels and much more fully than Sealsfield's few prefaces and letters, the foundations of his political and literary outlook. Sealsfield's outlook originated from the Josephinist Enlightenment, and was powerfully influenced by Bernard Bolzano, his philosophy teacher in the Kreuzherrenstift at Prague. He transferred his liberal views to politics, where they were strongly marked by the political reality of the Jackson era in the United States.

Aside from their part in the development of Sealsfield's outlook, however, these two early works have a further significance, which scholarship is only beginning to recognise. In their intentions and in their modes of representation they already point forward to essential features of the later novels.

In 1828 Sealsfield defined his first novel in these words: 'Es ist ein Werk, das die häuslichen, politischen, religiösen Verhältniße der westlichen Bewohner der V. St. [...] charakteristisch darstellt' ('It is a work which depicts the character of domestic, political, and religious conditions in the US').[5] This formulation is almost identical with the title he had given shortly before to his book on the United States. When Sealsfield continues: 'das ganze ist in einen *Roman* [...] eingekleidet' ('the whole thing has been given the form of a novel'), it becomes clear that content is primary and form secondary. Numerous remarks indicate how little he cared about genre terms. Thus he writes in connection with his *Transatlantische Reiseskizzen* ('Transatlantic Travel Sketches'): 'Wie Sie ersehen werden, sind diese Reise- oder vielmehr Stationen-Skizzen zugleich Roman' ('As you will perceive, these travel or rather staging-post sketches are at the same time a novel', XI, p. 9).

Given Sealsfield's indifference towards questions of genre, why did he give all his work after 1830 'the form of a novel'? The conclusive answer to this question is to be found in his view of this genre as an outstanding 'means of enlightenment'. This conception is set out in his most important programmatic text on the poetics of the novel, the preface to *Morton oder die große Tour* ('Morton or the Grand Tour', 1835; later entitled *Lebensbilder aus beiden Hemisphären*, 'Pictures of Life from Two Hemispheres').[6] Here he recounts how Walter Scott raised the novel's status from that of an inferior and despised literary genre by bringing it close to history and thus helped it to become a 'Bildungshebel, der sich mit den mächtigsten der Gesammtliteratur messen kann' ('an educational lever which ranks with the most powerful in the whole of literature', X, p. 6). By dealing in his novels with history and reality, Scott made a crucial contribution to the 'politische Erziehung' ('political education', X, p. 15) and to the enlightenment of his nation, creating 'ein Lesebuch zur Erholung und Belehrung' ('a book to read for relaxation and instruction', X, p. 17). It is clear from numerous remarks that these are also the principles on which Sealsfield's conception of the novel is based. For example: 'Ich wünsche das Meinige beizutragen, dem geschichtlichen Roman jene höhere Betonung zu geben, durch welche derselbe wohlthätiger auf die Bildung des Zeitalters einwirken könne' ('I want to do my part in giving the historical novel the higher emphasis by which it may have a more beneficial influence on the education of the age', X, p. 18). For Sealsfield, the novel is the best means of enlightenment and education, because it can accommodate any subject-matter and is diffused among all classes, from 'den Aufgeklärtesten, den Ersten des Landes' ('the most enlightened, the foremost people in the country', X, p. 17) via the middle classes to the 'weniger Gebildeten' ('the less well-educated', *ibid.*). With these statements the author, consciously or not, is following a type of argumentation which had become widespread among Germany's leading liberal critics since the July Revolution of 1830. Sealsfield's importance lies not least in the fact that he not only described and analysed these developments in the theory of the novel, but also acted on them, embodying these ideas in a fictional oeuvre which none of his liberal contemporaries could match.

If the novel is to perform its task of political enlightenment, the first condition it must fulfil, in Sealsfield's opinion, is that of life-like depiction. This introduces the problems associated with realism in his work. In older scholarly literature Sealsfield was often called one of the first important realists. Such a classification presupposed a concept of realism that stressed subject-matter, factual 'reality', 'truth', and the demonstrable 'accuracy' with which nature and people were depicted. This concept was suggested by the affinities between realist fiction and non-fictional descriptive writing. In the last twenty years, however, such a concept of realism has been challenged from many quarters, and with some justification, as 'naively mimetic'. Hence Sealsfield's work has been wholly excluded from recent discussions of realism. However, the 'reality' of the depicted data is far from being the only way in which Sealsfield fulfils the basic requirement of 'faithful' depiction. It is more important that he also sought to grasp the 'reality' of an age and of a nation. He announces programmatically that the novel he aims to write will depict 'das gesellschaftliche Leben in allen seinen Nuancen' ('social life in all its nuances', X, p. 20), or in other words, political and social life in the most comprehensive sense.

For the crucial question – *how* to depict the reality of an age – the character of the hero became an increasingly important touchstone in German fiction. The hero was no longer an outstanding personality but, under Scott's influence, a middling, average person, who was not so much psychologically interesting in his own right but rather a representative of the people or the reader. This choice was based on the assumption that the novel with a middling hero distributed its interest among many characters; as the 'Volksroman' ('novel of the people') it replaced the single, dominant personality with a large number of heroes – the people.

How Sealsfield arrived at this type of novel can be illustrated from the changes he made to his first novel, *Tokeah; or, the White Rose*, when translating it into German. In the English version the novel has a hero, the Indian chief Tokeah named in the title, together with individualised characters and a love story; the depiction of the people and of social problems remains in the background. Even the title of the German version, *Der Legitime und die Republikaner*, indicates the change. The chief's name is replaced by a term ('the legitimate ruler') that defines him as the representative of a position within the social conflict depicted in the novel, and he is placed in opposition to a body of people ('the Republicans'). Altogether, the revised version gives prominence to Sealsfield's concern with social, national, and ethnic groups and their problems.

Sealsfield pursued this course consistently in his next novel, *Der Virey und die Aristokraten* (1835). The hero of this novel is stated in the subtitle: 'Mexico in the year 1812'. Scarcely any characters are singled out as individuals. Instead, a very large number of people are presented to us, many of them identified not by name but by their status, their party, their social position, their ethnic origins or their profession. Thus they are deliberately treated as the representatives of specific social groups. Often, indeed, the populace takes part in the action, as in crowd scenes. Hence the novel embodies an early form of what Karl Gutzkow later developed into the 'Roman des Nebeneinander' ('novel of contiguity'). This method was discerned and described by contemporary critics. Thus the reviewer in the *Zeitung für die elegante Welt* for 1839 emphasises that the author has

> ein unzweifelhaft neues Romangenre erfunden, worin nicht die romanhaften Intriguen, Verwickelungen, Abenteuer in Leben, Liebe und Tod, und alle sonst gebräuchlichen Zuthaten eines Romans im gewöhnlichen Sinne die Hauptsache sind, sondern [...] die Menschenracen, die Stände, die Nationen und die Charaktere, insofern sie eine Nationalität repräsentiren (Spiess, p. 94).

> [... invented an unquestionably new genre of novel, in which the main concern is not the romantic intrigues, entanglements, adventures involving life, love, and death, and all the other customary accessories of a novel in the usual sense, but the races of mankind, classes, nations, and characters, insofar as the latter represent a nationality.]

Later, in a letter of 1854, Sealsfield again explained his method, which in his view made him the founder of a new type of novel, established on a broad national and social basis:

> Statt daß wie früher im Familien-Geschichtlichen Schelmen oder wie er sonst heißen möge Romane der Held des Romanes die Hauptperson war, um den sich die andern Persönlichkeiten im Rahmen herumreihten, ist hier der Held – wenn wir so sagen dürfen – das ganze Volk seine sozialen sein öffentliches sein Privatleben, seine materiellen politischen religiösen Beziehungen, tretten an die Stelle der Abentheuer, seine Vergangenheit seine Zukunft werden als historische Gewänder benutzt – Liebesscenen und Abentheuer nur gelegentlich als Folie um zu beleben hervorzuheben angewandt.[7]

> [Earlier, in domestic, historical, picaresque novels, or whatever they may be called, the hero of the novel was the main character, round whom the other personalities were ranked as a framework. Here, however, the hero – if we may use the word – is the people as a whole; its public and private life, its social, material, political, and religious relations, take the place of adventures; its past and its future are used as historical garments – love-scenes and adventures are used only occasionally as a foil, for animation and emphasis.]

By dissolving his fiction into descriptions and scenes, without any immediately recognisable thread of continuous action, Sealsfield not only incurs criticism for lacking unity and harmony, but risks damaging the readability of his novels. This becomes a serious objection if one bears in mind that the author's intention of spreading political enlightenment expressly required that the novels should be widely read.

In some works, including *Das Cajütenbuch*, Sealsfield tried to solve this problem in a way that recalls Balzac's *Comédie humaine*. While Balzac largely retains the individual hero as the central figure serving to integrate his novel, he allows this hero to play a secondary role, often seen from a different narrative perspective, in other parts of the fictional cycle. Sealsfield does something similar within a single novel, admittedly one that includes several relatively self-contained parts linked by a framework. Some figures appear several times in different situations, at different periods, in different social and political circumstances. Thus the Texan Colonel Morse, an experienced and self-assured character in the framework, also appears as a greenhorn in the inset story 'Die Prärie am Jacinto' ('The Prairie on the Jacinto'), set ten years earlier, and as a languishing lover in the concluding episode. This simultaneously reveals the interaction of private and public experience which is repeatedly shown throughout the novel. Such changes, and the juxtaposition of heterogeneous narratives, have been seen as inconsistencies. Before reaching this conclusion, however, one should consider Sealsfield's reason for adopting this kind of composition. The positive hero as central figure invites identification; his opinions are consciously or unconsciously accepted as correct; the authority of the individual is dominant. By showing this hero from another perspective as well, however, Sealsfield provides a safeguard against one-sided idealisation. Hence it never happens in this novel that one individual remains in the right for long; in every situation and at every time he must submit to a discussion from which other opinions and judgements may emerge as correct. Not only are individual episodes of the novel based on the principle of discussion as the democratic forum for the discovery of truth; this principle applies also, in a figurative sense, to the treatment of the hero in the overall design of the novel. This of course is not apparent when one episode is taken in isolation, as the opening narrative, 'Die Prärie am Jacinto', often was until recently. If this story is read on its own, considerable weight must be placed on the patriarchal and authoritarian figure of the Alcalde, who regards himself as an 'aristocratic democrat'. Undoubtedly this figure with his maxims expresses Sealsfield's own political ideas in many ways; his position in a larger context, however, makes clear that even his standpoint is not presented as exemplary, but has certain limitations and is open to discussion.

I suggest, therefore, that to appreciate Sealsfield's 'realism' one should examine his depiction of contemporary reality, his portrayal of the people as his hero, and his narrative perspective, in the manner just indicated. This is a better way of locating his novels in the context of the general discussion of realism than the scrutiny of their factual data would be.

Since the concept of realism is still confused, it may never be possible to decide once and for all whether Sealsfield's works were realistic or not. At all events, however, it is important to bear in mind that many contemporaries felt them to be realistic. While this is certainly not conclusive evidence for their realism, it does show that Sealsfield managed to carry out his intentions and convey them to his readers. Contemporary critiques offer ample evidence of this. In a great variety of phrases they acknowledge that Sealsfield's novels succeed in describing reality, taking characters directly from reality, and writing in accordance with nature.[8] It is no coincidence that one of these critiques makes programmatic use of the term 'realistic', which was still very rarely used in the

1840s (Spiess, p. 131). Elsewhere in the same review it is emphasised that this mode of depiction is particularly successful in bringing home to us questions of political freedom (*ibid.*, p. 135), and this points to an important aspect of Sealsfield's realism. Since his readers – whether on the basis of a naive or a more elaborate conception of reality – regarded his portrayals as life-like and hence as 'true', they were also much more inclined to accept his political message as 'true'. Enlightenment and republicanism did not appear as 'ideas' or 'tendencies', as in most other German works of this period – those of the Young Germans, for example; instead, they appeared as given reality. This helped Sealsfield's views to assume an exemplary character.

Sealsfield's desire to influence the reader is also responsible for the second purpose which he assigns to his novels, in accordance with his task of political enlightenment: his works must be entertaining. Sealsfield realised that it was not enough to describe the behaviour and views that he considered correct; they must be brought to life for the reader, so as to stimulate and seduce him. In deciding to write novels, Sealsfield also decided to adopt the genre which, being in prose, was accessible to a large number of readers and throughout its history had always been closely allied to entertainment. This function of entertainment ensured that the novel's enlightened didacticism could not become too obtrusively instructive. Here, too, Sealsfield is in agreement with numerous contemporary critics, especially the Young Germans, for whom the novel's popularity and wide diffusion made it particularly suitable for 'Ideenschmuggel' ('smuggling ideas'). For the Young Germans, admittedly, entertainment was only a means to a political end; their works are very forced, they can scarcely be called entertaining, and as a result they found only limited favour with the reading public.

In Sealsfield's work, by contrast, entertainment is of more value in its own right: it is freed from the narrow function of enlightened didacticism, without becoming an end in itself. Sealsfield does not scruple to employ all the devices current in the popular fiction of his day: the plot is often crammed with adventures, intrigues, fights, revolutionary and military combats; accidents, crimes, struggles for political positions, and the power of money are just as much part of the novels' spectrum as are stories of happy and unhappy love, of loyalty and treachery.

Besides these 'romantic' materials, we find a colourful, exciting, often intricate plot, told in a relaxed fashion with much conversation – including dialogue and short exchanges as well as lengthy discussions – and recurrent humour; the exotic backdrop, especially the descriptions of natural settings unfamiliar to German readers, is a further source of enjoyment. By adopting this mode of representation Sealsfield is following the example of British and American popular fiction, to which his model Walter Scott as well as authors like James Fenimore Cooper and Edward Bulwer-Lytton are also indebted. In Germany, of course, there is a similar tradition, though after the beginning of the nineteenth century it is seldom carried on by novelists who receive critical attention. The fiction of entertainment in Germany at this period tends increasingly to be equated with popular fiction in the eyes of literary scholars.

This is one of the reasons for the division of the German novel into the novel with literary merit and the novel of entertainment, a division which has often been noted and sometimes deplored, and which does not exist in this form in France or Britain. From the standpoint of a classicistic conception of the genre, the novel's varied plot and exciting narrative – everything that produces a 'good story' – were judged to be disreputable, if not downright reprehensible.

By the standards of the 1830s and 1840s, critiques of Sealsfield were remarkably receptive to the entertaining aspects of his novels. In the general discussion of the novel, *Vormärz* writers like Hermann Marggraff and Robert Prutz increasingly approved of influencing the public by adopting the traditions of the Enlightenment, but after 1848 the earlier negative attitude came more strongly to the fore. This was doubtless among the reasons for Sealsfield's exclusion from the literary canon in the second half of the century.

As has already become apparent, contemporary critical documents provide a basis for discussing numerous questions connected with aspects of Sealsfield's reception. To the detriment of scholarship, these documents have hitherto been noted only in isolated cases; they have not been thoroughly exploited, partly because of scholars' ignorance, partly because of their contempt for literary criticism as such. This is particularly serious in the case of Sealsfield, for in the fifteen years between 1833 and 1847 there appeared over eighty reviews of his works, some of them very detailed. Such intensive preoccupation with a fictional oeuvre is unusual, and in the history of German poetics it has no precedent. It certainly provides a better starting-point for the discussion of Sealsfield's influence than the speculations and conjectures which have been current hitherto. The sheer number of reviews is of course less important than what their content reveals. In particular, these critiques can show whether, and to what extent, Sealsfield managed to convey his enlightened and political intentions, and the resulting conception of the novel, in the works themselves.

As Sealsfield himself often stressed, one of his essential goals was to address the German people, familiarising it in an entertaining fashion with the ideas of the Enlightenment and republicanism. The best-known formulation of this desire is the dedication to the second edition of *Lebensbilder aus der westlichen Hemisphäre* (1842):

> Der zum Bewußtseyn ihrer Kraft und Würde erwachenden deutschen Nation sind diese Bilder des häuslichen und öffentlichen Lebens freier Bürger eines stammverwandten, weltgeschichtlich groß werdenden Staates als Spiegel zur Selbstbeschauung hochachtungsvoll gewidmet (XI, p. [5]).

> [These pictures of the domestic and public life of free citizens in a state which is ancestrally related to us, and which is rising to greatness in world history, are dedicated, with the deepest respect, to the German nation which is awakening into consciousness of its strength and dignity, as a mirror for self-contemplation.]

Many scholars have doubted whether Sealsfield attained his goal of addressing German readers in order to bring the influence of liberal and democratic ideas to bear on them. A glance at contemporary critiques may take us beyond speculation. For a whole series of reviews shows that readers managed to apply Sealsfield's hints to their own situation. Thus a review in the *Blätter für literarische Unterhaltung* for 1834 formulates one of the novels' doctrines as follows: one must 'deutsche und europäische Engherzigkeit aus seiner Seele treiben' ('expel German and European small-mindedness from one's soul'), and the Germans must discard 'die geistige Aermlichkeit ihrer Begriffe von Bürgerthum und Staat' ('the intellectual poverty of their conceptions of citizenship and the state') if they wish to find their place in the free world (Spiess, p. 32).⁹

The difference between attacking German conditions and conduct on the one hand, and close attachment to the course taken by the German nation on the other, is seen clearly by many reviewers. Thus a critic writes in 1839:

> Der Verfasser hat sein americanisches Bewußtsein und seine republicanische Ueberlegenheit in hinlänglichem Maße bewahrt, um auf die kleinlichen Institutionen der deutschen Länder und Ländereien, Völker und Völkchen, Staaten und Staatchen verachtend herabzublicken, aber für das große leidende, so arme und doch so reiche Herz der deutschen Nation, das im Mittelpuncte Europas sehnsüchtig schmerzlich klopft, fühlt und offenbart er die innigste Sympathie (Spiess, p. 94).
>
> [The author has retained his American consciousness and his republican superiority in sufficient measure to look down contemptuously upon the petty institutions of German lands, nations, and states, both great and little; but for the German nation's great suffering heart, so poor and yet so rich, which beats with such yearning pain in the centre of Europe, he feels and discloses the warmest sympathy.]

Time and again the novels deal with problems that the German reader could easily relate to his own circumstances. This applies, for example, to the forces mentioned in the title of the first novel, *Der Legitime und die Republikaner*. For the reader of the post-1815 Restoration period, 'legitimacy' was a familiar slogan, one of the three basic principles on which the European order rested after the Congress of Vienna. The novel shows how the legitimate ruler is compelled to yield to the republicans, not because the latter are stronger or morally better, but because of the logic of historical progress. The republicans' spokesman, General Jackson, who was President of the United States when the novel was published, stands for the victory of 'enlightenment' and 'humanism' over 'barbarism' and 'tyranny'.[10] Here, too, the reviews once more confirm that the European reader could easily adopt the perspective Sealsfield wanted. The tabooed theme of legitimacy, which had acquired particular urgency since Louis Philippe had ascended the French throne in 1830, could here come under discussion in a context remote from the current political situation and hence immune to the strictures of the censorship.

In Sealsfield's second novel, *Der Virey und die Aristokraten*, what German readers beheld in the 'mirror for self-contemplation' was the situation in Mexico in 1812. Mexico is a feudal state, ruled by a viceroy and a dominant class of aristocrats, and characterised by arbitrary government, lack of freedom, and horrifying ignorance among the mass of the population. A revolution is inevitable. The narrator recounts events from the standpoint of a citizen of the United States, a republican and a devotee of the Enlightenment. The harsh judgements passed on the ruling class are to be understood in this light, as are the comments on the revolutionary exertions of the masses, which are said to be destined to failure because of the people's ignorance. Over and over again political enlightenment is described as a precondition for self-government and thus for a republic: 'Weil eine Republik, ich meine eine wahre Republik, nicht ohne Selbstherrschaft jedes einzelnen Bürgers bestehen kann, und diese Selbstherrschaft wieder nicht ohne einen hohen Grad politischer Aufklärung, die über die ganze Nation verbreitet seyn muß' (IX, p. 306). ('Because a republic, I mean a true republic, cannot exist without self-government on the part of each and every citizen, and this self-government in turn cannot exist without a high degree of political enlightenment, which must be diffused throughout the entire nation.') 'Political enlightenment' thus reveals itself as the most important message of this novel, as of the previous one. Such remarks can scarcely be directed at American readers, for the latter live in 'einer Republik, wie sie seyn soll, [...] der einzig wahren, die je bestand' ('in a republic as it ought to be [...] the only true one that ever existed'), as we are told in this context (IX, p. 307). They are addressed rather to German readers, whose political circumstances in 1834 bore so much resemblance to those described. Here, too, the reviews show that reviewers and readers clearly recognised the thought-provoking parallels with their own situation in the Restoration period.

In the course of the 1830s, as the *Lebensbilder* continue to appear, criticism becomes increasingly willing and able to recognise Sealsfield's intentions and apply his enlightened political judgements to German conditions; in the early 1840s hardly any of the longer reviews lack observations to this effect. In 1841 Arnold Ruge ends a review of *Das Cajütenbuch* in the *Deutsche Jahrbücher* with the stirring rhetorical appeal: 'Möge das gute, tapfre politische Element, die Ehre und der Stolz dieser großartigen republikanischen Völker auf uns Deutsche übergehn' (Spiess, p. 109). ('May the good, courageous political element, the honour and the pride of these fine republican peoples pass to us Germans.') In a review of the same novel Alexander Jung praises Sealsfield because he '[in] den amerikanischen Sitten, Gebräuchen, Lebensentwicklungen, immer auch Europa mit zur Darstellung bringt, [...] *unsere* eigensten Zustände mit den treuesten Zügen abschattirt' ('always includes Europe in his depiction of American manners, customs and biographies, [...] shades *our* most personal circumstances with the most faithful strokes'), and thus fits the '*politischen* Charakter' of the present (Spiess, p. 110; emphasis in original).

In 1842 a critic writes in a review of *Süden und Norden* ('South and North'): 'Was können wir eifriger wünschen, als unsre eignen Schwächen, namentlich unsre ganze politische Verkommenheit in dem Spiegel des amerikanischen Jungbrunnens recht deutlich, ja recht grell zu erblicken?' (Spiess, p. 135). ('What can we desire more eagerly than to see our own weaknesses, especially our state of political degradation, distinctly, indeed harshly, mirrored in the rejuvenating well of America?') This rhetorical question may illustrate the challenge which the element of political enlightenment in Sealsfield's novels obviously represented for many German readers. This shows how far readers managed to respond to the effect Sealsfield intended (formulated most clearly in the dedication of the *Lebensbilder*) and to apply it to their own situation.

In the years before 1848, a number of critics with very diverse standpoints regarded Sealsfield's fiction as pointing the literary and political direction in which they hoped the German novel would develop. As early as 1837 the reviewer in the *Literarische Zeitung* described it as 'für die Romanliteratur [...] Epoche machend' ('marking an epoch in the literary novel'), and as creating 'eine neue Gattung für die Romanpoesie' ('a new genre for the poetry of the novel'; Spiess, p. 85). In the same year Hermann Marggraff writes that Sealsfield has 'die Grenzpfähle auf dem Terrain des deutschen Romans weiter hinausgeschoben' ('pushed forward the boundary posts on the terrain of the German novel') and is the leading figure among contemporary novelists (*ibid.*, pp. 371f.). Writing in the *Königsberger Literatur-Blatt* in 1842, Alexander Jung prophesies that 'dieser Schriftsteller, wie ganz er der *Gegenwart* angehört, und namentlich auch ihren wichtigen *politischen* Charakter trefflich in Worte überträgt, für die Zukunft unendlich mehr Gewicht noch haben [wird] als etwa der bloße *Geschichtschreiber* der Jetztzeit; denn jener ist Dichter und Psycholog und Politiker und Historiker *zugleich*' ('completely as this writer belongs to the *present*, and, above all, admirably puts into words its important *political* character, he will have infinitely more significance for the future than the mere modern-day *historian*; for he is a poet and psychologist and politician and historian *at once*'; Spiess, p. 110). In the *Dresdner Abend-Zeitung* of 1846 it is stressed 'daß Sealsfield's Schriften eine neue Bahn in der deutschen Literatur eröffnet haben' ('that Sealsfield's writings have blazed a new trail in German literature'; Spiess, p. 157). The *Gesellschafter* observes in 1847:

> Kein Roman-Dichter der Gegenwart verbindet mit solchem Erfassen der Lebens-Wirklichkeit aus dem Vollen ein so klares Verständniß seiner Zeit, seines Volkes und eine so großartige Anschauung der politischen Bewegung, welche die Welt-Geschichte unaufhaltsam in ihre Bahnen reißt. *Sealsfield* ist ebenso phantasiebegabter Dichter wie tiefblickender Politiker, die Dichtung wird bei ihm geschichtliche und philosophische Wahrheit, wie seine Philosophie und Politik treibendes, wogendes Leben (Spiess, p. 146).

> [There is no other novelist at the present day who combines such a grasp of life's full reality with such a clear understanding of his age and his people and such a lofty view of the political movement which is dragging world history irresistibly in its wake. *Sealsfield* is both a poet endowed with imagination and a far-sighted politician; in his hands poetry becomes historical and philosophical truth, just as his philosophy and politics are moving, surging life.]

While Sealsfield's achievement in establishing the 'democratic' novel is widely praised by critics,[11] this also supplies one of the principal reasons why this author came to be disparaged and ignored after the middle of the century. Political aspects, especially liberal democratic ones, were excluded from literary criticism's scale of values. From the 1850s onwards, democratic fiction was downgraded in favour of novels that were committed to liberal nationalism under the guise of self-styled objectivity.

Once the political content of Sealsfield's novels is lost from sight, all that is left are works of exoticism and ethnography. For a long time histories of literature classified Sealsfield in these categories, as the author of a special type of novel, thus isolating him from the mainstream of German fiction. It followed logically that the works were deprived of their historical and political context, with their political references and reflections being dismissed as irritating excrescences. Thus purged and reduced to adventure stories, the novels were treated as harmless books for teenage boys.

The political developments after 1848 also brought about far-reaching changes in conceptions of the novel and of realism, as the bourgeois liberal values of the programmatic realists triumphed over the democratic outlook of the *Vormärz*. As a result, serious formal and stylistic objections were raised against Sealsfield's works. Critics who relied on a stricter conception of form, based on values like order and measure, charged them with lack of discipline ('Zuchtlosigkeit'). The ideal of a balanced linguistic register, aiming at the middle style, also caused their rhetorical diversity of tones to be questioned.

On all these counts, Sealsfield's novels came to be regarded negatively. Only in the last twenty years have we begun to appreciate some of their peculiarities. The link between literature and enlightened political aims is now seen without prejudice. Thanks to our tendency to place literature in a historical framework and to take seriously the way in which it was understood by contemporaries, normative judgements seem increasingly problematic. Now that novel theory and criticism form part of the history of the novel, the traditional image of this genre is being modified. Prejudices against lack of formal discipline have diminished since the development of the genre in the early twentieth century has accustomed us to the expansion of the novel by the insertion of learned disquisitions. Our interest in the effect of literature on its readers has made us pay more attention to its critical reception and reduced our reservations against its capacity to entertain.

In my view, however, the most important recent insight is that Sealsfield, as I have described, was led by his political views to new themes and social models, and in the course of depicting them found his way to new modes of writing and communication. It was not least his political conception of the novel as a means of liberal enlightenment that enabled him to enrich German fiction by aspects that it had previously lacked.

Charles Sealsfield

Notes

This essay summarises the findings of various earlier studies of Sealsfield; the second part is a revised translation of the chapter 'Romane als "Aufklärungsmittel". Charles Sealsfields Werke in der Gattungsdiskussion des Vormärz' from my book *Romanpoetik von Goethe bis Thomas Mann: Entwicklungen und Probleme der 'demokratischen Kunstform' in Deutschland* (Munich, 1987), pp. 116–29. I am grateful to the publisher, Wilhelm Fink Verlag, for permission to have parts of this chapter translated.

1. My views on the questions about the nineteenth-century German novel raised in the introductory sections are developed and substantiated at more length in various works, most recently in the book cited above, where I also provide a fuller analysis of the extensive critical literature on this topic.
2. Thomas Mann, 'Die Kunst des Romans', in his *Gesammelte Werke*, 13 vols (Frankfurt, 1974), vol. X, p. 361.
3. For an introductory appreciation of Sealsfield's novels, see Jeffrey L. Sammons, 'Land of Limited Possibilities: America in the Nineteenth-Century German Novel', *Yale Review*, 68 (1978), 35–52.
4. Sealsfield's works are quoted from the reprint edition, *Sämtliche Werke*, ed. Karl J. R. Arndt (Hildesheim and New York, 1972 —). The most important recent studies are: Frank Schüppen, *Charles Sealsfield: Karl Postl: ein österreichischer Erzähler der Biedermeierzeit im Spannungsfeld von Alter und Neuer Welt* (Frankfurt and Berne, 1981); Walter Grünzweig, *Das demokratische Kanaan: Charles Sealsfields Amerika im Kontext amerikanischer Literatur und Ideologie* (Munich, 1987); Günter Schnitzler, *Erfahrung und Bild: Die dichterische Wirklichkeit des Charles Sealsfield (Karl Postl)* (Freiburg, 1988).
5. Sealsfield, letter to Cotta, 3 January 1828. Quoted from Eduard Castle, *Der große Unbekannte: Das Leben von Charles Sealsfield (Karl Postl). Briefe und Aktenstücke* (Vienna, 1955), p. 144.
6. See *Charles Sealsfields Werke im Spiegel der literarischen Kritik: Eine Sammlung zeitgenössischer Rezensionen.* ed. Reinhard F. Spiess (Stuttgart, 1977), quoted as Spiess. The influence of the preface is revealed by long quotations and critical reactions in several reviews: see Spiess, pp. 59, 60, 61f., 70, 72ff., 86.
7. Sealsfield, letter to Brockhaus, 21 June 1854, in Castle, pp. 291f.
8. See Spiess, pp. 34, 86 ('Roman der Wirklichkeit'), 122, 131 ('[will] eine wirkliche Welt schildern'), 138, 144, 146 ('Erfassen der Lebens-Wirklichkeit'), 150 ('getreuer Spiegel der Wirklichkeit').
9. For similar parallels and moral applications see Spiess, pp. 59, 98, 109, 117, 127, 136.
10. On the political problematic represented by such models, and in general on the content of Sealsfield's political concepts, see Schüppen, pp. 280ff.
11. The first history of the German novel by Oskar Ludwig Bernhard Wolff, in its second (1850) edition, ends with an enthusiastic reference to Sealsfield, whose works are said to have established the democratic principle in the novel: Wolff, *Allgemeine Geschichte des Romans, von dessen Ursprung bis zur neuesten Zeit*, 2nd edn (Jena, 1850), p. 727.

Josephinism, 'Austrianness', and the Revolution of 1848

R. J. W. Evans

Joseph II had his share in the outbreak of the Viennese Revolution of 1848. Monday 13 March, when the Lower Austrian estates assembled on the Herrengasse for a meeting of the opposition which many expected would critically embarrass the government, was the anniversary of his birth; a fact not lost on the crowds who drifted past the Emperor's statue on the Josefsplatz to witness developments at the Landhaus, and invoked his name in their protests.[1] It might seem ironical that Joseph, who had done so much to assert the authority of the Habsburgs, could be thus associated with events which over the next months came close to destroying their state. But in the death-throes of the Metternichian age, Joseph stood both for the evils of the system and for remedies to them. That fact, and the conflicting, even contradictory, sets of loyalties which it mirrored, deserve some elucidation in the context of the lasting cultural impact of the Austrian Enlightenment.

'Josephinism', the governmental programme particularly associated with Joseph – though his mother, Maria Theresa, played a large part in conceiving and implementing it – had consisted of three broad overlapping areas of domestic policy.[2] Firstly it had sought a reform of society, reducing the corporate privileges of nobles and urban elites, encouraging prosperity and promoting welfare. Secondly it had aimed to enhance state control in the ecclesiastical sphere, harnessing the material and spiritual resources of the churches, above all of the dominant Catholic interest, to more rational, tolerant and secular purposes identified by the regime. Thirdly it had constructed a large central administration based in Vienna, into which it tried to inculcate the virtues of efficiency, commitment, and loyalty. At root this last quality was crucial, and Joseph constantly endeavoured to advance in his servants and in the population at large an identity with the Austrian state and a sense of common citizenship within it. Advisers to the dynasty, like Sonnenfels, propagated a semi-official cult of patriotism (*Vaterlandsliebe*) which prepared the way, psychologically at least, for the dissolution of the Holy Roman Empire and its replacement with a kind of 'Austrian Empire' (the approved designation was 'vereinigter österreichischer Staatenkörper') in 1804–6.[3]

The measures adopted by Maria Theresa and especially by Joseph II were, of course, very controversial; many proved ineffective, some were stillborn. Yet they did generate enthusiasm, particularly within the expanding ranks of those who made careers as government employees. Moreover – a highly important consideration for our purposes – they became intimately associated with the rising German culture of the redirected body politic. Not only had German clearly taken over from Latin, Italian, French and Spanish as the language of public affairs in Austria, leaving only limited scope and subordinate status for the other vernaculars of the Monarchy; it assumed modern literary pretensions at the same time, finding an intellectual focus in the Habsburg court theatre, renamed National-Theater by Joseph when he brought it under his personal management from 1776. Vienna witnessed feverish intellectual activity and a spate of publications in the 1780s and earlier 1790s, whose inspiration derived directly from the Josephinist political debates of the day. The Emperor's headstrong onslaught on tradition and superstition, as Bodi has argued, furnished Austrian writers with their *Sturm und Drang*.[4]

The onset of European revolution and war restrained, but did not extinguish these initiatives. The most tangible witness to the Josephinist legacy was the massive equestrian statue of the Emperor, commissioned in the 1790s, which took the sculptor Franz Zauner years to complete.[5] Its eventual unveiling in November 1807 coincided with a further serious attempt to generate patriotism for the reconstituted Austrian Monarchy, now under desperate threat from France. Again the chief means adopted was a literary campaign in German under official sponsorship, orchestrated by the historian Hormayr and symbolised by his new journal with its revealing title, *Vaterländische Blätter für den österreichischen Kaiserstaat* ('Patriotic Pages for the Austrian Imperial State'). Native-born intellectuals, like Hormayr and the poet Castelli, co-operated with some notable immigrants – Gentz, the Schlegel brothers, Eichendorff, Brentano – to broadcast the message of German–Austrian solidarity under Habsburg aegis, although it soon fell victim to Napoleon's invasion and victory at Wagram.[6]

With the consolidation of Austria's international position after 1815, conditions might have appeared fruitful for a return to the principles of Josephinism at home. Reformist ideas were available: in the new code of civil law, for example, enacted in 1811; or in the economic management of the Hofkammer under Stadion, who had been foreign minister in 1807–9; or in the powerful progressive impetus in medicine and public hygiene. The civil constitution of the Austrian clergy remained in force, with firm restraints laid upon any manifestations of ecclesiastical autonomy, not least in the sphere of education. The administrative machine continued to expand, and no real concessions were made to any devolution of decision-making. With it the sense of German cultural mission survived intact; indeed, it was to yield rich fruit in the writings of the *Vormärz*.

We can identify the adherents of this Josephinist tradition at various levels of officialdom, from the very top, where it continued to find important carriers among aristocrats, mainly from Bohemia and Moravia, with their long record of service to the dynasty. Dietrichsteins and Kolowrats, Liechtensteins and

Colloredos, Chorinskys and Choteks still formed something of a governmental *parti de mouvement*, and dispensed lavish patronage (not least upon the theatre). But these Whiggish ministers and heads of department entertained somewhat divided loyalties: their commitment to social change, to Erastian churchmanship, even to thoroughgoing centralism had its limits – Count Franz Anton Kolowrat illustrates both their strengths and their weaknesses in the decades before 1848.[7] Middle-rank government officials (*Beamte*), mainly bourgeois, anti-clerical, and strongly involved in the intellectual life of Vienna, afford more classic evidence of *homo Josephinus*; they demonstrate, moreover, a clear line of filiation from the 1780s, through the salon formed at that time by Hofrat Greiner and continued by his daughter, Caroline Pichler (if not by her bureaucratic husband who, as readers of Caroline's sprightly memoirs will recall, was always too busy with his papers at the Hofkammer to participate).[8]

Prominent in the Pichler circle was Franz Grillparzer, likewise a Josephinist by extraction: his lawyer father had compiled an anti-papal dissertation in the 1780s and died full of mortification at the failure of the new Austrian state after 1800. Resentful of privilege, dismissive of ecclesiastical authority, convinced of the need for administrative action to hasten the civilising process in the Monarchy, Grillparzer embodied the precepts we have identified, and he lived them out during his long career with the Hofkammer, which culminated in the post of archive director (albeit Joseph II had actually abolished the Hofkammer in an abortive institutional purge!).[9] So did his friends and fellow dramatists Eduard Bauernfeld, who spent decades as an official in the state Lottery, and Ignaz Castelli, a tax collector with the Lower Austrian estates. Castelli's reminiscences are full of further *Beamte* of similar persuasion, as are the pages of a younger monument to the same ideals, Wurzbach's *Biographisches Lexikon*: a good example would be the Silesian poet, Joseph Christian von Zedlitz, who served in Metternich's State Chancery.[10] These were the men who did most to sustain the personal cult of Joseph. Verses inspired by the statue on the Josefsplatz belong among Grillparzer's best-known; the same theme also occupied Zedlitz and – as we shall see – Anastasius Grün, who powerfully captured the self-willed Emperor's tragic flaw:

> Ein Despot bist du gewesen! Doch ein solcher wie der Tag
> Dessen Sonne Nacht und Nebel neben sich nicht dulden mag.
>
> [Thou wert a despot! But such a one as the day whose sun cannot tolerate night and mist beside it.]

A less honourable character, Anton Gross-Hoffinger, who pursued a devious career in and out of the Habsburg service, compiled the first extensive biography of the Emperor. 'All that Austria is and can still be', he wrote, 'it has become through Joseph.'[11]

Such sentiments evinced that loyalty to the state which was typical of Josephinists. When Grillparzer, who may well have used the late and great ruler of Austria as prototype for the figure of Rudolf I in his *König Ottokar*, applied for promotion, he pointed out that 'I have done honour to my Fatherland through works of literature'.[12] But here lay the fundamental problem for patriots in the *Vormärz* Monarchy: for if these were official postures, they were not, most of the time, governmental ones. The regime increasingly set its face against any manifestations of popular enthusiasm, even those supportive of the state. Meanwhile the tide of legislation initiated by the enlightened absolutists, with its strident calls for devotion to the common weal, was stilled; the administration lost its direction and sense of purpose. From the turn of the century, then especially after the events of 1809, an arid dynastic loyalism resumed the place of the *Staatsgefühl* so dear to Joseph. In 1813 Franz I crossed the word 'Vaterland' out of an imperial manifesto and wrote 'Kaiser' instead. In 1821 the 'national' theatre was ordered to revert to the designation 'Hofburgtheater'. In 1828 the ideologue of Austrian patriotism, Hormayr, quit the country in dudgeon.[13]

The most notorious aspect of the age of Metternich in the Habsburg lands was its panoply of censorship and surveillance, built up from the late 1790s in close association with the forces of public order and the secret police.[14] This clumsy apparatus of restraint, besides working to squander sympathies for the Austrian Monarchy at home and abroad, showed its cutting edge precisely against *Beamte*. They stood to lose their livelihood if convicted, or even suspected, of any contravention of the elaborate, often impenetrable regulations against misuse of office or breach of official confidentiality (*Amtsgeheimnis*); black marks on their personal file (*Conduiteliste*) could block the promotion of 'patriots' or even 'friends of literature' who transgressed the bounds of a passive, filial devotion to the dynasty.[15] Thus censorship alienated many of the state's best servants, without achieving the suppression of their ideas. At the same time, all attempts to evade it *ipso facto* appeared as anti-Austrian gestures: they pointed towards an alternative, German identity which the authorities, apart from ineffective measures of an isolationist kind, did nothing to counteract.

There is no doubt that Austrian intellectuals in this period saw themselves as indissolubly part of some wider German culture. First and foremost in the linguistic sense, of course, a fact vindicated by their use of a literary language which rested rather on a northern than on a southern dialect; but in a geopolitical sense too. Grillparzer could only assert his essential Austrianness by differentiating himself from 'the rest of Germany' (*sic*). His tribute to the shade of Joseph II twice employs broader Teutonic imagery ('des deutschen Adlers Sonnenflug', 'Spiegel deutscher Lehr'), but pointedly avoids any Austrian epithets – only Grillparzer's withering criticisms of contemporary conditions were clearly reserved for his own land. We may recall that his King Ottokar, in a rousing speech, calls for the injection of German, not Austrian, values into thirteenth-century Bohemia.[16] Bauernfeld, while recognising the division of Germany into a multiplicity of fatherlands, by 1844 looked to the Zollverein to draw them together; and his play of that year, *Ein deutscher Krieger* ('A German Warrior'), stood squarely on the terrain of the national movement. Even the homespun Adalbert Stifter, at the end of his poignant fable *Brigitta*, set in Hungary, has his narrator don 'deutsches Gewand', grasp a 'deutscher Stab', and make his way back to his 'deutsches Vaterland', whereas it is evidently Austria to which he is returning.[17]

With the German orientation went a frequent espousal, from the end of the 1820s onward, of the prevailing liberal mood of intellectual criticism in the rest of the Confederation. The first Austrian milestone in this direction was *Austria As It Is* by Karl Postl (Charles Sealsfield), which appeared anonymously in English in 1828. That celebrated but rather crude diatribe coincided with Julius Franz Schneller's maturer historical reflections on *Oesterreichs Einfluß auf Deutschland und Europa seit der Reformation* ('Austria's Influence on Germany and Europe since the Reformation') which contain fulsome praise of Joseph and draw a sharp contrast between him and subsequent emperors. The second milestone soon followed, with the no less virulent *Spaziergänge eines Wiener Poeten* ('Strolls of a Viennese Poet') published anonymously by the aristocrat Anton Auersperg, alias Anastasius Grün. His witty and polished verse abounds in generalised Teutonic allusions: 'Germanias Geist', 'deutsche Ehre', 'der deutschen Sprache Einheit ... der deutschen Treue Reinheit'.[18] He also illustrates another characteristic of Austrian authors of this committed German literature: they tended to originate on the peripheries of the Monarchy, where Germans were outnumbered by other nationalities. Grün came from Carniola (Krain), 'im äußersten Süden Deutschlands' ('in the extreme south of Germany') as he put it. Moritz Hartmann, composer of verses on 'Deutsche Poeten', 'Deutsche Freiheitslieder', and 'Der deutsche Knecht', was Bohemian, like his fellow poet Alfred Meissner, as well as the pamphleteers Kuranda and Schuselka (and Postl). Lenau, who inserted into his *Faust* one of the most powerful indictments of the Metternichian system, had grown up in Hungary, like Karl Beck.[19]

Such writers, it may be argued, formed from afar an idealised model of German culture – the more so as several of them were assimilated Jews – and carried it with them from the Austrian provinces into that larger Fatherland where they could publish, and where, in most cases, they had to settle as emigrés. Their sentiments may certainly be reckoned liberal, even radical, by the standards of the day; but they were also good Josephinists for the most part in their concern with material advance, their anti-clerical stance, their enthusiasm for efficient central administration on German lines ('das Übergewicht des deutschen Prinzips auf freiwilligem Wege', or 'the voluntary predominance of the German principle', in Grillparzer's words). By the mid-1840s this programme began to reassert itself uneasily within the Habsburg regime – as the mordant Beidtel observed, a good deal of it had survived in the interstices of government, provided it called itself 'Cultur' rather than 'Aufklärung' and made much of its 'virtue' and devotion to the authorities.[20] Bureaucratic tensions hardened, while progressives like the acting Bohemian-Austrian Chancellor Pillersdorf gained ground. New forums for intellectual activity were created, notably the Imperial Academy of Sciences, and censorship began to crumble. From November 1846, with Kolowrat's help, Bauernfeld was able to stage his new comedy *Großjährig* ('Of Age') in which the young Baron Hermann manages to turn the tables on his egregious, scheming guardian Blase. The play's success rested, not on any action, but on the contest between the latter (literally 'Blister' or 'Bubble'), with his ludicrous Metternichian slogans ('Abwarten ... das ist das Hauptgeheimniß einer guten Administration' – 'Wait and see – that is the main secret of good administration') and his equally absurd foil Schmerl, the apostle of opposition for its own sake.[21] Patriotic reformers now found themselves manoeuvring between the conservative Scylla and a constitutional Charybdis.

The latter-day Josephinists of the *Vormärz* faced a third rival too, historically the most fundamental of all: renascent clerical intellectuals. Eighteenth-century Erastianism had laid low the Baroque forms of Austrian Catholic observance and encouraged new rational and reformist kinds of churchmanship. After 1800 the regime viewed progressive priests with as much suspicion as other kinds of progressive; it took action to muzzle and, if necessary, to chastise them, especially by its campaign against Bernard Bolzano and his adherents in Bohemia. But the government of Franz I and Metternich did not undo state controls over the Church: jurisdictional rivalries, particularly over marriage and education, remained a basic issue, as in contemporary Prussia, or just across the border in Hungary. When Catholic revival reached the Habsburg lands in the Romantic age, it could not identify itself with official Austrian positions any more than could liberalism.[22]

The early years of the nineteenth century witnessed the gathering in Vienna of a thoroughly international group persuaded of the need for a reassertion of clerical values. Its focus was the Redemptorist priest, Clemens Maria Hofbauer, who, though born in Moravia, had returned from over twenty years in Poland; its leaven a number of prominent Catholics, mainly converts, from Germany – the Schlegels, Adam Müller, Zacharias Werner – and other outsiders like the Hungarian magnate, Ferenc Széchényi. Later immigrants, among them Jarcke and Phillips from Prussia, Hurter and Meyer from Switzerland, sustained the cosmopolitan ideals of these ultramontanes, who remained for the most part as remote from the traditions of the Austrian Baroque as they were hostile to the Austrian Enlightenment. When Friedrich Schlegel lectured in 1812 on 'National-Erinnerungen' as 'the most glorious inheritance which a people can have', he seems to have been blissfully unaware of the incendiary implications for Austria of that proposition.[23]

Like their intellectual enemies – for whose ideology they appear at some point just before 1848 to have coined the term 'Josephinism'[24] – the clericals unleashed literary venom against the immobility of the *Vormärz* regime. Young Sebastian Brunner's satirical tirades against the administrative elite furnish the best evidence of that. Again like the Josephinists, however, the ultramontane movement had footholds within the governmental system and began to gain ground there in the 1840s. Reading the memoirs of Castelli and Caroline Pichler, or Beidtel's anatomy of the Habsburg bureaucracy, one is reminded of the continued loyalties to traditional Catholicism of some public servants. A number of bishops, like Zängerle of Seckau, waged an effective campaign from within for the immunities and privileges of the Church.[25] The affair of the Zillertal Protestants and the readmission of the Jesuits indicated a shift in the same direction after the death of Franz I. With time Metternich's own attitude towards the Church clearly changed: he now came to regard it as at least a useful ally. Witness his patronage of the clerics Rauscher and Brunner from 1844, and then of Meyer and Hurter, who was created court historiographer.[26]

This cautious accommodation between government and clerical opposition only provoked among Josephinists the most furious anti-clerical backlash of the whole period, including poetic invective from Grillparzer and Grün and Lenau's dramatic adaptation of episodes from the history of the Albigensians and Hussites. It culminated in the support shown from inside the Habsburg lands for the breakaway sect of German Catholics. One of the founders of the *Deutschkatholiken* was Franz Schuselka, a publicist from Budweis, whose editorial accomplishments included a revised version of the notorious 'Constantinople Letters', that spurious testimony to Joseph's enlightened principles. Schuselka and his like evidently saw themselves as thus linking the ideal of the Austrian state with that of the German nation. Now it was the turn of Catholics to reply with fury, and to visit both spiritual and civil anathemas on the upstart national church.[27]

On the whole, nevertheless, Austrian intellectual life, whether Josephinist or anti-Josephinist, remained more marked on the eve of 1848 by its alienation from government than by its half-hearted moves towards conciliation. Yet that did not mean an absence of Austrian patriotism. After all, the notion of 'patriot' had strong associations with oppositional movements through the late eighteenth century and beyond;[28] and critics of the *Vormärz* ancien regime in the Habsburg lands retained domestic loyalties alongside their wider German or ultramontane orientation. The most famous case is probably that of Grillparzer, who gave one of the lesser characters in his *König Ottokar* – a play badly mauled by the censor – a rousing set speech about the attractions of Austria. The timorous and conservative Grillparzer always tended to emphasize the advantages of Habsburg rule, at least as an ideal of stability and humanity; important themes in his later play, *Ein Bruderzwist in Habsburg*, have been recognised to form a commentary on the perils of radical and doctrinaire change in the 1840s.[29] But his fellow writers likewise incorporate local colour prominently, whether in the Hungarian atmosphere invoked by Lenau and Beck, or in the Bohemian settings for Ebert, Hartmann or Stifter. Grün's *Spaziergänge* convey a clear Austrian, and mainly Viennese, flavour, for all their hostility to the political status quo there. Emigrés like Hartmann and Meissner bemoan at times their exile from the charms of the *Heimat;* even the rancorous journalist Kuranda in Leipzig looked to the creation of a 'große österreichische Nation' in the future.[30]

Such 'national' consciousness was markedly enhanced in these decades by enthusiasm for Austrian history. Again, the dramatic literature of the time furnishes rich evidence of patriotic plots, even if (or precisely because?) their subject-matter was often found offensive by the authorities. More sober scholarship started to address the evolution of the *Kaiserstaat* and to project back contemporary concerns accordingly. In such chroniclers as Hormayr and Schneller the rise of the Habsburgs found its *raison d'être* and retrospective vindication in the Josephinist legacy – both authors had fallen out with the government by the end of the 1820s. The Catholic camp identified different priorities: thus Caroline Pichler wrote a play about the Counter-Reforming Emperor Ferdinand II; though even that combination of Habsburg hero and irreproachably loyal authoress fell foul of the censor (incongruously enough it later reappeared under the title *Christian of Denmark*). Later Brunner began to appeal specifically to native cultural and religious traditions destroyed by Maria Theresa and Joseph, condemning the cosmopolitan cancer of liberalism in the name of Austrian peasants, teachers and workers through splenetic and earthy verse.[31]

The most influential of all *Vormärz* broadsides against the Habsburgs was likewise a plea for more, rather than less, Austrianness. Victor von Andrian-Werburg commenced the first volume of his *Oesterreich und dessen Zukunft* (Austria and its Future, 1842) with a lament at the absence of any national unity or even identity, and went on to indict the bureaucracy precisely as being an un-Austrian parasitical growth. He thus presented himself as an anti-Josephinist; yet his remedy, an increase in *Gemeinsinn,* or public spirit, besides drawing on the earlier Prussian reform model and on the contemporary Hungarian cult of civic virtue led by the younger Széchenyi, also evidently harked back to Joseph. The detailed proposals which Andrian-Werburg published four years later sought to awaken Austrian patriotism and to save the state before time ran out. So did the pamphleteering efforts of other loyalists, like the army officer Karl Moering, who on the eve of revolution still found himself forced to declare that 'the Austrian has no Fatherland'.[32]

Understandable as an expression of frustratedness, that was certainly an exaggerated claim. What anyway rendered it increasingly inaccurate was ironically the very intellectual process which we have been examining. Whether or not creative German-language writing of the 1830s and 1840s in the Habsburg lands amounted to a 'specific and autonomous Austrian literature', as has been claimed, it assuredly fed upon, and in its turn stimulated, a sense of distinctive achievements and of the peculiarities of the domestic situation.[33] We need not concern ourselves with the relative shares of Weimar classicism, of native tradition, and of the social and political milieu of the *Vormärz* in this development. Suffice it to conclude that in the age of Grillparzer and Bauernfeld, of Nestroy and Raimund, of Lenau and Stifter, the Austrian contribution to Biedermeier must form an essential part of the definition of that controverted style.[34]

The Revolution, so much prefigured in the writings of Andrian-Werburg and others, so unexpected when it actually broke out, drew explicitly and protractedly on the Josephinist heritage. Not only did the Emperor's statue, surrounded by a citizens' guard of honour and with a placard proclaiming press freedom placed in its grasp, provide a symbolic focus, as we have already seen. Not only was the Emperor's personality much invoked, whether in public debate, especially when peasant emancipation came before the Reichstag, or in anecdotal publicity like Gräffer's *Josephinische Curiosa*.[35] The actual conduct of government fell to men reared in the centralist administrative tradition: Pillersdorf, Doblhoff, Bach, Schmerling, and others, all active in Viennese politics before 1848, now had their chance to achieve measured reform through the same official channels. Pillersdorf, chief minister between May and July, saw revolution as a temporary disturbance in a continuous process, which – in his own topical metaphor – put better drivers into the cab of the locomotive of state.[36]

The events of March 1848 reopened the question of identity. At first they seemed to herald a revived enthusiasm for Austria's mission. Early pamphlets urged the need for patriotism in this sense, to underpin new open, popular government. Grillparzer's first poetic response began simply:

> Sei mir gegrüßt, mein Österreich![37]
>
> [Hail to you, my Austria]

Grün and Bauernfeld glossed this sentiment in their own initial appeal for calm:

> Let us not be led by distant influences from some foreign part, and let us reflect that we are in the first place sons of a great and glorious Fatherland which we have to sustain, that we are Austrians and as such called to order for ourselves our own affairs. Harmony and concord for order and right. Österreich über alles!

Their friend Ernst von Feuchtersleben, a prominent anticlerical scholar and poet of the *Vormärz*, whose Josephinist sympathies were underlined by his work as a medical reformer, joined the Ministry of Education and set himself to institute major progressive legislation there, training 'future citizens' in the service of the 'holy will of the Fatherland'.[38]

During the spring of 1848, however, more conservative commentators became disillusioned by the ever accelerating pace of change. Bauernfeld, who had resigned his post in the Lottery in order to participate in the riskier venture of political mediation, soon withdrew, from a mixture of frustration and illness. Castelli, having joined the National Guard and written explanatory reform tracts for the peasantry, had to retreat to Lilienfeld Abbey to evade his detractors.[39] Most spectacularly, Grillparzer penned a salute to the Habsburg army in Italy, as the repository of Austrian identity (apart from its famous first stanza surely one of his feeblest pieces of doggerel), and found himself the subject of a torrent of abuse from progressives. He too fled into the country, then returned to pass the rest of the summer in the highly un-revolutionary occupation of shifting the Hofkammer archive from one Viennese repository to another.[40]

These months witnessed also the summoning of the Pre-Parliament and then the Parliament to Frankfurt, and thus the renewed blandishments of a German orientation, enhanced by an obvious reluctance on the part of the Habsburg court to accept its changed circumstances with good grace. Grün, who accepted a mandate to represent Carniola at Frankfurt, laid out his view of the issue clearly:

> My attitude (*Gesinnung*) is in truth decidedly German. ... But unfortunately the long separation has left behind it a deep gulf of mutual alienation

which only appeared to have been overcome by the goodwill of the first fresh exchange of greetings. ... German-Austria is a branch (*Expositur*) of the German Motherland with a special mission in the interests of Germany.

Yet Grün, as a modest and aristocratic liberal, soon withdrew from active politics, and left the field to more radical spirits. These continued to acknowledge a debt to Joseph: they decorated his statue with a black-red-gold banner for the visit of Frankfurt deputies to Vienna in July.[41]

As in Joseph's time, so in 1848, Austria's 'German question' was partly a practical one, with the problem of the language of administration now overshadowed by that of the language of debate at the Reichstag.[42] In the mid-nineteenth century, however, the emotional pull of German linguistic culture had become vastly more intense; and as in the *Vormärz* period its extreme votaries tended to be intellectuals from the periphery of the Habsburg lands and/or the periphery of established society, like Hartmann, Meissner and Herloßsohn from Bohemia or Fischhof and Goldmark from Hungary. Yet this party too resisted any full association with Great-Germandom at the expense of suitably reconstituted domestic structures based on Vienna: even the insurrection of October, after all, represented a last desperate bid to capture the existing apparatus of government. As Karl Beidtel put it in a speech to the Frankfurt Parliament on 24 October: 'Austrian Germans will be Germans – so long as you do not unreasonably insist that they cease being Austrians.'[43]

The awkward postures dictated by the dilemma of 'Germanness' versus 'Austrianness' furnished good material for satire. The arch-Viennese Nestroy poured scorn on all concerned in his *Freiheit in Krähwinkel*. More inconsequential as theatre, but also more revealing, is the extended new conclusion which Bauernfeld wrote to his *Großjährig* and which was performed to 'großes Brouhaha' early in 1849.[44] Hermann returns as a 'neuer Mensch' and after some uncertainty is really engaged to Blase's niece (exactly what the old guardian had intended, but for quite different reasons). This fresh episode reveals all the participants to have had some share in the novelties of the intervening year – even Blase sports a moustache – while the German cause clearly enjoys general favour. 'German spirit and word, language and culture,' says Hermann, 'and now German freedom, which is no longer a mere figment: that is our German present (*Gegenwart*).' Nearer to the taste of the jaundiced author, however, is perhaps the grotesque figure of Schmerl, wearing a black-red-gold sash – beneath his waistcoat.

Although the appropriation of Josephinism to Great-German purposes during 1848 did not seriously compromise the reputation of the *Volkskaiser* as patron saint of reformists at home, it did allow the anti-Josephinist camp to speak with a more unambiguously Austrian voice. The clericals remained a cosmopolitan band, but in Rauscher and the still youthful Brunner they now had vigorous and authentically Viennese leaders, attempting to wrest control of the Catholic Church from the older conciliatory generation epitomised by the venerable

Archbishop Milde (whose name quaintly matched his character). Brunner's *Wiener Kirchen-Zeitung* waged war on alien influences; as in the *Vormärz*, this campaign was tinged with anti-Semitism – again a clear repudiation of the principles of Joseph. One of its foremost targets in 1848 were the *Deutschkatholiken*, whose movement made converts rapidly during the Revolution. By the summer their services in Vienna had become so popular that they moved to the main hall of the Musikverein, where prominent liberal and German-national leaders addressed the throng.[45]

Altogether, religious questions occupied a much more important place in the imbroglio of 1848–9 in Central Europe than historians have tended to accord them. And whereas Austrian representatives left Vienna ceremoniously for the Frankfurt Pre-Parliament with an archiepiscopal blessing, the clash between liberals and ultramontanes came to dominate the debate. Weeks of the Reichstag's time were given over to confessional issues, and Josephinists in government and at the assembly found themselves caught between two stools.[46] As the bureaucratic ministry of Pillersdorf and his successors gradually ceded power to a military and aulic faction around Windischgrätz and Schwarzenberg, so a new and militant clerical establishment could assert itself. Its first strike was against the German Catholics: like their Christian Social descendants at the end of the nineteenth century, Rauscher and his supporters proved more than equal to this prototype of *Los von Rom* agitation. By 1849 Austrian bishops were at last ready to proceed in a similar fashion, and with official backing, against the vestiges of state control over the Church. In this crucial aspect of Josephinist activity, the Revolution seemed to have precipitated the final demise of the Emperor's work. The stage was set for the Concordat of 1855, a dramatic retreat from national sovereignty, but also distinctively Austrian, not least – paradoxically – in the extent of its sell-out to the cosmopolitan principles of nineteenth-century Roman Catholicism.

In other respects, however, the new Habsburg absolutism of the 1850s, under a young ruler who deliberately added his great predecessor's name to the plain 'Franz' he had been born with, did much more to sustain Josephinist initiatives than had that of the *Vormärz*. Ruthlessly centralised administrative machinery was instituted, both as an end in itself and as a vehicle for the pursuit of material progress and social justice. Initially, at least, many of the liberal bureaucrats of 1848 and before joined the regime. Moreover, deliberate efforts were made to cultivate more of an Austrian image, with official publicity of all kinds, especially through the educational system as reconstructed by Count Leo Thun, who as a rising aristocratic politician before 1848 had already made a serious attempt to combine Josephinist reform with Romantic loyalty to the Roman Catholic cause. The 1850s thus saw the development of a consciously *großösterreichisch* ideology of state, which proclaimed a tighter confederacy in Central Europe under Habsburg aegis and the dominance of German values within the lands of the dynasty. Many of the most energetic propagators of this ideology were actually German immigrants, like the Minister of Commerce, Karl Bruck, or the political theorist, Lorenz Stein, or the former hero of the Jungdeutschland movement, Heinrich Laube – even a younger brother of Heinrich Heine, who became editor of a government newspaper. But it swept local Josephinist tradition along with it. 'The glorification of my Fatherland', wrote Grillparzer in 1856, when requesting retirement on full pay because of failing eyesight, 'was always one of my prime considerations.'[49] Stifter was not the only intellectual to discover a mission of service to the public good (in his case as a school inspector); nor Meissner the only poet to flaunt openly nationalist sentiments.

The experiment carried the seeds of its own failure. On the one hand, internal conflicts within the Austro-German camp between liberal-progressive and conservative-clerical positions proved unbridgeable. Thun was a rare exception in embracing both standpoints, and he earned much opprobrium as a consequence. Thus was underlined the costly failure of Josephinism earlier to harness deeper spiritual values or a harmonious ecclesiastical establishment to its social and political programme. On the other hand Austro-Germans found themselves outflanked in the Habsburg lands by rival national claims which, having exploded into prominence in 1848, could no longer be contained within Pandora's Box. Their virulence destroyed the illusions of Josephinists that the public good and general enlightenment could be served through the medium of German language and culture without offending ethnic sensibilities. The weakness, indeed counter-productivity, of that presumption had already been manifested in the response to the Emperor's own measures; still more did it become clear by the 1850s. But even then, Joseph's disciples found it impossible to adapt to realities: witness Grillparzer's withering disdain for Czech and Hungarian linguistic culture, or Grün's disparagement of that of the Slovenes.[50]

By the 1850s it grew apparent that Austrian Germans would not be Germans. At a banquet for Friedrich List during the *Vormärz*, the toast was amended by Metternich's specific order from 'deutsche Einheit' ('German unity') to 'deutsche Einigkeit'[51] ('German unanimity'); in this case the Chancellor's preference actually coincided with the reality. Yet they did not become Austrian either, in any clear-cut or coherent way. We still know too little about how they did perceive themselves, or how others perceived them – a semantic investigation of the word 'Österreicher'/'österreichisch' and its cognates in neighbouring languages would be fruitful (and a new study of 'Moravians' *vis-à-vis* Bohemians/Czechs points the way to fruitful comparisons).[52] The failure to establish such an identity entailed crippling uncertainties in the last decades of the Monarchy. Even though it left continuing scope for less exclusive kinds of loyalty, the absence of any Austrian nation-formation in the earlier nineteenth century may well be accounted fundamental to the eventual shipwreck of the Habsburg Empire.

Notes

Thanks are due to John Warren (Oxford Polytechnic) for many valuable suggestions and much kind help during the preparation of this article.

1. [Franz de Paula Hartig], *Genesis der Revolution in Oesterreich im Jahre 1848* (Leipzig, 1850), pp. 161ff.; Viktor Bibl, *Die niederösterreichischen Stände im Vormärz* (Vienna, 1911), pp. 324ff.

2. The two standard accounts are by Fritz Valjavec, *Der Josephinismus* (2nd edn, Munich, 1945), a very general treatment, and by Eduard Winter, *Der Josefinismus. Die Geschichte des österreichischen Reformkatholizismus, 1740-1848* (2nd edn, Berlin, 1962), who concentrates on ecclesiastical issues. For more recent studies and bibliography see *Österreich im Europa der Aufklärung. Kontinuität und Zäsur in Europa zur Zeit Maria Theresias und Josephs II*, 2 vols (Vienna, 1985).
3. Ernst Wangermann, 'Joseph von Sonnenfels und die Vaterlandsliebe der Aufklärung' in *Joseph von Sonnenfels*, ed. Helmut Reinalter (Vienna, 1988), pp. 157-69; R. J. W. Evans, 'Joseph II and Nationality in the Habsburg Lands', in *Enlightened Absolutism: Reform and Reformers in Later Eighteenth-Century Europe*, ed. H. M. Scott (London, 1990), pp. 209-19.
4. Leslie Bodi, *Tauwetter in Wien: Zur Prosa der österreichischen Aufklärung, 1781-95* (Frankfurt, 1977).
5. Wolfgang Häusler, '"Des Kaisers Bildsäule"', in *Österreich zur Zeit Kaiser Josephs II* (Vienna, 1980), pp 288-90.
6. A. Robert, *L'Idée nationale autrichienne et les guerres de Napoléon* (Paris, 1933); Hellmuth Rössler, *Österreichs Kampf um Deutschlands Befreiung. Die deutsche Politik der nationalen Führer Österreichs, 1805-15*, 2 vols (Hamburg, 1940); Antal Mádl, *Politische Dichtung in Österreich, 1830-48* (Budapest, 1969), pp.19 ff.
7. See in general Ignaz Beidtel, *Geschichte der Österreichischen Staatsverwaltung*, ed. A. Huber, 2 vols (Innsbruck, 1896-8) vol. II. On Kolowrat himself there is little; but cf. ibid. vol. II, pp. 225 ff., 341 ff., and, most recently, Ronald E. Coons, 'Reflections of a Josephinist', *Mitteilungen des Österreichischen Staatsarchivs*, 36 (1983), 204-36.
8. Caroline Pichler, *Denkwürdigkeiten aus meinem Leben*, ed. E. K. Blümml, 2 vols (Munich, 1914).
9. Besides the Autobiography (*Sämtliche Werke*, vol. IV (Munich, 1965), pp. 28 ff. and *passim*), I have found Wilhelm Bücher, *Grillparzers Verhältnis zur Politik seiner Zeit* (Marburg, 1913), most useful on this aspect of Grillparzer's life. For his career in state service see G. Wolf, *Grillparzer als Archivdirektor* (Vienna, 1874), and the documents edited by Carl Glossy in *Jahrbuch der Grillparzer-Gesellschaft*, 2 (1892).
10. Emil Horner, *Bauernfeld* (Leipzig etc., l900); J. F. Castelli, *Memoiren meines Lebens*, ed. J. Bindtner, 2 vols. (Munich, n.d.), esp. vol. II, pp. 258 ff.; C. von Wurzbach, *Biographisches Lexikon des Kaiserthums Oesterreich*, 60 vols (Vienna, 1856-91). On Zedlitz see the articles by Eduard Castle in *Jahrbuch der Grillparzer-Gesellschaft*, 8 (1898), 33-107, and 17 (1907), 145-64, with documents; and by Zdeňko Škreb, ibid. 3rd ser. 12 (1976), 317-42.
11. *Der österreichische Vormärz*, ed. O. Rommel (Leipzig, 1931), pp. 167 ff.; Anastasius Grün, *Sämtliche Werke*, ed. A. Schlossar, 10 vols (Leipzig, n.d.), vol. V, 152f.; G. Tampier-Metzker, 'Anton Johann Groß-Hoffinger. Leben und Werk eines Publizisten des Vormärz', *Mitteilungen des Instituts für Österreichische Geschichtsforschung*, 75 (1967), 403-30; Márta S. Lengyel, *Reformersors Metternich Ausztriájában* (Budapest, 1969).
12. Edith Rosenstrauch-Königsberg, 'Stützen der Gesellschaft? Blumauer und Grillparzer – beamtete Dichter', *Jahrbuch der Grillparzer-Gesellschaft*, 3rd ser. 13 (1978), 85-100; Wolf, pp. 20 ff.
13. Viktor Bibl, *Die Tragödie Österreichs* (Leipzig/Vienna, 1937), pp. 81 ff.; James J. Sheehan, *German History, 1770-1866* (Oxford, 1989), pp. 430f.
14. See, in general, Donald E. Emerson, *Metternich and the Political Police. Security and Subversion in the Hapsburg Monarchy, 1815-30* (The Hague, 1968), and Julius Marx, 'Die Zensur der Kanzlei Metternichs', *Österreichische Zeitschrift für öffentliches Recht*, IV, 2 (1951), 170-237. The fact that this police had its sinister antecedents under Joseph II is not relevant here, since posterity largely overlooked the illiberal reaction of the late 1780s.

15. Beidtel, vol. II, pp. 44, 77 ff., 106 f., 110 ff.: an acerbic, but well-informed witness.
16. André Tibal, *Etudes sur Grillparzer* (Paris/Nancy, 1914), pp. 151 ff., draws together some quotations from the writer on this subject. *König Ottokars Glück und Ende*, Act 1, lines 462 seqq.
17. *Der österreichische Vormärz*, pp. 201 ff.; Horner, pp. 95 ff.; 'Aus Bauernfelds Tagebüchern', ed. C. Glossy, *Jahrbuch der Grillparzer-Gesellschaft*, 5 (1895), 1-217, 6 (1898), 85-223, at vol. 5, 87 f., 95, 104 ff. Stifter describes his narrator as crossing the river Leitha to encounter 'die lieblichen blauen Berge des Vaterlandes'. I owe this reference to Professor Peter Branscombe.
18. Grün, vol. V, pp. 115-76.
19. Grün, vol. I, 54 (quoted). *Der österreichische Vormärz*, pp. 101 ff. Lenau, *Sämtliche Werke*, 2 vols (Leipzig, n.d.), vol II, 117 ff.
20. Bücher, pp. 81 ff., for Grillparzer. Beidtel, vol. II, p. 23; cf. ibid. pp. 385 ff., for what follows, together with Hanns Schlitter, *Aus Österreichs Vormärz*, 4 vols (Zurich etc., 1920), vol. IV, and the earlier sections of Karl Eder, *Der Liberalismus in Altösterreich* (Munich, 1955). See also the wider arguments about Jewish assimilation in David Sorkin, *The Transformation of German Jewry* (New York/Oxford, 1987), and Steven Beller, *Vienna and the Jews, 1867-1938: A Cultural History* (Cambridge, 1989).
21. *Großjährig. Lustspiel in zwei Aufzügen, und dem Nachspiel: Ein neuer Mensch* (Vienna, 1849); cf. 'Aus Bauernfelds Tagebüchern', vol. 5, pp. 124 ff.
22. Winter, pp. 204 ff.; Eduard Hosp, *Kirche Österreichs im Vormârz, 1815-1850* (Vienna/Munich, 1971); Alan J. Reinerman, *Austria and the Papacy in the Age of Metternich*, vol. I (Washington, 1979).
23. Sebastian Brunner, *Clemens Maria Hofbauer* (Vienna, 1858); Rudolf Till, *Hofbauer und sein Kreis* (Vienna, 1951). On the literary Romantics: Herbert Seidler, *Österreichischer Vormärz und Goethezeit. Geschichte einer literarischen Auseinandersetzung* (Vienna, 1982), pp. 117 ff.; Anton Mádl, *Auf Lenaus Spuren. Beiträge zur österreichischen Literatur* (Vienna/Budapest, 1982), pp. 30 ff.
24. Historians of the phenomenon do not seem to have addressed this semantic question. 'Josephinism' was certainly an expression current in a pejorative sense among those who loosened the grip of the state over the Church in and after 1848.
25. Beidtel, esp. vol. II, pp. 156 ff., 275 ff.; Coons, pp. 222 ff.
26. C. Wolfsgruber, *Joseph Othmar Kardinal Rauscher* (Freiburg i.B., 1888); Johannes M. H. Ritzen, *Der junge Sebastian Brunner in seinem Verhältnis zu Jean Paul, Anton Günther und Fürst Metternich* (diss. Nijmegen, 1927).
27. Franz Schuselka, *Oesterreichische Vor- und Rückschritte* (Hamburg, 1847), pp. 168 ff. and *passim*. For the 'Constantinople Letters' see Derek Beales, 'The False Joseph II', *Historical Journal*, 18 (1975), 467-95. On the German Catholics see Winter, pp. 298 ff., and Wolfgang Häusler in *Die Habsburgermonarchie, 1848-1918*. Vol. IV: *Die Konfessionen*, ed. A. Wandruszka and P. Urbanitsch (Vienna, 1985), pp. 596-615.
28. See most recently *Nationalism in the Age of the French Revolution*, ed. O. Dann and J. Dinwiddy (London, 1988).
29. *König Ottokar*, Act 3, lines 1667 seqq.; but Gerhart Baumann, *Franz Grillparzer: Dichtung und österreichische Geistesverfassung* (2nd edn, Frankfurt/Bonn, 1976), vastly overstates this case. For the background to *Ein Bruderzwist in Habsburg* see P. Kuranda, 'Grillparzer und die Politik des Vormärzes', *Jahrbuch der Grillparzer-Gesellschaft*, 28 (1926), 1-21, and A. Grenville, 'Grillparzer and the French Revolution', in *The Impact of the French Revolution on European Consciousness*, ed. H. T. Mason and W. Doyle (Gloucester, 1989), pp. 172-87; and cf. R. J. W. Evans, 'Rudolf II and his Historians: The Nineteenth Century', in *Prag um 1600. Beiträge zur Kunst und Kultur am Hofe Rudolfs II.* (Freren, 1988), 45-50.
30. Cf. *Der österreichische Vormärz*, pp. 104, 106 f. (Hartmann, Meissner). Friedrich Heer, *Der Kampf um die österreichische Identität* (Cologne/Vienna, 1981), p. 199.

31. Pichler, vol. II, pp. 36 ff., 52 f.
32. Cited in Heer, pp. 198 f. Josef Redlich, *Das österreichische Staats- und Reichsproblem*, 2 vols. (Leipzig, 1920-6), vol. I, pt. l, pp. 40 ff., argues that Vienna-based, bourgeois German culture in Austria had embraced the idea of a *Vaterland* by 1848, and makes shrewd, but not decisive, points in favour of this claim.
33. Mádl, *Politische Dichtung*, p. 19; cf. id., *Auf Lenaus Spuren*, pp. 13 ff.
34. Cf. the viewpoints of Seidler, and of Friedrich Sengle, *Biedermeierzeit. Deutsche Literatur im Spannungsfeld zwischen Restauration und Revolution, 1815-1848*, 3 vols (Stuttgart, 1971-80), esp. vol. I, pp. 110 ff.
35. Friedrich Engel-Janosi, 'Kaiser Josef II in der Wiener Bewegung des Jahres 1848', *Zeitschrift des Vereins für Geschichte der Stadt Wien*, 11 (1931), 53-72; Franz Gräffer, *Josephinische Curiosa, oder ganz besondere, teils nicht mehr, teils noch nicht bekannte Persönlichkeiten, Geheimnisse, Details, Aktenstücke und Denkwürdigkeiten der Lebens- und Zeitgeschichte Kaiser Josephs II*, 5 vols (Vienna, 1848-50).
36. F[ranz Xaver] von P[illersdorf], *Rückblicke auf die politische Bewegung in Österreich in den Jahren 1848 und 1849* (Vienna, 1849), esp. pp. 65 f.; cf. the broader reflections in his *Handschriftlicher Nachlaß* (Vienna, 1863).
37. See, for example, *Des Oesterreichers richtiger Standpunkt. Geschrieben im Februar 1848* (Cologne, 1848). Grillparzer, *Werke*, ed. R. Franz (Leipzig/Vienna, n.d.) vol. I, p. 181; cf. other early 1848 poems in *Die Dichtung der ersten deutschen Revolution, 1848-1849*, ed. E. Underberg (Leipzig, 1930), pp. 42, 61, 91.
38. Grün, vol. I, p. 40. Paul Gorceix, *Ernst von Feuchtersleben, moraliste et pédagogue, 1806-49* (Paris, 1976), pp. 157 n. (cited) and *passim*.
39. Horner, pp. 118 f.; Castelli, pp. 251 ff.
40. The poem is in *Werke*, vol. I, p. 181. For Grillparzer's activities in 1848 see W. E. Yates, *Grillparzer: A Critical Introduction* (Cambridge, 1972), pp. 29 f.,and Wolf, pp. 46-8.
41. Grün, vol. I, pp. 50 f. Häusler, '"Des Kaisers Bildsäule"', pp. 289 f.
42. Peter Burian, *Die Nationalitäten in 'Cisleithanien' und das Wahlrecht der Märzrevolution 1848-9* (Graz/Cologne, 1962), pp. 40 ff.
43. Cited in Lewis Namier, *1848: The Revolution of the Intellectuals* (London, 1946), p. 99.
44. Bauernfeld, *Großjährig*; 'Aus Bauernfelds Tagebüchern', vol. VI, pp. 87, 89. Further clues to Bauernfeld's attitudes in 1848-9 are in his *Gesammelte Aufsätze*, ed. Stefan Hock (Vienna, 1905), pp. 57-136.
45. Beidtel, vol. II, pp. 437 ff. Häusler, in *Die Habsburgermonarchie*, vol. IV, reviews the whole episode.
46. Grün, vol. I, p. 143; Erika Weinzierl-Fischer, 'Die Kirchenfrage auf dem Österreichischen Reichstag, 1848-49', *Mitteilungen des Österreichischen Staatsarchivs*, 8 (1955), 160-90.
47. Walter Rogge, *Oesterreich von Világos bis zur Gegenwart*, vol. I (Leipzig/Vienna, 1872), pp. 131-4, provides a liberal view of these events; *Habsburgermonarchie*, IV, pp. 22-4.
48. Christoph Thienen-Alderflycht, *Graf Leo Thun im Vormärz* (Graz etc., 1967), for Thun's earlier career. On the 1850s reforms, Hans Lentze, *Die Universitätsreform des Ministers Graf Leo Thun-Hohenstein* (Vienna, 1962), and Richard Meister, *Entwicklung und Reformen des österreichischen Studienwesens*, 2 vols (Vienna, 1963), do not see altogether eye to eye. This is not the place to cite further literature on Austrian neo-absolutism, a subject which I plan to treat in its own right on another occasion.
49. Wolf, p. 79. There is good information on some of these German immigrants in Giles Pope, 'The Political Ideas of Lorenz Stein and their Influence on Rudolf Gneist and Gustav Schmoller' (diss. Oxford, 1985).
50. Bücher, pp. 120 ff., and Tibal, pp. 227 ff., assemble some quotations. Grillparzer's bias was ideological rather than ethnic: he attributed the 'leidiger

Nationalitätenschwindel' in the Monarchy to the pernicious influence of German speculative philosophy. But he ignored the responsibility of Joseph II himself. Likewise Grün's views were by no means straightforwardly anti-Slav: he had earlier been a friend of the Slovene poet Prešeren.
51. Grün, vol. I, pp. 67 f.
52. Jaroslav Mezník,'Dějiny národu českého na Moravě', *Český Časopis Historický*, 88 (1990), 34-61.

Austrian Writers of the Enlightenment and Biedermeier
A Biographical Directory

Since some of the articles in this volume refer in passing to writers unlikely to be listed in anglophone reference works, there follows a concise biographical directory of these figures. With a few exceptions, the writers listed are those not dealt with in *The Oxford Companion to German Literature*. This is not of course a comprehensive guide to Austrian writers of the period 1780-1848, but may serve to stimulate further interest in the writers concerned. The information is drawn chiefly from the standard reference works: Constant von Wurzbach, *Biographisches Lexikon des Kaiserthums Österreich*, 60 vols (Vienna, 1856-91), and J. W. Nagl, Jakob Zeidler and Eduard Castle, *Deutsch-österreichische Literaturgeschichte*, 4 vols (Vienna, 1899-1937).

ALXINGER, JOHANN BAPTIST VON (1755-97). Although he studied law and held various official posts, including that of secretary to the Hoftheater, Alxinger had private means which enabled him to devote himself to literature and to help less fortunate writers. He corresponded with many of the best-known German writers and scholars of the day, including Wieland, Heyne, and Adelung. Besides much lyric poetry, he wrote epic poems, *Doolin von Mainz* and *Bliomberis*, on the model of Wieland. A Freemason, he joined the famous lodge 'Zur wahren Eintracht' ('True Harmony') in 1785.

ARNSTEIN, BENEDIKT DAVID (1761-1841) belonged to a well-known Jewish family; his grandfather, Adam Isaac Arnstein, founded a major banking house, and another relative, Franziska ('Fanny') von Arnstein (1758-1818), kept a salon which acquired international fame during the Congress of Vienna. Benedikt Arnstein worked in the family bank, but his literary interests were encouraged by Alxinger. He wrote several comedies, including *Eine jüdische Familienszene* (1782).

AYRENHOFF, CORNELIUS HERMANN VON (1733-1819) was an army officer who devoted his spare time to writing neo-classical dramas, some on the model of Racine. One, *Der Postzug*, was praised by the francophile Frederick the Great. Like Frederick, Ayrenhoff had old-fashioned tastes, and detested the drama of Shakespeare and Goethe. He was himself attacked by Sonnenfels and others, and long outlived his own reputation.

BAUERNFELD, EDUARD VON (1802-90), a state official, dramatist, and liberal journalist, was also a close friend of Schubert and the painter Moritz von Schwind. His many comedies include *Bürgerlich und romantisch* (1838), *Ein deutscher Krieger* (1844), *Großjährig* (1846); also important are his memoirs, *Aus Alt- und Neu-Wien* (1872). During the revolutionary upheavals of March 1848 he and Grün tried to exert a moderating influence; he refused election to the Frankfurt Parliament because of illness. In later life he was regarded as a grand old man of Austrian literature.

BECK, KARL (1817-79) came from a Jewish family in Hungary. Though well known as a revolutionary poet in the 1840s, especially for *Lieder vom armen Manne* and *Gepanzerte Lieder*, he is now remembered mainly for writing the text of the Strauss waltz 'An der schönen blauen Donau'.

BLUMAUER, ALOYS (1755-98) joined the Society of Jesus in 1772, but on the Society's dissolution the following year had to earn his living as a private tutor, librarian, and writer. He was court censor from 1782 to 1793, thereafter a bookseller. Together with Ratschky, he edited the important poetic journal *Wienerischer Musenalmanach* from 1781 onwards. He also edited the *Journal für Freymaurer*, published quarterly by the lodge 'Zur wahren Eintracht', which he joined in 1782. He wrote many fine lyric poems, besides the valuable essay *Beobachtungen über Österreichs Aufklärung und Literatur* (1782), describing the effects on literature of Joseph II's liberalisation of the censorship laws. His main work is his anti-clerical travesty of the *Aeneid*.

BORN, IGNAZ VON (1742-91) joined the Jesuits early in life, but left after sixteen months; he studied law and then natural history, especially mineralogy. In 1776 he was placed in charge of the Imperial natural history collection. His scientific publications resulted in his election to learned societies in London, Padua, and Stockholm, while in Vienna he was well known for his anti-clerical satires and his prominence in the lodge 'Zur wahren Eintracht', to which he tried, unsuccessfully, to recruit Joseph II.

BRUNNER, SEBASTIAN (1814-93) was ordained a priest in 1838, and in 1843 was entrusted by Metternich with the task of collating ambassadors' reports on religious and political unrest; he later attained high clerical office under Pope Pius IX. He wrote many satires against liberalism, Hegelianism, and the spirit of the Enlightenment, such as *Don Quixote und Sancho Pansa auf dem liberalen Parnasse*, which is aimed at Bauernfeld and Grün.

CASTELLI, IGNAZ FRANZ (1781-1862) was a state official, librarian, dramatist and poet. He adapted many plays from the French of Pixérécourt, Scribe and others, and formed a large collection of plays, play-bills and theatrical memorabilia. Some of his poems are in Lower Austrian dialect; he wrote a dialect dictionary, as well as *Wiener Memoiren* (1838), an important source for the literary life of the period.

COLLIN, HEINRICH JOSEPH VON (1772-1811), was a court official and dramatist. His tragedies, modelled on Schiller, enjoyed great success, especially *Regulus* (1802), as did his patriotic poems and ballads. His complete works were edited after his death by his brother Matthäus von Collin (1779-1824), himself a historical dramatist of note.

DEINHARDSTEIN, JOHANN LUDWIG VON (1794-1859), a dramatist, was also employed as a censor. His poetic drama *Hans Sachs* was performed with great success in 1827, the year in which he succeeded Haschka as Professor of Aesthetics at the Theresianische Ritterakademie in Vienna. From 1832 to 1841 he was deputy director of the Hoftheater. He had much contact with writers in Germany, including Goethe, Humboldt, Schelling, and Carus, and published writings by them in his *Wiener Jahrbücher der Literatur*.

DENIS, JOHANN MICHAEL KOSMAS PETER (1729-1800) was educated by Jesuits at Passau; he entered the Society as a novice in 1747 and was ordained in 1756. He taught rhetoric at the Theresianische Ritterakademie. On the dissolution of the Society in 1773 he became a librarian and published important bibliographical studies. He translated Macpherson's 'Ossian' poems into German (1768-9) and also wrote, under an anagrammatic pseudonym, *Die Lieder Sineds des Barden* (1772).

EBERT, KARL EGON (1801-1882) was born in Prague, and employed as librarian and later as estate manager by his patron, Prince von Fürstenberg. He celebrated Czech history in his epic *Wlasta: Böhmisch-nationales Heldengedicht in drei Büchern* (1829) and his dramas, notably *Bretislaw und Jutta* (performed in 1829).

FESSLER, IGNAZ AUREL (1756-1839) entered the Capuchin Order in 1774, but by the time of his ordination in 1774 he was already disaffected with the Church. He took advantage of Joseph II's relaxation of the censorship laws by writing the pamphlet 'Was ist der Kaiser?', and was deeply involved in Freemasonry. He was tried and punished on the charge of breaking his vows, but in 1784 he was appointed Professor of Oriental Languages at the newly founded University of Lemberg. His drama *Sidney* was performed at Lemberg in 1788, but was interpreted as an attack on Joseph II, and he was obliged to flee to Silesia. In 1791 he became a Lutheran; he married, was divorced, and married again. To make money, he wrote many historical novels, beginning with *Marc Aurel* (1790). After much wandering and poverty in Germany and Russia, Fessler was appointed Lutheran Bishop at St Petersburg in 1819, and retained this post until his death.

GRÜN, ANASTASIUS, pseudonym of Anton Alexander, Count von Auersperg (1806-76), was a poet and close friend of Nikolaus Lenau; he was famous for his satirical attack on the Metternich regime, *Spaziergänge eines Wiener Poeten* (1831). As a well-known liberal, he was elected to the Frankfurt Parliament in 1848, but soon resigned; in later life he again took a prominent part in Austrian politics.

HARTMANN, MORITZ (1821-72) was born of Jewish parents in Bohemia and educated at Prague University, where his friends included Alfred Meissner. His poems published at Leipzig in celebration of Hussitism, *Kelch und Schwert* (1845), drew the attention of the police. In 1848 he was elected to the Frankfurt Parliament, and was on its extreme left wing. On its dissolution he went into exile in Paris. With his former fellow-student Franz Szarvady he translated the poems of Sándor Petöfi from Hungarian into German; he also wrote poems, travel books, and biographies.

HASCHKA, LORENZ LEOPOLD (1749-1827) was a Jesuit who, on the dissolution of the Society, became a writer, a librarian, and later Professor of Aesthetics at the Theresianum. He was helped financially by Alxinger and was closely associated also with Blumauer, Denis, Leon, and Ratschky. He wrote many poems, especially odes, and composed the anthem 'Gott erhalte Franz den Kaiser', which was set to music by Haydn. Although in the 1780s Haschka shared Blumauer's anti-clericalism, on the accession of Leopold II in 1790 he is said to have become a police spy.

HERLOSSSOHN, GEORG KARL REGINALD (1804-49) was born at Prague, his real name being Herloss; it is not known why he changed it. After early poverty in Vienna, he settled in Berlin, where during the 1830s and 1840s he edited the literary periodical *Der Komet* and wrote many stories and novels.

HOFFMANN, LEOPOLD ALOYS (1748-1806). Encouraged by Denis to pursue a literary career, he lived as a freelance writer first in Prague and then in Vienna. In the early 1780s he edited a series of sermon critiques, and joined the Illuminati. With the help of Gottfried van Swieten (whose father Gerhard had been an enlightened adviser to Maria Theresa), he became Professor of German at Pest, returning to a similar post in Vienna in 1790. During the anti-Josephinist reaction Hoffmann, a police spy, conducted a witch-hunt against Jacobins, but after Leopold II's death he was attacked by Alxinger and other former friends, fell into disfavour, and was compelled to retire from his chair. He retreated to Wiener Neustadt, where he spent the rest of his life in seclusion.

HORMAYR ZU HORTENBURG, JOSEPH FREIHERR VON (1781-1848) was born in Innsbruck, and helped to organise the Tyrolean uprising of 1809. In 1816 he was appointed official historiographer to the Imperial family; in 1828 he moved to a government post in Munich, where he had a distinguished diplomatic career under the Bavarian crown. The best known of his many historical works is *Österreichischer Plutarch oder Leben und Bildnisse aller Regenten und der berühmtesten Feldherrn, Staatsmänner, Gelehrten des österreichischen Kaiserstaates* (1807-12), containing 76 biographies; Grillparzer made extensive use of it when writing his historical dramas *König Ottokars Glück und Ende* (1819) and *Ein Bruderzwist in Habsburg* (completed 1848).

HURTER, FRIEDRICH EMANUEL (1787-1865), a historian, was educated at Göttingen. Deeply conservative and opposed to what he considered shallow progressivism, Hurter became a Protestant clergyman at Schaffhausen in Switzerland, but got into increasing trouble through his evident sympathy with Catholicism. Having been obliged in 1841 to resign from all his ecclesiastical offices, he became a Catholic in 1844, and was appointed by Metternich court historiographer at Vienna. His main historical work was *Geschichte Papst Innocenz des Dritten und seiner Zeitgenossen* (1834-42).

KURANDA, IGNAZ (1811-84), born in Prague of poor Jewish parents, became a journalist in Vienna and attained fame with his play *Die letzte weiße Rose* (based on Schiller's fragment *Warbeck*). He spent some time in Brussels, where he gave highly popular lectures on German literature. In Leipzig in 1841 he founded *Die Grenzboten*, an important Vormärz periodical in which Hartmann, Meissner, and others were published. His history of Belgium, *Belgien seit der Revolution* (1846), advocated constitutional government. In March 1848 he returned to Vienna and was elected to the Frankfurt Parliament. Afterwards he was

A Biographical Directory

prominent in Vienna as a newspaper editor and Liberal politician.

MASTALIER, KARL (1731-95) was a Jesuit and teacher of rhetoric; after the Society's dissolution he became a canon at Laibach (Ljubljana). He published numerous odes and orations, strictly following classical models.

MEISSNER, ALFRED (1822-85) was born at Teplitz (Teplice) in Bohemia. Inspired by Czech history, like his fellow-student Hartmann, he published a historical epic, *Žižka* (1846), and many plays and novels. Having gained a reputation as a political poet, he was elected to the Frankfurt Parliament, where he sided with the extreme left. He spent time in Leipzig, London, and Paris, where he became acquainted with Heine. His recollections of Heine and others are in *Geschichte meines Lebens* (1884).

PEZZL, JOHANN (1756-1823) was born in Bavaria and studied law at Salzburg, but lived in Vienna from at least 1783, when he applied for admission to the Masonic lodge 'Zur wahren Eintracht'. In 1785 he became secretary to the Chancellor, Prince Kaunitz. His most important works are *Marokkanische Briefe*, in which Vienna is described by a supposed Moroccan envoy (on the model of Montesquieu's *Lettres persanes*); the lively *Skizze von Wien* (1786-90), to which he wrote several sequels; and the novel *Faustin oder das philosophische Jahrhundert* (1783), which earned him the description 'the Austrian Voltaire'.

PICHLER, KAROLINE, or Caroline (1769-1843), was the daughter of the official Franz von Greiner, in whose house she met such writers as Alxinger, Blumauer, Denis, Haschka, Leon, Ratschky, and Sonnenfels, and heard Mozart's playing. Alxinger, Haschka, and Leon guided her extensive reading. She married Andreas Pichler in 1796 and in turn kept a salon frequented by distinguished Austrians (the Collin brothers, Grillparzer, Hormayr) and visitors (the Schlegels, Brentano, Tieck). Though she wrote many plays and historical novels, she is best remembered for her excellent *Denkwürdigkeiten aus meinem Leben*, published posthumously in 1844.

PRANDSTÄTTER, MARTIN JOSEPH (1750-?) was a poet employed in the Vienna magistracy, and an enthusiastic supporter of Josephinism; he belonged to the Masonic lodge 'Zur wahren Eintracht'. He was charged with participation in a Jacobin conspiracy and sentenced to thirty years' imprisonment in a fortress; it is not known how long he survived.

RATSCHKY, JOSEPH FRANZ (1757-1810) was educated by Jesuits, and obtained, thanks to Sonnenfels' influence, a position in the state service. He belonged to the Masonic lodge 'Zur wahren Eintracht'. He was the founder and first editor of the *Wienerischer Musenalmanach*; he translated Horace and wrote many poems in the rococo style, besides a humorous poem, *Michael Striegel. Ein heroisch-episches Gedicht für Freunde der Freiheit und Gleichheit* (1794), directed against the French Revolution.

RAUTENSTRAUCH, JOHANN (1746-1801) was born in Erlangen, but spent most of his life in Vienna; a writer, official, and enthusiastic Josephinist. When the liberalisation of the censorship produced a flood of pamphlets, Rautenstrauch is said to have written the first of a series of pamphlets on Viennese parlourmaids. He also wrote anti-clerical pamphlets, which brought him into fierce disputes with clerics.

A Biographical Directory

RETZER, JOSEPH FRIEDRICH VON (1754-1824) was employed under Joseph II in the censorship office. He belonged to the Masonic lodge 'Zur wahren Eintracht'. Besides a history of the censorship from 1766 to 1787, he wrote poems and short biographies, including that of Richter, and edited the works of Ayrenhoff, Denis, and others. As this suggests, Retzer's tastes were old-fashioned. He became known as an eccentric bachelor, who persisted in wearing a pig-tail and a three-cornered hat long after these eighteenth-century adornments had gone out of fashion.

RICHTER, JOSEPH (1748-1813) is remembered for his pamphlet 'Warum wird Kaiser Joseph von seinem Volke nicht geliebt?' (1787) and especially for his *Eipeldauerbriefe*, begun in 1785 and published regularly in 1793-7, 1799-1801 and 1802-13, in which a peasant, supposedly visiting Vienna, provides a cousin with humorous and sometimes covertly critical commentaries on events of the day. After Richter's death this publication was continued by Franz Karl Gewey (1813-19) and Adolf Bäuerle (1819-21).

SCHNELLER, JULIUS (1777-1832), born at Strasbourg, studied mathematics and history at Freiburg and Vienna. He was friendly with Karoline Pichler, Heinrich von Collin, Castelli, and others. In 1803 he became Professor of History at the Lyceum at Linz, and in 1806 he moved to a similar post at Graz. Further promotion was hindered, however, by his passionate admiration for Josephinism, Napoleon's reforms, and the constitutional governments of Britain and the United States. In 1823 he therefore left Austria to become Professor of Philosophy at the University of Freiburg. A prolific writer, he wrote numerous histories of Austria, Bohemia, and Hungary.

SCHREYVOGEL, JOSEPH (1768-1832) began his literary career as a contributor to Alxinger's short-lived *Österreichische Monatschrift* (1793-4); from late 1794 to 1797 he lived in Jena, in contact with Goethe, Schiller, Herder, and Wieland. Back in Vienna, he founded, edited, and largely wrote the very popular weekly, *Das Sonntagsblatt* (1807-9). As 'Dramaturg' at the Hoftheater he was successful in promoting young talent, including that of Grillparzer, but was dismissed in 1832 after prolonged conflicts with its director, Count Czernin. His own best dramatic works were adaptations from Calderón.

SONNENFELS, JOSEPH VON (1733-1817), son of the Jewish rabbi Perlin Lipmann, was baptised in 1735 together with his father. Sonnenfels senior was given the title 'Edler von Sonnenfels' by Maria Theresa, and Sonnenfels junior was appointed by her to the newly founded chair of political science at Vienna University. His textbook for Austrian state officials, *Grundsätze der Polizey, Handlung und Finanz* (1765-7), went on being reprinted until 1819. His main contribution to literature was his weekly journals, notably *Der Mann ohne Vorurteil*, which were modelled on the English *Spectator* and *Tatler*. A close friend of Ignaz von Born, he joined the Masonic Lodge 'Zur wahren Eintracht' in 1782 and encouraged the founding of the *Journal für Freymaurer*.

SONNLEITHNER, JOSEPH (1766-1835) was secretary to the Hoftheater from 1804 to 1814, and in 1814 founded the Gesellschaft der Musikfreunde des österreichischen Kaiserstaates. He also wrote comedies and edited the works of other authors, including the comedies of Philipp Hafner.

A Biographical Directory

ZEDLITZ, JOSEPH CHRISTIAN VON (1790-1862) was born in Silesia and became an army officer and fought at the battles of Aspern and Wagram. In his lifetime he enjoyed a high reputation as a poet, especially for his *Todtenkränze* (1828), commemorating great figures of the distant and recent past such as Petrarch, Tasso, Byron, Goethe, Joseph II, and Napoleon.

Part Two
Review Articles

The Austrian Enlightenment
An Essay on Publications, 1975–1990
Leslie Bodi

The last twenty-five years have seen a remarkable increase in publications on the Austrian Enlightenment, including its most radical phase 1780–90, when Joseph II was reigning alone. Historical factors have brought about a certain recovery from the 'Josephinist trauma' (R. Bauer) which in earlier times made it so difficult to deal with that singular combination of enlightened modernisation and absolutist centralism which radically changed the history of the Habsburg Monarchy and its peoples. Recent reappraisals of this fascinating period of Austrian history seem to me not unconnected with the renewal in the Western world's interest in the Enlightenment project and its social and revolutionary consequences that were typical of the 1960s and culminated in the years around 1968. In Austria itself, this development shows up most clearly in the Kreisky period of 1970–83. The proclamation of an 'Austrian Way' included a revaluation of the Austrian historical tradition. which aimed at overcoming the rift between the forces of 'Red' and 'Black', of 'reactionaries' and 'progressives' in the nineteenth-century meaning of the word. This made it possible to commence a more balanced valuation of Enlightenment traditions which had often been consciously eliminated by an official 'Austrian ideology', constructing an unbroken line between Baroque–Catholic traditions and the pious Biedermeier of Metternich's repressive rule. The material at hand also points to the impact of the new world-wide paradigm change of the 1970s which aims at a better understanding of questions of national and cultural identity in an increasingly pluralistic world. In this respect the history of the multilingual and multicultural Habsburg Monarchy has developed into an interesting paradigm of past mistakes and future perspectives.

This article does not aim at a full bibliography nor a fully 'objective' assessment of the literature on Austrian reform absolutism and Enlightenment of the last fifteen years. It was born out of my personal interest in recent research on eighteenth-century Austria; work done after the publication of my own book on Viennese prose writings of the years 1781–95 (Bodi, 1977). I am not a professional historian, so the selection of books was based on personal choice, my interest being in the literary, cultural and ideological aspects of the period. Since I believe in a broad interdisciplinary approach, I had to exclude many valuable specialist books and articles. I have, instead, given more space to writings on those social changes and developments that contributed to the definition of an 'Austrian' identity, and the identities of the emerging nations of Central Europe.

It is well known that there is no modern comprehensive history of the Danube Monarchy in the eighteenth century. Such a work could be compiled only by the close collaboration of numerous European scholars from many disciplines. It is therefore of great importance that over the past fifteen years an extensive range of material has been published on eighteenth-century Austria. The bicentennials in 1980 of both Maria Theresa and Joseph II played a particularly significant role. In keeping with the established Austrian tradition, special weight was given to the commemoration of Maria Theresa's death in 1780. W. Koschatzky edited an authoritative volume of studies on 'Maria Theresa and her Age' (Koschatzky, 1980). Its tone is set by Hofmannsthal's well-known 1917 essay commemorating the Empress's birthday and contrasting her exemplary piety and motherly humanity with the Prussian–German ideal personified by Frederick II (pp. 11–16). This attitude is reflected in the editor's 'Preface', where we read that 'being an Austrian has always meant having a well-defined attitude to life and not just a certain citizenship' (p. 9). A. Wandruszka's well-balanced historical introduction (pp. 17–39) is followed by essays on a wide range of topics in the Theresan period such as 'Politics and General History', 'Economy and Society', science, education and technology, as well as the visual and performing arts, including highly specialised studies of the applied arts and trades. These include studies of furniture, porcelain and the fashion articles which are still important items of Austrian industry.

There are first-class essays devoted to the image of Maria Theresa in the Austrian tradition (pp. 447–61), reinforced, as it has been, by some of her surviving foundations, including the Theresianum (pp. 239–57) and the Vienna Stock Exchange (pp. 233–8). The book is enriched with copious illustrations, many of which can also be found in the lavish catalogue of the monumental Schönbrunn exhibition 'Maria Theresia und ihre Zeit' of October 1980. Here the rule of the Empress is characterised, by the Minister for Education, as the period 'which brought about the decisive change of Austria from a Baroque to an Enlightened state' (MTK, 1980, p. 6). The exhibits and their descriptions give a broad panorama of contemporary history and everyday life.

It is interesting to compare this treatment of Maria Theresa with that given to Joseph II in the documentation of 'Austria in the Age of Joseph II' staged from March to November 1980 as the 'Landesausstellung' of Lower Austria at the Baroque monastery of Melk (JIIK, 1980). The choice of venue itself indicated the uneasy relationship of the Austrian establishment to the radical Emperor; it was a joke in Vienna at the time that it could be paralleled only by a Voltaire Exhibition in Notre Dame, or a Marx Exhibition in Cologne Cathedral. The introductory essays of the Catalogue give a somewhat embarrassing indication of the inappropriateness of the venue (JIIK, 1980, pp. XVII–XXI; 1–5), but the text itself presents, in more than 300 pages, an encyclopedia of the period. Over sixty well-researched and documented articles cover various aspects of political, social, economic, artistic and cultural life, as well as the Emperor's biography and reform policies. Special articles deal with the 'Länder' of the Monarchy, including studies on Vienna (pp. 139–45) and developments in the non-German-speaking territories. Articles by H. Feigl, E. Bruckmüller and H. Jungwirth (pp. 44–69) give a good summary of the economy. Even a marginal topic like changing court etiquette is revealed as an important marker of social and political change (Haupt, pp. 76–81). Essays by W. Häusler, K. Vocelka and K. M. Kisler on the survival to the present of the Emperor's image and ideas conclude the volume (pp. 282–305).

An International Symposium held in connection with the Melk Exhibition also focused on the question: 'What has survived of Joseph II?' (*Was blieb*, 1980). The introductory summary is by A. Wandruszka (pp. 14–24), and W. Ogris assesses the contradictions arising from Joseph's attempt to establish the rule of law within the framework of bureaucratised absolutism (pp. 43–4). Further articles investigate the impact of Josephinist policies on such fields as education, medicine, social welfare and religion; others study developments in Hungary and the Netherlands. A clever journalistic essay by H. Magenschab concludes the volume, asking pertinent questions about Maria-Theresan and Josephinist elements in Bruno Kreisky's rule (pp. 124–8).

Another landmark is provided by a volume edited by Erich Zöllner (Zöllner, 1983). The editor suggests that some clarification of the characteristics of the age has been achieved by the bicentennial exhibitions and proposes to define the period 1740–1790 as 'reform absolutism' (p. 4), in view of the often purely instrumental use of the terminology of European Enlightenment by the rulers and administrators of the Monarchy. The volume lives up to the high standards set by Zöllner. Interesting studies discuss many of the questions arising from the legal, military, economic and administrative reforms as well as the relationship of the Church and the State (E. Kovács, pp. 29–53). Günther Hamann describes the development from the collecting activities of aristocratic patrons to modern science and technology (pp. 151–77), while concise essays by H. Lengauer (pp. 178–87) and G. Heinz (pp. 188–209) attempt definitions of the specific character of the literature and the arts of the period. In an important study, R. A. Kann criticises eighteenth-century Austrian reform absolutism for not coming to grips with the problem of the evolving nationalities of the Empire. Because they were unable to understand the 'Enlightenment' elements of early nationalism, the rulers' German-language-based centralism led to the development of romantic nationalism and, ultimately, to the dissolution of the Monarchy (pp. 12–14); see also Kann's essay in Plaschka/Klingenstein, 1985 pp. 557–66). Materials dealing more specifically with the interrelationship of Austria and Hungary in the period are to be found in the discussions of a conference of Austrian and Hungarian historians in 1980 (Drabek/Plaschka/Wandruszka, 1982).

The most representative collection of bicentenary essays is the two-volume edition of the papers read at the Austrian Academy of Sciences' International Symposium held in Vienna in October 1980, under the sponsorship of the Ministry for Science and Research (Plaschka/Klingenstein, 1985). This project arose from the somewhat belated reaction of the Kreisky Government to the Schönbrunn and Melk exhibition and was intended to give the Austrian Enlightenment a clearly defined place in the national consciousness of the country. It was held in Vienna in recognition of the urban–metropolitan core of the reform movement. At the same time, the title of the Conference ('Austria in the Europe of the Enlightenment') was meant to emphasise the broader European context of Austrian reform absolutism, while the subtitle, 'Continuity and Caesura in Europe in the Age of Maria Theresa and Joseph II', expressed the organising committee's desire to highlight the factors of explosive change as well as those of tradition and continuity. In her introductory essay, G. Klingenstein opens up the European perspective (pp. 19–28); R. A. Kann takes a moderately conservative, Maria Theresa-centred attitude (pp. 29–36), while a left-wing point of view marks E. Wangermann's talk on 'Progress and Reaction' in Joseph's reforms. He stresses the importance of the caesura of 1784–85 as the crisis point for enlightened absolutism in Europe and Austria. In line with traditional Marxist scholarship, however, he does not fully recognise nascent nationalism as a substantial constituent of the dynamics of reform politics in Central Europe, seeing all national movements only as manifestations of reactionary 'political romanticism' (p. 43). The following fifty essays are organised in three large groups followed by summaries of the points raised in the discussions. E. Zöllner concludes the proceedings of the whole conference.

Section One, 'Economy and Society', comprises a set of basic essays on the development of the social structures of the period. H. Feigl demonstrates the importance of peasant smallholders for the future of Austria (p. 66; see also JIIK, pp. 45-51); H. Stekl describes the marginalisation of the lower strata of society in Vienna (pp. 291–304), while R. Bauer places the discussion of 'Luxuries' in its European context (pp. 319–34). Further articles deal with the economic and social developments of the individual provinces of the Monarchy, such as Galicia, Hungary and Bohemia, or analyse the impact of Austrian trade policies on the peoples of the Balkans. Useful statistical data on the development of the state budget, incomes and income distribution are given by G. Otruba and R. Sandgruber (pp. 197–263).

The second section deals with the political institutions of the absolutist state and its attempts to establish the rule of law. Topics include the conflicts arising in the process of modernisation and centralisation, and the inevitable clash of traditional estates and corporations with the new tenets of natural law and enlightenment (e.g. H. Liebel, W. Ogris, and G. Kocher, pp. 339–96). E. Kovács discusses the political separation of Austria from the Holy Roman Empire as a function of the changing relationship between Pope and Emperor and shows the emergence of a specific Austrian state religion (pp. 421–36). Some of the central problems of the reform process are demonstrated in case histories from Hungary, Lombardy, Luxembourg and Trient (pp. 437–508). K. O. v. Aretin sees Josephinism as a prime example of 'Catholic Enlightened Absolutism' (pp. 509–24), while Austrian foreign policy is the subject of articles by R. A. Kann, D. A. Beales and E. Donnert (pp. 557–92).

'Art, Literature and Education' is the title of the third section. Taking the development of historicism in painting as her starting point, Klára Garas points to the new function of patriotism and historical consciousness in Austria and Hungary around 1780, and P. Preiss discusses the Bohemian aspects of this process (pp. 623–51). Essays on music, architecture, ballet and theatre include a lucid article by H. Haider-Pregler (pp. 701–16). The literary essays are somewhat disappointing, touching only on the popular comedy (pp. 717–41) and the relatively insignificant comic epics of the period (pp. 743–66). These studies (by H. Zeman and W. M. Bauer) show traditionally trained Austrian Germanists ill at ease with this literature of strong social and political engagement. In an article on tertiary education, N. Hammerstein sees the reforms as reflecting the inner contradictions of Catholic Enlightenment in Germany (pp. 787–812).

The impact of Habsburg educational policies on Serbia is well shown in articles on primary education (S. K. Kostic, pp. 847–66) and the development of historical consciousness and nationalist ideologies (D. Medakovic, pp. 883–94). E. Rosenstrauch-Königsberg's is the only article of the collection that directly tackles the question of the emergence of an 'Austrian' national self-identification in the course of the reform period. She stresses the role of Freemasons, Illuminati and the 1784 language regulation, but is not quite free of the illusion that a victory of Austrian and Hungarian 'Jacobins' could have prevented nineteenth-century 'romantic nationalism' (pp. 916–18).

This work of over 1100 pages has an extensive bibliography of secondary literature on 'The Age of Maria Theresa and Joseph II' compiled by K. Vocelka, I. Mayer and M. Wakounig (pp. 969–1063), bringing up to date K. Vocelka's earlier bibliography (Koschatzky, 1980, pp. 467–90). It is an indispensable working tool, even though the subject categorisation could have been more user-friendly. *Österreich im Europa der Aufklärung* is not free of overlapping information, but the articles are well researched, with excellent footnotes. Some of the authors find it difficult to adapt their essays to the categories of 'continuity' and 'caesura', even though these concepts can prove very fruitful, as in P. Hersche's comparison of the modernisation and reform policy models of Austria and Switzerland (pp. 397–419). This massive work is the most important among the collections of the last fifteen years.

Before discussing more specialised areas, it should be mentioned here that the past decade has seen the emergence of some important research periodicals, besides the proceedings of the Mátrafüred Colloquia from 1971 onward (summary in Köpeczi 1985). The 'Austrian Society for Eighteenth Century Research' began publishing its Yearbook in 1984 (*Jahrbuch*, 1984) and it contains many relevant studies. The latest special issue is devoted to questions of 'nationalism' and 'patriotism' in eighteenth-century Austria (Csáky/Hagelkrys, 1989). For this topic, an important classic is still R. Bauer's collection of essays on the self-identification of Austrian literature from the time of reform absolutism (Bauer, 1977).

Looking at material published on specific disciplines, my main interest is in literary research. Here the representative collection of building blocks is H. Zeman's assemblage of essays on Austrian Literature (1750–1830) (Zeman, 1979). It is based on an Eisenstadt Symposium of September 1977, which predates the bicentennial collections and catalogues. Its two volumes contain over 40 contributions and were published under the auspices of the Burgenland Government in collaboration with the Institute for Austrian Cultural History. The first section is devoted to questions of 'sociology of literature' with useful essays on the basic rhetorical, stylistic and poetic assumptions underlying eighteenth-century Austrian literature as conveyed in the teaching methods and programmes of the schools of the Monarchy. W. Martens's analysis of poems of the Vienna Theresianum in 1772–74 (pp. 1–22) is supplemented by F. Keller's investigation of M. Denis's place in the Jesuit tradition (pp. 55–83). W. Neuber traces the survival of these traditions into post-enlightenment times (pp. 23–53). For our understanding of the attitudes of writers throughout the Monarchy to questions of literature, the knowledge imparted by Austrian 'Gymnasien' is of the first importance; it is thoroughly investigated by G. Jäger (pp. 85–118), both in a study of the syllabuses for stylistics and the teaching of classical authors, and in a comparison of the German literary texts used in readers and educational anthologies. These materials provide a good basis for understanding the fundamental differences between the Austrian and the German literary traditions. More might have been said on the survival of 'Latinitas' in the Austrian culture – as opposed, for instance, to what E. M. Butler called the 'tyranny of Greece over Germany'. A. Martino devotes an excellent survey to the 'reading cabinets' and lending libraries in Vienna (pp. 119–42) and H. Zeman and W. M. Bauer study the impact of such important printers, publishers and booksellers as Kurzböck, Degen and Wallishausser (pp. 143–202).

Further articles deal with the journals of the period: there is a basic bibliography by H. W. Lang (pp. 203–27), and the reception of 'Josephinist Literature' from outside Vienna is illustrated in E. Beutner's analysis of the *Oberdeutsche Allgemeine Literaturzeitung* from 1788 to 1811. This shows how hard it was to transmit the attitudes and achievements of Austrian Enlightenment to the rest of Germany (pp. 229–56). The working of literary and theatre censorship is elucidated by F. Hadamovsky on the basis of lists of prohibited books from 1751–1848 (pp. 289–305).

Zeman's collection also devotes a group of studies to the cross-fertilisation of texts and music. How strong was the Italian impact on Austrian musical culture is evident in the eighteenth-century imperial court poets (E. Kanduth, pp. 307–30) and in essays by H. Rüdiger, H. Zeman and C. Kritsch on Lorenzo da Ponte (pp. 331–77). W. Pross shows the interplay of neo-Latin traditions and Austrian Enlightenment in a discussion of Mazzola/Mozart's *La Clemenza di Tito* (pp. 379–401).

Evidence of increasing English influence is provided by H. Zeman (pp. 403–25) and H. Foltinek (pp. 445–62). The interrelations between Hungarian and Austrian literary developments are clearly set out by A. Tarnai (pp. 463–74) and M. Csáky (pp. 475–89). Tarnai makes a case for different periodisations in Austrian and Hungarian literary history and points to the importance of Latin and German within the multilingualism of Hungarian writers (p. 471). Analysing the 'presence of Hungarian literature in Vienna', Csáky stresses the need for understanding the importance of language-bound nationalism, but also draws attention to the benefit Hungarian writers derived from the multicultural atmosphere of Vienna. He shows how these writers' simultaneous self-definition as 'Hungarus' (i.e., their political self-understanding as 'members of the Natio Hungarica') and their ethnic-linguistic 'Magyar' identification, made possible the evolution of a 'gesamtösterreichisch' literature overcoming ethnic and linguistic differences. Csáky sees with regret this pluralist option being later suppressed by the victory of nineteenth-century nationalism (pp. 487–9; see also Drabek/Plaschka/Wandruszka, 1982, pp. 71–89). This question has remained one of the leading themes of Csáky's further work, his studies on 'early liberalism' in Hungary (Csáky, 1981) and, more recently, on problems of Central Europe.

Further essays in the Zeman collection deal with the impact of the reform period on the evolution of Serbo-Croatian and Czech literature, showing again and again the clash between Josephinist Enlightenment and nascent nationalism (pp. 491–504; 545–62). H. Zeman writes about the self-identification of Austrian literature at the turn of the century; he notes the survival of tenets of Enlightenment in the development of a specifically 'austriakisch' tradition (p. 565). His otherwise competent assessment of this development in the secondary literature up to the mid-nineteenth century fails, however, to gauge the full importance of the explosive radical criticism of enlightened absolutism in the pamphlets of the second half of the Josephinist decade (e.g., pp. 575; 578). H. Lengauer usefully contributes to the theory of drama in the period (pp. 587–621), and W. M. Bauer shows how the theories of classical stylistics conflicted with the reality of the evolving Austrian novel (pp. 623–52). Among the concrete literary analyses of writers and individual works there are informative articles by F. Sengle on Alxinger (pp. 773–803), and R. Bauer on the poetry of F. J. Ratschky (pp. 891–907). C. Siegrist analyses Pezzl's *Faustin* as a synthesis of 'anti-theodicy and engaged literature' (pp. 829–51), while W. Griep identifies F. W. v. Meyern as the author of one of the most outstanding novels of the period, *Abdul Erzerums neue persische Briefe* (Vienna/Leipzig, 1787), which has traditionally been attributed to Pezzl (pp. 805–28). Articles by the ethnographer L. Schmidt investigate the relationship of popular poetry and peasant songs to the tenets of Enlightenment (pp. 865–90). In the concluding essay of the collection, K. Garas looks at the literary inspirations for the visual arts (pp. 929–43).

Zeman's collection touches on many questions of literature and literary theory which have been, in the past fifteen years, the subjects of substantial monographs. In the area of theatre studies, H. Haider-Pregler's book on the educational function of eighteenth-century theatre is of paramount importance (Haider-Pregler, 1980). It looks at the way the stage was made to serve the educational ideals of the emerging middle classes, ideals which were then utilised by the absolutist state for the education of 'civilised' and also obedient subjects. The author traces the development of the concept of the state as a 'school of the nation' (pp.66–8) from the time of the early cameralists and the seventeenth-century theatre groups who had to fight against the marginalisation of actors and producers by church and municipal authorities. She summarises the German discussion of the time aiming at the creation of a national theatre as the concretisation of middle class utopias (pp. 174–8), and points to the interrelationship between theatre arts, journalism and the increasing self-confidence of the actors involved in 'literary' plays. Vienna is seen as the model for the development from 'popular' forms of theatrical entertainment to the establishment of high drama and comedy with the foundation of the National Theatre in 1776. Special weight is given both to the activities of Gottsched and his followers in Vienna, and to the growing recognition by Sonnenfels and his circle of the need to establish a forum for the artistic expression of Austrian reform absolutism. The fight against improvisation was also meant to serve the enforcement of state control and censorship (p. 202). Haider-Pregler demonstrates very well the dangers inherent up to the present day in making the theatre an 'educational' and representational tool of the state (p. 18).

W. M. Bauer's extensive study on the novel of the Austrian Enlightenment tackles an interesting theoretical problem: the relations between fiction and social and political criticism in literature (Bauer, 1978). He is concerned with the difficulties that arise when stylistic and rhetorical prescriptions of contemporary normative poetics are applied to the changing social reality of the reform period. This leads to interesting observations on the interplay of traditional literary genres, types and concepts with aspects of contemporary reality. On the whole, however, this well-researched book is not altogether convincing, owing to an over-emphasis on formal categories and the lack of a coherent analysis of the socio-historical context of Austrian enlightened absolutism.

Further valuable work has been done, in recent years, in many of the fields mapped out in the essay collections published around 1979/80. Previous research on eighteenth-century Austrian journals is now superseded by an extensive bibliography of the German- and Hungarian-language periodicals from 1740 to 1809 (Seidler, 1988). It lists 420 items with detailed commentaries and informative indices. The only suggestion for improving this valuable book would be to attempt a clearer distinction between 'periodicals' and once-only published pamphlets. This could have usefully contributed to the definition of the 'Broschüre' as one of the most important printed media of Josephinism throughout the Danube Monarchy. The scope of this article, as well as the wealth of material at hand, limits me to the more extensive publications and monographs. It might, nevertheless, be useful to draw attention to work-in-progress in areas of special significance. In the field of publishing and the book market, the enigmatic G. P. Wucherer was responsible, in the years following the crisis of Austrian reform policies in 1784–85, for some of the most radical pamphlets against Joseph II. There is now an unpublished thesis by M. Winter which argues that Wucherer was a genuine opponent of absolutist rule. Winter also draws on valuable archive material, and provides an extensive listing of Wucherer's publications (Winter, 1988).

The past fifteen years have seen a number of substantial studies dealing with Josephinism as a religious movement. A wide-ranging volume of essays was published by E. Kovács on Catholic Enlightenment and Josephinism (Kovács, 1979), and there are interesting books by P. F. Barton, mainly on I. A. Fessler

(Barton, 1978), and the problematic of religious toleration (Barton, 1981).

The most informative book about the religious component of Austrian reform absolutism is P. Hersche's study of 'late Jansenism' (Hersche, 1977). It offers thorough analyses of attitudes of personal piety, enlightened ideology and pragmatic absolutist politics, putting these questions firmly into the general framework of the development of Austria and of the 'dialectics of Enlightenment' (pp. 404–5). The secular aspect of the relationships between state absolutism, Enlightenment and education is very well summarised in E. Wangermann's study of Gottfried van Swieten (Wangermann, 1978). I have myself recently tried to present the literary policies of Austrian reform absolutism as a model for 'glasnost' within recurrent movements of liberalisation in Central and East European literatures and cultures (Pavlyshyn, 1990, pp. 17–36).

The central figure for an understanding of the ideological aspects of our period is Joseph von Sonnenfels. His work articulates, better than any other, both the theoretical assumptions underlying the Austrian Enlightenment and the guidelines for their practical application. A full Sonnenfels biography is badly needed; the well-written journalistic survey by D. Lindner is not meant to fill the gap (Lindner, 1983). There is, however, a recent collection of essays on Sonnenfels which comes close to a more coherent study (Reinalter, 1988a). The editor notes the lack of a comprehensive modern Sonnenfels monograph and presents a range of articles designed to give a well-rounded picture of his activities. W. Ogris describes Sonnenfels's moves to establish the rule of law in the Habsburg lands, his basically pragmatic attitudes and his full endorsement of the tenets of the absolutist state (pp. 11–95). J. Garber and H. Reinalter discuss Sonnenfels's position as a social theorist of the late Enlightenment, concentrating on his writings at the time of the French Revolution. They show his unflinching support for 'enlightened absolutism' (pp. 97–156). H. Kremers very thoroughly analyses the source materials used by Sonnenfels for his essays and lecture courses. She defines his place in the traditions of European economic thought and his adaptation of the international material at hand to the specific conditions of Austria (pp. 171–90). The concept of 'patriotism' is shown by E. Wangermann to have remained basically constant in Sonnenfels's work since his well-known pamphlet of 1771 on the subject (pp. 157–69), and H. Haider-Pregler demonstrates Sonnenfels' importance for the establishment in Vienna of a 'national theatre' (pp. 191–244). Some of the essays of this volume overlap with the studies published by the same authors in other collections: here, however, they come together to show the work of Sonnenfels from a number of complementary perspectives. We are constantly reminded that Sonnenfels's teachings cannot be overrated, if only because generations of university students – prospective lawyers, teachers, public servants, writers and artists – were brought up on the study of his textbooks, which were prescribed examination material at Austrian universities from 1769 to more than forty years later.

Discussion of the impact of the Enlightenment on the emergence of radical movements in the Danube Monarchy at the time of the French Revolution, as well as the interrelationships of 'Jacobinism' with the activities of secret societies like the Freemasons and the Illuminati, remains based on the source materials and scholarly analyses of historians like E. Wangermann, A. Wandruszka, K. Benda, G. Silagi, A. Körner and E. Rosenstrauch-Königsberg in the 1960s and early 1970s. Much of this information is used and further developed in collections of articles by internationally-renowned scholars on 'Jacobins in Central Europe' (Reinalter, 1977) and 'promoters of Enlightenment in Central and Eastern Europe' (Balázs, 1979). H. Reinalter has subsequently attempted to provide the long overdue full presentation of the activities of the 'revolutionary democrats' in the Habsburg Monarchy (Reinalter, 1980, p. 9). Although his book contains interesting archive material in connection with the Austrian aspects of the Jacobin Trials of 1794–5, it shows a somewhat simplified approach to the development of a new intelligentsia in the course of the reform movement and the complexities of nascent nationalism. A more thorough attempt to understand the struggle between the adherents of Josephinist reform policies and their opponents is undertaken by G. Lettner (Lettner 1988). Her detailed analysis of the events in the last months of the rule of Leopold II and the interaction of rebellious students, enlightened bureaucrats, conservative politicians and clever pamphleteers is an important contribution to our understanding of the inner conflicts of adherents and opponents of reform absolutism. Like many publications written from a traditional Marxist perspective, however, this interesting study suffers from its reduction of complex social situations to a confrontation of clear-cut 'reactionary' and 'progressive' forces.

The bicentenary of the French Revolution reactivated interest in questions of reform absolutism and its suppression in Austria. H. Reinalter's collection of essays on Austria and the French Revolution consists mainly of reformulations of the author's earlier studies (Reinalter, 1988b). The Hungarian developments in the last decade of the eighteenth century, including the presentation of the strengthening national aspirations in the lands of the Hungarian Crown, are well covered by K. Benda and others in the relevant volume of the 'History of Hungary, 1790–1848', first published in 1980 (Mérei/Vörös, 1980).

Many of the books discussed in this article demonstrate that the almost complete inaccessibility of primary materials has made it extremely difficult to conduct research in eighteenth-century Austrian social and cultural history. For the study of strictly historical topics some older editions of documents have at least been available since the second half of the last century. However, work on popular texts, especially the pamphlets published in the years after the easing of censorship in 1781, can still only be done in the libraries of Vienna, in some other centres of the old Danube Monarchy, and in the Stanford Library collection, assembled with indefatigable dedication by Dr P. R. Frank. Reliable modern scholarly editions are very scarce. The great reprint-wave of the 1960s and 1970s almost completely by-passed the Austrian reform period.

Even now, we cannot lay our hands on a full and reliable edition of the seminal works of Sonnenfels. A reprint of the ten-volume *Gesammelte Schriften* (Collected Writings) of 1783–87 and a critical edition of his basic university textbooks are urgently needed. Students of Austrian theatre, culture and literature are fortunate to have an excellent modern edition of his *Briefe über die Wienerische Schaubühne* (Letters on the Viennese Theatre) by H. Haider-Pregler; it contains a well-documented study of Sonnenfels's ideas and his attitudes to the theatre, as well as a thorough commentary on the text (Sonnenfels, 1988; pp. 347–563).

One of the important satirical novels of the time, often seen by contemporaries as the most typical expression of the intellectual climate of the first half of the Josephinist decade, Pezzl's *Faustin* (1783), has been published in a well-annotated reprint by W. Griep (Pezzl, 1982); it also indicates the significant changes that appeared in the fourth edition of 1788. Some of the pamphlets discussing Joseph II's decree of 1785 establishing state control over the Masonic lodges of the Monarchy are reprinted in a volume by H. Reinalter *(Joseph II/ Freimaurerei*, 1987). The central discussion on the relations between absolutist practice and the ideas of European Enlightenment of 1784–86 was, however, conducted in pamphlets grouped around J. Friedel's *Briefe aus Wien* and J. Grossing's *Unwahrscheinlichkeiten* (Improbabilities). They are still not available in reprint.

A broad selection of the Austrian literature of the Enlightenment period, 1765–1800, has recently been published (Rosenstrauch-Königsberg, 1988). It contains some poetry, excerpts from Sonnenfels's journals and the novels of Pezzl and F. X. Huber, pamphlets by Richter, and Blumauer's seminal essay on the 'Broschürenflut'. Excerpts from Pezzl's description of Vienna help to provide local colour. The accompanying essay gives the rationale for the selection and brief survey of the period. This volume is far superior to J. Schondorff's superficial and rather impressionistic compilation of texts illustrating Viennese literary life in the era of Joseph II (Schondorff, 1980). The sketchy form of the book points to its editor's main interest, the birth of the Viennese 'feuilleton' after the liberalisation of the press in 1781 (p. 296).

We can only mention here some of the additional recent publications about Austria in the eighteenth century intended for a broader reading public. There is an unbroken interest in Maria Theresa, extending to television scripts (Sebestyén, 1980) and children's books (Hamann, 1985). The 'popularisation' of Joseph II has always been a much more onerous task. H. Magenschab's book on Joseph as a 'revolutionary by divine right' (Magenschab, 1979) is a chatty narrative adopting a collage technique of lengthy inserted quotations. It uses a rather trivialised psychology to come to grips with the personality of Joseph II and his relevance for the present-day Austrian reader (p. 9). A somewhat more serious attempt to describe Joseph as a 'ruler between the ages' by L. Mikoletzky is not very informative (Mikoletzky, 1979). I have not yet seen K. Gutkas's new biography (Gutkas, 1989).

Joseph's 'system' and his personality have kept their fascination for intellectuals throughout the world. B. O. Jones, one of Australia's most dedicated believers in enlightened modernity – and a Labor Minister for Science from 1984 to 1990 – started his writing career with a lucid booklet on Joseph II (Jones, 1966, not included in earlier bibliographies). The Hungarian intelligentsia has always regarded the withdrawal of most of Joseph's reforms 'with a stroke of the pen' some weeks before his death as both an allegory for the defeat of Enlightenment and the victory of national forces over foreign despotism. A booklet by J. Barta provides an intelligent discussion of the historical forces behind Joseph's notorious signing and its relevance for the ambivalent situation of Hungary in the 1970s (Barta, 1978). The last years of the Kádár regime also produced a readable biography of Joseph as the 'imperial Don Quixote' (Molitor, 1987). The author ascribes the Emperor's tragic failure to his having been a 'class traitor' to the aristocracy in the interest of an underdeveloped bourgeoisie (p. 384). The schematic use of Marxist categories makes it difficult, however, for Molitor to come to grips with the complexities of reform and 'Enlightenment from above', one of the pivotal problems of the political traditions of Central and Eastern Europe.

Such difficulties are patently evident in contemporary attempts at presenting Joseph II and his rule in imaginative literature. Retelling popular anecdotes about Joseph is an easy option (Mahovsky, 1980). A more demanding form is chosen by K. Böser who writes a 'political comedy' on the clash of state power and activist Enlightenment in its first modern manifestation – the Austria of Joseph II (Böser, 1978, p. 63). A lengthy whimsical essay by K. M. Gauss satirises the Austrian and Central European intellectuals' and artists' dream of fully bureaucratised state patronage under the rule of a 'benevolent despot' identifiable as both Joseph II and Bruno Kreisky (Gauss, 1989). His protagonist is J. Rautenstrauch, a leading figure of Viennese journalism in the 1780s and author of numerous satirical 'dream-visions'. Rautenstrauch has fallen asleep after Joseph's death and awakes in post-Kreisky times. The book itself takes the form of a late eighteenth-century Austrian pamphlet and shows how attitudes of cantankerous nagging and carping are born from the political immaturity and disillusioned servility which are characteristic of the 'Nörgler' and 'Raunzer' figures in Nestroy's, Kraus's and Bernhard's works. A comprehensive history of the Josephinian legend in imaginative literature has still to be written; it would be of special relevance today not only for Austria but for the whole of Central and Eastern Europe. The best expert in the field, E. Beutner, has not yet published a full account of his research. He has, however, contributed some important building blocks for a future synthesis (Beutner, 1987, pp. 111–23; see also some essays in the bicentennial anthologies).

This article cannot deal in any detail with three books of recent years which go beyond accumulations of raw materials or specialised studies and are already substantial parts of a major history of the Habsburg Empire in the age of the Enlightenment. All three come from outside German-speaking Europe. F. Venturi's great synthesis of eighteenth-century Italian cultural and intellectual history, *Settecento Riformatore*, now contains a discussion of the reform period in Austria (Venturi, 1984, pp. 615–779). I believe that the full importance for Central European studies of this remarkable work has yet to be understood. Venturi is aware of the great social and political differences between the easily definable centres of Italy, though recognising the unifying forces of language and traditions. His monumental work takes in the main political events and ideological issues of eighteenth-century Europe as seen by the different social and regional groupings of Italian writers and intellectuals. Venturi can thus present a multi-dimensional history of both the development of Italian Enlightenment and the main movements in the history of ideas of the Western world, not excluding their popularised and highly effective expression in pamphlets and short-lived journals. His account of Austrian Enlightenment, as seen by the Italian intelligentsia, can greatly enlarge our understanding of this movement. A comprehensive history of the Habsburg Monarchy could, with profit, use a similar method.

It is of the greatest importance for our understanding of eighteenth-century Austria that the long expected *History of Hungary* from the end of Turkish occupation (1686) to the death of Joseph II has now been published in its final form (Ember/Heckenast, 1989). It is one of the last volumes of an impressive project of the Institute of History of the Hungarian Academy of Sciences: the whole venture is a characteristic product of the post-1956 liberalisation period, demonstrating the intention of Hungarian historians and intellectuals to keep in contact with their Western and, more specifically, their Austrian colleagues. The editors' introduction emphasises the special importance of change in eighteenth-century Europe, as well as in the Habsburg Empire, at a time when Hungary had already become an integral part of the Danube Monarchy. It also emphasises the problems raised by the unequal development of the individual parts of the region. Additionally, the work is designed to show the emergence and strengthening of national aspirations and movements in the ethnic groups within the lands of the Hungarian Crown (pp. 17–22).

The finest Hungarian scholar in this field, É. H. Balázs, lucidly characterises 'the Habsburg variant of enlightened absolutism' (pp. 831–926) and discusses the Josephinist decade as 'the drama of the 80s' (pp. 1023–1123). She firmly sets these years into the context of the overall European crisis of absolutism, and evaluates with sensitivity the dialectics of the Emperor's reforms and conservative feudal resistance, the latter strengthened by the imposition on Hungary in 1784 of German as the 'official language'. She traces the rise of a progressive, pragmatic and economically (as well as socially) well-informed layer within the Hungarian nobility that was later able to lead the reform movement of the 1830s (pp. 1121–3). This thoroughly documented and substantial work covers the whole period in detail. Analyses of the ideological, educational and cultural aspects of Maria Theresan and Josephinist absolutism are given by D. Kosáry (pp. 763–824; 1125–1205). I would think that more attention could probably have been given to the most important form of public debate and discussion of the era, the writings of Viennese pamphleteers and their Hungarian followers and translators. On the whole, however, it will be difficult in future to arrive at a valid synthesis of eighteenth-century Austrian and Central European history without making reference to this extremely useful publication. É. H. Balázs's history of life in Vienna and Pest-Buda at the turn of the eighteenth century (Balázs, 1983) covers the same ground in more popular form.

A full understanding of the role of Austrian reform absolutism in the shaping of Eastern Central Europe to the present day is now made possible by the three-volume 'History of Transylvania' (in Hungarian, Makkai/Szász, 1986). A substantial section, with ample bibliographical documentation, by Z. Trócsányi deals with eighteenth-century developments (pp. 972–1185).

Absolutism in whatever form and however 'enlightened' can never be separated from the personality of the absolute ruler. There is ample (though not always up-to-date) material to help the scholar needing information about Maria Theresa's rule and personal characteristics, and the personality of Leopold II has been investigated thoroughly by A. Wandruszka in his definitive biography of 1963–5. It is a well known and often lamented fact, however, that there is nothing comparable for Joseph II, the key figure of Habsburg enlightened absolutism. This work is now being undertaken by D. Beales in his biography of the Emperor, the first volume of which, covering the period of Joseph's youth and the years of his co-regency, was published in 1987 (Beales, 1987). The author tells me we shall have to wait some time for its continuation. As it stands, however, the work is already an indispensable tool for the student of the period. The introduction summarises the present state of research and defines the scope of the book and the intentions of the biographer (pp. 1–16).

In this survey we can mention only some of the main aspects of Beales's book, but at long last we have a biography of Joseph II, prepared with the greatest scholarly care, that gives, for the first time, a meticulously annotated modern portrayal of a historical personality whose story has often been used and distorted for opposing political and ideological purposes. The thorough confrontation of published materials with archival sources furnishes a reliable basis for our understanding of Joseph and his age. The analysis of Joseph's seminal memoranda on the principles of government of 1763 (*Rêveries*, pp. 97–106), 1765 (pp. 164–76) and 1768 (pp. 176–91) provides a good insight into both the main tenets of Josephinism in the broad sense of the word (i.e., not only the religious or the ecclesiastic) and the continuity of Joseph's ideas. Beales constantly reminds us of the interplay between the 'triumvirate' of Maria Theresa, Kaunitz and Joseph (pp. 139–49; 422–7), and shows how Joseph's views and intentions played an important role in all crucial decisions (e.g. pp. 418; 476–79). He also takes great pains to dispute and invalidate the image of Joseph as an aggressive militarist expansionist (e.g. pp. 302–5).

A fascinating image of Joseph's multi-faceted personality emerges. We are shown his egalitarianism and aristocratic arrogance; his activism, irony and hatred of etiquette, as well as his skilled handling of public relations; and the inevitable merging in an absolute ruler's existence of the private and the public sphere (e.g. pp. 306–7). Beales gives us the clearest insight into the personality of a typical intellectual, constantly longing for broad-minded, stimulating conversation but condemned to an existence of unfulfilled loneliness even while creating for himself a group of intimate companions from among the côteries of courtly society (e.g. 314–37). Obviously much more will emerge with the continuation of the book. I am thinking here of Joseph's increasing difficulties in coping with the fatal clash between the Enlightenment project and the forces of public indolence and feudal resistance in the midst of the escalating international crisis of the 1780s. The awakening nationalism of the peoples of the Monarchy was an unexpected and unwanted by-product of the policies of openness, change and reform. This paradox must have exceeded the Emperor's comprehension. We can be certain, however, that Beales's biography of Joseph II, when finished, will be a decisive step towards an up-to-date synthesis of the history of eighteenth-century Austria, the Danube Monarchy and the whole of Central Europe.

This multifarious array of publications on eighteenth-century Austria reminds the reader how topical this period of reform and modernisation remains. Many of the changes brought about by the revolutions of 1989–90 in Eastern Central Europe have their roots in the unresolved conflicts created by the late eighteenth-century 'revolution from above' in the Habsburg Monarchy. Clashes between bureaucratic Enlightenment and traditional creeds, state patriotism and language-bound nationalism, the pressures of public opinion and of normative authoritarianism appeared here in their first modern manifestation. At the same time, the foundations were laid for the rule of law, the 'Rechtsstaat', with its secularised system of education and social welfare, crucial then and crucial now for the successful 'Europeanisation' of the region.

Bibliography

This is a short-title listing of the books mentioned in the article: in some cases with the abbreviations under which they are quoted.

Balázs, Éva H. et al. (eds.) 1979 *Beförderer der Aufklärung in Mittel- und Osteuropa*, Berlin.
Balazs, Éva H. 1987 *Bécs és Pest-Buda a régi századvégén*, Budapest.
Barta, János ifj. 1978 *A nevezetes tollvonás*, Budapest
Barton, Peter F. 1978 *Jesuiten, Jansenisten, Josephiner*, Vienna/Cologne/Graz.
Barton, Peter F. (ed.) 1981 *Im Zeichen der Toleranz*, Vienna.
Bauer, Roger 1977 *Laßt sie koaxen, Die kritischen Frösch' in Preußen and Sachsen!* Vienna.
Bauer, Werner M. 1978 *Fiktion und Polemik*, Vienna
Beales, Derek 1987 *Joseph II vol. 1. In the Shadow of Maria Theresa 1741–1780*, Cambridge.
Beutner, Eduard et al. (eds) 1987 *Dialog der Epochen. Walter Weiss zum 60. Geburtstag*, Vienna.
Bodi, Leslie 1977 *Tauwetter in Wien*, Frankfurt.
Böser, Knut 1978 *Joseph II oder das Ende der Unsterblichkeit, Komödie*, Cologne.
Csáky, Moritz 1981 *Von der Aufklärung zum Liberalismus*, Vienna.
Csáky, Moritz; Hagelkrys, Reinhard (eds) 1989 *Vaterlandsliebe und Gesamtstaatsidee*, Vienna.
Drabek, Anna M.; Plaschka, Richard G.; Wandruszka, Adam (eds) 1982 *Ungarn und Österreich unter Maria Theresia und Joseph II*, Vienna.
Ember, Győző; Heckenast, Gusztáv (eds.) 1989 *Magyarország története, 1686–1790*, 2 vols, Budapest.
Gauss, Karl-Markus 1989 *Der wohlwollende Despot*, Klagenfurt.
Gutkas, Karl 1989 *Joseph II, Eine Biographie*, Vienna/Darmstadt.
Haider-Pregler, Hilde 1980 *Des sittlichen Bürgers Abendschule*, Vienna/Munich.
Hamann, Brigitte 1985 *Ein Herz und viele Kronen*, Vienna.
Hersche, Peter 1977 *Der Spätjansenismus in Österreich*, Vienna.
Jahrbuch 1984 ff. Das achtzehnte Jahrhundert und Österreich, Vienna.
JIIK 1980 *Österreich zur Zeit Kaiser Josephs, Katalog Niederösterreichische Landesausstellung Stift Melk*, Vienna.
Joseph II und die Freimaurerei im Lichte zeitgenössischer Broschüren, 1987, ed. H. Reinalter,

Vienna.
Jones, Barry O. 1966 *Enlightenment in Politics*, Melbourne.
Köpeczi, Béla et al. (eds) 1985, *L'absolutisme éclairé*, Budapest.
Koschatzky, Walter (ed.) 1980 *Maria Theresia und ihre Zeit*, 2nd ed., Salzburg/Vienna.
Kovács, Elisabeth (ed.) 1979 *Katholische Aufklärung und Josephinismus*, Vienna.
Lettner, Gerda 1988 *Das Rückzugsgefecht der Aufklärung in Wien 1790-1792*, Frankfurt/New York.
Lindner, Dolf 1983, *Der Mann ohne Vorurteil, Joseph von Sonnenfels 1733-1817*, Vienna.
Magenschab, Hans 1979 *Josef II, Revolutionär von Gottes Gnaden*, Graz/Vienna/Cologne.
Makkai, László; Szász, Zoltan (eds) 1986 *Erdély története*, Vol. 2. *1606–tól 1830–ig*, Budapest.
Mahovsky, Ekhard 1980 *Die Furche von Slawikowitz und andere Anekdoten um Kaiser Joseph II*, Vienna/Munich.
MTK 1980 *Maria Theresia und ihre Zeit, Katalog Ausstellung Schloß Schönbrunn*, Vienna.
Mikoletzky, Lorenz 1979 *Kaiser Joseph II, Herrscher zwischen den Zeiten*, Göttingen/Zürich/Frankfurt.
Mérei, Gyula; Vörös, Károly (eds) 1980 *Magyarország története 1790-1848*, 2nd ed. 2 vols, Budapest.
Molitor, Ferenc 1987 *II. József, a császari Don Quijote*, Budapest.
Plaschka, Richard Georg; Klingenstein, Grete, et al. (eds) 1985, *Österreich im Europa der Aufklärung. Kontinuität und Zäsur in Europa zur Zeit Maria Theresias und Josephs II*, 2 vols, Vienna.
Pavlyshyn, Marko 1990 *Glasnost' in context*, New York/Oxford/Munich.
Pezzl, Johann 1982 *Faustin oder das philosophische Jahrhundert*, ed. Wolfgang Griep, Hildesheim 1982.
Reinalter, Helmut (ed.) 1977 *Jakobiner in Mitteleuropa*, Innsbruck.
Reinalter, Helmut 1980 *Aufgeklärter Absolutismus und Revolution*, Vienna/Cologne/Graz.
Reinalter, Helmut (ed.) 1988a *Joseph von Sonnenfels*, Vienna.
Reinalter, Helmut 1988b *Österreich und die Französische Revolution*, Vienna.
Rosenstrauch-Königsberg, Edith (ed.) 1988 *Literatur der Aufklärung 1765-1800*, Vienna/Cologne/Graz.
Schondorff, Joachim (ed.) 1980 *Aufklärung auf wienerisch*, Vienna/Hamburg.
Sebestyén, György 1980 *Maria Theresa*, Vienna.
Seidler, Andrea; Seidler, Wolfram 1988 *Das Zeitschriftenwesen im Donauraum zwischen 1740 und 1809*, Vienna/Cologne/Graz.
Sonnenfels, Joseph von 1988 *Briefe über die wienerische Schaubühne*, ed. Hilde Haider-Pregler, Graz.
Venturi, Franco 1984 *Settecento Riformatore*, Vol. 4 *La caduta dell'Antico Regime (1776–1789)*. Pt. 2 *Il patriottismo repubblicano e gli imperi dell'Est*, Torino.
Wangermann, Ernst 1978 *Aufklärung und staatsbürgerliche Erziehung. Gottfried van Swieten als Reformator des österreichischen Unterrichtswesens 1781-1791*, Vienna.
Winter, Michael 1988 *Georg Philipp Wucherer. Ein Buchhändler und Verleger oppositioneller Schriften gegen Joseph II*, Diss. Univ. Vienna.
Zeman, Herbert (ed.) 1979 *Die österreichische Literatur. Ihr Profil an der Wende vom 18. zum 19. Jahrhundert (1750–1830)*, 2 vols, Graz.
Zöllner, Erich (ed.) 1983 *Österreich im Zeitalter des aufgeklärten Absolutismus*, Vienna.
Was blieb von Joseph II? 1980 *Eine Dokumentation. Internationales Symposion Melk*, St. Pölten/Vienna.

Leslie Bodi

Note

My thanks are due to Dr Ritchie Robertson, for having provided reviewer's copies from a number of publishers. I also wish to thank Monash University Library and its Interlibrary Loan Service. Some interesting publications have, nevertheless, remained unavailable to me. I have received valuable advice and publications for this article from D. Beales, E. Beutner, M. Csáky, H. Lang, G. Klingenstein, H. Haider-Pregler, A. and W. Seidler and A. Tarnai. D. C. Muecke helped to put the text into shape. I am grateful for all their assistance. More detailed reviews have been published by me on Haider-Pregler, 1980, in *Journal of Modern History*, 55 (1983), 156-8; on *Joseph II/ Freimaurerei* 1987, in *Internationales Archiv für Sozialgeschichte der deutschen Literatur*, 14 (1989) 244-8; and on Lettner 1988, in *ibid.*, forthcoming.

The Mozart Bicentenary
Peter Branscombe

Brigid Brophy, *Mozart the Dramatist: The Value of his Operas to Him, to his Age and to Us*, 2nd edn (London: Libris, 1988), 332 pp., £29.95 hardback, £9.95 paperback.

Baird Hastings, *Wolfgang Amadeus Mozart: A Guide to Research*, Garland Composer Resource Manuals, vol. 16 = Garland Reference Library of the Humanities, vol. 910 (New York and London: Garland Publishing, Inc., 1989), xxx + 412 pp., $69.00.

Hans-Josef Irmen, *Mozart: Mitglied geheimer Gesellschaften* (Mechernich: Prisca-Verlag, 1988), 360 pp., DM 49,50.

H. C. Robbins Landon, *Mozart: The Golden Years 1781–1791* (London: Thames and Hudson, 1989), 272 pp., £14.95.

Richard Maunder, *Mozart's Requiem: On Preparing a New Edition* (Oxford: Clarendon Press, 1988), [vii] + 227 pp., £25.00.

Frederick Neumann, *Ornamentation and Improvisation in Mozart* (Princeton: Princeton University Press, paperback, 1989), xiii + 301 pp., $24.95.

J. W. Smeed, *Don Juan: Variations on a Theme* (London and New York: Routledge, 1990), xi + 190 pp., £25.00.

Andrew Steptoe, *The Mozart-Da Ponte Operas: The Cultural and Musical Background to Le nozze di Figaro, Don Giovanni and Così fan tutte* (Oxford: Clarendon Press, 1988), [x] + 273 pp., £25.00 hardback, £12.95 paperback.

Neal Zaslaw, *Mozart's Symphonies: Context, Performance Practice, Reception* (Oxford: Clarendon Press, 1989), xxv + 617 pp., £50.00.

As we remember the second centenary of Mozart's death, at the age of 35 on 5 December 1791, we cannot help being aware of a profound irony: that a single manuscript volume in his hand can now command at auction a sum that in comparative values probably exceeds his entire income for the whole of his short life. Readers whose memories go back to 1956 will recall the major publications that appeared in celebration of the second centenary of his birth – A. Hyatt King's *Mozart in Retrospect*, *The Mozart Companion*, edited by Donald Mitchell and H. C. Robbins Landon, three major congress reports and the catalogues of several exhibitions, Alois Greither's *Die sieben großen Opern Mozarts*, Paul and

Eva Badura-Skoda's *Mozart-Interpretation* (translated as *Interpreting Mozart on the Keyboard)*, and above all, the early volumes of that superb, if mildly flawed undertaking, the *Neue Mozart-Ausgabe*.

By comparison with the events of 1956 there is every sign that the Mozart industry will in the course of 1991 surpass not only all its own earlier efforts, but those hitherto marshalled in the cause of any artist. The *Neue Mozart-Ausgabe* proceeds on its stately and impressive course: over one hundred volumes have appeared by spring 1990, with the remainder promised by spring 1991 (and an India-paper edition in twenty volumes at bargain price is to come out at that time); regrettably, the *Kritische Berichte* are far behind schedule. 1991 will see the launching of several symposia, congress reports and other special publications (including lavish catalogues of the large-scale national and international exhibitions that have been announced). Every single one of Mozart's works, sketches included, is to be performed in New York during the anniversary year, and Philips have announced a similarly complete recording project on 180 CDs.

One of the most valuable books to have appeared in the aftermath of the last Mozart year was *Mozart-Handbuch: Chronik – Werk – Bibliographie* by Otto Schneider and Anton Algatzy (Vienna, 1962). By contrast, Baird Hastings's *Wolfgang Amadeus Mozart: A Guide to Research* is a great disappointment. Monoglot readers will approach it with high hopes, as its table of contents suggests great promise. There are five main divisions: profile (with chronology 1756-1956, a register of towns that Mozart visited, and an iconography with brief comments); Mozart's compositions, editions, Mozartiana and sources (including inevitably incomplete and out-of-date listings by location); Mozart's writings (a brief outline of editions of the letters, and of material connected with Mozart's activities as teacher); bibliography (general publications, specialised references, background, biography, music, and films and videos about Mozart); and an alphabetical dictionary of his contemporaries. Appendices cover listings of Mozart's pupils, his patrons, characters, and identifiable locales in his works, and lists of organisations and publications concerned with Mozart and his music; there are also indexes of authors, editors and translators; of names; and of works (a mere eighteen works are included!).

The most depressing aspect of this book is that one can take nothing for granted. Practically any page examined in detail reveals an embarrassing number of errors – in dating, spelling of names, copying down of bibliographical details. One cannot blame Mr Hastings for the incompleteness of his coverage – no one man, hardly even an international team of scholars, could hope to include every single item of value – yet there are startling gaps as well as some trivia in the 500-odd items listed. This is one of those books of which Otto Erich Deutsch said (self-deprecatingly) that it should only appear in a revised second edition; nothing short of a total re-working could make this a reliable book.

Of a totally different order is Richard Maunder's *Mozart's Requiem*. This is the companion to Dr Maunder's recent edition (OUP, 1988) of the work itself, which not surprisingly gave rise to some adverse criticism, taking as it does a stern line with regard to those movements for which no material survives in Mozart's hand. Thus, no Sanctus and 'Osanna', no Benedictus; and the

'Lacrymosa' and Agnus Dei are retained in a revised form. Maunder has based many of his editorial decisions on analogous passages, and on practices in other works of the composer's last year. The results can readily be heard in, for instance, Christopher Hogwood's recording of the work for L'Oiseau-Lyre. The book is a lucid, intelligent and refreshingly straightforward account of a highly complex set of problems; I have not come across anywhere so unsensationally gripping, and clear, a study of the genesis and history of the work. For once we are given detailed evidence about the strengths and (mainly) the weaknesses of Mozart's pupil Süssmayr as a composer at the time of his completion of the score (he was then probably not quite 26). No attempt is made to gloss over the mysteries and uncertainties: where the author permits himself a degree of surmise, he make it clear that this is what he is doing. And the argument he puts forward is, if occasionally debatable in point of detail, almost totally convincing overall. A valuable bonus is the concluding chapter, 'Performance', in which, apart from such obvious matters as the size and kind of forces for which Mozart was writing, Maunder has trenchant advice on the pronunciation of the Latin text (hard G; sibilant C before E, I, OE or AE; QU as KV, etc., as in the traditional Austro-German rather than the Italian manner). A challenging, stylish and uncommonly useful book.

Hans-Josef Irmen's new volume is even more important than it is difficult to obtain, which is saying something! *Mozart: Mitglied geheimer Gesellschaften* should be in the hands of every Mozartian, and indeed of everyone with an interest in the activities of Freemasons and other secret societies in the late eighteenth century. It is divided into five main sections; it has numerous tables, facsimiles and diagrams, and an index of persons, but no bibliography (sources are, however, normally cited in footnotes).

There is a wealth of new material here. Who was aware until now that Mozart had an organ in his apartment that he announced for sale (anonymously, but giving his address) in the *Wiener Zeitung* in January 1791 (he presumably found a buyer for it, as the instrument is not listed among his effects later that year)? And Irmen adduces evidence that Schikaneder was close to bankruptcy at that same period, and thus really did need the box-office success that early anecdotes speak of, but that later scholars (including the present writer) have been inclined to pooh-pooh.

The first four chapters are of outstanding importance, with their analysis of the intellectual and aristocratic background of Vienna in the 1780s; numerous documents, here made generally available for the first time, including lodge rituals (even one for female Masons, dated 1783, is mentioned though not reproduced); and a detailed study of the various other secret societies and branches of Masonry that existed (Irmen argues that Mozart had links with the Asiatic Brethren).

The most controversial chapter is the fifth, in which Professor Irmen argues for a commitment to numerology on Mozart's part that must have been obsessive to the point of frenetic. Anyone who has examined the autograph score of *Die Zauberflöte* in facsimile will recall that Mozart counted up the number of bars in each of the items (larger units, especially the finales, are sub-divided at changes of key-signature and/or tempo). Irmen would have us believe that Mozart found time in the busy summer of 1791 not merely to count the notes within his score, but to compose in such a way that, for example, the sum of the notes in the second violin part in the orchestral introduction to the Queen's first aria magically adds up to 80, which by substitution of letters for numerals (A = 1, B = 2, etc.) gives us 'Königin'. The trouble is, it could perfectly easily give us other words too ('Nachtnebel', for example); and my own inspection of the second violin part stubbornly refuses to yield the required total of 80 notes (what happens with ties, rests, accidentals?). Did Mozart really have nothing more pressing to do than play the numbers game? Readily corrected in a second edition are the numerous minor printer's errors and other slips; and one can hope that Professor Irmen will cite the (few) sources that he uses but does not identify. This is a very significant addition to the Mozartian literature; one will need time and careful, repeated study to assimilate all that it contains.

Mozart's symphonies, apart from the last six, have not had the same attention devoted to them as have the operas, concertos and chamber music. As Neal Zaslaw demonstrates in his magnificent and massive volume, *Mozart's Symphonies: Context, Performance Practice, Reception*, this comparative neglect is (or rather, has until now been) understandable: symphonies were usually unidentified in concert announcements, expendable or recyclable preludes and postludes to other musical works. It is largely thanks to Professor Zaslaw (as musical adviser to the splendid Schröder/Hogwood complete recordings of the symphonies, and now and above all thanks to this book) that the situation has changed. Here is much more than a *catalogue raisonné* of Mozart's symphonies authentic, possible, dubious and spurious, precious as that is: it is a profound, elegant, beautifully produced study of an age, its sociology, aesthetics, musical theory and practice. One does not know whether to admire more the judicious and perceptive analysis of the music or the thoroughness, originality and clarity of the presentation of the context in which the works came into being and were first performed. Various minor corrections are promised for the second edition, which will be an even more irreplaceable (and in paperback, even more welcome) possession for every Mozartian.

Considerations of space make it impossible to cover several of the recent books with the thoroughness they deserve. Frederick Neumann's *Ornamentation and Improvisation in Mozart*, now available in a paperback edition the generous margins of which will invite the careful reader's annotations, is of great practical value for performers. Neumann takes us through the treatises of Mozart's predecessors and contemporaries, pointing out the disagreements between them (attributable to geographical distance as well as stylistic differences), suggesting on the basis of analogy and musical common sense the most likely solution to a particular problem. The note of caution he sounds is one of the most healthy features of an invigorating book: 'to "apply" a rule from a treatise to another master's music, let alone to that of a unique genius, is a dangerous procedure ...' (p. 3). Throughout, Professor Neumann observes Mozart's own 'pervasive stress on musicianship, expression, and taste – "gusto" as he calls it – as final arbiter in matters of execution' (p. 5). The body of the book (which is followed by bibliography, and indices of works cited and of names and subjects) is in two sections. Part I covers the ornaments, Part II improvisation. The wealth of evidence about the appoggiatura, both theoretical and in actual performance, will prove especially helpful.

Andrew Steptoe has written a valuable and attractively presented study of *The Mozart-Da Ponte Operas*. Though there is no lack of perceptive and nicely illustrated analysis of the music, for many readers the depiction of the historical, social and cultural context will be quite as valuable, based as it often is on neglected or quite unfamiliar material. For the connoisseur, the heart of the book is the intricate detail, embedded in sound, lively and more general argument, about the three great operas: about parody in *Così*, problems of adaptation and pacing triumphantly solved in *Figaro*, or the role of cohesion and contrast in *Don Giovanni*, to cite three examples. This is a fine book.

H. C. Robbins Landon, having devoted much of three decades to the neglected and infinitely deserving cause of Haydn, has in recent years put his prodigious talents to work on Mozart. *The Golden Years 1781–1791*, soon to be followed by a *Mozart Compendium* he has edited for the anniversary year, is in the same rewarding vein as its forerunner *1791: Mozart's Last Year*: a fascinating kaleidoscope of narrative, excursus, generous and well-chosen illustrations, some kite-flying and the occasional plain error, with important new information in the appendices about Masonry and the Illuminati, Mozart's patrons, his colleagues and audiences. This is a very well documented book, atmospheric, easy to use, difficult to put down. And by present-day standards it is a real bargain.

Though J. W. Smeed's *Don Juan: Variations on a Theme* ranges over a wider chronological and geographical field than can legitimately be encompassed here, the da Ponte/Mozart *Don Giovanni* is the most frequently mentioned and, in Hoffmann's famous interpretation, the most thoroughly examined of all versions of the story. Gluck's ballet, the *Don Juan* of the Laufen boatmen, and Marinelli's *Dom Juan, oder Der steinerne Gast ... mit Kaspars Lustbarkeit* also make briefer appearances. Dr Smeed's book contains a great deal of carefully presented information within its 200 pages, and *Don Giovanni* could hardly be more shrewdly and clearly covered.

Brigid Brophy's *Mozart the Dramatist* was accorded a very mixed reception when it was first published in 1964. It reappears in a handsome revised edition, with a new subtitle, an eight-page preface mainly devoted to the two mature *opere serie* that were rather overlooked in the first edition, and as appendix a four-page 'Note on Professor Chailley's "Magic Flute"'. A number of larger or smaller revisions have been incorporated in the main text, but the pagination, like the attractive typesetting, has been retained. It remains a book that will tease, occasionally infuriate, often challenge the informed reader; some of the more glaring errors have been corrected, but there is much that will continue to vex the pedant and delight the irreverent.

Inevitably there is an element of chance about the inclusion or exclusion of this or that title in a survey of this kind, as well as something invidious about the relative attention accorded to a particular book. The well-informed reader may wonder at the absence of recent books by Alan Tyson, Volkmar Braunbehrens and Gunthard Born, to name but three. Mozart studies are in a vigorous state of health, though there is every sign that the dedicated Mozartian will be suffering from indigestion well before the end of 1991.

Histories of the Viennese Jews
Sander L. Gilman

Steven Beller, *Vienna and the Jews 1867–1938: A Cultural History* (Cambridge: Cambridge University Press, 1989), x + 271 pp., £27.50.

George E. Berkley, *Vienna and Its Jews: The Tragedy of Success, 1880–1980s* (Cambridge, Mass.: Abt Books; Lanham, Md.: Madison Books, 1988), xxii + 422 pp., £14.50/$24.95.

William O. McCagg, Jr., *A History of Habsburg Jews, 1670–1918* (Bloomington, Ind.: Indiana University Press, 1989), xiv + 290 pp., $27.50.

Ivar Oxaal, Michael Pollak, and Gerhard Botz (eds.), *Jews, Antisemitism and Culture in Vienna* (London/New York: Routledge & Kegan Paul, 1987), xiv + 300 pp., £30.00.

Peter Pulzer, *The Rise of Political Anti-Semitism in Germany and Austria*, revised edition (London: Peter Halban, 1988), xxvi + 358 pp., £20.00 (hardback), £9.95 (paper).

Robert S. Wistrich, *The Jews of Vienna in the Age of Franz Joseph*, The Littman Library of Jewish Civilization (Oxford: Oxford University Press, 1989), 696 pp., £45.00.

There is no doubt that there has been an explosion of interest in the Jews of Vienna following the election of Kurt Waldheim to the Austrian presidency. Not that there has not also been an equivalent literature on Berlin or Frankfurt Jewry, but that has been almost exclusively in German (with one or two notable exceptions). But six books in English (only one a reissue and that in much revised form) in two years is quite a formidable number for an anglophone public. Are readers in the English-speaking world so very interested in the Jews of Vienna, or are we dealing here with a generational phenomenon – the attempt to recapture something of a lost Jewish past in a city considered (as we shall discuss) to have a very special place in the history of the Jews in the *Galut*? If we remember that except for Grunwald in the early 1930s and the statistical study of Rosenblit in 1983, virtually no systematic studies of the Jews in Austria were published during the preceding fifty years, it becomes clear that these six volumes reflect an obsessive preoccupation with 'closing the gap' on the history of Viennese Jewry.

Let me proceed – at least in the beginning of this review – rather informally and survey these volumes individually and then, at the close of the review, see whether a pattern emerges from them which may (or may not) tie their various undertakings together. Pride of place belongs to Peter Pulzer, who is in every way the 'dean' of historians of Austrian Jewry. When first published in 1964, his study of the rise of political anti-Semitism shaped all of our understanding of the process by which anti-Semitism became part of the political culture of central Europe during the late nineteenth century. The book has retained its centrality: I cannot imagine an undergraduate class in the history of Central Europe (or the history of anti-Semitism – my own teaching interest) which does not assign at least one chapter from Pulzer's book. Now we have a revised 'Pulzer', and one which is available in paperback for classroom purchase. The volume is quite up to date. Reflecting the literature since 1964, Pulzer has brought the volume into the 1990s. It remains a solid, well researched, non-speculative study which provides a basis for any discussion of the political use of Jew-hatred. Whether or not one agrees with the radical subdivision of Jew-hatred into self-contained categories, such as 'political anti-Semitism', Pulzer's study remains valuable. It is a narrative history of people and events, one which is clearly organised and plays the events in Vienna off against the events in Berlin. This was the greatest strength of the first edition and remains the strength of this edition. It is a strength which becomes evident only when we consider the pitfalls of writing a 'history of Jews of Vienna'. For the comparative dimension helps stress the uniqueness (or the continuities) of certain patterns seen in a Protestant, Northern, 'German', i.e. Hohenzollern tradition or in a Catholic, Southern/Eastern, 'multi-cultural' k.u.k. tradition. What seems absolutely clear is the central role of Christianity as the focus of any Central European representation of the Jews. The specific vocabulary of Jew-hatred seems to be more closely linked to 'Christianity' than to any specific version of Christianity. While Pulzer stresses the representations of the Jew, his book has little on Jewish self-representations. It also has little on the history of culture, little on institutional structures. But then again, that was never its intent. The book remains a central teaching tool and a spur to all research in this area.

Pulzer's best student of recent years is Steven Beller – whose dissertation on Vienna and the Jews is self-consciously subtitled 'a cultural history'. Beller's intent is to complement the work of his teacher. He begins, however, by attempting to place his study in relation to Carl Schorske's work on Vienna. Unlike Pulzer, Beller needs to counter the lack of centrality which Jews seem to have in Schorske's world – at least as Jews. Schorske's focus is on the middle class. For him, the role of the Jews as a special category of middle-class identity was not paramount. Beller's intent is twofold: to show that the *Verjudung* (to use the contemporary, nasty term) of Austrian middle-class society was a reality, not merely a fantasy of the anti-Semites; and that the ubiquitousness of the Jews and their institutional structures form a 'real' focus for the anti-Semitism of the *fin de siècle*. Now, I too find Schorske's underemphasis of the 'Jewish' component in Viennese culture problematic, but for quite different reasons than does Beller. For being 'Jewish' is an inherent category of difference for the *fin de siècle*. It is a category of organisation, as certain as class. But it has little to do with the 'realities' of Jewish life in so far as it is an external set of categories. It is clear that some Jews of the *fin de siècle*, becoming aware of this unbridgeable abyss of difference, began to question the possibility of acculturation. But most Jews of the time internalised this sense of their own difference and dealt with it as well (or as badly) as they could.

In his answer to Schorske, Beller is caught in an odd bind: 'real' history demands that you go into an archive, find 'real' facts, compile them and then – tell it as it 'really' was. Beller is a good member of the guild and does exactly this. Here he is the mirror of his teacher. His archives are the extant school records of the Gymnasia in Vienna and he concludes that an overwhelming percentage of the students in a number of the schools were Jews. And, through these school records, he is able to track their parents' occupations and thus to present us with a picture of social mobility. Now this sounds fine, until we stop and think about the real problem many of us have had in figuring out what the occupation of one of these parents, Jacob Freud, 'really' was. Though he called himself a 'merchant' the best guess today is that he was a middleman selling for the pennies of profit between other middlemen and the retailer, not a 'merchant' in the sense of any economic definition but a virtual *Luftmensch* living from non-production and commodification. Beller 'believes' the designations outlined in the records without asking about the myth-making which they represent. Likewise he indulges in his own myth-making which in 1989 is a bit embarrassing, at least for an American Jew to read. The heroic era of Jewish history is over. We have been through the period (in the 1930s and 1940s) where tracing the 'Jewish' heritage of anyone could help satisfy our need for Jewish heroes; we are passing through the era where it is necessary for Afro-American scholars to claim Beethoven as a black in order to make a claim on Western culture. Beller 'really' needs to categorise everyone who had 'Jewish blood' as a Jew, whether it was Johann Strauss or Ludwig Wittgenstein. He misses the point. What one wants to tabulate are those individuals who were labelled as Jews in whatever context, whether they were 'Jewish' or not, to see whether an arena of public culture could be labelled as *verjudet*. It has nothing to do with 'real' Jews but with the shaping of public perception. Indeed, I find the 'mislabelling' of individuals as Jews in Fritsch and the *Semi-Gotha* interesting, because it provides a matrix for how the label 'Jew' could be used. It is not a random label and it often has less to do with perceived ancestry than with present-day activity.

Here a comparative dimension would have been very helpful for Beller. Medicine (or at least specialities such as psychiatry) in Berlin could never be labelled 'Jewish', nor were they in Vienna. For academic psychiatry in its clinical and administrative (asylum) functions showed virtually no 'Jews', no matter how defined. In taking psychoanalysis, which Freud in his fantasy about his age saw as isolated from the mainstream of psychiatry because of its 'Jewish' practitioners, as representative of a 'Jewish' quality to this arena, Beller misreads the institutional history of psychiatry. But it would be true to say that psychiatry was sensed as permeated by the Jews and as part of the conspiracy to control the existence of the Austrian middle class, at least in the popular press and fringe leaflets. This has nothing to do with Jews. Beller has not learned the basic rule of the history of anti-Semitism: you don't need Jews to have anti-Semitism.

The edited volume by Oxaal, Pollak and Botz comes much closer to being a cultural history (i.e., a history of political culture) than does Beller's dissertation. Beller is represented in this study also, but is balanced by clever pieces by the Parisian sociologist Michael Pollak on cultural innovation and social identity (which makes my earlier point about Beller self-evident); the ubiquitous Allan Janik on self-hatred as a model of identity formation; Sigurd Paul Scheichl on the language of anti-Semitism (from which Beller should have learned much) and Walter R. Weitzmann on Jewish communal politics from 1890 to 1914. This is not just a collection of essays, but a tentative attempt to sketch the complexity of internal and external definitions of the Jew. And maybe that is the way one must proceed. For a single voice tends to represent a single perception of the Jew on the 'Mazzesinsel' as well in the suburbs.

William O. McCagg, Jr., who has already given us a first-rate history of Hungarian Jews, has now expanded his field of vision and given us a broad-based history of Habsburg Jewry from 1670 to 1918. This is much closer to the comparative dimension which can produce a clearer portrait of the complexity of any aspect of Jewry in the Empire. For Buda and Pest are quite different from Prague or Vienna. And 1670 is very different from 1870. The book works as an overview and provides a solid narrative survey of the complexities of Jews and their acculturation or assimilation into the various parts of the Empire and their relationship to the 'centre', to Vienna. Little space is given to anything but 'political' history (from the state to the community), but the gaps are easily filled from other histories of Vienna.

The only study which brings the story of Viennese Jewry up to date is George E. Berkley's *Tragedy of Success, 1880–1980s*. In this popular history of the century spanning the Shoah, Berkley is the one historian who knows (or at least makes explicit) why anyone would care about the history of *fin-de-siècle* Viennese Jewry. For Hitler was there in 1907; Vienna shaped him (according to his own myth-making) into an anti-Semite and, so the story goes, without this moment there would have been no Shoah. Thus Viennese Jewry is responsible for the Shoah. Well, you can take this narrative or leave it, but it is clear that some version of this myth is the reason that Jewish scholars are, and continue to be, fascinated with Vienna and its Jews. Relying on existing research, Berkley's finely argued and reasonably well-written book compiles extraordinary amounts of material and places the political, cultural and historical dimension of Viennese Jewry in a general context. He deals with the Shoah in Vienna and with the post-war reconstruction (or perhaps resurrection? – but that term belongs to another discourse) of Viennese Jewry out of the spirit of the *Ostjude*. Despite occasional inaccuracies, this is a good attempt to write the complete history from the rise of political anti-Semitism until today.

The final volume on my shelf is Robert Wistrich's study of the Jews of the 'age of Franz Joseph'. As with all Wistrich's books, this study is a mine of material. He seems to have read everything on the topic and I have only rarely caught him out on using his sources. He is interested in the communal history of Viennese Jewry and places this in the context of the rise of anti-Semitism. He knows the history of the squabbles within the Jewish community and attempts (often quite successfully) to co-ordinate them with the external pressures placed upon the Viennese Jewish community from the Hofburg or the City Hall. He stresses the institutional roots of Zionism from Kadimah to the anti-Zionist voices in the Jewish community. And he concludes this volume with a spectacular series of individual readings (Kraus, Weininger, Freud, Schnitzler, Zweig and Roth), which give the reader more insight into the culture of the late nineteenth-century Viennese Jewish 'mind' than any other such history. Here is 'cultural' history as it must be undertaken, through the eyes of the participants and in sufficient detail that we sense the individual variations within the overarching responses. Indeed, the chapter on Freud is a must for anyone who has qualms about answering Peter Gay's claims about the nature and meaning of Freud's 'Jewish' identity. Wistrich's book is the most solid of these contributions and is indeed the only one of them which attempts to break truly new conceptual ground. But we have come to expect this from him and would be very disappointed if he did not deliver on our assumptions.

Now we must come to a conclusion: what do all of these books have in common and why have they all appeared at this time? What they have in common is an attempt to understand the complexity of Viennese (or Austrian) Jewry in a greater or lesser context. Their motivation is clear – the Austrian 'case' is a special one, one needing a close reading. And that because of the centrality in all of these studies – whether stated or not – of the Shoah. Only McCagg and Pulzer attempt a comparative study. And even they constantly stress the uniqueness of the Austrian situation. This may be true, but the reasons for the uniqueness of Austrian or Viennese Jewish experience cannot be found by pointing out the cultural diversity of the k.u.k. Empire (was it any more diverse than the stretch from Ostfriesland to the Bavarian Alps or from Glasgow to Delhi?) or the 'centripetal' structure of the Empire (was it any more centripetal than the Ottoman Empire?). What Wistrich begins to sketch is of interest – how ideas about the Jew and self-images of the Jew come to be reflections of commonly held understandings of the spectre of race as mirrored in social institutions. We can find a clue in the variations on widely held beliefs about the nature of the 'Jew' which are structured by the particular internal need of Austrian culture for its own variety of Other. Had Beller followed up his attempt to classify with an attempt to understand the fantasies of classification and the need to classify which he shares with the records he was examining, he would have come closer to the matter. All in all, for those of us working in the history of Viennese Jewry, these volumes prove an interest in the field but (thankfully) do not block further work in this area with a 'definitive' answer to a most complex and puzzling problem, the history of anti-Semitism in Austria and the Jewish response.

Part Three
Reviews

H. C. Robbins Landon and David Wyn Jones, *Haydn: His Life and Music* (London: Thames and Hudson, 1988), 383 pp., £24.00.

Over the last forty years our knowledge and understanding of Haydn's music have been transformed out of all recognition. Much of the credit for this must go to H. C. Robbins Landon, whose founding of the Haydn Society in 1949 marked the beginning of a complete re-evaluation of the composer. The supervision of a collected edition of Haydn's works, the preparation of a five-volume documentary biography, *Haydn: Chronicle and Works*, the editorship of the *Haydn Yearbook*, and the publication of numerous specialist books and articles, have now given him unchallenged supremacy. The appearance of a one-volume biographical and musical study consequently raises great expectations, abundantly fulfilled in a publication which will surely become one of the classics of Haydn literature.

The task which Robbins Landon has set himself, 'a summary based on what might be called the collective view of Haydn just over a quarter of a millennium after his birth', is a formidable one. Despite numerous minor revisions, the standard studies of Geiringer (1932, 3rd edn 1982) and Hughes (1950, 5th edn 1974) both fail adequately to reflect the current state of knowledge and are now more of historical interest. Other recent publications on Haydn are either too short to do justice to the subject, concentrate on only one aspect of his career, or are written from a perspective too far removed from the coal-face of research. But Robbins Landon's study presents a good, highly readable account of Haydn's life and music, drawing on the latest documentary and archival research.

The biographical chapters are basically an abridgement and adaptation of material from *Haydn: Chronicle and Works* and the slightly later *Haydn: A Documentary Study*, although more recent discoveries are also incorporated. Lively and engaging discussion links a judicious selection of documentary matter, producing a rounded picture of the composer and his activities. In this respect the present volume sometimes scores over the more comprehensive *Haydn: Chronicle and Works*, since essential facts receive greater prominence. For example, the description of the architecture and organisation of Eszterháza, as well as Haydn's activities, are here thrown into bold relief, whereas previously they tended to be submerged in a mass of archival detail and authorial comment unhelpful to the average reader. But by means of brief notes in the body of the text, Robbins Landon constantly refers to *Haydn: Chronicle and Works* for those readers who wish to consult such minutiae as a bill of 1763 for replacement double bass strings, or Haydn's petition to Prince Esterházy for hay and oats to feed the two horses he was presented with by Count Erdödy in 1776.

Interspersed between the biographical chapters are discussions of Haydn's music for the relevant period, provided by David Wyn Jones. On the whole, these deal admirably with the problem of describing and evaluating a vast and varied corpus of music. To take one example, the chapter for the years 1766–80 makes sense of perhaps the hardest and least accessible part of Haydn's output, namely his operas. It frequently comes as a surprise to those acquainted only with the concert and chamber works of Haydn to discover that he was a highly esteemed opera composer, as well as an influential interpreter of other composer's stage works. In somewhat less than twenty pages Wyn Jones manages to set Haydn's operas against the conventions of the day, explain their structure, and account for the weaknesses which are often perceived in them today. He is no less consummate in his handling of symphony, string quartet, and oratorio.

If any criticism may be levelled, it is perhaps that the *Rezeptionsgeschichte* of Haydn's music, which is dealt with largely in the Introduction, might profitably have been expanded. But this is a minor matter when set against the considerable achievements of the book as a whole. The combined efforts of Robbins Landon and Wyn Jones have produced a masterful insight into a composer, the ingenuity and complexity of whose music has vexed many previous commentators. *Haydn: His Life and Music* completely dwarfs any earlier attempts and is much the best one-volume study of the composer available today.

EWAN WEST

Briefe von und an Friedrich Kaiser (1814–1874), ed. Jeanne Benay, Contacts: Theatrica, 1 (Berne: Lang, 1989), xxx + 181pp., 44 Sw.F.

Friedrich Kaiser was a fertile dramatist, the author of over 150 plays. He and Nestroy together dominated the repertory of the commercial theatres in Vienna in the 1840s and 1850s. The style that the impresario Karl Carl required him to adopt was strongly influenced by Nestroy, who acted in many of his plays; but the 'Lebensbild' genre that he invented, a sentimental comedy with a moral, corresponded to the demands of Viennese critics for a more edifying type of didactic *Volksstück* in explicit contrast to Nestroy's farcical satires. Kaiser's first success in the genre, *Wer wird Amtmann?* (performed in 1840), is now remembered mainly as an object of Nestroy's mockery in the salon scene in *Der Talisman*; but it ushered in the last significant shift of taste in the tradition of Viennese dialect comedy before that tradition was swallowed up by operetta in the expanding industrialised city of the 1870s. Anzengruber's admiration for Kaiser (alone among the playwrights of his generation) is indicative of his pivotal importance.

Over and above his work as a playwright (and minor actor), Kaiser was an active journalist and the author of three valuable volumes of theatrical memoirs. He was prominent in the events of 1848 (it was he who rode through Vienna in the uniform of the Academic Legion on 13 March with the proclamation of a new constitution), and his memoirs of the revolution were edited posthumously by Franz Hadamowsky in 1948. He was also a leading figure in various clubs which functioned as centres of liberal sympathies for the artists and men of letters in mid-century Vienna. He founded the *Concordia*, to which Grillparzer and Bauernfeld belonged, in 1840; after the revolution he was the first president of its successor, the *Grüne Insel*. His letters show him on intimate terms with figures such as Castelli, the Burgtheater actor Carl La Roche, and Constant von Wurzbach, the compiler of the *Biographisches Lexikon des Kaiserthums Österreich*, whose entry for Kaiser in Volume 9 (1863) is still a useful source of information for the main part of his career.

His plays, moreover, lived on for some time. One, *Stadt und Land* (1844), appeared in Reclam's *Universal-Bibliothek*. The Deutsches Volkstheater in Vienna, founded fifteen years after his death, mounted productions of two dating from 1849, *Die Posse als Medizin* in 1895 – Schnitzler was among those attending the première – and *Mönch und Soldat* as late as 1914. In 1914, too, the city of Vienna honoured his memory by erecting an *Ehrengrab* in the Zentralfriedhof.

Inevitably Kaiser has been overshadowed by Nestroy in literary histories; but the publication of his letters to complement those of Raimund and of Nestroy (edited by Eduard Castle and Walter Obermaier in 1926 and 1977 respectively) is very welcome, all the more so since it has been undertaken by Jeanne Benay, who is established as the leading authority on Kaiser through her work on his use of French sources. Her edition contains sixty-eight letters, most of which are preserved in the Wiener Stadt- und Landesbibliothek and other Viennese libraries (plus two in Innsbruck and Bonn). Sixty are by Kaiser himself. Many deal with club activities. Others document the story of his lifelong love for Marie Pospischill, who abandoned an arranged marriage to live with him and who bore him an actress daughter. An appendix contains letters from both mother and daughter and also from Kaiser's elder brother, a writer on educational subjects. Among Kaiser's own letters one to Wurzbach on the family of Johann de Pian, the leading scene-designer for Carl's (and subsequently Nestroy's) company, is of special interest in illustrating the way Wurzbach collected biographical material.

Kaiser had a clear hand, illustrated in a facsimile, and Dr Benay's text is a diplomatic transcription. It is supplemented by an essay outlining Kaiser's career and by a detailed commentary on the letters. This tends to rehearse their content more than necessary but is valuable for a wealth of reliable background information. It is to be hoped that the appearance of this edition will stimulate the discovery and publication of other letters, particularly those in private hands. The journal *Nestroyana*, which specialises in the Viennese popular theatre, would be an obvious place for such finds to be publicised.

W. E. YATES

Miriam J. Levy, *Governance and Grievance: Habsburg Policy and Italian Tyrol in the Eighteenth Century* (West Lafayette, Ind.: Purdue University Press, 1988), x + 231 pp., $17.50.

The critical situation faced by Leopold II when he became ruler of the Habsburg Monarchy in February 1790, and his efforts to resolve this during his brief two-year reign, have inspired a large literature. Open disaffection in the Austrian Netherlands, near rebellion in Hungary, unrest in Galicia and, in some measure, throughout the Monarchy were compounded by a series of interrelated problems in foreign policy. The most acute of these were the unfinished and disastrous war with the Turks and relations with Prussia. Responsibility for this unpromising inheritance has been fixed to the shoulders of Joseph II, whose reckless foreign adventures and remorseless pursuit of unpopular reforms had brought the Monarchy to the brink of disaster by the time of his death. Miriam J. Levy's scholarly and carefully-researched monograph adds an additional and unfamiliar dimension to this well-known story, that of the Habsburg province of Tyrol. It exemplifies Professor Grete Klingenstein's recent remarks about full knowledge of the Monarchy arising only from detailed investigations of *all* its constituent parts,[1] and it makes available important information on one of the least known areas in the Habsburg Lands.

Eighteenth-century Tyrol was substantially larger than its present-day counterpart and sprawled south of the Brenner into what are now Alto Adige and part of the Trentino: the influence of Lombardy (itself governed from Vienna) and more generally of the Italian Enlightenment on its southern regions were clearly considerable. It contained a significant and prosperous Italian minority, who by the closing decade of the century amounted to some 16% of the population. The prosperity that came from the wine trade and from silk production had been imperilled by the tariff policies of Maria Theresa and Joseph II, while the Italian community also resented the Emperor's attempts to impose German as the language of law, administration, commerce and schooling. In 1790, and especially at the Innsbruck Estates during the summer and early autumn, this minority made a stand against the prevailing social, economic and political discrimination, and even demanded separation and unification with Italian territory. The new Emperor, Leopold II, a noted constitutionalist and ruler of the Grand Duchy of Tuscany for a quarter of a century, was himself sympathetic to the Italians' cause, which he appeared initially to support against the German majority.

A careful narrative of events in 1790–1 is at the heart of Professor Levy's book. The sharp divisions at the Tyrol Diet of 1790 (the first full meeting for 70 years) and the reaction of the government in Vienna are carefully outlined on the basis of substantial research on the German and Italian sources and wide reading in the secondary literature. She demonstrates how, in order to gain time, the new Emperor skilfully played off one group against another: his support for the Italians in the Tyrol paralleled his backing for the Romanians in Transylvania and for the Serbs and the burghers in Hungary. But if Professor Levy establishes Leopold's tactical skills beyond question, she does so at the expense of his strategic grasp and reputation for statesmanship. Her conclusion (p. 126) that 'many problems' had been 'resolved' by spring 1791 is surprising, in view of her own evidence that only one minor issue had been settled and that it was Bonaparte's armies rather than Habsburg government which ended agitation. Her pages provide considerable ammunition for those historians who believe that Leopold II shelved problems rather than trying to solve them.

The value of Professor Levy's book lies in introducing some complex and unfamiliar events to an English readership. Its limitations are those of many published doctoral theses. The narrative is one-dimensional, the author is occasionally reluctant to engage with some of the larger questions and too often loses sight of the broader picture: her remark at the outset, that the Tyrol ranked fourth in the scale of *internal* problems faced by the new Emperor, is not integrated into the narrative that follows. Yet Leopold's pressing domestic and foreign difficulties would seem to have shaped his actions – and periodic immobility – over the Tyrol. It is especially surprising that the influence of Freemasonry is nowhere discussed in the text. The valuable biographical Appendix makes clear that a surprising number of the leading figures in this story were Masons. Though events in the Tyrol are not sufficiently related to developments elsewhere in the Habsburg Monarchy, Professor Levy's book deserves attention as a reliable examination of a neglected dimension of Leopold II's reign.

H. M. SCOTT

1. 'Revisions of Enlightened Absolutism: "The Austrian Monarchy is like no other"', *Historical Journal*, 33 (1990), 155-67, especially p. 155.

Lawrence Sondhaus, *The Habsburg Empire and the Sea: Austrian Naval Policy, 1797–1866* (West Lafayette, Ind.: Purdue University Press, 1989), 326 pp., $24.50.

Sondhaus has pulled off an astonishing feat in writing an engrossing book about the history of a backwater navy which ends right at the point of its greatest victory at Lissa in 1866. In up-dating the older two-volume history of the Austrian navy from 1802 to 1847 by Khuepach and Bayer, he has broadened the perspective considerably by taking account of financial, commercial and political factors and, above all, treating the navy as a social organism with a life of its own. He follows the splits and rivalries not only of German and Italian officers, but of Trieste vs. Venice, of Napoleonic officers and French emigrés at the beginning of the period, and of rival cliques of predominantly German officers (like Wüllerstorff vs. Bourgoignon and Tegetthoff vs. Pöck) in the 1850s and 1860s. The supposed dullness of pre-1848 history is thrown into perspective by the 'Era of Big Spending' between 1824 and 1833, when the navy not only benefited from loose financial strings, but won the respect of Metternich by keeping a close eye on Greek privateering. The financial crisis following upon the costly anti-revolutionary fervour of the early 1830s plus the notoriously lax discipline of the Marchese Paulucci, its long-time commander, in turn led to a stagnation that climaxed in the Bandiera mutiny of 1844 – an episode that Sondhaus, for the first time, follows through from the point of view both of Austrian and Italian sources.

In summing up, Sondhaus gives greater credit than most naval enthusiasts to the fairness of army leaders in dealing with naval matters and lays stress on the individual efforts of sundry archdukes, in particular Ferdinand Maximilian (the later Emperor of Mexico) who managed to persuade his imperial brother to pursue a naval arms race in a period of retrenchment, thus in fact laying the foundations of victory at Lissa. This famous last-minute victory may not have changed the course of the war, but it was instrumental, Sondhaus insists, in holding all of Dalmatia for Austria, thus keeping Austria within the ranks of naval powers for half a century longer. To say that this is easily the best account of the Austrian navy so far, will not do justice – for want of modern competition – to a splendid work of historiography that might serve as a model of how military history ought to be written.

LOTHAR HÖBELT

Alan Sked, *The Decline and Fall of the Habsburg Empire 1815–1918* (London: Longman, 1989), 296 pp., £8.95 (paper)

Alan Sked's valuable and provocative book rests on a paradox. Ostensibly concerned with 'the decline and fall' of the Monarchy, it is really more a continuation of the theme of his previous book, *The Survival of the Habsburg Empire*. This is not a book about the Empire's inevitable decline; instead Sked argues that there was no real decline until 1918. Rather it is a study of how the Habsburgs, that is to say Franz Joseph, threw away their perfectly viable empire for the sake of honour.

The book takes the form of a historiographical discussion of recent literature on the history of the Monarchy. (It should therefore be very useful for teaching purposes.) Sked uses this recent research to argue, often convincingly and always with great plausibility, that although Austria appeared to lurch from crisis to crisis throughout the nineteenth century, it was seriously threatened with dissolution only once before 1918, and that was in 1848, when Radetzky's victories in Italy saved the Habsburg cause. Even here Sked suggests that 1848 was, in most parts of the empire, no real threat to the dynasty's rule. If anything, it was the ruling house's clumsy handling of affairs which sparked the revolution. Once some sort of order was restored in Habsburg policy it proved relatively easy to subdue the Austrian populace, which had, in any case, only sought reform and not revolution. Sked further asserts that the Hungarian revolution was, eventually, put down by the Austrians, not the Russians.

With the Italians beaten, the threat of 1848 proved an empty one. It was not internal strife which caused the Monarchy's subsequent problems so much as its repeated ability, in 1859 and 1866, to lose wars. The result was the Compromise of 1866 between the dynasty and the Hungarians. This is often taken to have been a fatal mistake, limiting Habsburg policy so much as to make it impotent in constitutional matters, and in foreign policy beholden to the anti-Russian Magyars. Similarly, the economic aspect of the relationship is supposed to have resulted in unfair advantage for the Hungarians. While not rejecting these criticisms out of hand, Sked does question them, and puts them in a proper perspective. On foreign policy he points to long periods of co-operation with the Russians over the Balkans. In the economic sphere he cites recent research which emphasises the beneficial effects of the post-1866 economic settlement. Finally, while appearing to side with those who see the Compromise as hindering efforts to remedy the problem of the nationalities, Sked rightly argues that this was not in itself fatal for the Monarchy.

Despite what conventional wisdom might suggest, Sked argues that the problem of the nationalities in the last decades of the Empire, while causing serious domestic disruption, never really threatened to dissolve that Empire. In other words, the policy inspired by Taaffe of keeping every group in a state of 'mild dissatisfaction' worked. While all were discontented, none but the most extreme fanatics sought to achieve their goals outside the context of the Monarchy.

Sked rejects the idea that it was the South Slav question which caused Austria to go to war. Instead he claims the 'irrational' policy of hostility to Serbia stemmed from Franz Joseph's sense of honour, and the obsessive wish of the ruling circles to do down an emergent and pugnacious Serbia before it became too powerful in Austria's 'backyard', to use a modern metaphor. It was thus foreign policy, not a domestic crisis, which caused the war, and hence the Empire's demise as it proved incapable of sustaining the war effort. Even here Sked stresses just how loyal the nationalities were until well into 1918.

Against Sked one could argue that a large part of the reason why Austria felt threatened by little Serbia, and why its war effort proved ultimately so ineffective, was that the Compromise and the nationalities question had absorbed and wasted so much of the state's resources that there was little left over for the real costs of being a great power. Thus the army was tiny relative to those of the other powers, and even worse equipped. One could also object that a book on the decline and fall of the Monarchy should have rather more pages devoted to the period from 1866 to 1918 than those allotted here. That is when, after all, things are supposed to have gone wrong, yet less than a third of the book is so assigned.

Nevertheless, this is a most interesting and well-argued account of the Monarchy's last century. Sked's ability to see this period with unsentimental detachment, in a field where nostalgia is often hard to avoid, is especially praiseworthy. His central contention that there was, in fact, no real threat to the Monarchy before 1914 comes as a salutary corrective to much of Austrian historiography. Whether admirers of Franz Joseph will so welcome the book is another matter.

STEVEN BELLER

Otto Dahinten, *Geschichte der Stadt Bistritz in Siebenbürgen*, ed. Ernst Wagner, Studia Transylvanica 14 (Vienna and Cologne: Böhlau, 1988), xx + 541 pp., DM 128.

Franz Greszl, *Ofen-Buda: Entwicklungsgeschichte der königlichen Residenzstadt Ungarns im 18. Jahrhundert* (Munich: Verlag des Südostdeutschen Kulturwerks, 1984), 144 pp., DM 39.

Carl Göllner (ed.), *Die Siebenbürger Sachsen in den Jahren 1848–1918*, Siebenbürgisches Archiv 22 (Vienna and Cologne: Böhlau, 1988), xiv + 448 pp., DM 128.

Hans Rothe (ed.), *Deutsche in der Habsburger Monarchie*, Studien zum Deutschtum im Osten 21 (Cologne and Vienna: Böhlau, 1989), viii + 171 pp., DM 44.

Perhaps the most striking thing about the Germans in the Habsburg Monarchy is not so much their dominance as their diversity. For every inhabitant of the ethnically homogeneous Alpine provinces, there was another living as a member of the German minority in one of the ethnically mixed provinces of the Empire. But dominance always played its part too: whether as a landed elite, or as prosperous burghers, or simply as more efficient peasant farmers, Germans set themselves off against the rest of the local population. That formed an underlying reason for their almost total expulsion from the successor states after 1945, the tragedy which has cast its shadow over all subsequent writing about them.

Dahinten's posthumously published work was written in the immediate aftermath of the collapse, and covers what had been one of the remotest, but strongest, of such communities: as late as the 1930s, 40,000 Saxons comprised almost 50 per cent of the population of Bistritz and its surrounding district. As history, it is amateurish and pedestrian. The liveliest sections, on the municipal Gymnasium in the 1840s and on the revolutionary events of 1848–9, are actually eye-witness accounts written by others; and the most scholarly portion of the book is the editor's supplementary bibliography. But it prints much interesting archival material, especially on matters of professional relevance for Dahinten, who was director of the Bistritz *Stadtbauamt*: detailed chronicles of public buildings, the water supply, and fortifications are complemented by miscellaneous legal cases, guild documents, and *Kleiderordnungen*. Moreover, it conveys an authentic sense of the viewpoint of the author, who lived from 1882 to 1955. His dislike for Hungarian administrative methods after 1867 is easily trumped by his withering contempt for the inter-war Romanian regime, corrupt and primitive – in 1934 the new authorities changed every single street name (a table lists all 139 of them) to commemorate freshly-baked Romanian heroes.

Dahinten's book shares common ground with the next two volumes under review here. Greszl too provides an old-fashioned and narrowly focused account of certain buildings and their uses in a single Hungarian town. He concerns himself exclusively, though only an absurdly wordy sub-subtitle makes this clear, with the development of churches and their congregations as revealed by visitation records for specific years (mainly 1732, 1761, 1783, 1795, and 1832). The general picture of Buda as peaceful and pious, an 'ordentlicher, ruhiger Ort' to which 'Religiosität ist im allgemeinen vorzüglich eigen', as the topographer Schams put it in 1822 (p. 81), is confirmed with some valuable details. Ecclesiastical statistics show how the Orthodox South Slavs who repopulated the town after the expulsion of the Turks were progressively outnumbered by Catholic Germans – a policy specifically favoured by the municipal administration. They also tell us about the linguistic competence of individual priests, who often spoke two or more modern languages with varying degrees of facility, mainly German and Hungarian or Croatian, sometimes Slovak. There are sidelights on the cult of particular saints and other forms of piety; on education and poor-relief. Yet no kind of argument or larger thesis emerges, and even the antiquarianism is flawed by an almost complete neglect of Hungarian literature on the subject.

Like Greszl, the contributors to the volume on the *Siebenbürger Sachsen*, the second in a series which began life a decade ago as 'Geschichte der Deutschen auf dem Gebiete Rumäniens', ignore much relevant Magyar literature. They also misspell Hungarian names (and on occasion seriously misunderstand them: thus the governmental party from 1910 was not a 'Munk*á*spart' or an 'Arbei*te*rpartei' [p. 208]). Like Dahinten's work, this account of the Transylvanian Saxon community as a whole is essentially a political chronicle, all compiled by the editor, with further, and rather more rewarding, chapters on economy, society, and culture. Despite disclaimers (e.g. pp.164 f.), the historical animus against Hungarian rule lives on vigorously, with useful, albeit unoriginal, discussion of the formation of Saxon parties and interest groups to resist it. Yet the loss of their communal autonomy had only a limited effect on the Saxons: the bulk of their parliamentarians usually supported the government (a matter not properly developed here); economic well-being was guaranteed through various kinds of self-help; the educational system retained its quality and separate identity (if Trefort had really succeeded in the 'forcible Magyarisation' of elementary schools in the 1870s [p.171], the Lex Apponyi of 1907 would not have been necessary); the Lutheran Church even consolidated its position by assuming the residual functions of the old *Landesuniversität*. The volume lacks any kind of conclusion; indeed, its narrative sections simply tail off into nothing. They do not begin to broach the issue of Romanian take-over after 1918, and they are mealy-mouthed about German-Romanian relations earlier. It is a pity that a work which has eventually, through no fault of its authors, had to appear in the West, should still bear the impress of its origins under the Ceausescu dictatorship.

Deutsche in der Habsburger Monarchie is a curious publishing venture in a different way, which returns us to the problem of diversity raised at the beginning of this review. Eight essays could hardly be more heterogeneous, and their collective *raison d'être* remains a puzzle. A preface qualifies the title, announcing a concentration upon those parts of the Monarchy 'die selten im Zusammenhang mit deutscher Sprache behandelt werden'; and we duly find a very serviceable account of German traditions in Southern (now Yugoslav) Styria by Othmar Pickl, a similar but briefer summary for the Saxons of the Hungarian Zips region by Gabriel Adriányi (whereas their Transylvanian compatriots and co-religionists are ignored), and a sketch of some relevant themes in the work of the Galician novelist, Karl Emil Franzos, by Joseph P. Strelka. But the rest of the volume comprises a technical paper on the reception in Germany of the Austrian *Bürgerliches Gesetzbuch*, a breathtakingly abbreviated history of Austro-German literature, a reprinted contribution on Rudolfine culture in sixteenth-century Bohemia, a linguist's introduction to Yiddish, and some idle musings on Hungarian painting. All four of these books leave one wondering when Teutonic scholarship will rise above the level of *Heimatgeschichte* in its treatment of the Germans of the eastern Habsburg lands (as it has so conspicuously done for Bohemia with the publications of the Collegium Carolinum in Munich); when it will rediscover its native traditions there of professional *Gründlichkeit* and *Ordnung*. Even the terrible events of October 1944 did not find those traditions entirely wanting: Dahinten relates (pp. 203-4) how, as final catastrophe impended, the treasury in Bistritz still managed to pay all its municipal officials their salary a month in advance, and to provide them with a detailed financial statement.

R. J. W. EVANS

Karl Kraus, *Frühe Schriften, 1892–1900*, I and II, ed. J. J. Braakenburg (Munich: Kösel, 1979), 308, 324 pp.; *Erläuterungen*, ed. J. J. Braakenburg (Frankfurt: Suhrkamp, 1988), 256 pp., DM 160.

Rainer Dittrich, *Die literarische Moderne der Jahrhundertwende im Urteil der österreichischen Kritik. Untersuchungen zu Karl Kraus, Hermann Bahr und Hugo von Hofmannsthal*, Europäische Hochschulschriften, Reihe I, Deutsche Sprache und Literatur, 1088 (Frankfurt, Berne, New York, Paris: Peter Lang, 1988), 286 pp., 63 Sw.F.

While Kraus's youthful writings may lack the critical vision and the stylistic mastery of the later work – from which perspective he distanced himself from them – some biographers have too easily dismissed the years 1892–98. The reviews and feuilletons which make up the bulk of the two text volumes of *Frühe Schriften* (taken over by Suhrkamp) testify to two formative influences: Germany's socially committed Naturalists, and the unnerving political repercussions of Badeni's language ordinances of 1897. The view of satire and the norms which preceded his linguistic criticism have meanwhile been documented, but it is time for the relation of his early journalism to his later critique of journalism and theatre to be scrutinised; for the obsession with combing for his opinions of Jung-Wien (exemplified by Rainer Dittrich's book) to be corrected; and for the relation of satire and polemic, of genres and style, to be clarified. In the absence of extensive archive material like that for Kraus's later work, at least the reader of *Die demolirte Literatur* can now see the development of motifs and word-play in contemporaneous feuilletons. The competent edition of *Frühe Schriften* can facilitate such approaches, even if the apparatus is not exhaustive.

The new volume III comprises notes, corrigenda, index and two newly discovered unpublished feuilletons. Viennese topography and dialect expressions, biographical and bibliographical information, political and other topical allusions are registered with great diligence. Thus apart from *Mélange* or Mark Twain, we are initiated into the 'Kußaffaire', 'Wasmuth's Ringe', a Jean Paul allusion, the pseudonym 'Crêpe de Chine' and Kraus's unpublished gloss on a feuilleton by Alfred Kerr. However, the 'lyre-form', which caused the editor problems (III,163), refers to the shape of the Burgtheater auditorium which was modified in these years (II, 54); and the newspaper sources (III, 97) given for Kraus's 'Gänsefüßchen' satire appear incorrect. The apparatus is generally factual, but at times pedantic or even trivial, as when Kraus is given a 'phobia' about postal delivery which is 'a major topic' of his correspondence; or as when Kraus's comment on characterisation in Schnitzler, 'der Dichter, der das Vorstadtmädel burgtheaterfähig machte' ('the writer who enabled the girl from the suburbs to enter the Burgtheater'), is taken as alluding to the dramatist's private life.

At times we learn less from the notes than from the text: '*Panem et circenses*' (III, 27) was in fact the motto of the book by Emil Reich whose title we learn later (III, 58); its author is described as a literary historian and popular educator, but his career as a philosophy lecturer whom Kraus admired (I, 125) is not covered. Theatre production data are frequently not of the specific performance being reviewed, but of a play's first performance, sometimes decades previously.

No details are given for Berlin premières like Strindberg's *Gläubiger* (22.1.1893 at the Residenztheater) and Sudermann's *Heimat* (7.1.1893 at the Lessingtheater). We have to wait till (III, 78) for details on Nestroy's *Der Flüchtling* which are relevant to (III, 62).

Secondary literature is, consciously but inconsistently, not acknowledged, whereas information received orally is. Continuing from the bibliographer Otto Kerry, the editor has traced press sources, but has made little use of unpublished sources which could have shed light on Kraus's literary relations. It is particularly unfortunate that a review by Kraus from 1896, which the editor himself discovered, is not reprinted here, and that no use has been made of the new unpublished material on *Eine Krone für Zion* from the Theodor Herzl archive, promised us in *Kraus-Hefte*, 13 (1980). These omissions, however, are no doubt due to Johannes Braakenburg's sad death in October 1988, before his third volume appeared in print.

The annotations seldom take into account Kraus's later work, or how his opinions and relations changed. The editor has explicitly valued facts, to avoid 'premature interpretation'. He has wisely cautioned that not all satirical or humorous articles in journals signed with a '-k' are by Kraus; he has rightly excluded a book-review ascribed to Kraus by Paul Schick, and queried a 'Brief aus Gmunden' from the *Neue Freie Presse* (I, 220f.). However, he has been too insistent on such initials as proof of authorship in placing a feuilleton from the spa Ischl in 1892 (T 92.4) for the short-lived journal *Das Rendez-vous*. Having encouraged 'premature interpretations' by including it in volume I, the editor has second thoughts in volume III, since the initials C-a were not used by Kraus elsewhere, but also on stylistic grounds, which are not specified. The confusion is compounded by the (for once) imprudent speculation that the older C. Karlweis was the author. The anomalous piece dates from a time when Kraus's style was still unformed, and his emulation of Daniel Spitzer, which has begun to be researched, suggests that there is more to discover about his relation to the conventions and rubrics of Viennese feuilleton culture before 1900.

Rainer Dittrich's book is not of comparable importance. The two-page conclusion, which ends with a lapidary 'etc.', speaks for the generalisations which precede it: Hofmannsthal is recrowned a champion of classicism and baroque, and his early appreciation of contemporary literature is panned; his interpretation of Balzac is taxed for eschewing the literary historian's label – and correct labelling is this book's concern. This is not, then, an original study of the relation of traditionalism and modernism, or of the relationship of criticism to creative oeuvre in the trio of authors. This lack distorts the perspective on their intense, if inconsistent, engagement with modern literature: Kraus's attacks on 'isms' are taken as his 'literary criticism', Hofmannsthal's paradigm of 'Kunstabsicht' meets with almost equal irritation.

Modernism is dogmatically defined, enabling examples which defy the book's simplistic verdicts either to be neglected (Kraus and Strindberg, Wedekind) or excluded (Werfel or Ehrenstein from 'Expressionism', Schnitzler from Bahr's Jung-Wien). There is no appraisal of the works whose reception by the trio is at stake, scant reference to regular Austrian critics, neglect of secondary literature and 'archive-based research', whose alleged absence is lamented. The clichés echo work on Kraus and Heine from the late sixties. At every turn the author comes up with the same disappointing conclusion: these Austrians, even Bahr, are simply too 'traditionalist'.

GILBERT J. CARR

Friedrich Schröder, *Die Gestalt des Verführers im Drama Hugo von Hofmannsthals* (Frankfurt am Main: Haag + Herchen, 1988), 299 pp., DM 35.

Margit Resch (ed.), *Seltene Augenblicke: Interpretations of Poems by Hugo von Hofmannsthal*, Studies in German Literature, Linguistics, and Culture, Vol. 40 (Columbia, S.C.: Camden House, 1989), 226 pp., $34.00.

Friedrich Schröder's thoroughly researched doctoral thesis examines the adventurer figure in Hofmannsthal's works, often referring to Kierkegaard's Don Juan interpretation and to Casanova's memoirs. Having sketched the already extensive research on Hofmannsthal's adventurers, he analyses convincingly Kierkegaard's distinction between the seducer who calculates his assaults on womankind and the Don Juan who instinctively capitalises on a favourable situation. The 'intensive', intellectual seducer delights in the dalliance of conquering one woman; the 'extensive', spontaneous philanderer enjoys satisfying his desires with many. Kierkegaard's Johannes is a latter-day Narcissus, Mozart's Don Giovanni dependent on struggle with the enclosed world of bourgeois respectability based on the Christian ideal of marriage. Against a contrast between 'seducer' and 'adventurer', Schröder develops his view of Casanova as a lover sensitive to the physical and psychological needs of his cast-off conquests, letting his acts of seduction accrete some of the qualities of the adventurer. Using the Bellino episode from his memoirs, where Casanova is faced by the challenge of a woman dressed as a boy, Schröder points out how far Casanova has moved away from the 'intensive' seducer seen in Kierkegaard's Johannes to become the model of an 'erotic adventurer' not dissimilar to Don Juan.

The major part consists of four chapters on *Der Abenteurer und die Sängerin*, *Cristinas Heimreise*, *Der Schwierige* and *Der Unbestechliche*. In the first of these plays, Weidenstamm is a poetic enfiguration of Casanova, and Venice the ideal ambivalent scenario for the erotic adventurer. Schröder shows how Hofmannsthal used Casanova's Bellino episode selectively, contrasting especially Thérèse, who changes lovers, and Vittoria, whose first meeting with Weidenstamm becomes the decisive experience in her life. Lorenzo too is far more complex than his model in Casanova's memoirs. In showing Weidenstamm incapable of appreciating the musical talent he has inspired in Vittoria, Hofmannsthal opened up an extra problematical dimension.

In the discussion of *Cristinas Heimreise*, *Florindo und die Unbekannte* is applied to good effect. Schröder emphasises Cristina's development from naive peasant girl to knowing woman as a necessary encounter with Eros. In renouncing Florindo for married life, she incorporates the focal point of Hofmannsthal's interest: the struggle between Eros and ethos, further intensified in the contrast between Venice and the mountain village Capodiponte of Act 3. Schröder, however, schematises the struggle perhaps too far when he relates Eros to the self and ethos to the 'du'-figure. Hofmannsthal surely allowed each 'representative' to be determined in part by both worlds.

In *Der Schwierige* both Neuhoff and Kari are examined as 'seducer' figures, yet little mention is made of Kari's nephew Stani who perhaps represents a parallel to Kari's earlier persona on whom Schröder bases much of his argument. Neuhoff is rightly dismissed as a personality with no substance and less success, a failure in social conversation and in personal dialogue. Indeed, one wonders whether he deserved analysis except as a complete foil to the complex involvement of Kari with a society sensitive to every faux-pas, and represented memorably in the Furlani clown-episode. Schröder uses previously unpublished fragments to excellent effect in his analysis of Kari's two major scenes with Helene. His explanation of the difficulties implied by the relationship between Eros and ethos convinces, particularly in the wished-for synthesis of the 'Ganze' or 'Innerste'. It is however disappointing to see how Schröder jibs at using the word 'Rasse' to apply to Helene, revealing laudable sensitivity yet a lack of awareness of the social implications in the play hinted at by the English concept of '(good) breeding'.

Dr Schröder is the first to link Hofmannsthal's knowledge of Julie de Lespinasse's letters and her biography by Pierre Marquis de Ségur with Jaromir in *Der Unbestechliche*. He sees Lespinasse's lover Guibert as a Don Juan and model for Jaromir, a would-be chronicler of his experiences with women. One would like to see further discussion of the relationship between writer and charlatan, actor and picaro, with reference perhaps to Hofmannsthal's earlier reflections on the actor (not forgetting his dedication of this play to Max Pallenberg) and to Thomas Mann's use of Nietzsche's long Aphorism Number 361 from *Menschliches, Allzumenschliches* in connection with the *Bekenntnisse des Hochstaplers Felix Krull*. The conclusion relating Jaromir with Guibert, Casanova and Johannes is probably his most searching comment: 'Aus den aufgezeigten Parallelen läßt sich nach meiner Auffassung der Schluß ziehen, daß der erotische Abenteurer auch Züge des reflektierten Verführers annehmen kann, wenn er altert und die Ausstrahlungskraft seiner Erscheinung nachläßt' (p. 154). ('In my opinion, the parallels that have been revealed permit the conclusion that the erotic adventurer can also assume traits of the reflective seducer, once he grows old and the radiance of his appearance wears off.') Unfortunately the implications are not analysed. Jaromir is examined against Theodor, Marie, Melanie and Anna with useful appraisal of Theodor's dual role as servant to and manipulator of his master's existence. Schröder rightly emphasises the fewer strata of meaning in *Der Unbestechliche* than in *Der Schwierige* and shows how ethos in the person of Theodor eventually triumphs over the Eros of Jaromir.

In a much shorter final section Schröder sketches his theme in *Idylle, Der Kaiser und die Hexe, Der Rosenkavalier, Ariadne auf Naxos* and *Die ägyptische Helena*, where one catches sight of material elsewhere given far more satisfactory treatment. Some women 'seducers' (Hexe, Zerbinetta, Helena and even the Marschallin) give further proof of the importance of the 'Verführer'-figure in

Hofmannsthal's dramas. An appendix includes nine previously unpublished notes by Hofmannsthal on Casanova. As in much previous research, Dr Schröder has found how difficult it is to fit Hofmannsthal's works and characters into a single pattern. His major contribution is to have pinpointed the evidence of Hofmannsthal's awareness of the Casanova legend and to have pursued this in four of his main comedies.

The collection of essays edited by Margit Resch is intended to encourage further appreciation of Hofmannsthal's lyrics, especially of lesser-known ones. The collection was originally planned in German, then in English. There are finally ten interpretations in German and one in English, a general introduction and a section 'Zum Geleit' (by Richard Exner), seven other planned contributions not appearing. Most of the better-known poems are omitted, and the treatment is primarily of interest to the Hofmannsthal specialist. The editor's introduction bravely tries to present Hofmannsthal as a person rather than a poet, badly needed when so much of what follows proves her point that 'ein Gedicht interpretieren ist ein akademischer Willensakt' (p. 10: 'to interpret a poem is an academic act of will'), a game whose fashionable rule is to consider why Hofmannsthal allowed certain of his poems to be published, others not. Exner hopes these essays will bring the poems 'eine erhöhte Aufmerksamkeit', and in as much as they are addressed to members of the flourishing and urbane Hofmannsthal-Gesellschaft, they are assured of success. Only two contributions, however, and those by far the shortest: Lore Muerdel Dormer's on 'Das kleine Stück Brot' and Rudolf Schier's comparison of 'Siehst du die Stadt?' and Wordsworth's sonnet 'Composed upon Westminster Bridge, September 3, 1802' come near to achieving Hofmannsthal's own lightness of touch without losing out on scholarly reference and precision.

Richard Exner's 27-page analysis of 'Wir gingen einen Weg ...' is a restructured version of an article first published in 1976, ten pages of which are footnotes and illustrations. This is rivalled in length by Werner Schwan's use of 'Zum Gedächtnis des Schauspielers Mitterwurzer' as a pretext for discussing Hofmannsthal's detailed interest in acting techniques and his need to present his ideas to the public through the theatre, Mitterwurzer's career, *Lebensphilosophie* at the turn of the century and parallels between Hofmannsthal's relation to this and the relations between the Sturm und Drang and the Enlightenment. Equally expansive is the contribution in English by Steven P. Sondrup on 'Terzinen', based in part on Heidegger's methodology and including among useful sections (on the use of 'gleiten', the poet's terror, hair imagery and the intuitive understanding of death) one alarming example of academic style: 'Whereas the intellection of the first section alienated the speaker from the world and from himself in its objectifying reification, the simple looking, the staring, the openness to the world conjoins and relates the speaker to his world in such a way that the anticipation of death, presaged in these lines and fulfilled in more explicit terms at the end of the section, becomes the ground for a freedom toward death' (p. 193). Alas, poor Hofmannsthal!

Janette C. Hudson on 'Nox portentis gravida' offers a detailed account of the poet's harmonisation of opposites, referring the work to Nietzsche's concepts of Apolline and Dionysiac, and seeing it as an example of what Hofmannsthal was hoping for in the essay *Gespräch über Gedichte*. More effective, because more articulate on the actual processes at work in 'Dein Antlitz', is David E. Jenkinson's carefully formulated essay on the poet's precision in using the simplest linguistic methods to articulate a thoroughly complex inner situation. Jenkinson neatly fits the text into a process of poetic maturing from aestheticism to sociability and love. Ruth Lorbe establishes the importance of 'Welt und ich' to point out Hofmannsthal's struggle with the 'Mangel eines Centrums, einer Weltanschauung' (p. 104) as a poet, relating this to other texts of the early 1890s. Here we see his partially successful encounter with the reflected aesthetic world within himself. Identification with Atlas or Orpheus was not enough to still his latent uncertainty. Only by seeing death as the symbol of life, as in *Alkestis*, could Hofmannsthal produce the concepts of sacrifice and change to lift the uncertain poetic self out of its inability to define and contain the outside world.

Karl Pestalozzi emphasises in 'Großmutter und Enkel' playful allusions to *Jugend*, the periodical where it first appeared. He also finds interesting parallels and contrasts with *Das Bergwerk zu Falun* then being written. He relates it to Hofmannsthal's Goethe-prologue of the same year, showing how the poem's language recalls spiritual and literary worlds that exemplify self-surrender and rebirth in the form of a miniature erotic drama of the soul. Finally, Martin Stern reveals 'Der Jüngling in der Landschaft' as a moral metanoia on the threshold between Hofmannsthal's early and late work, interpreting it as being covertly the most Christian of the poems Hofmannsthal chose to publish ('das auf verborgene Weise christlichste [...]', p. 216). The attainment of insight, not social involvement, is at its core.

This volume is handsomely produced and will doubtless enlighten many readers, but its dense scholarly apparatus will probably deter rather than attract potential admirers of Hofmannsthal.

BRIAN KEITH-SMITH

Stefan Zweig, *Briefwechsel mit Hermann Bahr, Sigmund Freud, Rainer Maria Rilke und Arthur Schnitzler*, ed. Jeffrey B. Berlin, Hans-Ulrich Lindken and Donald A. Prater (Frankfurt: Fischer, 1987), 526 pp., DM 58.

While reservations concerning Stefan Zweig's literary talent are not likely to disappear, his energetic promotion of translations and his popular intellectual biographies have gained him a deserved reputation as a cultural mediator of European stature. The published correspondence with Maxim Gorki, on the one hand, and with Romain Rolland, on the other, delineates the Eastern and Western poles of literary culture between which Zweig moved with grace and ease. The present collection of 'four of the most interesting' (p. 7) unpublished correspondences to have survived the destructive vagaries of war and exile contains lively dialogues with a quartet of Zweig's most distinguished Austrian contemporaries. Not only do the letters provide valuable information that has not been adequately interpreted by his biographers, they also offer insights into major topics of Austrian modernity, including the complex interaction between psychoanalysis and literature and the intellectual response to World War I.

As the younger writer and, in the case of Rilke, the one who knew himself to be less talented, Zweig tends in these exchanges to assume a deferential and sometimes adulatory tone. His attitude of respectful reserve breaks down most dramatically in the correspondence with Hermann Bahr, which is the most extensive and in 1904 the first to begin. Although Zweig must have initiated the exchange with Bahr in the hopes of gaining an influential literary friend, he rather abruptly slipped into the precocious role of editor and adviser. In 1912, he enjoins Bahr to write 'what compels you, not merely what entices you' (p. 26) and suggests that a still-be-written autobiography would be his first 'immortal book' (p. 28). This is one of two letters in their correspondence where a spirited or even angry response might have been expected. In both cases, Bahr apparently kept silent. In the second, even more challenging letter, Zweig tried in 1917 to enlist Bahr in his peacemaking endeavours and urged him to buy up and destroy the edition of *Kriegssegen*, a collection of chauvinistic essays. In a compromising expression of sympathy, however, Zweig admits that he can understand Bahr's nationalistic passion: 'Ich sehe keine Schande darin, durch Leidenschaft zum Nationalismus verleitet worden zu sein (ebensowenig wie zu Schändung oder Gotteslästerung, denn jede Leidenschaft ist heilig) aber ich sehe auch keine Schande darin, zu sagen, meine Leidenschaft war töricht und gefährlich' ('I see no shame in having been misled into nationalism by passion (any more than into rape or blasphemy, for every passion in holy), but I also see no shame in saying, "my passion was foolish and dangerous"', p. 49). With all due respect for Zweig's pacifist sentiments, his own choice of words demonstrates that there is indeed 'Schande' in 'Schändung'. The implication that rape has anything to do with passion indicates a profound moral confusion about personal relations that could not help but compromise any oppositional political convictions Zweig might have nourished.

As we now know from Klaus Heydemann's meticulously researched article, 'Der Titularfeldwebel – Stefan Zweig im Kriegsarchiv', Zweig participated more enthusiastically in the propagandistic work of the military than his private declarations of anti-war feeling once seemed to indicate. (A summary of Heydemann's documentation, which is merely cited in the notes to Rilke's letters, would have provided useful commentary on the correspondence with both Bahr and Rilke.) Rather than there being what the editors call an 'essential incompatibility' (p. 9) between Bahr and Zweig, it seems more likely that there was a basic sympathy between these two tireless, sometimes careless writers, who in later years frequently undertook Alpine walking tours together. One can hardly imagine Zweig writing to any of his other correspondents in this volume that he had 'sprayed Germany as far up as the North Sea with a machine gun salvo of lectures' (p. 104).

A rather more anxious affinity predominates in the exchange of letters between Freud and Zweig. Freud takes a pronounced pleasure and interest in Zweig's fiction that sometimes seem to overwhelm the author. In a letter of 1926, for example, Freud delivers an astonishingly detailed interpretation of the three stories in *Verwirrung der Gefühle*. Zweig's faltering response clearly shows that he is unnerved by Freud's effusive praise and energetic explications; he even confesses to having been unable to wield his pen ('die Feder führen', p. 180) the day before. Little wonder, for while admiring Zweig's 'Darstellungskunst' ('art of depiction', p. 179), Freud had questioned the constrictions it places on the reader's imagination. The letters also reveal a Freud who was less enthusiastic about Zweig's biographical essays, his 'Panoptikum' (p. 211) as Freud admits to calling it 'jokingly' (p. 211). The discoverer of psychoanalysis does not spare Zweig some testy remarks about the analytical essay on himself in *Die Heilung durch den Geist*, nor does he fail to demand corrections, which Zweig, by the way, failed to make. Zweig's insistence that he owed much to Freud's courageous example but not to his theory (p. 173) is but one indication of how valuable this correspondence would be for a study of what might be called submissive resistance to psychoanalysis.

Some of the earliest and longest letters between Zweig and Rilke concern Zweig's plan for an inexpensive 'anthology' of Rilke's poetry that would have made his work available to a larger reading public. Despite a considerable degree of sympathy and mutual admiration between the two men, Rilke seems reluctant in this and in other matters to succumb to Zweig's apparent need to promote and promulgate his colleague's work. One of the apparent curiosities in the correspondence, Rilke's request for information about the sacrament of Extreme Unction from the Jewish bourgeois Zweig, is perhaps not as outlandish as it first seems. Zweig is after all able to consult a priest friend and to pass on the answer he 'expected' (p. 276). That at least Zweig's later work made a 'Catholic' impression is verified by Bahr's reaction to *Die Augen des ewigen Bruders* (1921). He calls it 'tief katholisch' ('profoundly Catholic') (p. 70) and insists that if he did not know who the author was he would bet that he was a Jesuit.

The correspondence between Zweig and Schnitzler displays a sustained interest in each other's work and reveals particularly on Zweig's part a careful and insightful reading of his older colleague's publications. Given Hofmannsthal's deliberate neglect of *Der Weg ins Freie*, Schnitzler must have been particularly pleased to read that Zweig openly recognized the novel's attempt to depict the 'idea of a Jewish-Viennese amalgamation' (p. 355). Yet the generally cordial tone of this correspondence apparently glossed over intermittent personal and aesthetic misgivings. Schnitzler, for example, gives a friendly, but decidedly less positive assessment of *Verwirrung der Gefühle* than Freud while stating bluntly in his diary: 'not truly poetic, but artificial' (p. 483). In the same letter, Schnitzler confides to Zweig that he has considered appending 'variants' (p. 423) to certain novellas, a tentative gesture towards a radical modernist aesthetic that future Schnitzler scholarship will definitely want to consider.

Considering the participation of all the correspondents in the birth of Austrian modernism and in its insistent questioning of the meaning and value of language, it is not surprising that the seminal event of this epoch, the First World War, is often as conspicuous by their silence about it as by their discussion of it. Not only Bahr's failure to respond to Zweig's demand that he retract his nationalistic essays, but also the absence of any letters between Freud and Zweig during the war years, as well as Zweig's comment to Schnitzler in 1916 that 'words and conversations are sometimes [...] detestable' (p. 398), bear witness to the war's debilitating effect on intellectual discourse. Even though Zweig writes on Christmas Day in 1914 that he is waiting for 'a powerful man in this time who will utter a curse against all those committed to hatred' (p. 42), neither he nor his friends ever mention the one writer who on 19 November 1914 began to do just that. With his public reading of the satirical essay 'In dieser großen Zeit' ('In these great times'), Karl Kraus began to articulate a radical critique of the fatal connections between war and culture.

The use of an editorial team for such a diverse collection of letters has obvious advantages, but it has also resulted in wasteful duplications, especially in the bibliographies, and in an apparently arbitrary system for deciding what constitutes appropriate commentary. When Zweig refers to 'German authors' (p. 180) whose work profited from psychoanalysis, for example, the notes supply five conjectures, four Austrians and Thomas Mann (p. 239), but one of Freud's characteristic Heine quotations is left unidentified (p. 187). The latter is only one of several examples where the reader is given no indication whether an attempt at identification or explication was even made. On the positive side, the notes reflect skilful integration of unpublished letters to and from Zweig as well as of pertinent passages from his diaries and those of Schnitzler. Curiously, however, only Schnitzler's published diaries are cited, which means that valuable, easily accessible information regarding the letters written after 1919 has been omitted. Despite these imperfections, this edition of Zweig's correspondence represents an importance new source for the interpretation of Austrian culture in the crucial era between the turn of the century and the Anschluss.

LEO A. LENSING

Texte des Expressionismus: Der Beitrag jüdischer Autoren zur österreichischen Avantgarde, ed. Armin A. Wallas (Linz: edition neue texte, 1988), 322pp., 256 Sch./DM 39.

The Austrian Expressionist movement has been up until now a largely unexplored chapter. As A. A. Wallas points out, until this very day Austrians deal rather reluctantly with the Expressionist movement when discussing Austrian culture around the turn of the century and between the two World Wars. This reluctance is mostly due to the fact that the dissonances the Expressionist writers exposed do not readily fit into the harmonising picture official Austrian cultural politics likes to paint of those times. Even less explored is the contribution of Jewish writers to this avant-garde movement.

The anthology on review here sets out to fill this void in both areas of scholarship. Its goal is to reintroduce a literary movement that was thought of as 'un-Austrian' by the 'völkisch' ideologists of that era. By focusing on the Jewish contributors to this movement it also aims to (re-)open the dialogue with traditions of Jewish Austrian ideas within Austrian culture.

Wallas presents texts of poetry, prose and drama by 55 writers whose works were banned and burned during the Nazi era. As a result most of these authors are nowadays virtually unknown, so much so that even biographical data are difficult to ascertain. The bio-bibliographical register at the end of the volume reveals that most of the authors died in concentration camps or in exile.

It is quite an impressive choir of voices of this lost generation that Wallas has selected for his anthology. Arranged alphabetically, the volume starts with the powerful poetry of Paul Adler and ends with the opening scene of Stefan Zweig's drama *Jeremias*. In between we find an extraordinary variety of literary forms, styles and themes that give expression to the sense of crisis and doom which beset that generation and especially the Jews among them. Ranging from the religiously inspired verses of Uriel Birnbaum to the sarcastic social satires of the brothers Carl and Albert Ehrenstein we also find, just to mention a few, Jakob Moreno Levy's utopian visions of a world united in brotherly love next to excruciating scenes from the battlefields of World War I by Richard Ghuttmann and Andreas Latzko, ecstatic paeans to life by writers like Arnolt Bronnen next to lamentations over the devastations of war and technology by Hugo Sonnenschein.

If the styles and contents of these works are varied, so are their authors' attitudes towards their Jewish identity. Religious believers like Uriel Birnbaum are to be found, as well as the likes of an Arnolt Bronnen (i.e. Arnold Bronner) who reject their Jewish origins. Zionists like Max Brod and Eugen Höflich (later to be known as Moshe Yaakov Ben-Gavriel) are in company with writers like Albert Ehrenstein who thought of Zionism as a nationalistic anachronism, clearly disproved in its validity by World War I as well as by the socio-political reality of Mandate Palestine. This anthology therefore also provides fascinatingly varied insights into the very complex problems of Jewish identity in Austrian society.

Common to most of these writers, however, is a tendency to identify with the secular humanistic aspect of Judaism and to be driven by a desire to fulfil an ethical humanising mission. Common to them all is also a deep sense of being social outsiders in a society where a decisive criterion of identity was being a member of the Catholic state religion and where the anti-Judaism of the Catholic church as well as the economic anti-Semitism of the petit-bourgeoisie had a long-running and deeply-rooted tradition. They also shared a common fate of persecution and extinction in body and spirit, either in the concentration camps or through the loneliness of their exile and finally by the official Austrian policy of extinguishing all memories of an unacknowledged past.

With his anthology, which also provides a very informative and sensitive introduction to the special problematic of these writers, Wallas has taken a step in the right direction of recovering this lost generation. It is to be hoped that this timely anthology will spark a new interest in a hitherto repressed chapter of recent German literature.

HANNI MITTELMANN

Reviews

Stanley Corngold, *Franz Kafka. The Necessity of Form* (Ithaca and London: Cornell University Press, 1988), xx + 321 pp., $ 32.95.

Detlev Kremer, *Die Erotik der Schrift* (Frankfurt: Athenäum, 1989), 182 pp., DM 24.80.

The volume by Stanley Corngold contains ten already published and two new essays. There are commentaries on the diaries, *The Trial*, and various aphorisms and stories, above all *The Judgement* and *The Metamorphosis*. Comparative chapters link Kafka with Cervantes, Nietzsche, Flaubert and Expressionism. The critical context is an argument with deconstruction: Kafka's literalisations destroy empirical reference in common metaphors, but they go beyond aporetic suspension between antitheses, which deconstruction uncovers, to generate an endless process of self-reflective writing about writing. In *The Metamorphosis*, for example, literalisation of the metaphor generates metamorphoses of both tenor and vehicle. The tenor is not reduced to properties of the vehicle, but through unfolding tranformations the man-insect becomes an opaque, indecipherable *parole* lifted out of *langage;* it becomes a signifier reflexively signifying itself as 'an aesthetic object – the unique correlative of a poetic intention' (p. 68); more precisely, it signifies the birth of *The Judgement*. Professor Corngold's readings are, in his own terms, allegorical; they seek allusion to non-empirical truth. While occasionally this may be a mystic apperception of the 'splendor of life' (p. 135), that about which one must be silent, but to which literature may allude, generally turns out to be literature.

Allegorical reading is apodeictically set above symbolic readings which retain reference to the empirical world: the latter preserve the sense of familiar metaphors, the former stresses their transformation into the utterly strange which cannot be translated into another discourse. Yet Corngold does perform translations which are almost always the same: the concrete metaphor or chiasm is translated into its abstract structure. This can become impoverishing, as when he argues of the man-insect in *The Metamorphosis* that the empirical identity of both tenor and vehicle are inconsequential; paramount is the form of the metaphor as such: 'any metaphor would do' (p. 67). Similarly, the bachelor is 'the figure for the misery of nonbeing' (p. 22); that Kafka chose *that* particular word, denoting a social identity in a historical world, is inconsequential; the bachelor is purely the anti-self of literature. Thus literature is excised from history and Kafka as *writer*, or occasionally as mystic, elevated over Kafka as critic. The hierarchical ordering of the allegorical over the symbolic leads to strong but narrow readings which rarely build bridges (a metaphor demolished in a chapter on literary history) to connect allegorical allusion with symbolic critique or to explore specific modes of life which might be implicated in the radical separation of literature from life which Kafka expresses. In a chapter on Expressionism, Corngold does momentarily ground the separation in a history of modernity and reads Kafka's literalisations as uncovering the ideological function of common metaphors. But the chapter on literary history concludes that 'a literary history including Nietzsche and Kafka halts before the interminable reversal, the unstable chiasm, indwelling in their positions' (p. 163) and a chapter on principles of interpretation reasserts the primacy of the ahistorical: 'Kafka's social alienation follows from a primordial experience of separation which his relation to writing forced on him' (p. 295), for – and here the authorities are Barthes, Derrida and Deleuze – 'writing responds to the (non) origin of articulation, difference and deferral' (p. 295).

For these same authorities, Corngold asserts, 'literature incessantly figures desire and death as writing' (p. 295). This could be a summary of Detlev Kremer's thesis. But Dr Kremer connects Kafka's retreat into literature with a psychology of the author and a historical context. The core of Kafka's life as of his art, he argues, is the rejection of fixed identity. The writer of the letters to Felice performs the same movement as the fictional figures, of approach towards then retreat from identifications, like the parabola which the paths to the castle describe. The ends of the parabola tend towards fluid lack of definition at one extreme and anorganic stasis or death at the other. Eros is the motor propelling the movement: driven by desire, the author of the letters advances towards then retreats from the identity of husband, from which he escapes into writing fuelled by deflected desire. The bachelor is threatened by writer's block; he needs the erotic fuel to go on writing, yet Eros threatens to drag the author away from literature into entanglement with women. The perfection of writing tends towards escape from desire for the filth of life and towards total emancipation from identity, as figured in Odradek, for example; the threat is the cessation of movement in the deathly purity of the anorganic, the rock of Prometheus, for example. Kremer links the parabola to a Hegelian history of the unhappy consciousness of the bourgeois (male) subject and a literary history of figures of the female in writing by men since Romanticism. Rather than extended readings, he alludes to a wide range of texts, but there are notable interpretations of *A Country Doctor* and *The Trial*.

Both volumes emphasise writing about writing in often similar readings, notably of *In the Penal Colony* and *The Burrow*. Kremer's parabola illuminates a wider range of elements in Kafka's writing than Corngold's ascetic demonstrations of the chiasmic logic which drives the transformations of metaphor, and where Corngold elevates Kafka's priestly celibacy, Kremer recognises a priestly misogyny afflicting the servants of Literature, that attentuated post-Romantic successor to God. But if Corngold's tone is sometimes hagiographic, Kremer tends towards a knowing superiority as he plots, again and again, the curve of the parabola, and the context he offers remains literary-historical. For illumination of the social identities from which Kafka fled into literature readers must look elsewhere than to these two volumes which are, however, of value for strong readings.

ELIZABETH BOA

Lothar Huber (ed.), *Franz Werfel: An Austrian Writer Reassessed* (Oxford: Berg, 1989), viii + 237 pp., £27.50

British scholars have long been indebted to the Austrian Institute for its readiness to mount symposia on authors whose standing in academic fashion may be low but whose intrinsic interest is high. This volume, based on papers delivered at the 1987 London Werfel symposium, thus forms a welcome addition to the rather thin field of secondary literature on a writer who was frequently better than second-rate. As ever with such volumes, contributions tend to be diverse both in methodology and content, but the volume can be recommended for its original contributions to our knowledge of all three areas in which the protean Werfel worked: the lyric, the prose narrative and the drama.

It was of course as a lyric poet that Werfel first found fame, and though his reputation has plummeted since the heady days of *Der Weltfreund*, the contributions here may lead us to reconsider our responses to his poetic output. Margaret Ives provides a telling analysis of 'Eine alte Frau geht', based on her teaching of that poem, whilst Fred Wagner delivers a judicious survey of Werfel's entire poetic work. In terms of stimulus to further research, perhaps the volume's greatest contribution comes from W. E. Yates's essay on Werfel and Austrian poetry of the First World War. For this reviewer at least, he opens up hitherto unknown vistas, and the bibliography alone is worth having.

It may well be that Werfel's academic unfashionability is linked to his ability to write commercial blockbusters like *Jacobowski und der Oberst*, but in examining the many guises in which this play has appeared J. M. Ritchie shows it is quite possible to be both intellectually rigorous and entertaining at the same time. Georgina Clark enlarges our understanding of Werfel's collaboration with Max Reinhardt, and in particular the spectacular American staging of *The Eternal Road (Der Weg der Verheißung)* when the Manhattan Opera House had to be rebuilt to accommodate the combined egos of author and producer. John Warren's sympathetic survey of the three historical dramas *(Juarez und Maximilian; Paulus unter den Juden; Das Reich Gottes in Böhmen)* reveals their common concerns with the politics of the inter-war years as well as with Werfel's commitment to Christian love and forgiveness. Such qualities had not been overly apparent in the symbolic drama *Spiegelmensch*, which Lothar Huber treats with greater respect than Karl Kraus was ever able to. His case might have been better made had he decided which language he wished to write in. A sentence like 'His Doppelgänger, the Spiegelmensch, provides the impetus for this "Aufbruch" into a new life' (p. 67) is perhaps an extreme, but not untypical, example of the hybrid style which also mars the synoptic survey of Werfel's work with which Huber introduces the volume.

Despite the volume and variety of both his lyrical and dramatic output, it may well be that for modern readers now rediscovering Werfel his novels and stories have the most to offer. David Midgley analyses the fascinating *roman à clef*, *Barbara oder die Frömmigkeit*, in which Werfel provides a panoramic assessment of Austria in the First World War and its chaotic aftermath. In counterpoint to Michael Reffet's review of Freudian elements in Werfel, Midgley points out how useful Jungian categories are in understanding the author's fictional strategies in this uneven but compelling work. R. S. Furness brings to his vigorous discussion of *Verdi: Roman der Oper* an awareness not only of the literary but also the musical aesthetics of the late nineteenth and early twentieth centuries. Critics have hitherto had little time for this best-seller, but Furness's informed comparative criticism reveals Werfel as a writer whose appreciation of musical issues is just as lively as that of Thomas Mann.

For many readers Werfel's greatest epic work is *Die vierzig Tage des Musa Dagh*, his novel about the Armenian genocide at the hands of the Turks in 1915, and any work reassessing Werfel's achievement clearly requires a discussion of this novel. It is thus fitting that Werfel's distinguished biographer Peter Stephan Jungk, whose work has led the revival of interest in the author, should contribute an essay on this novel. Excellent though it is, his contribution is not new, being a translation of the relevant section of his book, which has now also appeared in English translation. It is sad that a novel of such distinction could not have occasioned an original contribution. Malcolm Pasley's essay on Werfel and Kafka is also something of a missed opportunity. Pasley acknowledges his debt to Roger Bauer's essay of 1980, but unfortunately he does not appear to know the story *Der Tod des Kleinbürgers* (1928) with its overwhelming echoes not only of 'Vor dem Gesetz', as Willy Haas points out in the Reclam edition of the story, but also of *Das Urteil*. Affinities between Werfel and a rather less eminent author, Lothar Schreyer, co-editor of *Der Sturm*, are examined in Brian Keith-Smith's contribution. Here, as frequently elsewhere in the volume, the discussion revolves around Werfel's concern for the relationship between individual expression and the integration of self into a community.

While the volume has been conscientiously edited by Lothar Huber, some editorial problems have not been fully addressed. Indexes are provided but are unreliable. On p. 140, for example, Furness mentions both Adolf Loos and Peter Altenberg, but neither name appears in the index. Most disturbingly, the thorny problem of whether or not to provide English translations of German quotations remains unresolved. Sometimes there is a translation, sometimes there is not, and this naturally raises the question of the volume's intended readership. Germanists will not normally require English versions, whereas non-Germanists attracted to the book by Werfel's fame as a best-seller will never know where they are.

ANDREW BARKER

Harald Klauhs, *Franz Theodor Csokor: Leben und Werk bis 1938 im Überblick*, Stuttgarter Arbeiten zur Germanistik, 204 (Stuttgart: Heinz, 1988), 583 pp., DM 70.

At first sight, this published dissertation seems to suffer from many of the faults of such works. Much of it is not directly relevant to its professed subject, being an amalgam of quotations (often second-hand) from too many critics in the general field of modern Austrian literature and culture, and even digressing to analyse works not written by Csokor. The author is also far too fond of loose suggestions introduced by formulations such as 'Es darf vermutet werden ... ' or 'Es ist anzunehmen ... ' That said, however, all those concerned with Austrian literature will find much here that is rewarding; for Csokor was not only a good dramatist in his own right, but had a finger in many pies and a wide range of friends.

Among the interesting areas well covered by Dr Klauhs are Csokor's early years, when we see him on the edge of the Viennese literary scene, and his position as one of the few Viennese Expressionist authors. His involvement in the theatre as *Dramaturg* and producer, working closely with Rudolf Beer and Karl Heinz Martin, is also well described. During this period Csokor had a significant share in the staging of plays by Ernst Toller and his friend Georg Kaiser; with youthful impetuosity, he tried to help Kaiser at the time of the latter's sensational trial by publishing a brochure on his behalf. Other important topics are Csokor's ambivalent relationship to the politics of the period, and the time which he spent, like so many Austrian writers of the 1920s, travelling and working in Weimar Germany. We receive a clearer picture of the events at the 11th Congress of the International PEN Club in Dubrovnik in 1933, and of the split in the Austrian delegation. Csokor's role was less forthright than in his own later account, but in the ensuing conflict between what he was to call 'gutes Gewissen and gutes Geschäft' ('good conscience and good business') he came down firmly on the side of the former, and at the time of the Anschluss he went into voluntary exile.

Solid assessments are given of all Csokor's works for the stage; this is doubly useful when information about them is so scanty and so many key texts are unavailable. Special emphasis is given to the play generally regarded as his most impressive work, *3. November 1918* (1936). Here Klauhs is interesting in his judgement of the role of Radosin, who represents the aristocracy of service or 'Dienstaristokratie', and in relating the play to the new Austrian ideology of the *Ständestaat*. However, he is not fully aware of the play's contemporary resonance: it offers an ambivalent reflection of those Nazi institutions and ideas which were being parallelled in Schuschnigg's Austria.

The range of Csokor's work and of his literary development up to 1938 is remarkable. From Expressionism he moved via the attempt at a more revolutionary type of drama (the play about Büchner, *Gesellschaft der Menschenrechte*, 1929) to a drama about contemporary politics, *Besetztes Gebiet* (1930). There followed the two successful works which served the *Ständestaat*: the translation of Zygmunt Krasinski's play *Die ungöttliche Komödie*, for which Csokor received a medal and an invitation to Poland which enabled him to leave Austria in 1938, and of course *3. November 1918*. But not to be forgotten either are his radio plays, his poetry, and his prose. In the last analysis, however, we remember him for his friendships (with Kaiser, Horváth, Carl Zuckmayer, Lina Loos, and Rudolf Beer, to name but five) and for his position (consolidated after the war) at the very heart of Viennese literary life. Anyone exploring Csokor's literary connections will find this book particularly useful, providing as it does a well-documented account of Csokor set against the background of the intellectual, political and social climate of his time.

JOHN WARREN

Heinz Steinert, *Adorno in Wien: Über die (Un-)Möglichkeit von Kunst, Kultur und Befreiung* (Vienna: Verlag für Gesellschaftskritik, 1989), 239 pp., 278 Sch.

A criticism often voiced in discussion of Adorno's work, and of the Frankfurt School in general, is its refusal to apply its sweeping analysis of bourgeois ideology to the specific configurations of given socio-historical moments. The tension between a penchant for global theoretical pronouncements and a desire for their demonstration through detailed historical analysis was, after all, at the centre of the Frankfurt School's *Positivismusstreit* and continues to characterise responses to the use of Critical Theory in the humanities, including literary studies, today. Heinz Steinert, Professor of Sociology in Frankfurt and Director of the Institut für Rechts- und Kriminalsoziologie in Vienna, implicitly seeks to address this issue by analysing Adorno's arguments against the background of the cultural content from which they developed – Vienna in the 1920s.

Steinert reminds us that the Frankfurt School, as far as Adorno's contribution is concerned, was in large part a Vienna School; Adorno's sociological and philosophical works are not as extensive as, and represent a continuation of, his work on music, which itself grew out of his experience as a student of Alban Berg and as an ancillary figure in the Schoenberg circle. Steinert's book is based on the premise that by ignoring (and by this he means not discussing) the social and historical background of Schoenberg's work, Adorno idealised and misunderstood the New Vienna School even as he assimilated many of its ideas. Steinert believes that the pervasive pessimism of Adorno's thought is not attributable to his disappointment with the workers' movement or with the failed revolutions of 1917 and 1918/19, but primarily with the person of Arnold Schoenberg, whose musical 'revolution' had become canonised by the time Adorno arrived in Vienna for his short stay there in 1925 and with whom he always found personal interaction difficult. Adorno thus came to glorify a past moment in the development of Schoenberg's work, and this notion of a past and failed or all-too-cursory revolution laden with missed possibilities came to characterise a cognitive model within Critical Theory. According to this argument, by concentrating on the aesthetic dimension of an idealised former revolution Adorno made light of the very socio-cultural forces which had shaped Schoenberg's self-understanding: rampant anti-Semitism, a widespread trend among avant-garde artists in turn-of-the-century Vienna toward isolation, their rejection of the public, their emphasis on the concept of *Arbeit* in interaction with aesthetic material, and their desire to control the vehicles disseminating artistic works (cf. Kraus's *Die Fackel*, the Secession project, and Schoenberg's *Verein für musikalische Privataufführungen*).

Thus, Steinert's book applies the interests of sociology to an analysis of the development of Adorno's theories concerning aesthetics and society, and in so doing seeks to highlight their characteristic features as symptomatic of a specific moment in Viennese culture. While this approach is illuminating, I do not find much in it that furthers our understanding of Adorno's works or of the culture under discussion.

In order to advance his argument, Steinert describes in detail the biographical connections between many of the leading figures of Viennese cultural life from 1900 to 1925, and recounts the familiar tales of the Secession scandal, Wittgenstein's frustrating attempts at finding a publisher for his *Tractatus*, the role of anti-Semitism in Mahler's resigning as Director of the Vienna Opera, and of the personal interrelations of the Schoenberg circle. Though he paints a remarkably vivid picture of the period, those interested in turn-of-the-century and early twentieth-century Vienna will find little new material in the first two-thirds of the text, and specialists may wish to skip the first 122 pages and proceed directly to discussion of Adorno himself.

For this reviewer, the most informative passages in the book were not those devoted to the applicability or historical validity of Adorno's theories (the focal point of Steinert's interest), but those concerning features of Adorno's biography which, until now, had been known in only the vaguest outlines. These include a comparatively detailed discussion of Adorno's frustrating work in the editorial staff of the *Musikblätter des Anbruch* (pp. 133–40) and of his interaction with his teacher in Frankfurt, the Director of the Hochschen Conservatory Bernhard Sekles, and with Hindemith, Berg, and, above all, Schoenberg. Thus it is regrettable that, when revising his original manuscript, Steinert chose to edit out much biographical material (p. 232), an admission he makes when lamenting the difficulty of gaining permission to quote from Adorno's letters. If the informative, extensive, and entertaining footnotes are any indication of this earlier version, the omission of such material is lamentable. True to its subject, the style of Steinert's book is witty, ironic, and self-reflective. His forthright, passionate, and yet critical commitment to his subject is inspiring and, when reading him, I repeatedly found myself in sympathy with his political standpoint and his ideological criticism. Thus I was disappointed to find a provocative thesis (that Critical Theory developed out of a misunderstanding of Viennese culture) presented in a way that offers comparatively few novel insights and even seems, on occasion, beside the point. Perhaps Steinert's forthcoming book on Adorno's work on jazz will be historically and critically more illuminating, or will he simply argue that Adorno failed to take into consideration the material basis for jazz production from the 1920s to the 1960s, and that therefore his work is not applicable to jazz today?

MARC A. WEINER

Gernot Heiss *et al.* (eds), *Willfährige Wissenschaft: Die Universität Wien 1938 bis 1945*, Österreichische Texte zur Gesellschaftskritik, 43 (Vienna: Verlag für Gesellschaftskritik, 1989), 340 pp., 248 Sch.

Christian Brünner and Helmut Konrad (eds), *Die Universität und 1938* (Vienna and Cologne: Böhlau, 1989), 180 pp.

Both these books raise questions, many of them disturbing, about the role of Austrian academics after the Anschluss. The thrust of Gernot Heiss's collection (originally a series of lectures at Vienna University) is that the behaviour of Vienna's academics in 1938 differed morally not a jot from the rest of society. In the words of the preface: 'Der ganze Stolz von Aufklärung und Wissenschaft – Methodik, Kritik, Offenheit und Rationalität – zerbricht an der Existenz der Universitätslehrer selbst' ('The whole pride of enlightenment and scholarship – methodology, criticism, openness, rationality – shatters on the existence of the university teachers themselves'). The difference was that the clerks could articulate their treason in the claptrap of the 'world-historical' mission and the unreflected faith in the scientific method.

This conclusion is not perhaps surprising in itself but the detail in which it is illustrated in the Heiss collection is new. The Vienna University archives – made available to researchers for the first time – and the 'Gauakten' held by the Ministry of the Interior have produced the first convincing account of Austrian academic politics after the Anschluss. The result is a further debunking of the view that March 1938 led to a *Gleichschaltung* from above – whether Nazi or merely Prussian.

For both Vienna and Graz, the Anschluss was as much the culmination as the start of an era. A prime example is anti-Semitism, which had steadily taken hold of much of both the student and the teaching body in the course of the twenties and thirties. It starts after the First World War with the attempts of the University authorities to stem 'fortschreitende Levantisierung' by applying a *numerus clausus* to Jewish applicants. The growth of the 'akademischer Ungeist' in the following years is shown by Oliver Ratholb's account of the 1925 intrigue to get rid of the Jewish law professor, Stephan Brassloff, for allegedly making 'obscene remarks', which apparently amounted to no more than calling an anti-Semitic student who had been disrupting his lectures 'Lausbub' and 'Rotznäsiger'. Neither of the ringleaders of the campaign against Brassloff were Nazis, and one – Othmar Spann, the theoretician and philosopher of the *Ständestaat* – was considered by the Nazis to be one of their most dangerous enemies. Five years later the Glaispacher Studentenordnung aimed at segregating Jewish students. It was praised after the Anschluss by the 'minority expert' and former Schuschnigg supporter, Theodor Veiter, as a move to provide protection against 'jüdische Überflutung' ('Jewish swamping'). By then a silent Aryan paragraph ('stille Arierparagraph') ensured that a disproportionately large number of Jews were given insecure posts as 'Privatdozenten', which made their removal after the Anschluss administratively all the easier.

Closely linked with anti-Semitism was Greater German ideology, whose dominance in the Historical Institute is well illustrated in Gernot Heiss's discussion of such leading figures as Heinrich von Srbik, Otto Brunner and Wilhelm Bauer. Advocacy of Austria's German mission in Central Europe could easily be invoked after the Anschluss to curry favour with the new regime. Srbik, for example, trumpeted his role in the 'Begründung und Führung der "gesamtdeutschen Geschichtsauffassung"' ('establishing and guiding a conception of history based on the unity of all Germans') when applying to join the party. After the war the tradition survived almost unscathed, remodelled retrospectively as Austrian subversion of what Brunner called 'Parteiphraseologie und kleindeutsch-preußische Vorurteile' ('party phraseology and prejudices in favour of a small, Prussian-based Germany'). (Its most recent incarnation is as a defence of 'pluralism' against the taboos allegedly imposed by an Austrocentric historiography.)

The first fruit of the Anschluss was a whirlwind purge of Jewish personnel. By April 1938 over 40% of teachers had left the university (p. 304), the overwhelming majority of them Jews. Michael Hubenstorf estimates that in the medical faculty the number of victims was between 151 and 170. One hundred and eleven of them were forced to flee while six died in concentration camps. Among the victims in the law faculty was Brassloff, who died in Theresienstadt. A second wave of persecution – less violent and methodical – affected the supporters of the Schuschnigg regime.

Besides purging the university teaching staff the new regime encroached on the institutional, financial and personnel autonomy of the university in a variety of ways. But it was often met more than half-way by ambitious scholars tailoring their subject to Nazi ideology in order to obtain funding. Patronage and what Edith Saurer calls 'the logic of clan formation' were stronger than ideology. And when Berlin did try to force change through, it might face resistance by the authorities, as was the case with the attempt to found an 'Institut für Zeitungswissenschaft'. Other attempts were more successful, for example the 'Fächer des Frauenschaffens', the 'Hochschulinstitut für Leibesübungen', the 'Dolmetschinstitut' and, curiously, an 'Institut für die Geschichte des Postwesens'. Heinz Kindermann's 'Zentralinstitut für Theaterwissenschaft' on the other hand, though an Austrian initiative, was personally sponsored by Baldur von Schirach in his attempt to curry favour with the disgruntled Viennese – even to the point of receiving accommodation in the Hofburg.

The many individual careers traced here also cover a wide spectrum – from ideological commitment to non-political withdrawal, and occasionally dissent. The case of Alfred Verdross is a good example of the shifting, complex path a biography might follow. He was a Catholic conservative, who protected Nazis but never shared their ideological presumptions and in the end was involved in Catholic resistance circles. (He also supervised Kurt Waldheim's dissertation.)

Die Universität und 1938 does not, unfortunately, provide a comparably rich account of Graz University after 1938. Apart from Maximilian Liebmann's informative account of the fate of the theological faculty, the university archives could apparently not be tapped. There is also too much padding, with little direct relevance to the book's subject, which might more interestingly have been replaced by, for example, an account of Graz's role in the Nazi *Drang nach Süden*, especially in the 'Germanification' of Southern Styria after 1941. Among the more valuable essays is an account by Dieter Binder of the steady erosion from the late 1920s of the Catholic fraternities (*Verbindungen*) in the face of the 'actionism' of their German National, and increasingly Nazi rivals.

Both these collections – in particular the one on Vienna – underline how varied Austrian experiences under the Anschluss could be. They confirm that a large amount of empirical research is needed in all areas of society before an alternative explanatory framework to the debunked and discredited 'victim thesis' can be arrived at. They show indisputably that the return to the university after 1945 was generally far easier for compromised Nazis than for Nazi victims. Finally, on a more positive note than that adopted by many of the contributors, the very fact that they emerged out of Austria's 'Bedenkjahr' points to the huge change – even, dare one say, progress – in the role of Austrian universities over the past forty-five years.

ROBERT KNIGHT

Reviews

Theodor Haecker, *Tag- und Nachtbücher 1939–1945*, ed. Hinrich Siefken, Brenner-Studien 9 (Innsbruck: Haymon, 1989), 352 pp., 420 Sch.

This work originally appeared posthumously in 1947, though it was planned and to some extent organised by the author himself before he died in April 1945, shortly before the end of the war which the diaries reflect and record. From the manuscript at the Literaturarchiv in Marbach, Professor Siefken has now produced the first complete and correctly ordered edition of a remarkable work, which he aptly describes in his preface as consisting mainly of aphoristic criticism of the author's times, philosophical and religious reflections, polemical notes, self-contemplation and self-definition in solitary self-communing, as well as dialogues, diatribes and prayers.

Theodor Haecker (1879–1945) is perhaps best known as a satirist, a philosopher and also as a classical scholar: *Vergil, Vater des Abendlandes* (1931) is still a standard work. He was the translator and virtually the discoverer of Kierkegaard for German-speaking countries: *Sören Kierkegaard und die Philosophie der Innerlichkeit* (1913). He also translated a number of John Henry Newman's works, notably *The Grammar of Assent*, a philosophical inquiry into the nature of faith, by the composition of which Newman himself in 1845, and then his German translator in 1921, came to accept Catholicism. But in the early years of his life as a writer – he was a late student, having begun his career in commerce and then, via university studies, found his way into publishing – he was best known for his satirical polemics during and about the First World War, which appeared in journals like Ludwig von Ficker's literary and philosophical *Der Brenner*, published in Innsbruck. This has given its name to the fine series in which the present new edition of Haecker's work appears. The name of this journal, which first appeared in 1910, pointed to Ficker's aim of forging closer links between South and North, of establishing a viable intellectual and literary pass between German-speaking nations and across the symbolical mountain barrier which divides them. It was through the *Brenner* that the Swabian, Haecker, formed a close and lasting friendship with the Austrian, Karl Kraus, following him in exploring and revelling in satire which, in the end, he renounced, though with regret: satire lingers on in his analysis of the far more terrible leaders of the Second World War. Through his early journalism Haecker became rather better known in Austria, to begin with, than in his own country. He eventually made his home in Munich where he spent the war-years and was bombed out of house and home in one of the most devastating air-raids in June 1944. For a time he then found refuge with the family of the Scholls, of 'Die weiße Rose' fame, executed in 1943, to whom he had been friend and mentor.

It was in Austria, too, during one of the earliest post-war 'Salzburger Hochschulwochen' to which English and American guests were invited, and where German writers such as Bergengruen, Guardini and Gertrud von Le Fort met Austrian fellow-Catholic scholars and writers, that I first heard about Haecker's war-time journal. And it was in conversation with the Stifter editor, Max Stefl, who, like Haecker, was a bitter enemy of the regime, that the high esteem in which Haecker was held first became clear to us. Forbidden all public activity, living and writing in danger and solitude, Haecker continued, only more intensively, a life-long habit of writing in the midnight hours – and one might ask whether this, too, was in some way connected with Karl Kraus as a model. Haecker's midnight reflections are, as with Kraus, most diverse in content, but his predominant theme is of course the war and the bitter shame of having to be a German during the reign of the devilish 'Herrgott', as he calls Hitler, and of the 'Herrgott-Religion'. The 'Notaten' are varied, too, in structure and form: there are actual essays of several pages, for instance on the nature of evil [770], the philosophy of being and not-being [723]; there are actual dialogues in Socratic form, speculations on the idea of the absurd and of paradox, bitter, quite desperate outbursts as he listens to Nazi radio speeches. He was not only deeply aware of the possibilities and limitations of language and of its terrible misuse by these speakers, but he was, again like Kraus, whom he quotes on this subject [188], quite abnormally sensitive to the quality of the human voice ('stinkender Leichnam der vox humana', as he called the Nazi voice); he shared what he calls Kraus's almost uncanny power of rightly judging character just by a voice.

A selected few of the less dangerous 'Notaten' did, in fact, still somehow manage to appear in the periodical *Hochland* in 1940, the year for which there are over six hundred entries, this one year by far exceeding all the other years in length. As Siefken points out in his survey for this year (p. 259), Haecker was still at this time, and in vain, trying to formulate some redemptive meaning to all this evil. The question of obedience to an evil authority continues to haunt him and, in a sense, to defeat him. As a writer, he has the idea of using the actual language of 'enemy' countries, French and English, to make points against his own language now debased by Nazi slogans and usage. The 'Notaten' are, in fact, very interesting from the linguistic point of view; sometimes, as often with aphorisms, one has the impression that Haecker is quite happily playing about with words as counters, seeing what kind of pattern emerges when words are arranged in one sequence or another. Quite a few of the entries are speculations, and in part word-games, not primarily valid realisations or statements of belief.

Although Haecker was writing, as he seems to imply, only for himself [749], he was too much of a seasoned communicator and philosophical moralist not to be all the time aware of a possible reader: 'Es is doch ein Unterschied ob ein Stilist seinen Leser durch eine unerwartete Wendung plötzlich überraschen kann oder ob schon erwartet wird, daß nun sicher etwas Unerwartetes komme. Es ist auch ein Unterschied, ob man dieses Unerwartete zweimal lesen kann, oder bloß einmal' (No. 1084, 22 December 1944). ('It does make a difference whether a stylist can suddenly surprise his reader by an unexpected turn of phrase, or whether the reader is already expecting that something unexpected is sure to come. It also make a difference whether one can read the unexpected phrase twice or only once.') Musil, too, never forgetting his reader, courteously invited him to read his similarly aphoristic comments not only once, but twice. Like Hugo von Hofmannsthal, Haecker remains constantly aware of his function and duty as a writer, to as it were create his reader even as he writes, and describes this as 'Miterschaffen des Lesers'. In Haecker's diaries this creative effort in the solitude of war-time vigils was eminently successful. One may say that although these diverse, disparate and usually unconnected 'Notaten' are not easy to read straight through in sequence, they yet manage to convey, as one looks back on one's reading, a sense of unity and wholeness; one finds that one has been readily responding to the process of being formed into a willing and receptive reader.

Hinrich Siefken and the Brenner-Studien editors are to be warmly thanked for making available a reliable text of Haecker's journal in a well-produced and beautifully printed book. An introduction (pp. 8–17) gives a brief biographical account of Haecker the writer, providing the essential background for the diary and its wide frame of reference. The text of the entries (pp. 21–241), with their numbers enclosed in square brackets, is followed by the editor's commentary (pp. 245–348), brief, succinctly informative and always to the point, so that what are often cryptic entries are made intelligible. Each of the war years in question is preceded by a short summary and finally the editorial procedures are outlined (pp. 245–9). Running headings giving the year of the entries throughout the text and the commentary facilitate reference and confer a sense of continuity and wholeness upon a mass of mostly brief aphoristic entries. This is an exemplary edition which it is a pleasure to use, study, and return to at leisure, for that is how the work can best be appreciated and understood.

ELISABETH STOPP

Austrian Studies

Acknowledgements: The Editors gratefully acknowledge the support of the Austrian Institute in London. They also wish to record their great personal and professional indebtedness to the late Martin Spencer, without whose encouragement *Austrian Studies* might never have been founded.

Advisory Board: Andrew Barker (Edinburgh), Peter Branscombe (St Andrews), Amy D. Colin (Pittsburgh), R. J. W. Evans (Oxford), Sander L. Gilman (Cornell), Murray G. Hall (Vienna), Leo A. Lensing (Wesleyan), Eda Sagarra (Dublin), W. G. Sebald (East Anglia), J. P. Stern (London), Joseph Peter Strelka (New York), Robert Wistrich (Jerusalem), W. E. Yates (Exeter).

Books for review should be sent to Ritchie Robertson, St John's College, Oxford OX1 3JP, England.

Manuscripts for publication should be submitted to Edward Timms, Gonville and Caius College, Cambridge CB2 1TA, England.

Guidelines: Articles should be written in English and should not exceed 7 500 words. They should be typed double-spaced, using endnotes (not a numbered bibliography) to identify the source of quotations. Quotations should normally be given in the original language, followed by an English translation. A detailed style sheet is available from either of the Editors, on request.

Austrian Studies may be ordered through any bookshop. Since it is designed as an annual publication, it may also be obtained by subscription direct from the publishers, Edinburgh University Press, 22 George Square, Edinburgh EH8 9LF, Scotland.